The Quest
for the Plausible Jesus

The Quest for the Plausible Jesus

The Question of Criteria

GERD THEISSEN AND DAGMAR WINTER

Translated by M. Eugene Boring

Westminster John Knox Press
LOUISVILLE • LONDON

German text copyright © University Press Fribourg Switzerland

Originally published as *Die Kriterienfrage in der Jesusforschung*. First published by University Press Fribourg Switzerland.

First American edition
Published by Westminster John Knox Press
Louisville, Kentucky

Translation © 2002 Westminster John Knox Press

Book design by Sharon Adams
Cover design by Eric Walljasper

This book is printed on acid-free paper that meets the American National Standards Institute Z39.48 standard. ∞

PRINTED IN THE UNITED STATES OF AMERICA

02 03 04 05 06 07 08 09 10 11—10 9 8 7 6 5 4 3 2 1

Library of Congress Cataloging-in-Publication Data

Theissen, Gerd.
    [Kriterienfrage in der Jesusforschung. English]
    The quest for the plausible Jesus : the question of criteria / Gerd Theissen and Dagmar Winter : translated by M. Eugene Boring.
      p. cm.
    Includes bibliographical references and index.
    ISBN 0-664-22537-3 (pbk.)
    1. Jesus Christ—History of doctrines. 2. Jesus Christ—Historicity. 3. Church history—Methodology. I. Winter, Dagmar, 1963– II. Title.

BT198.T47413 2002
232.9'08—dc21   2002017335

Contents

Foreword

This book presents a critical history of the "criterion of dissimilarity" and proposes that it be replaced by a "criterion of historical plausibility." According to this latter criterion, it is not what is dissimilar to its Jewish and early Christian environment that is to be regarded as authentic. Rather, each individual historical phenomenon is to be considered authentic that plausibly can be understood in its Jewish context and that also facilitates a plausible explanation for its later effects in Christian history. In our opinion, the decisive criteria in historical Jesus studies are contextual plausibility in tandem with the plausibility of later effects.

The book is a cooperative project. It is based on the dissertation of D. Winter accepted by the faculty of theology of Heidelberg University in 1995. The dissertation focused on the history of the use of the criterion of dissimilarity and concluded by proposing the criterion of plausibility here suggested. In the course of supervising the dissertation, G. Theissen developed the hermeneutical reflections that constitute the last chapter of this book. The volume is thus the product of a years-long discussion of the criteria for research in the study of the historical Jesus.

The first chapter of the work presents the material problematic of the criterion of dissimilarity in the present situation of historical research; we composed this section together, with the intention of showing why precisely this criterion is so important in Jesus research.

The extensive second chapter was written by D. Winter. It shows how the criterion of dissimilarity came to be formulated in the different phases of Jesus research: for the old liberals, the dissimilarity between Jesus and earliest Christianity became methodologically the primary criterion, while in the so-called "New Quest" the distinction from Judaism received the central place. The two-sided criterion of dissimilarity dominated Jesus research programmatically during this period of the "New Quest," that is, from about 1953 to 1980. But the presuppositions emerging from the intellectual history of the times are bound up with the origins of historical-critical research from the time of the

Renaissance and the Reformation, and they cannot be understood apart from their background in the Enlightenment and the historicism of the nineteenth century. This section brings these presuppositions to light.

The third chapter, again written cooperatively by both authors, formulates a new criterion of historical plausibility on the basis of the preceding history, a material criterion that is related to the "Third Quest for the historical Jesus" that began about 1980. This criterion is not so much interested in prescribing something new, but wants rather to gather up and clarify what has changed in the last fifteen years of research.

The final section, composed by G. Theissen, presents hermeneutical reflections that probe more deeply into the methodological considerations involved in the reformulation of a criterion. Research on the historical Jesus often wanted to find a way to leap over the "ugly ditch" between history and faith. Although the attempt never succeeded, Christian faith remains bound to history. The question remains: How can the relatively plausible results of historical study ever be bound to unconditional certainty? What degree of reliability can be attained by historical study as such? We have intentionally kept these fundamental questions separate from the questions of historical methodology. Our new formulation of a historical criterion can thus be shared by those who do not share the hermeneutical presuppositions developed in the last chapter.

A book on the historical methodology of Jesus research may seem superfluous to many, especially in view of the fact that the methods used in scholarly study of the New Testament have become ever more precise and sophisticated, so that they are often criticized because of their "scholasticism." We may thus name two reasons for the importance of the issue of criteria in Jesus research.

First, "Jesus" is a disputed topic. The plurality of scholarly and prescholarly reconstructed pictures of Jesus cannot be limited in a free society. We have comparable problems in other areas. In view of the pluralism of opinions and perspectives in ethics and politics, open societies have long since united around a "meta-consensus:" legitimacy is not produced by material criteria but by formal procedure. The rules of the game of dialogue make pluralism legitimate. In the realms of religion and church, we confront similar challenges. The methods of historical criticism, themselves in a constant process of development, present rules for dialogue that make it possible to debate the factual, historical foundations of a religion. Methodological considerations are thus not an alien scholasticism but are aids in creating the conditions for living together—in the churches, between the religious communities, and in the midst of a secularized, pluralistic world.

The second reason concerns our specific problem: the criterion of dissimilarity programmatically marks Jesus off from both Judaism and the church.

By means of the plausibility criterion we are proposing, Jesus is considered, from the point of view of a history of origins, an individual historical phenomenon integrated in his Jewish context and, from the point of view of a history of effects, an individual related to Christianity. We thereby come to terms methodologically with one of the most important results of more than two hundred years of Jesus research: the historical Jesus belongs to two religions, to Judaism and to Christianity. This discovery irritates the members of both religions, Christians more than Jews. Our criterion of historical plausibility transforms this discovery into a presupposition of historical-critical work with the Jesus tradition. That means that anyone who applies historical methods to the study of Jesus cannot do so without accepting in advance the guideline that Jesus belongs in the context of Judaism and also that his influence continued to affect Christianity in the form of the sources that testify to him. In our opinion, it is only the transformation of theological claims into research strategies that could "interrupt" and abolish the connection between historical methodology and the embedding of Jesus within the matrix of Jewish origins and Christian effects. (This is what happened on the basis of the hero and genius cult of the nineteenth century, and on the basis of the reduction of the historical Jesus to a mere "Dass" in the kerygmatic theology of the twentieth century.) If now—judged from a theological point of view—the connection to the historical Jesus is an aspect of Christian identity, and—judged from a historical point of view—Jesus belongs within Judaism, it follows that in the historical foundations of Christianity there is contained an obligation to reconfigure its relation to Judaism (and to other religions). Two huge challenges of modern times for the church are here directly combined: the challenge of historical criticism and the challenge of interreligious dialogue—in this case, especially, Jewish-Christian dialogue.

The two authors thus do not share the inclination widespread in these times of postmodern mentality that the problems of historical methodology are important for scholars of history but irrelevant for a living faith. Without methodology we have no rules for dialogue by means of which we can reasonably debate what is important to us. For Christians, dealing with the problem of the historical Jesus has central importance. To be sure, for some time now an enormously creative stream of Protestant intellectual history has caused quite a stir by arguing that the problem of the historical Jesus is unimportant for Christians. To theological common sense (especially outside German Protestant theology), this thesis has never seemed quite reasonable.

It is thus no accident that this book represents the cooperative work of a male German theologian with a female Anglican theologian who is at home in the tradition of the Church of England. In the last fifteen years the center of gravity of study of the historical Jesus, located in German research for a long period, has shifted to English-speaking lands. The following section on the history of research will also acknowledge that the beginnings of historical-critical study of the Bible are to be located in England.

The writing of this book obligates us to thank many people: the doctoral work of D. Winter was generously supported by a grant from the Hanns-Seidel-Stiftung. Professor K. Berger was the second reader of the dissertation; the term "criterion of plausibility" goes back to him and was understood by him as a criterion for the investigation of the whole history of early Christianity. Professor M. Küchler accepted this work in the series Novum Testamentum et Orbis Antiquus. The Protestant Church of Hesse and Nassau supported its publication by subsidizing its printing costs.

In addition, we thank all those who have personally helped us in the writing of this book. Annette Merz read the manuscript and suggested important material improvements. Helga Wolf and Heike Goebel typed the manuscript at its different stages and gave it a readable form. All these have helped to eliminate mistakes. In addition, Dr. Rosemary Selle and Annette Weissenrieder helped in correcting the page proofs. We express our heartfelt thanks to them all. Dagmar Winter also offers special thanks to the congregations of the English Church in Heidelberg, St. Michaels Protestant Church in Reichelsheim/Odenwald, and St. Mark's Church in Bromley/Kent.

Dagmar Winter   Gerd Theissen
Bromley   Heidelberg

Translator's Note

I have used standard English translations of cited material where available. Occasionally the English translation was made from an earlier edition of the German text cited by the authors. In such cases I have adapted the standard translation to the later edition, or translated the text that appears in Theissen/Winter and retained the German pagination, with the corresponding page in the English translation sometimes appearing in brackets. I have occasionally added a translator's note where sensitivity to particular terms seemed to be important (e.g., on "Anti-Judaism").

Gerd Theissen supplied the original German disks, which made translation from the computer screen a less arduous task than constant reference to the printed book. He also shared the authors' expansions and modifications of the original text, making this English translation the definitive edition of this work. Dagmar Winter graciously read extensive sections of my translation and made helpful suggestions for its improvement. Joe Weaks, doctoral student at Brite Divinity School, helped with bibliographical, editing, and indexing details. Sandy Brandon, Administrative Assistant in the New Testament department of Brite Divinity School, handled typing, duplicating, and mailing chores with cheerfulness and efficiency. Jack Keller, Editorial Director, Julie Tonini, Senior Associate Managing Editor, and the staff of Westminster John Knox ushered the manuscript through the press with dispatch. To all these I here extend sincere gratitude, while taking responsibility for any errors that remain.

M. Eugene Boring
Fort Worth

Abbreviations

ARW	Archiv für Religionswissenschaft
BBB	Bonner Biblische Beiträge
BEvT	Beiträge zur evangelischen Theologie
BETL	Bibliotheca ephemeridum theologicarum lovaniensium
BHT	Beiträge zur historischen Theologie
BiLi	Bibel und Liturgie
CBQ	*Catholic Biblical Quarterly*
ChW	Christliche Welt
CSR	Christian Scholars Review
Cyprian ep	Epistles of Cyprian
EncBib	Encyclopaedia Biblica, ed. T. K. Cheyne. London, 1800–1903
EHS.T	Europäische Hochschulschriften. Theologie
EKL	Evangelisches Kirkenlexikon
EvFo	Evangelisches Forum
EvT	*Evangelische Theologie*
ExpTim	*Expository Times*
FGLP	Forschungen zur Geschichte und Lehre des Protestantismus
FSThR	Forschungungen zur systematischen Theologie und Religions-philosophie
GA	Gesamte Ausgabe
GNT	Grundrisse zum Neuen Testament
Greg	Gregorianum
GThW	Grundriss der theologischen Wissenschaften
GuV	Glauben und Verstehen
HerKorr	Herder Korrespondenz
HHS	Harvard Historical Studies
HTh	History and Theory
HThK.S	Supplements to Herders theologischer Kommentar zum Neuen Testament
HTR	*Harvard Theological Review*

HWP	Historisches Wörterbuch der Philosophie
JAC	Jahrbuch für Antike und Christentum
JBL	*Journal of Biblical Literature*
JR	*Journal of Religion*
JSNT	*Journal for the Study of the New Testament*
JSOT	*Journal for the Study of the Old Testament*
KP	Kleine Pauly
KSGW	Kritische Studien zur Geschichtswissenschaft
KuI	Kirche und Israel
KVR	Kleine Vandenhoeck-Reihe
LTK	Lexidon für Theologie und Kirche
MPTh	Monatsschrift für Pastoraltheologie
MThA	Münsteraner Theologische Abhandlungen
MThZ	Münchner Theologische Zeitschrift
NovT	*Novum Testamentum*
NTOA	Novum Testamentum et Orbis Antiquus
NTS	*New Testament Studies*
NZST	Neue Zeitschrift für Systematische Theologie
PrM	Protestantische Monatshefte
QD	Questiones Disputatae
RGG	*Religion in Geschichte und Gegenwart*
RoMo	Rowohlts Monographien
RV	Religionsgeschichtliche Volksbücher für die deutsche christliche Gegenwart
SaeSp	Saecvla Spiritalia
SBEC	Studies of the Bible and Early Christianity
SBS	Stuttgarter Bibelstudien
SBT	Studies in Biblical Theology
SCC	Studies in Creative Criticism
SHCT	Studies in the History of Christian Thought
SJT	*Scottish Journal of Theology*
SPLi	Studia Patristica et Liturgica
SThGG	Studien zur Theologie und Geistesgeschichte des 19. Jahrhunderts
TANZ	Texte und Arbeiten zum NT Zeitalter
TLZ	*Theologische Literaturzeitung*
TRu	*Theologische Rundschau*
TToday	Theology Today
TRE	*Theologische Realenzyklopädie*
TSTP	Tübinger Studien zur Theologie und Philosophie
USQR	*Union Seminary Quarterly Review*

UTB	Uni-Taschenbücher
WA	Martin Luther, Kritische Gesamtausgabe ("Weimar" Edition)
WF	Wege der Forschung
WUNT	Wissenschaftliche Untersuchungen zum Neuen Testament
ZdZ	Die Zeichen der Zeiten
ZNW	*Zeitschrift für die neutestamentliche Wissenschaft*
ZTK	*Zeitschrift für Theologie und Kirche*

I

The Quest for Criteria
in Jesus Research

The Essential Problem of the Criterion of Dissimilarity

1. PHASES OF JESUS RESEARCH
AND THE CRITERION OF DISSIMILARITY

"Jesus research," as a scholarly effort to reconstruct a picture of the historical Jesus, is a product of the Enlightenment. Accompanied by changing interests, paradoxically including the interest that manifested itself from time to time in Protestant theology as studied lack of interest, it has lived through several phases.

After its beginnings in the eighteenth century (the English deists, Reimarus), "life of Jesus research" flourished in the nineteenth century—making its mark most clearly in the theology of the old Liberals. It was concerned with presenting a historically true life of Jesus that functioned theologically as a critical force over against churchly Christology. This historical Jesus represented an alternative to the dogmatic-christological tradition of the church and was of great relevance in terms of theological ethics. To the extent that criteria for Jesus research were formulated, their content approximated a "criterion of dissimilarity." Such criteria were one-sidedly applied to distinguishing Jesus from early Christianity: that which contradicted the later church's exalted view of Jesus was considered especially authentic.

In Germany at the beginning of the twentieth century, this tradition experienced a sharp turning point. Albert Schweitzer wrote his history of life-of-Jesus research, which was described as the funeral dirge for this phase of the quest.[1] It was especially Rudolf Bultmann, however, who rejected the theological

---

1. To be sure, in his book Schweitzer set forth an outline of the life of Jesus. But his reconstructed picture of Jesus still had such a shattering effect precisely because he had come to the conclusion that the eschatological-apocalyptic ideas by which Jesus was

approach of the liberal lives of Jesus that had wanted to derive theological affir-
mations directly from historical data. As a leading figure in the influential dialectical theology, Bultmann denied that the "historical Jesus" had any theological
significance. He categorized Jesus (or in Bultmann's terms, Jesus' *"preaching"*)
historically as belonging entirely within Judaism, as one of the presuppositions
of early Christianity,[2] but not as the foundation that determined its essential
character. He saw this as constituted by the (post-) Easter kerygma of the cross
and resurrection. Against the background of this theological and historical
assessment, form criticism became the domineering method of Gospel
research.[3] In the field of theology, this alliance of "kerygma theology" and form
criticism led to a crisis of historical interest in Jesus. It was ground between the
millstones of form-critical skepticism "from below" and a kerygmatic claim
"from above." However, this second phase of Jesus research turned out to be
only transitional.

While in English language scholarship—despite Schweitzer and Bultmann—a broad stream of interest in the historical Jesus continued without
interruption, in Germany this interest was reawakened in the Bultmann school
in the 1950s. One spoke of the "New Quest" in contrast to the "Old Quest"
of the preceding century. While those in the nineteenth century were concerned to write a "life of Jesus" in the biographical sense, with the intent of
reconstructing a portrayal of Jesus that liberated one from the ecclesiastical
picture of Christ, for the "New Quest" (J. Robinson) the issue of the continuity between the historical Jesus and the Jesus Christ of post-Easter faith stood
at the center of the discussion. Thereby the difference between the historical
Jesus and early Christianity was relativized, but the distinction between Jesus
and Judaism was emphasized all the more. Bultmann had dated the beginning
of Christianity at the emergence of the kerygma of the cross and resurrection,

---

fundamentally guided were conditioned by his own times and were mistaken. What
remained was "only" a basic ethical principle. And it should finally not be overlooked
that Schweitzer's critique of life-of-Jesus research with his "awe . . . in the presence of
historical truth" itself stood entirely in the tradition of liberal theology (H. Pleitner,
Das Ende der liberalen Hermeneutik am Beispiel Albert Schweitzers [TANZ 5; Tübingen:
Francke, 1992] 230).

2. Cf. R. Bultmann, *Theology of the New Testament* (trans. Kendrick Grobel; New York:
Charles Scribner's Sons, 1951) 1:§§1–4.

3. "Its goal did not consist of the reconstruction of original sources, but it proceeded
on the basis that texts handed on in the tradition initially gave more information about
the transmitters than about what was transmitted. . . . The point of departure is accordingly not the historical Jesus, but the community that confesses Jesus as its exalted and
present Lord" (D. Lührmann, "Die Frage nach Kriterien für ursprüngliche Jesusworte.
Eine Problemskizze," in J. Dupont, ed. *Jésus aux origines de la christologie* (BETL 40;
2nd ed.; Leuven: Leuven University Press, 1989) 63.

that is, at the formation of post-Easter Christology. For Bultmann, it was here that something new over against Judaism first began. In contrast, his students, who sought the material point of contact for such a Christology in elements already present in the historical Jesus, had to look for the beginnings of the exodus from Judaism already in the life of Jesus. Everything they regarded as distinguishing Jesus from Judaism appeared to them to be especially important. Thus, for the "New Quest" the "criterion of dissimilarity" became programmatic, as formulated by E. Käsemann in an essay that introduced this new phase of Jesus research:

> In only one case do we have more or less safe ground under our feet: when there are no grounds either for deriving a tradition from Judaism or for ascribing it to primitive Christianity, and especially when Jewish Christianity has mitigated or modified the received tradition, as having found it too bold for its taste.[4]

To be sure, (as an inheritance from the "Old Quest" of the historical Jesus) the difference between Jesus and early Christianity continued as a methodological principle. Distinguishing Jesus from Judaism, however, became the more important procedure. When Jesus was distinguished from early Christianity the emphasis lay on that part of early Christianity in which Jewish traditions had their strongest effects, namely Jewish Christianity. This procedure corresponds to the material result expressed in the same essay, in which for the first time the double-sided criterion of dissimilarity was formulated. This essay also declared that Jesus' sovereign freedom "shakes the very foundations of Judaism and causes his death." This statement is only somewhat moderated by seeing late Judaism as sharing "the distinction (which is fundamental for the whole of ancient thought) between the *temenos*, the realm of the sacred, and the secular:"[5] according to Käsemann, the critique of first-century Judaism embodied in Jesus strikes at every ancient religion.

Equipped with the array of tools provided by the classical methods of form criticism and redaction criticism, as well as the criterion of dissimilarity from the realm of the history of religions, numerous Jesus books were written in the following period by well-known New Testament scholars: among others, one may mention Günther Bornkamm, Herbert Braun, Kurt Niederwimmer, and Eduard Schweizer. Among scholars in this period who did not belong to the

---

4. E. Käsemann, "The Problem of the Historical Jesus," in *Essays on New Testament Themes* (SBT 41; London: SCM Press, 1964) 37. First published in *ZTK* 51 (1954): 125–53. Originally a lecture given at the reunion of the "Old Marburgers," 20 October 1953.

5. Käsemann, "Problem of the Historical Jesus," 40, 39.

Bultmann school but who must be mentioned because they were widely read, one may mention Ethelbert Stauffer and Joachim Jeremias. The first volume of Jeremias's *New Testament Theology*[6] was a portrayal of Jesus' message and can be considered within the "New Quest" in terms of its content.

Though relatively unnoticed in Germany, a new phase of Jesus research began in the early 1980s primarily in the English-speaking world, the "Third Quest" (T. Wright)[7] or "Jesus Research" (J. H. Charlesworth).[8] The common denominator of the various efforts at recovering the historical Jesus grouped together by these terms is the emphasis on truly historical research that will satisfy the demands of secular historical scholarship and that distinguishes itself more or less sharply from historical study carried on from churchly, theological motives. This demarcation manifests itself in a threefold manner:

1. Jesus is consistently classified as belonging within Judaism. There are frequent disavowals of any attempt to provide legitimization for Christian faith in Jesus by historical research. For the turn toward the *Jewish* Jesus in the "Third Quest," a significant role is played by the growing insight into the problem of anti-Judaism in theology (not only in Germany) and the study of the persecution and murder of Jews under German fascism. However, the engagement of Jewish scholars with Jesus research has been especially important for the genesis of the Third Quest.
2. The preferential treatment of canonical sources for Jesus is intentionally challenged. In principle, all "apocryphal" gospels and Jesus traditions are considered equally valid sources, the actual value of each source being determined exclusively on the basis of historical insight—while the traditional theological orientation to the canonical Gospels is neglected.[9] Impetus for this development was provided especially by the discovery of the *Gospel of Thomas* (1945), in particular by those scholars who wanted to find in it traditions independent of the Synoptic Gospels.
3. While the "New Quest" was especially interested in the theological significance of the proclamation of Jesus and his destiny, within the "Third Quest" Jesus is deliberately interpreted in the context of the secular and

---

6. Joachim Jeremias, *New Testament Theology. The Proclamation of Jesus* (New York: Charles Scribner's Sons, 1971). No further volumes appeared.

7. The term "Third Quest" was coined by N. T. Wright in Stephen Neill and N. T. Wright, *The Interpretation of the New Testament 1861–1986* (2nd ed.; Oxford: Oxford University Press, 1988) 379.

8. The designation "Jesus Research" derives from J. H. Charlesworth, "From Barren Mazes to Gentle Rappings: The Emergence of Jesus Research," *Princeton Seminary Bulletin* 7/3 (1986): 221–30.

9. A title such as C. W. Hedrick's "The Tyranny of the Synoptic Jesus" (*Semeia* 44 (1988): 1–8) shows what high expectations can be aroused by the utilization of non-canonical sources: liberation from the dictatorship of the Synoptic (and that means the canonical) Jesus!

social history of Palestine.[10] Thereby several studies of Jesus maintain a "secular accent"—quite independently of whether the advent of Jesus is seen in correlation with a social crisis or in the context of a relatively calm social situation.

In the meantime, the "Third Quest" has sprouted numerous branches. A unified picture of Jesus has by no means been attained. The differences between the various authors are even greater than among the authors in the "New Quest." That can be explained partly in terms of the sociology of scholarship. There is, in fact, a remarkable difference between the authors active in the "Third Quest" and those in the "New Quest." Almost all the authors within the "New Quest" originated from one academic tradition, namely, the Bultmann school, and within this school a new question was raised, or an old question was reformulated. At a 1953 meeting of the "Old Marburgers"—disciples of Bultmann—Ernst Käsemann presented his pioneering lecture on "The Problem of the Historical Jesus." This lecture, published the following year, set the discussion in motion.

The situation is completely different with the "Third Quest." Without any particular starting signal, all at once a number of studies emerged that we classify together as the "Third Quest." This new beginning was just in the air, without having been intentionally placed on the agenda by anyone with a specific point of view.

Basically, in the United States and Great Britain, historical research had never been made so theologically problematic as had happened in the German-speaking world. Hence, improved knowledge about the first century C.E. was unhindered in giving occasion to return to the quest of the historical Jesus. That the center of gravity of this fresh beginning is located in the Anglo-Saxon world could also be related to an increased measure of self-confidence vis-à-vis German theology. It appears that since German scholars had avoided the subject of the historical Jesus,[11] English-speaking scholars were "all the more" keen to deal with it. One expression of this interest in the historical figure of Jesus is the organization of the so-called "Jesus Seminar" in 1985 at the Westar Institute in the United States, initiated by R. W. Funk. This seminar set its dual goals as fostering Jesus research by coordinating the work of qualified scholars, on the one hand, and, on the other, making the results of its work

---

10. Cf. also W. Stenger, "Sozialgeschichtliche Wende und historischer Jesus," in *Kairos* 28 (1986): 11–22.

11. Interestingly enough, Jesus books innocent of scholarly learning have, of course, always enjoyed a great popularity without regard to how they were regarded in theological circles.

accessible to a broad spectrum of the public, which finally stood to benefit from research on the historical Jesus.[12]

As the previous phases of Jesus research had been associated with the reformulation of criteria, so also in the case of the Jesus research of the "Third Quest." On the one hand, we note a gradual and almost imperceptible erosion of the criterion of dissimilarity and, on the other hand, an abrupt new beginning with the help of a criterion previously considered second-rate.

First, with regard to the erosion of the criterion of dissimilarity: its use had in any case always been provided with precautions. Objections were raised that separating Jesus from Judaism and early Christianity overlooked the continuity between Judaism, Jesus, and early Christianity, a continuity that doubtless was present. In addition, in view of our fragmentary knowledge of both Judaism and Christianity, deviations from each of the historical realities could hardly be ascertained with confidence. In view of the plurality of both Judaism and Christianity, the demand for "dissimilarity" or "distinctiveness" would lose its selective power: within the manifold variety of both Judaism and early Christianity, every traditional statement of Jesus would fit somewhere. Such provisos often served only to rob the criterion of dissimilarity of its critical power. With good conscience, the critic could well regard as authentic more than what remained after the sharp knife had done its work. With the advent of the "Third Quest," however, the criterion of dissimilarity basically fell by the wayside. Once it is programmatically asserted that Jesus belongs within Judaism, one can no longer use "dissimilar from Judaism" as a fundamental methodological principle. It would then make more sense to ask which variation of Judaism we meet in Jesus. Along the same line, when it is made a programmatic principle that Jesus research must deal with all early Christian literature, including the apocryphal books and works with a "heretical" slant, then Jesus cannot simply be contrasted with all of early Christianity. Rather, one must ask, With which stream of early Christianity is Jesus being contrasted? Should it be, as in Käsemann's classical formulation, Jewish Christianity? Or is it perhaps the case that several streams of Jewish Christianity (which can by no means be considered a unity) have preserved Jesus traditions more faithfully than Gentile Christianity? How was the image of Jesus further developed in the different streams of early Christianity? And what points do these different images have in common? There can be no doubt: a new formulation of criteria is overdue.

It is thus no coincidence that in this situation scholars wanted to reexamine and resolve all methodological issues from the ground up. In his Jesus

---

12. The first results were presented in 1993: R. W. Funk and R. W. Hoover, eds., *The Five Gospels: The Search for the Authentic Words of Jesus* (New York: Macmillan, 1993).

book,[13] for example, J. D. Crossan abandons the criterion of dissimilarity and by reevaluating the apocryphal sources is inspired to formulate a criterion that combines the age and number of sources in which a purported feature of the historical Jesus is documented. He begins by claiming an early date for several apocryphal documents and sources reconstructed from literary analysis. According to Crossan, the earliest layer includes the undisputed Pauline letters; the oldest layer of the *Gospel of Thomas*; three papyri that contain fragments of an unknown gospel (the Egerton Papyrus, the Fayum fragment, and Oxyrhynchos Papyrus 1224); and the fragments of the *Gospel of the Hebrews*, to which are added four reconstructed sources: the Sayings Source Q, a collection of miracle stories, an apocalyptic scenario (behind Mark 13 and *Didache* 16), and a "Cross Gospel" that he postulates as a source for the *Gospel of Peter*. Thus none of the canonical Gospels belongs to the oldest layer. They are dethroned.

In the second place, Crossan investigates how often a Jesus tradition is independently documented. The inclusion of apocryphal texts understandably gives preference to the traditions that are included in them. By means of a combined number, both criteria are registered in the documentation of each tradition: when a tradition is documented in the oldest stratum, and, in addition, (in different strata) is documented four times, it receives the number 1:4. The saying against divorce, for example, is documented in the oldest layer (in Paul and in Q), and, in addition, is documented four times in different layers, namely in 1 Cor 7:10–11, in Q (Luke 16:18 = Matt 5:31–32), in Mark 10:10–12, and in Herm. *Mand.* IV, 16b, 10. This procedure has an undeniable intellectual charm. Its clarity and methodological consistency are seductively alluring. But it suffers from its claims for early dating, which are hardly capable of attaining scholarly consensus. An additional factor is the element of randomness in the preserved traditions. Whatever happens to be preserved on a fragment of papyrus gains huge significance. Above all is to be noted, however, that with this procedure one can establish only one thing: the perceptible age of a tradition, without being able to exclude the early date of other traditions that are not so frequently documented. This problem remains even if the dating of documents were carried through more consistently, and even if they were more capable of producing a scholarly consensus.

Our brief sketch of the phases of modern Jesus research has shown that each of these phases is bound up with a new determination of criteria for authenticity and inauthenticity. For the most recent phase, this new determination

---

13. J. D. Crossan, *The Historical Jesus: The Life of a Mediterranean Jewish Peasant* (San Francisco: HarperSanFrancisco, 1991) xxvii–xxxiv; see also "Materials and Methods in Historical Research," *Foundations and Facets Forum* 4 (1988): 3–24.

has not yet been satisfactorily carried out. The quest for criteria must once again be fundamentally reexamined.

2. FUNDAMENTAL PROBLEMS IN THE QUEST FOR CRITERIA

Since Jesus research operates with historical-critical methods, it cannot base its work on a particular Gospel or Gospel harmony. The point of departure for Jesus research was in fact precisely the challenging of unlimited trust in the historical reliability of the Gospel texts. In other words, exegesis abandoned the bond of medieval historiography to "authorities" such as the Scriptures. Since the "affirmative power of tradition"[14] was no longer considered valid, "authorities" had to be legitimated by other means (e.g., as eyewitnesses[15]). As a result, it became necessary to develop criteria for dealing with and evaluating the available sources. Thus the historical-critical method of source analysis that had been developed in classical philology and transferred to the historical sciences was then adopted by exegesis. Source analysis (then called "literary criticism") was the "most distinguished method"[16] of the historical theology of the older life-of-Jesus research, supplemented by form criticism and redaction criticism, in which the primary concern was always for the oldest source and the oldest form of the tradition. When it became clear in form criticism and redaction criticism that the oldest form of the tradition was already shaped by kerygmatic perspectives and did not necessarily offer trustworthy access to history, scholars found it necessary to look for other criteria—and found the criterion of dissimilarity, based on a combination of critical reading of the sources and the comparative study of religions.

The criteria that derive from historical criticism deal with the source material in a reductionistic manner: the "unhistorical" elements are excised from the available texts and/or the "authentic" elements are distilled from them. One criterion is used to pin down the supposedly underlying distinguishing feature. Thus the determination of such criteria is also guided by unscientific factors. Some of the theological problems bound up with the quest for criteria may here be briefly listed.

---

14. G. Melville, "Kompilation, Fiktion und Diskurs. Aspekte zur heuristischen Methode der mittelalterlichen Geschichtsschreiber," in Ch. Meier and J. Rüsen, eds., *Historische Methode* (Beiträge zur Historik 5; Munich: dtv, 1988) 135.
15. Cf. Reimarus' catalogue of criteria with regard to eyewitness testimony in H. S. Reimarus, *Die Vernunftlehre als eine Anweisung zum richtigen Gebrauche der Vernunft in dem Erkenntniss der Wahrheit aus zwoen ganz natürlichen Regeln der Einstimmung und des Widerspruchs*, (Hamburg, 1766; 3rd ed. reprinted Munich, 1979 [ed. F. Lötzsch]).
16. Lührmann, "Die Frage nach Kriterien," 60.

In the Jesus research as carried on by Protestant scholars in particular,[17] special weight is attached to the *words* of Jesus, so that it became very important to establish the historical authenticity of particular sayings. This concentration on the message of Jesus is also to be traced back to the fact that, in the transmission of Jesus' sayings—in contrast to the tradition of Jesus *deeds*—"the medium of transmission is identical with that which was being transmitted, so that in the tradition *from* Jesus the word *of* Jesus can be preserved."[18] Of course, it is also the case that the high evaluation of the "word" in Protestant theology played a role in this concentration on the word of Jesus.

In view of the fundamentally positive significance of Jesus of Nazareth for Christianity, the proof of the historical *authenticity* for particular items of content could become a theological argument, all the more so since "truth" was understood as "historical truth"[19]—as in the age of historicism.

At the same time, the question was always posed as to what was *essential* for Jesus, his "essence." From time to time there was no clear distinction made between the material that had been judged "authentic" and the importance of this material, which may have been only incidental for the earthly Jesus.[20]

Moreover, the criterion of dissimilarity poses the question of that which was singular and unique in the figure of Jesus. The more the image of Jesus as the revelation of the transcendent God faded in modern consciousness, the more it depended on historical research to establish his uniqueness in immanent history—often as a disguised proof of his revelatory quality (or as a substitute for it).

Since the Gospels are the most important sources for Jesus, the theologically loaded question of the *trustworthiness of Scripture* plays a role.[21] As a result, christological questions emerged regarding the continuity and/or discontinuity between the historical Jesus and Jesus Christ as portrayed by canonical texts from the point of view of faith.

---

17. J. Gnilka, *Jesus of Nazareth: Message and History* (trans. Siegfried S. Schatzmann; Peabody, Mass.: Hendrickson, 1997) 7: "In the Catholic world there was no quest of the historical Jesus; exegesis began to unfold only in conjunction with the later Gospel studies."

18. Lührmann, "Die Frage nach Kriterien," 64–65.

19. However, the handing over of truth claims to the realm of history meant at the same time the relativizing of truth—a basic problem of historicism.

20. M. D. Hooker has pointed to this in her article "On Using the Wrong Tool" (*Theology* 75 [1972]: 574), in which she distinguishes between that which is characteristic and that which is merely different.

21. Cf. for example the obvious relief in the remark of A. Neumann, after referring to Schmiedel's "foundation pillars": "The existence of such statements is the salvation of the Synoptic Gospels, giving them a definite value as sources. The Gospels cannot be pure sagas or legends when material so intractable is enshrined in them." (A. Neumann, *Jesus* [trans. M. A. Canney, with a preface by P. W. Schmiedel; London: Black, 1906] 10.)

Thus in the background of Jesus research there always stands particular theological or christological concepts as well the discussion of the approach to the Bible. This all precipitated out in the formulation of methods and criteria of historical study of Jesus that sought authentic materials in the Gospels. Theological interests and historical methodology entered into a close alliance. This posed a fundamental problem. Since the beginning of Jesus research a call has regularly been issued for a methodology based on secular historical study or on the attempt to operate in a manner that satisfies the demands of secular historical research, and for the development of methods that are valid for all historical sources. Nevertheless, as a rule the criteria were developed only on the basis of the New Testament texts and applied only to them, in order to excavate from them the authentic Jesus material they contained. In their formulation, methodological considerations of general historical science play an amazingly small role. The results of this procedure in itself, however, will not lead to the "historical Jesus," nor even to a historical picture of the figure of Jesus. For this, one must take into account the historical background of Jesus' work as a whole, must consider the analogous problematic of the historical evaluation of other traditions, and must include the methodological approach common to historical science. Work on the issue of criteria in Jesus research has thus sometimes led to contradictory results. On the one hand, with the help of the criterion of dissimilarity the historical world beyond the New Testament is taken into consideration, but only as a background against which the figure of Jesus stands out by contrast. On the other hand, precisely by this procedure the historian distances himself/herself from general historical methodology, for as we have already suggested and will document more closely in the course of this book, behind the criterion of dissimilarity stand quite specific theological interests.

3. THE CRITERION OF DISSIMILARITY WITHIN THE FRAMEWORK OF THE CRITERIA FOR JESUS RESEARCH

This book concentrates on the criterion of dissimilarity. But is it the most important criterion? The most recent developments in Jesus research appear to raise questions about this. In the "Third Quest" we note both a gradual erosion of this criterion and the abrupt introduction of other criteria. It is thus necessary to sift through the numerous criteria that have been developed in order to determine the relative importance of the criterion of dissimilarity. We are not driven by any ambition to list and discuss every criterion that has ever been proposed.[22] We want merely to make a systematic categorization of the traditional criteria. Three groups can be distinguished: (1) source-evaluation arguments, (2) indices of distinctiveness, and (3) criteria of authenticity. As we will see, only the third group deals with criteria in the strict sense.

---

22. Three catalogues of criteria are here listed. The first is from D. G. A. Calvert, "An Examination of the Criteria for Distinguishing the Authentic Words of Jesus," *NTS* 18 (1971/1972): 221: "Those sayings are judged to be authentic which

(1) are positively distinctive from Jewish thoughts;
(2) are positively distinctive from the thought of the post-Easter church;
(3) contain elements that could not be from the church;
(4) exhibit Aramaisms in various forms and reflect Palestinian conditions;
(5) are found in more than one tradition or form;
(6) are characteristic of the known teaching of Jesus."

One can easily see that no. 3 is only a more particular form of no. 2., and that nos. 1–3 together represent the classical criterion of dissimilarity. The linguistic criterion no. 4 is weak, since all Syria spoke Aramaic and a semitizing biblical style can be documented throughout early Christianity. No. 6 is the classical criterion of coherence, and no. 5, the criterion of multiple attestation.

A more extensive list is presented by M. E. Boring, "Criteria of Authenticity: The Beatitudes as a Test Case," in *Foundations and Facets Forum 1*, (1985): 3ff.; cf. also his *The Continuing Voice of Jesus: Christian Prophecy and the Gospel Tradition* (Louisville, Ky.: Westminster John Knox, 1991) 192–206:

(1) Attestation in multiple sources
(2) Attestation in multiple forms
(3) The linguistic criterion
(4) The environmental criterion
(5) Tendencies of the developing tradition
(6) Dissimilarity ("in contrast to both Judaism and Christianity")
(7) Modification ("the more radical form is usually the earlier form.")
(8) Coherence
(9) Plausible tradition history
(10) Hermeneutical potential ("what the earliest form must have been in order to generate the others.")

One can easily see that nos. 5, 7, 9, and 10 are all variations of the same procedure in separating original material from secondary formulations that developed in the history of the tradition. Along with no. 3, the linguistic argument, they belong for the most part to the category of source-evaluation arguments that emphasize the age of a particular tradition. Nos. 1, 2, and 8 are different ways of evaluating one and the same set of facts: the coherence of sources. Nos. 4 and 6 refer in complementary ways to Jesus' environment, namely, on what connects him to it (no. 4) and what distinguishes him from it (no. 6). In our opinion both belong together under the heading of contextual plausibility.

Ten criteria are also listed in the comprehensive catalogue of C. A. Evans ("Authenticity Criteria in Life of Jesus Research," *CSR* 19 (1989): 6ff.). The following are already familiar: Multiple Attestation, Multiple Forms, Semitic Features and Palestinian Background, Dissimilarity, and Consistency (or Coherence). A new addition to the list is the criterion of "Contradiction," but this is only the flip side of the criterion of coherence: that which conflicts with the substance of traditions otherwise known to be authentic

3.1 Source-evaluation Arguments

Source-evaluation arguments speak to the issue of whether in a given body of source material we have any chance at all of finding historical tradition and/or of getting back to the historical event itself. That is to say, source-evaluation arguments assess the usability (or uselessness) of sources for the reconstruction of history but do not themselves carry through on this evaluation—unless one is convinced that he or she has found an absolutely reliable source. Since, however, there is no such thing as absolutely reliable sources in human history, even with the best sources available, the task of investigating them further still remains to be done. In order to do this, one needs additional arguments and criteria that go beyond the general issue of the reliability of the sources. Source-evaluation arguments thus, as a rule, formulate only the necessary, but not sufficient, conditions for the extraction of authentic Jesus tradition. In Jesus research the most important source-evaluation arguments have been the age of a tradition, that is, its temporal proximity to the event, its Palestinian local color (i.e., its having been stamped with appropriate features by the location of the event itself), and the independence of traditions from each other (or their interdependent relationship).

1. The *age of the tradition* can have something to say about the relative value of both written sources and the older (written and) oral sources contained in them. It is a fortunate circumstance when one can establish a *terminus post quem* or *terminus ante quem* by means of contemporary events to which it refers or to which it is related. Thus some of the traditions contained in Matthew and Luke, even though not formulated until after 70 C.E., go back to the time before the destruction of the temple, such as the requirement to pay the temple tax (Matt 17:23ff.) or the command to be reconciled to one's brother before offering sacrifice (Matt 5:23ff.). The Jewish war and the destruction of the temple were decisive events. They left their marks on later history. It would be even more relevant if the later effects of the crisis under Caligula could be identified, which would put us in the period after 40 C.E. For the most part, however, we must infer the age of traditions not by coordinating them to contemporary events but on the basis of their multiple attestation. In the 50s C.E.,

---

must be inauthentic. Two criteria distinguish later and earlier layers: "Least Distinctive" means that there is a tendency to secondary touching up and making more precise; "Tradition Contrary to Editorial Tendency" highlights the difference between tradition and redaction. Two further criteria deal with characteristic features of content, which presuppose the successful application of prior criteria, which we would designate "indices of distinctiveness:" "Proleptic Eschatology" and "Prophetic Criticism." Evans himself pleads for a careful application of the criterion of dissimilarity, so that much of what he says has points of contact with our own reflections.

Paul from time to time appeals to sayings of Jesus that he had received from tradition (and which therefore must have existed still earlier); the existence of Jesus traditions in the time before 50 is thus well documented. Since he falls back on sayings of Jesus only in regard to particular polemical and disputed issues (divorce, 1 Cor 7:10–11; obligation to support missionaries, 1 Cor 9:14; dispute regarding the eucharist, 1 Cor 11:17ff.), one may assume that he knew other Jesus traditions but did not cite them—either because there was no occasion to do so or because he was more oriented to the exalted Lord than to the earthly Jesus (2 Cor 5:16). Finally, as examples of verifiable old tradition, one may mention the numerous double traditions of Q and Mark, since they must be older than both sources. Since Q had already been composed prior to 70 C.E., and Mark about 70, we also have here documentation for older traditions that extend back into the first generation. Fixing the age of a tradition is, of course, no criterion of its authenticity or inauthenticity: that which is not documented until a later source can, in itself, be old and even authentic. On the other hand, that which stands in our earliest sources could go back only to the formulations of the earliest post-Easter church. Determining the age of a tradition thus sometimes functions only as a negative criterion: that which not only is documented late but which also with great probability first originated late must be excluded as evidence for Jesus. Only in this negative form can the determination of the age of a tradition be considered a "criterion of authenticity"—or better, a "criterion of inauthenticity."

2. The investigation of Palestinian *local color*[23] is also a factor in determining the relative source value of a document or tradition. Thus here also the principle applies: the presence of Palestinian local color does not verify the authenticity of a tradition but only the presence of Palestinian (or even Galilean) roots. This fact does, to be sure, increase the probability that Jesus too could have said or done this or that, but authenticity could be inferred only on the basis of additional arguments. Just as in the case of the determination of the date of a tradition, so also with the criterion of local color: sometimes a negative application of this tradition is possible. That which not only has clearly picked up secondary non-Palestinian features but also originated outside Palestine cannot be from Jesus. In the case of this source-evaluation argument, one must acknowledge, however, that whether we can really verify the Galilean or Palestinian provenance of a tradition depends on chance circumstances. It is a matter of Galilean local color, for instance, that the Jesus

---

23. Cf. G. Theissen, *Lokalkolorit und Zeitgeschichte in den Evangelien. Ein Beitrag zur Geschichte der synoptischen Tradition* (NTOA 8; Freiburg [Schweiz]/Göttingen: Universitätsverlag Fribourg/Vandenhoeck & Ruprecht, 1989), passim, for the following examples.

tradition is anchored in rural settings in which the two large cities of Galilee are bracketed—Sepphoris and Tiberias are never mentioned in the Synoptic tradition. References to the customs office in Capernaum could represent local color, since in the latter part of the first century the border no longer ran through there, although it probably did in the time of Herod Antipas. Local color could be represented by Jesus' trips into the territory of nearby Gentile cities of Tyre, Sidon, and the Decapolis, since Jewish minorities lived in the rural areas belonging to these towns. The association of reeds shaken by the wind with the palaces of kings (Matt 11:7) could be a matter of local color, since some coins of Herod Antipas are inscribed with a reed as Herod's emblem. Finally, local color could be indicated in the way the Galilean lake is portrayed, especially in those places where it is called a "sea" ("ocean"), as if it were the central body of water around which a small social world oriented itself. Stories of boat trips are only understandable against this Galilean background and so forth—this is the way the criterion works.

3. The *independence* of (at least) two traditions increases the relative source value of each of them, while their dependence decreases the value of the dependent one to that of its source, or, more precisely, makes it of even less value than its source. Nonetheless, a plurality of independent sources attesting a particular tradition is no guarantee of the authenticity of a tradition (no matter how numerous such sources may be), but only the authenticity of its age. At most, the argument for fixing the relative value of a source would be a positive criterion of authenticity only in an instance where we could be certain that two sources are related because they are independent witnesses of the event to which they commonly attest and thus, so to speak, represent two independent eyewitnesses. Of course, in the Gospels we can never be certain whether the variant traditions originated through independent access to the same historical event or go back to a single tradition that has secondarily branched out into two different traditions. One can say no more than that a majority of several independent witnesses increases the probability of having discovered authentic historical material. In some cases we can be almost certain that we have independent sources that reach back to the history itself, namely, where we can compare Christian and non-Christian texts. There are only a few such cases. But the importance of these for evaluating the source value of the Gospels as a whole has often been underestimated. With reference to Jesus, we have the *Testimonium Flavianum* (*Ant.* 18.63–64), the kernel of which probably goes back to Josephus. It has been edited in the process of Christian transmission and thus its value and usefulness as a comparison with the Gospels is limited. The case is different with three other figures mentioned in the Gospels: John the Baptist, Herod Antipas, and Pilate, all of whom are mentioned by Josephus. We have further information about the two political figures in the form of additional documentation, coins, and an inscription. It

is thus somewhat possible to compare Synoptic statements with statements of non-Christian origin in the form of spot checks, which give us some idea of the extent to which we might have historically trustworthy traditions. One could also assess this kind of source-evaluation argument as a contribution to the investigation of local color, since doubtless all discoveries about the environment and the figures within it help us to judge how deeply the Synoptic tradition is rooted in the social and political world of Palestine. The conclusion is repeatedly confirmed: the Synoptic tradition is inconceivable apart from this particular environment. As said above, only in supposedly borderline cases can the independence of traditions function directly as a criterion of authenticity. Conversely, the argument from dependence or independence can be applied as a criterion of inauthenticity: traditions that are clearly dependent and could not have originated independently have no claim to authenticity.

Source-evaluation arguments are thus as a rule not directly applicable as criteria of authenticity, but they can be used as negative criteria of inauthenticity. J. D. Crossan's argument that combines the age of traditions and their independence would thus not be primarily a criterion of authenticity in the strict sense, but it could presumably be a means for assessing the source value of a tradition. In addition, it can be applied negatively as a criterion of inauthenticity. But here too a word of caution needs to be raised: not everything that appears in a late literary layer or is found in texts of a late date must immediately be considered inauthentic on this basis alone. One example will suffice. The private instruction in the house after the public dispute about marriage and divorce in Mark 10:10–12 is clearly a secondary addition to a unit of tradition already complete in itself. Nonetheless, the saying about divorce, placed in this context of private teaching, is in itself probably authentic. This judgment is based not only on the saying's good documentation in independent tradition, but also on the fact that, within Jewish traditions, it has its own distinctive accent and provoked demonstrable difficulties in early Christianity. Matthew adds the "immorality clause," and Paul adds a "mixed marriage clause," in order to provide the apodictic negation of any divorce with exceptions (cf. Matt 5:32; 19:9; 1 Cor 7:10–11).

3.2 Indices of Distinctiveness

We designate all the characteristics peculiar to the Jesus tradition as "indices of distinctiveness."[24] The basis for establishing them is the comparison with other contemporary traditions. Indices of distinctiveness are thus logically

---

24. J. Jeremias, "Characteristics of the *ipsissima vox Jesu*," in *The Prayers of Jesus* (SBT 2.6; London: SCM Press, 1967) 108–15. Jeremias also attempted to work out the linguistic mannerisms preferred by Jesus as well as the general distinguishing marks of his

dependent on the criterion of dissimilarity and thus do not represent a standard that functions as a norm (*"norma normans"*) but a standard that has been set by another norm (*"norma normata"*). Nevertheless, there is a certain justification for the fact that such indices of distinctiveness repeatedly appear in catalogues of criteria. Thus the following are generally regarded as particularly characteristic features of Jesus' preaching: the nonresponsorial *amen* that introduces many traditional sayings of Jesus; the antimakarisms that pronounce blessing precisely on those who (still, in the here and now) suffer deprivation; and the antithetical form such as "You have heard it said to those of old . . . but I say to you." So also the expression "Son of Man" in its characteristic usage (without comparison and with no reference to a vision) belongs to the distinctive elements in the Jesus tradition. The importance of such indices of distinctiveness for reconstructing the historical Jesus has been both over- and underrated. They are overrated when they are applied as "criteria" supposed to confer the quality of "authenticity," for even these distinctive characteristics were also imitated in early Christianity. Because, in the earliest Christian period, they were already regarded as characteristic features of Jesus' speech, they intruded into many traditions that had either originated from Jesus or had been newly coined. Material was created and reformulated "in Jesus' style." It can thus be verified that the expression "Son of Man" was secondarily added to several sayings. Precisely for this reason the importance of the indices of distinctiveness for Jesus research has often been underestimated, since for most scholars there is little doubt that as a whole they must point back to Jesus himself. They are not, however, criteria that may be used to establish Jesus' "very words" (*ipsissima verba*), but are most likely indications of his "very voice" (*ipsissima vox*). While we remain uncertain in details as to whether this or that word really goes back to Jesus, we are still remarkably sure that this or that expression, a particular linguistic form, and the characteristic genres of his speech as a whole point back to him.

3.3 Criteria of Authenticity

In our opinion, among the traditional criteria, real criteria of authenticity[25] are to be found only in the two traditional criteria that have now become classical: the criterion of dissimilarity and the criterion of coherence. The criterion

---

language (parables, riddles, talk of the kingdom of God, *amen*, and *abba*) in *New Testament Theology: The Proclamation of Jesus* (trans. John Bowden; New York: Scribners, 1971) 8–36. His procedure is basically sound, but it is not a matter of "criteria," which are already presupposed.

25. A formulation of the criteria of authenticity that well expresses the consensus that occasionally appears is found in N. Perrin, *Rediscovering the Teaching of Jesus* (New York:

of dissimilarity had long since played a latent role but did not become pro-grammatic until formulated by Ernst Käsemann at the beginning of the "New Quest." That which cannot be derived from Judaism or Christianity has a claim to authenticity. The criterion of coherence is dependent on the criterion of dissimilarity. It increases the amount of authentic Jesus material in that addi-tional tradition can be declared authentic when it coheres with that which can-not be derived from Judaism or Christianity. By means of this supplementary criterion, a more comprehensive and encompassing picture of the figure of Jesus can be attained. The strict requirements for judging material to be authentic inherent in the criterion of dissimilarity were thus quantitatively relaxed but not so much qualitatively, for the strong historical and theological tendencies of the criterion of dissimilarity (to be pointed out below) could be continued in this way.

The criterion of coherence means in the first place *substantial agreement in terms of content* with a core of authentic Jesus material. It refers not only to par-ticular details. In the background there always stands an outline of the image of Jesus taken as a whole. In terms of content, this picture can contain inconsis-tencies, such as the tension between present and future eschatology. The deci-sive factor is that such inconsistencies can be interpreted as meaningful tensions.

Moreover, one could relate the criterion of coherence to a *biographical coherence*: almost everything we ascribe to Jesus must fit within the two authen-tic dates established for his life, namely, his baptism by John the Baptist and his crucifixion in Jerusalem. Here, too, one can reckon with developments. Whoever submits to baptism in order to flee from the coming wrath of God—and then emerges in public with a message of the kingdom of God that is pri-marily a message of grace, namely, a turning to the weak and lost—this person has distanced himself from the preaching of his master: Jesus nowhere makes baptism a condition of salvation!

Finally, one can relate the criterion of coherence to a *coherent history of tra-dition*, that is, to the agreement in substantive content found in different

---

Harper & Row, 1967). (1) The "criterion of dissimilarity:" "The earliest form of a say-ing we can reach may be regarded as authentic if it can be shown to be dissimilar to characteristic emphases both of ancient Judaism and of the early Church, and this will particularly be the case where Christian tradition oriented towards Judaism can be shown to have modified the saying away from its original emphasis" (39). (2) The "cri-terion of coherence:" "Material from the earliest strata of the tradition may be accepted as authentic if it can be shown to cohere with material established as authentic by means of the criterion of dissimilarity" (43). (3) The "criterion of multiple attestation," regarding which Perrin has some reservations, "is a proposal to accept as authentic material which is attested in all, or most, of the sources which can be discerned behind the synoptic gospels" (45).

strands of independent tradition. To the extent that it deals with one and the same tradition, the coherence of the history of tradition is often regarded as a criterion of multiple attestation and relegated to a third-class status behind the two primary criteria. However, it basically belongs to the source-evaluation arguments previously discussed: here the argument is based on the independence of traditions for which there is multiple attestation, which initially permits inferences about the age of a tradition, not its authenticity.

Our survey of the most important criteria in Jesus research shows that only the last-named criteria of dissimilarity and coherence are criteria of authenticity in the strict sense. Of these two, the criterion of dissimilarity is the more important. The other "criteria" are actually source-evaluation arguments that help us to identify within the many traditions and texts those in which one might expect to locate authentic Jesus material. They are themselves dependent on additional criteria, and in and of themselves can only be applied in a negative sense as criteria of *in*authenticity. Taken as a whole, then, the source-evaluation arguments belong to those issues that must be considered *before* the application of the real criteria of authenticity. In the case of the indices of distinctiveness, on the other hand, these criteria of authenticity are already presupposed. It is a matter of the belated acknowledgement and application of these criteria, since the peculiar features of Jesus' message presuppose that these have been established by their divergence from all other traditions by means of the criterion of dissimilarity. The traditional criterion of coherence is relativized by the indices of distinctiveness, since these have secondarily proliferated throughout the whole Jesus tradition and thereby given it a "coherent" character.

Source-evaluation arguments and indices of distinctiveness are, in our opinion, however, still important procedural elements in Jesus research: they decide whether it is the authenticity or the inauthenticity of a Jesus tradition that must be established. The higher we rank the source value of a particular tradition, and the more indices for the distinctiveness of Jesus we can show, all the more the burden of proof rests on those who advocate its inauthenticity. The lower the source value of a particular text or tradition and the less it contains what is "typically Jesus," all the more the burden of proof falls on those who advocate its authenticity. However, if source-evaluation arguments and indices of distinctiveness can influence the "rule for establishing burden of proof," then this shows that they function as a preparatory stage for the real proof but are themselves not already a (sufficient) proof of authenticity or inauthenticity. This proof is provided by other criteria—as a rule, the criteria of dissimilarity and coherence. We have previously shown, however, that, in the most recent developments in the quest of the historical Jesus, it is precisely the decisive criterion of dissimilarity that has become problematic. What is it about this criterion that is so essentially problematic?

4. INTRODUCTION TO THE PROBLEMATIC OF THE CRITERION OF DISSIMILARITY

4.1 Factual and Conceptual Explanations of the Criterion of Dissimilarity

a) Distinguishing Two Criteria behind the Criterion of Dissimilarity

A certain lack of clarity has tended to prevail in the discussion of the criterion of dissimilarity with regard to the fact that this criterion actually comprises two different criteria that must be legitimized in two different ways.[26] The *one* criterion is oriented to the post-Easter Christian community and its tradition and redaction, while the *other* is oriented to Judaism and to Jesus' Jewish environment. In order to distinguish the two criteria concisely and crisply from each other, in the following we will speak of the CDC (criterion of difference from Christianity) and the CDJ (criterion of difference from Judaism).

The CDC is derived from the oldest principles for evaluating sources. It proceeds on the assumption that historical sources were not composed by disinterested reporters. Thus in order to get closer to the authentic historical background of reported events, one must be aware of all the intentions and social circumstances of the sources' authors and editors. As a result, every item of content that fits awkwardly within the thinking of the author or editor and is foreign to his or her time is to be considered especially historically trustworthy. In Gospel research, the CDC functions according to this basic principle in the fields of redaction criticism, tradition criticism, and form criticism. Redaction criticism works out the concepts and theology implicit in the document's editing; form criticism provides insights into the function and meaning of particular textual units in the history of the early Christian communities ("*Sitz im Leben*"). All texts and textual elements that, according to our knowledge of the history of the traditions, were not of use to the early Christian community or conflicted with its interests were considered to be historically authentic on the basis of the CDC. The same principle is meant by "intentional" or "unintentional" transmission.[27]

---

26. This is also the case in D. Lührmann's otherwise very illuminating discussion. Thus he traces the criterion of dissimilarity back to the history-of-religions approach alone and neglects the—likewise original—aspect of source criticism (D. Lührmann, "Die Frage nach Kriterien," 65). E. P. Sanders and M. Davies speak of "the criterion of dual dissimilarity" [*Studying the Synoptic Gospels* (Philadelphia: Trinity Press International, 1989) 316].

27. M. Bloch, *Apologie der Geschichte oder Der Beruf des Historikers* (Anmerkungen und Argumente 9; Stuttgart: Klett, 1974) 73–74: "The indications that now and then unintentionally present past history to us make it possible for us . . . [among other things, not to] become the victims of every prejudice, exaggerated caution, and shortsightedness under which the view of this [earlier] generation suffered."

The CDJ is formulated analogously to the CDC: Everything in Jesus' words and deeds that distinguishes him from Judaism is regarded as having greater historical probability. This line of argument is based on considerations operative in the study of the history of religions. In this connection we need to point out two problems in advance:

In the first place, this procedure implies a view of Jesus and his disciples already determined by the "Christian" understanding of Jesus' later influence. Jesus is often seen a priori as one who has abandoned Judaism. But also when Jesus is regarded as "only" a reformer within Judaism, there is often already at work an assessment of Jesus that considers the aspects in which Jesus goes beyond Judaism to be his essential elements and wants to use them to establish Christian identity.[28] This kind of Jesus research for use within the church cannot satisfy the omnipresent demands of secular historical scholarship.

Second, difficulties emerge in the attempt to establish the CDJ on the basis of the history of the tradition and on redaction criticism, since the Jesus material in the Gospels has been handed on by the earliest Christians, that is, by disciples of Jesus who from the very beginning regarded him as a distinctive figure. Thus everything "distinctive" separating Jesus from Judaism could go back to the earliest Christian bearers of the tradition. One could, of course, argue with some justification that the first "Christians" were not yet Christians in the sense of the later separation from Judaism, and as "Jewish Christians" were more "Jews" than "Christians." But this argument makes the dilemma even greater. If in this case, too, everything Jewish were radically excised from the Jesus tradition, then Jesus would appear as the first Christian, whose Jewish Christian disciples could not possibly have understood him—in which case the reliability of the Jesus tradition it had transmitted would be dubious.

Thus whenever it is applied to the Gospels—and other extensive sources are not available—the CDJ implies a hypothesis about the origin of these sources. These sources are historical artifacts.[29] The reconstruction of the history of how they originated is often unconsciously guided by modern premises: the background of the CDJ is principally influenced by ideas about the philosophy of history that had been adopted for theological motives and thereby made even more dominant (cf. below under 4.2b).

---

28. This is quite clear in Käsemann when (with a lack of clarity that also pertains to his language itself) he says with regard to the dissimilarity to Judaism that "there is an *almost* complete lack of satisfactory and water-tight criteria" (emphasis D.W.) (Käsemann, "Problem of the Historical Jesus," 37).

29. Here the problematic involved in speaking of "authenticity" becomes especially clear. The term is mostly used to mean that the Gospels give historically reliable information about a saying or deed of Jesus, i.e., that they are historically reliable witnesses in the modern sense.

Both the CDC and the CDJ work with Gospel texts and function by means of comparison. The CDC remains in the realm of early Christian texts (although, of course, in form-critical considerations, issues of early Christian history play an important role) and compares the Christian background of the texts with precisely these texts themselves, while the CDJ compares the early Christian texts with the Judaism reconstructed on the basis of other texts and sources.

b) Linguistic and Material Vagueness of the Term "Dissimilar"

The term "dissimilar" is understood and designated in different ways. This criterion thus appears under the heading "dissimilarity criterion," "nonderivable criterion," "criterion of discontinuity," or "discrimination principle." The vocabulary used to describe the functional content of this criterion is even more varied: deviation, contradiction, contrast, distinguishable, standing out, sharply profiled, not fitting in, Jesus-specific, (not) on the level of Judaism, possible (as Jewish), inimitable, unrepeatable, not explainable from, not derivable on Jewish presuppositions, unprecedented, underivable, without parallel, without analogy, completely unique. This spectrum of variations not only reflects a divided mind with regard to form. It is also a matter of material "dissimilarities" about which there is likewise considerable lack of clarity. Thus when one speaks of "dissimilarity" between a saying attributed to Jesus and Judaism or Christianity, the following are among the possible meanings:

> The saying of Jesus is not documented elsewhere and *in principle* is not possible or conceivable within a Jewish or Christian framework, that is, no other human being could have said it.
> The saying of Jesus is, *in fact*, not derivable from Jewish tradition, thus cannot be placed in its context by means of a genealogy of the history of traditions.
> In this particular variation, it is unique within Judaism or Christianity and thus *concretely* not derivable although, in principle, it can well be imagined within its milieu and general analogies can, in fact, be found.

Moreover, the quest for Jesus' "dissimilarity" to his historical context (in the manifold sense described above) is problematic from the point of view of scientific logic. Speaking of "historical dissimilarity" presupposes a definite picture of both Judaism and Christianity,[30] a picture that is always limited in view of our fragmentary sources. Thus application of a "dissimilarity" criterion faces an enormous problem with regard to scientific logic. Every claim to dissimilarity

---

30. This picture can be based on fundamentally problematic judgments about the "essence" of Christianity and Judaism.

is necessarily an argument from silence,[31] for dissimilarity, not to speak of underivability, cannot be verified historically. Such a verification would demand a complete picture of history, but sources always have only a fragmentary character. Therefore universal negative claims are not possible, all the less when they are made about a complex historical entity pervaded by ambiguity. The now obsolete idea that in the first half of the first century C.E. we are dealing with a uniform "normative Judaism" may have contributed greatly to the fact that it took a long time for claims of "dissimilarity" to be perceived as problematic.

c) Positive and Negative Applications of the Criterion of Dissimilarity

By comparing the available textual material with its assumed background, the criterion of dissimilarity (both as CDJ and as CDC) divides the data into basically two groups, which, of course, have fluid boundaries in view of the complex traditions: one part *differs* from Judaism or Christianity; the other part *corresponds* to Judaism or Christianity. Then the criterion is applied in a positive or negative manner. A positive application means that, in a particular case, dissimilar material can be identified without excluding the other as possibly authentic. A negative application separates the nondissimilar material as basically inauthentic and takes only the dissimilar into consideration. Obviously, the negative application of the criterion is much sharper and has wider implications than the positive application. Presently the majority of scholars—to the extent that they use the criterion of dissimilarity at all—favor the positive application of the criterion.

4.2 Motives for the Application of the Criterion of Dissimilarity

a) Theological Motives

The theological motivation for the application of the CDC was originally grounded in the critical attitude toward dogma of the Jesus research of the eighteenth and nineteenth centuries. In this context, this form of the criterion of dissimilarity clearly prevailed over the CDJ. The Jesus research of the "Old Quest" was concerned with freeing Jesus from the chains of dogma so that theological relevance was granted to historical factuality alone. The results of his-

---

31. Cf. also a basic rule of the Pharisees, according to which "negative testimony is not allowed. In Israel no one can state before a court what an accused person has *not* said, or done, or been involved in. There is just as little ground for anyone today to testify who Jesus was not." (P. Lapide, in *Jesus in Two Perspectives: a Jewish-Christian Dialog*, by Pinchas Lapide and Ulrich Luz (trans. Lawrence W. Denef; Minneapolis: Augsburg Pub. House, 1985) 114.

torical study of Jesus could be used directly as theological arguments. The source-critical criterion of dissimilarity fit these presuppositions extremely well and, at the same time, anticipated the results: the historical Jesus had to step forth in contrast to the churchly sources. The clear formulation of the CDC as a fundamental methodological principle[32] in 1901 in the work of Paul Wilhelm Schmiedel was apologetically motivated in this (liberal) sense—as a reaction to the radical criticism of the historicity of the life of Jesus.

The CDJ in Jesus research was often applied for poor reasons that already presupposed a negative view of Judaism:[33] "It is a basic rule of drama that in order for the hero of a play to make his greatest impact there must always be a villain. Does the religion of love also require an eternal villain as a scapegoat in order to get rid of its hatred for unbelievers and in order to accentuate the light of Jesus against the dark background of 'the Jews'?"[34] For this purpose, corresponding christological concepts that emphasize the complete uniqueness of (Jesus) Christ encouraged the use of the CDJ.[35] On this basis, the CDJ was important for exegetes of the "New Quest" who were influenced by dialectical theology, especially since it appeared that they could thereby overcome the skepticism about Jesus research with a verifiable method. However, one did not want to completely isolate Jesus as a historical figure. Thus, alongside the "break with Judaism," one emphasized all the more the connections with early Christianity. The typical interest of this phase of Jesus research in the continuity between Jesus and Christianity thus allowed the CDC to slip into the background in the interests of the CDJ.[36] To the extent that the CDC was

---

32. "Foundation pillars of a truly scientific life of Jesus" (P. W. Schmiedel, *Das vierte Evangelium gegenüber den drei ersten* [RV 1; Reihe, 8 u. 10. Heft; Halle: Bebauer u. Schwetschke, 1906]. The first formulation of the foundation pillars had already been published in English in 1901.

33. This negative view of Judaism is already embedded in the Gospels, most clearly in the Gospel of John.

34. Lapide, *Jesus in Two Perspectives*, 16.

35. Cf. Luz (in Lapide and Luz, *Jesus in Two Perspectives*, 164) clearly addresses this problem: "Postulates of a dogmatic nature, e.g., that Jesus *must* have been exceptional or else Christians would not be able to relate exclusively to him and his interpretation of God, are not acceptable to me."

36. Both elements named above are found in Käsemann's classic formulation of the criterion of dissimilarity for the "New Quest" (1954): the emphasis on the difference from Judaism by pointing especially to Jewish Christian tradents (". . . especially when Jewish Christianity has mitigated or modified received tradition, as having found it too bold for its taste." [37]). The corresponding element is found in the high theological evaluation of the fundamental distinctiveness of Jesus ("However, it is even more important for us to gain some insight into what separated him from friends and foes alike." [Ibid.]).

considered applicable to Jewish Christianity, the CDC could even modulate into a concealed version of the CDJ.

Moreover, theological anti-Judaism played a role. There was a desire to dissociate Jesus as far as possible from Judaism, a dissociation that has been looked at with discriminatory eyes even until the present day. It was done especially by attempting to claim that Jesus had already broken with Judaism on the issue of the Torah.

b) Motives Related to Theories of Historical Science

From the point of history theory, that is, the theoretical foundations of history writing, the basis and motivation for the application of the CDC, and especially of the CDJ, is provided by the doctrine of individualism. This approach provides "an analytical procedure in which those characteristics are disregarded that the event to be recognized has in common with others, in favor of those features that . . . distinguishes it from them."[37] It is a matter of what is "peculiar" or "special" about a person, the specifics of his or her individuality. Since the historical, individual Jesus of Nazareth (along with his later influence on world history) is considered to be a historical entity, this concept of historical theory concentrates everything on the unique and special in this historically innovative person.[38] In the case of Jesus, attention was thus focused on the contrast between him and his Jewish milieu, as well as on what distinguished him from his followers (understood as epigones). In the light of this concept, an enlivened interest in judgments about historical authenticity and the relative value of the elements for reconstructing the figure of Jesus as a result of applying the CDJ was understandable. No distinction was made between the "authentic" and the "essential" or "typical" features of this figure.

5. ON THE WAY TO A MORE COMPREHENSIVE METHODOLOGY

The point of departure for this study is provided by the critical and analytical history of research on the criterion of dissimilarity presented in chapter 2. Here we distinguish four phases in the quest of the historical Jesus. For each

---

37. K.-G. Faber, *Theorie der Geschichtswissenschaft* (2nd ed.; Munich: Beck, 1972).

38. Along with this, the last century's scholarly ideal of solitary originality probably also played a role. Originality as the primary and obvious presupposition for advancement in the German university fostered originality at any price. In this environment it is understandable that such originality was also postulated and sought in the case of Jesus. (Cf. T. Nipperdey, *Nachdenken über die deutsche Geschichte. Essays* [Munich: Beck, 1986] 472, 475).

phase, after a comprehensive presentation of the issue of criteria, one Jesus book will be analyzed, namely, those by W. Bousset, R. Bultmann, G. Bornkamm, and J. H. Charlesworth. These four portrayals of Jesus are representative of each phase of the quest of the historical Jesus, and they are free from extreme theses and characterized by a prudent scholarly ethos. We could, of course, have chosen different representatives of each period. The analysis of these four Jesus books is only by way of example. In the history of research, we do not attempt to be complete. Rather, we have particular interest in the history of the ways the CDC and the CDJ have been combined and related to each other. The goal is to attain insights into the motives and tendencies of the criterion of dissimilarity, as well as into the problematic associated with it.

It is not merely a matter of criticizing the criterion of dissimilarity. We will also look at the *justified* concerns of the beginnings of the CDC in source criticism and the basis for the CDJ in the study of the history of religions. We will discover individual elements that are to be incorporated into future Jesus research. It will, however, become clear from our critique that these elements of the criterion of dissimilarity are to be placed in a new comprehensive methodological framework. In this regard, the "Third Quest" phase of Jesus research has brought about important changes. It indicates—by maintaining and reviving the CDC—an inversion of the CDJ. Approaching the historical figure of Jesus requires a new methodology for integrating the relationship of Jesus to the Judaism of his time into Jesus research. This deep-rooted methodological change is to be critically adopted and finally (in chapter 3) explicated in the form of new methodological principles.

The goal of chapter 3 is to come back to the ways of posing the question that have been justified by the criterion of dissimilarity and to extend them in order to attain a plausible concept from the point of view of theology and historical science. The "criterion of historical plausibility," that is, our new formulation of a criterion for Jesus research, will deal with this concern. We will formulate this criterion of historical plausibility as a double criterion intended to replace the criterion of dual dissimilarity, namely, as the criterion of plausibility in the Jewish context, on the one hand, and, on the other hand, as the criterion of Christian plausibility of effects. Thus, when the term *historical plausibility* replaces the term *dissimilarity*, this should signal that distinctions and differences between Judaism and early Christianity are not in themselves an adequate methodological basis for Jesus research. Rather, it suggests their historically "more plausible" connection and continuity—which can include continuity as well as discontinuity, analogy as well as difference, agreement as well as contrast. Moreover, with the term "*historical*" we include the claim of formulating criteria that correspond to the generally accepted methods of historical science and that can thus be applied not only to the Jesus traditions but mutatis mutandis to other comparable traditions. On this basis, chapter 3 concludes with an excursus on the question of the authenticity or inauthenticity of the sayings of Montanist prophets. The research procedure here corresponds much more to the criterion of historical plausibility here suggested than to the traditional criterion of dissimilarity.

A concluding hermeneutical section (chapter 4) will reflect on the relation of this criterion of historical plausibility to modern historical consciousness, on the one hand, and to the absoluteness of religious faith, on the other. Here we take up the criteria developed previously in order to show that they correspond to the fundamental axioms of modern historical consciousness, which have themselves become historically important.

The Appendix provides—in chronological order—a collection of quotations of formulations of the criterion of dissimilarity and of discussions of this theme. Again, it is, of course, only a selection.

In conclusion, we emphasize once again that the volume in hand is not devoted to the quest of the historical Jesus as such and does not claim to present a complete picture of Jesus research. This point is to be especially stressed in view of the flood of recent Jesus books. All the less do we claim to deal with all the criteria that have been used and discussed in Jesus research. Several criteria are treated only briefly. At the center of the study stands the criterion of dissimilarity, along with its history and the relationship of Jesus to Judaism and Christianity that it presupposed as the methodological foundation of Jesus research.

II

The Criterion of Dissimilarity in the History of Jesus Research

Aspects of the Quest for Criteria

1. THE PREHISTORY OF THE CRITERION OF DISSIMILARITY

The criterion of dissimilarity in its twofold form as CDC (criterion of difference from Christianity) and CDJ (criterion of difference from Judaism) presupposes specific questions and insights in dealing with historical texts. The term "criterion" as used in Jesus research points to an act that evaluates and distinguishes: a criterion designates the distinctive characteristic on the basis of which (relatively more) original material is selected. "Dissimilarity" states what this distinctive characteristic consists of.

In the case of the CDC the standard for comparison for this "dissimilarity" is found first of all on the level of the text itself. As the transmitter of the tradition, it was the post-Easter community that formed the text. To the extent that it is a matter of tracking down the differences between "Christian" and "original" expressions by means of a comprehensive analysis of the text, we are dealing with a philosophical issue.[1] In the case of the CDJ, the standard for comparison is located outside the text,[2] which presents us with a historical issue that goes beyond philological questions, since the form and contents of the text are compared with Jewish texts in order to establish dissimilarities. The CDJ, but also the CDC—to the extent that it presupposes the knowledge

---

1. The problematic involved in the underlying assumption that the secondary "Christian" reformation can be removed like an outer layer of paint will be discussed below.

2. A special case is constituted when one assumes that the tradition has received "(re-) Judaizing" elements at the hands of Jewish Christians.

27

of the history of the first Christians—implies an engagement with and critical analysis of the historical circumstances that stand behind the text.

The goal of the application of both forms of the criterion of dissimilarity is to discover historically reliable material in the sources by means of which a historically reliable picture of Jesus could be reconstructed. This motive, which first made possible the development of this criterion at all within the framework of the quest of the historical Jesus, is not conceivable before the development of modern historical science.

The basic presupposition for the formulation of a criterion of dissimilarity lies in the differentiation of the level of secondary interpretation from that of the original author on the one hand (CDC), and the level of the text from that of the historical reality on the other (CDJ). The one side touches on the development of philology; the other, that of historical science. This correlation with two academic fields is intended to represent a systematic distinction from the perspective of our question. The historical development of each is closely interwoven with that of the other.[3]

We here preface an oversimplified sketch of the stages in the process of increasing differentiation:

1. *THE MIDDLE AGES*: The levels of interpretation, author, and historical reality constitute a unity.
2. *RENAISSANCE HUMANISM*: The emergence of modern philology leads to the separation of contemporary interpretation and original intention at the level of the text. The goal is the reconstruction of the *text*.
3. *THE ENLIGHTENMENT*: The emergence of modern historical science leads to the separation of the textual level from that of the historical events themselves. The goal is the reconstruction of *the historical reality behind the text*.

1.1 Renaissance Humanism: Critical Method as the Reconstruction of the Original Text

The understanding of texts is subject to constant change. A further development and differentiation of this understanding that is directly relevant for our question emerged at the turn from the Middle Ages to modern times in the Renaissance and the advent of Humanism.

To be sure, sources were critically examined and their truth was questioned already during the Middle Ages.[4] The authorities of the tradition were defin-

---

3. On this, see especially the works of U. Muhlack.
4. On medieval historiography cf. G. Melville, "Kompilation, Fiktion und Diskurs. Aspekte zur heuristischen Methode der mittelalterlichen Geschichtsschreiber," in

itive, however, as is illustrated by the fact that they were synchronized with each other. It was presupposed that there was direct access to their texts so that—with no awareness of any historical gulf—a dialogue between "historical" contents of a text and the present could be carried on. Within the thought world of the medieval schools' fourfold meaning of Scripture, "historia" designated "the lowest, most literal understanding of a text."[5] This term, as hermeneutically defined by Hugo of St. Victor, remains at the literary level[6] and describes only the way the history is portrayed, not the historical event itself. The fundamental credibility of the literal meaning was not open to debate.[7] That is to say, here we have no critical distinction between literary and historical 'historia.'

In regard to its reliance on appropriate authorities, the revival of philology in Renaissance Humanism[8] is both continuous and discontinuous with the Middle Ages. There was the conviction "that every claim that rests on an earlier event can only be supported by an unassailable tradition of acknowledged authors about the event in question."[9] On the one hand, reliance on such texts was not given up, although by incorporating it into classical antiquity the Christian tradition's claim to absoluteness was surrendered. On the other hand, the tradition was subjected to a critical

---

Ch. Meier and J. Rüsen, eds., *Historische Methode* (Beiträge zur Historik, 5; Munich: dtv, 1988) and J. Knape, *'Historie' in Mittelalter und früher Neuzeit. Begriffs- und gattungsgeschichtliche Untersuchungen im interdisziplinären Kontext* (SaeSp 10; Baden-Baden: Koerner, 1984).

5. J. Knape, *'Historie,'* 92.

6. Formerly the term *historia* was understood only in the literary sense, applied namely to the historical works of Christianity or to the narration of past events. On this cf. J. Knape's study *'Historie,'* which provides rich resources on this topic; cf. 87–88 on Hugo of St. Victor.

7. The fixation on the given historical accounts is reflected in the medieval use of the term "historia:" it is used for the *account*, the portrayal of history, while other terms are used for the events themselves (J. Knappe, *'Historie,'* 92). Despite this terminological distinction, account and event were not critically played off against each other.

8. Here we can only point to the problem involved in the concept of "humanism," without elaborating on it. I follow Holeczek's definition: "At the center of what we understand by humanism is found the new linguistic-literary culture that arose in the late Middle Ages from the study and imitation of ancient literature and its content." (H. Holeczek, *Humanistische Bibelphilologie als Reformproblem bei Erasmus von Rotterdam, Thomas More und William Tyndale* [SHCT 9; Leiden: Brill 1975] 24). The designation "Renaissance Humanism" points especially to its advocates such as Erasmus, Valla, and their philological school of thought.

9. W. Setz, *Lorenzo Vallas Schrift gegen die Konstantinische Schenkung. De falso credita et ementita Constantini donatione. Zur Interpretation und Wirkungsgeschichte* (Bibliothek des Deutschen Historischen Instituts in Rom 44; Tübingen: Niemeyer, 1975) 43.

investigation,[10] and for the first time there developed a critical distance to the *traditional* text. The goal was "the encounter with the personality of the ancient author in his work,"[11] which must for this purpose be reconstructed as close as possible to its original form. The work then represents its author.

The return to the origins, "ad fontes," the motto this epoch had emblazoned on its banner, thus meant above all the grasping of the original meaning of ancient texts.[12] This led to a quest for ancient manuscripts and their chronological classification, that is, to historical text criticism, an inseparable aspect of the cultivation of ancient languages. It was in this text-critical and linguistic sense that Thomas More insisted "that in all doubtful cases one should attempt to get as close as possible to the 'apostolic wording'."[13] One can see that, for example, in L. Valla's *In latinam Novi Testamenti interpretationem ex collatione graecorum Exemplarium adnotationes* (1444). This humanistic philological work includes the New Testament, where it is treated in the same way as secular documents.

Moreover, the deeply rooted insight into the historicalness of a text and in the historical distance separating the interpreter from ancient texts calls for an interpretation that distinguishes the text from its historical context and that uses this insight as a means in commenting on it. This kind of historical interpretation is to be distinguished from the results of a historical evaluation of the texts themselves. The goal is the restoration of ancient documents, not the restoration of ancient history by means of these documents. For the humanistic mind-set, a normative importance is inherent in the ancient sources themselves, so that they are thereby in principle withdrawn from subjection to further historicization. To be sure, one finds historical data in historical com-

---

10. A. Buck, *Die humanistische Tradition in der Romania* (Bad Homburg: Gehlen, 1968) 138: "While the medieval reader sought to find in the ancient author confirmation for the fixed ideas of his traditional Christian worldview, the humanist attempted first to read the ancient author as a historical person, and then to resolve modern problems with the help of the ancient author." The turn to history did not occur for the sake of historical study itself. Thus alongside the emphasis on the literal sense, the humanist interpretation was always quite close to the tropological sense. The maxim was "Historia . . . magistra vitae" ("history . . . the mistress [director, teacher] of life," from Cicero, *De or.* 2.36).

11. Buck, *Die humanistische Tradition*, 133.

12. For the following comments cf. the clear presentations by U. Muhlack, "Zum Verhältnis von Klassischer Philologie und Geschichtswissenschaft im 19. Jahrhundert," in H. Flashar et al., eds., *Philologie und Hermeneutik im 19. Jahrhundert. Zur Geschichte und Methodologie der Geisteswissenschaften* (Göttingen: Vandenhoeck & Ruprecht, 1979) 51–52 and "Von der philologischen zur historischen Methode," in Meier and J. Rüsen, *Historische Methode*, 156–62, as well as G. Melville, "Kompilation."

13. H. Holeczek, *Humanistische Bibelphilologie*, 161.

mentary on these texts, but these are subordinated to textual interpretation. Historical-critical reconstruction of the actual history is not extended "beyond the editing of the ancient documents themselves".[14] For Erasmus, for example, this means in regard to Jesus that it is not the historical figure himself but the texts that tell about him that are the object of investigation.[15]

The famous work of Lorenzo Valla, in which he exposed the so-called "Donation of Constantine" as spurious, is typical in that it was based primarily on an analysis of the Latin.[16] "The question of the probability and evidence for the historical events contained therein plays a subordinate role."[17] The question of authorship, however, is important. As soon as humanistic philology began to deal with New Testament texts as literary artifacts, they come into view as works composed by particular individuals: "Unlike scholastic exegetes, humanists approached a text with a certain curiosity about the distinctive personality and style of each author."[18] We thus have here the first step that is also presupposed by the CDC: with the focus fixed on the text itself, it is a matter of restoring and understanding this oldest form in its specific style.

In addition, humanistic theory of history knows a criterion that likewise belongs to the prehistory of the CDC. Since historical factuality or the writing of history was connected with its usefulness, particular demands were made on the historian. These claims were not so much of a formal nature (e.g., the claim to have experienced the events oneself as an eyewitness—the "autopsy" claim) as a claim of a personal nature: "The realization of the truth-claim and the guarantee of factuality for the historical representation appears . . . [especially] to be a question of the personal ethos of the historian" and of his intellectual qualifications.[19] Impartial objectivity also belongs to the requisite attitude. This requirement applies both for the humanist historian and to the

---

14. U. Muhlack, "Von der philologischen zur historischen Methode," in Ch. Meier and J. Rüsen, eds., *Historische Methode* (Beiträge zur Historik 5; Munich: dtv, 1988) 166.

15. J. D. Tracy, "Ad Fontes: The Humanist Understanding of Scripture as Nourishment for the Soul," in J. Rait, ed., *Christian Spirituality II: High Middle Ages and Reformation* (World Spirituality: An Encyclopedic History of the Religious Quest, vol. 17; London: Routledge & Kegan Paul, 1987) 255.

16. R. Pfeiffer, *Die Klassische Philologie von Petrarca bis Mommsen* (Munich: Beck, 1982) 58.

17. W. Setz, *Lorenzo Vallas Schrift gegen die Konstantinische Schenkung. De falso credita et ementita Constantini donatione. Zur Interpretation und Wirkungsgeschichte* (Bibliothek des Deutschen Historischen Instituts in Rom 44; Tübingen: Niemeyer, 1975) 43.

18. Tracy, "Ad fontes," 255.

19. R. Landfester, *Historia magistra vitae. Untersuchungen zur humanistischen Geschichtstheorie des 14. bis 16. Jahrhunderts* (Travaux d'Humanisme et Renaissance 123; Geneva: Droz, 1972) 96–97. On the topic as a whole, cf. 94–108.

author of the ancient source.[20] Thereby another foundation stone for the CDC was indirectly laid, for it rests on the insight that the Christian authors and transmitters of tradition were certainly not "impartial," did not write objective history, and could not have done so.

1.2 The Enlightenment: Critical Method as the Reconstruction of the History behind the Text

The guiding principle for the humanists' criteriology was the question "Authentic or inauthentic?" The issue to be debated was the authenticity of the text in the philological sense. In the Enlightenment of the eighteenth century, a door was opened for a fresh approach to history by the new sense of the independence of rational, worldly wisdom that erupted into the scholarly consciousness. Historical science realized that its task was to investigate its sources with regard to the truth of their contents. "Truth as orthodoxy was replaced by *historical* truth. The task of the historian conceived as making a neat inventory of truth and error in history was replaced by the task of reconstructing the 'true history' itself."[21] To adopt Droysen's terms, "authenticity criticism" was supplemented by "correctness criticism."[22] This "correctness criticism" includes a testing of the credibility of a tradition in which the *inner* credibility is distinguished from the rationality that was so important for the Enlightenment: coherence with rational experience of the world and the evidence of natural morality[23] is a significant criterion of truth. Along with the testing of the *external* credibility, which investigated the trustworthiness of individual authors[24]—the "author's knowledge" as it was then called—these elements of "correctness criticism" were already present in the humanist criteria of

---

20. Examples of this demand for impartiality from the mid-sixteenth century in Georg Widman and Johannes Sleidan are found in the collection of quotations in the Appendix.

21. E. Stöve, *Kirchengeschichte zwischen geschichtlicher Kontinuität und geschichtlicher Relativität. Der Institutionalisierungsprozess der Kirchengeschichte im Zusammenhang neuzeitlichen Geschichtsverständnisses* (Habil. Heidelberg, 1978) 101–102.

22. J. G. Droysen, *Historik. Vorlesungen über Enzyklopädie und Methodologie der Geschichte*, ed. R. Hübner (Darmstadt: Wiss. Buchgesellschaft, 1974 [= unchanged reprint of the 7th ed., 1937]) 99, 122. The idea of applying these theoretical-systematic categories to the history of scholarship comes from H. W. Blanke, "Aufklärungshistorie, Historismus und historische Kritik. Eine Skizze," in H. W. Blanke and J. Rüsen, eds., *Von der Aufklärung zum Historismus. Zum Strukturwandel des historischen Denkens* (Historisch-politische Diskurse 1; Paderborn: Schöningh, 1984) 168ff.

23. E. Stöve, *Kirchengeschichte*, 1:144.

24. H. W. Blanke, "Aufklärungshistorie," 170.

verisimilitudo (verisimilitude) and *auctoritas* (authority).[25] But only reason plays the leading role. The Bible as such is no longer a "historical textbook,"[26] and the other classical authors of antiquity also lose their decisive authority.

To the extent that historical thinking here comes into play, a thinking that attempts to reconstruct the historical course of events without binding itself to their specific portrayal in the text, this approach lays another foundation stone for the CDJ.

The "earlier/later criticism"[27] that appeared as a diacritical procedure in historical scholarship at the beginning of the nineteenth century finally made possible a refined version of the CDC by distinguishing separate layers of the tradition. The underlying principle was later formulated by J. G. Droysen as follows: "It is a matter of . . . whether that which lies before us is still intact, preserved as what it was and was intended to be, and whether modifications can be recognized that must be discounted for the purposes of historical study."[28]

The application of historical-critical methods to *biblical* texts is the presupposition for the development of these procedures in general historical scholarship to become fruitful methods for Jesus research. At the level of historical criticism, Valla had already treated the New Testament no differently than secular texts. But for him, the critically reconstructed text was still sacred and an indisputable authority. However, the later Enlightenment's critical interest in a historical reconstruction of the events reported in the Bible presupposed a fundamental questioning of the Bible's total claim to truth.[29] That means that a new authority is required in order to displace the authority of the Bible: reason. This step means in turn a violent break with the inspiration theory of the old Protestant orthodoxy and necessitates a completely new understanding of

---

25. E. Kessler, *Petrarca und die Geschichte. Geschichtsschreibung, Rhetorik, Philosophie im Übergang vom Mittelalter zur Neuzeit* (Humanistische Bibliothek. I/25; Munich: Fink, 1978) 26.

26. K. Scholder, *Ursprünge und Probleme der Bibelkritik im 17. Jahrhundert. Ein Beitrag zur Entstehung der historisch-kritischen Theologie*, (FGLP 10/23; Munich: Kaiser, 1966) 82.

27. Droysen, *Historik*, 114.

28. Ibid., 115.

29. K. Scholder, *Ursprünge und Probleme*, 56–78: (astronomical worldview) and 79–104 (historical worldview), parallels this process with reference to history with the changes that had taken place in astronomy, methods that effected a drastic change in the worldview. The influence of the modern worldview of the natural sciences on biblical criticism claimed by Scholder has been challenged by Reventlow by citing Boyle's and Newton's piety and belief in the Bible (in my opinion too weak an argument in view of the general intellectual revolution; cf. H. Reventlow, "Wurzeln der modernen Bibelkritik," in H. Reventlow, W. Sparn, and J. Woodbridge, eds., *Historische Kritik und biblischer Kanon in der deutschen Aufklärung*, [Wolfenbütteler Forschungen 41; Wiesbaden: Otto Harrassowitz, 1988]) 58.

the Reformation's "sola scriptura," an understanding in which this scriptural principle is cut loose from its theological obligations.[30]

a) Preparation for the Enlightenment: Socinianism

From the point of view of our question, the seventeenth century may be understood as the time of the great transition.[31]

On the Protestant side, the Reformation period was followed by Protestant Orthodoxy, whose emphasis on the Scripture and the doctrine of inspiration made it impossible for critical study of the Bible to proceed beyond text criticism—for this would have called into question the whole dogmatic system of orthodox theology. It was rather the case that "all decisive progress in the development of historical criticism was the result of polemic interests,"[32] which were turned against Orthodoxy. This is seen in the movement of Socinianism, which was characteristic for that transitional period.

This movement pursued a polemical interest and posed the "question of the relation of Scripture, doctrine, and reason."[33] Like John Locke (1632–1704) and Johannes Clericus (1657–1736), who regarded reason as the critical standard by which Scripture is understood, they proceeded on the basis of the fundamental agreement between reason and Scripture. For the Socinians, Scripture and reason stood together against doctrine. The introduction of reason as a standard was laden with immense potential, but it was not yet applied to Scripture (the only exception).[34] It was rather the case that Socinianism was convinced that "it could maintain the authority of the Scripture along with the authority of reason, if it gave up the dogmatic tradition."[35] The facticity of events reported in the Bible was supported on the basis of reason. Arguments were developed that still play a methodological role even today: when something is claimed to be true that brings disadvantages to those who make the claim, the claim is pre-

---

30. The old Protestant orthodoxy, which subsumed exegesis under systematic theology, merely continued Luther, who had in fact only partly turned away from the older doctrine of inspiration. Cf. O. Merk, "Anfänge neutestamentlicher Wissenschaft im 18. Jahrhundert," in G. Schwaiger, ed., *Historische Kritik in der Theologie. Beiträge zu ihrer Geschichte* (SThGG 32; Göttingen: Vandenhoeck & Ruprecht, 1980) 37–59, see especially 39–41.

31. H. Reventlow, *The Authority of the Bible and the Rise of the Modern World* (Philadelphia: Fortress Press, 1985) 147, 223, passim.

32. E. Stöve, *Kirchengeschichte*, 2:36, n. 8.

33. Scholder, *Ursprünge und Probleme*, 41.

34. According to Scholder, *Ursprünge und Probleme*, 171, this is the reason that after 1680 the Enlightenment changed the historical emphasis but produced nothing essentially new.

35. Scholder, *Ursprünge und Probleme*, 54.

sumably true. Thus the Socinian catechism argued for the truth of the resurrection on the basis of the persecution of Christians.[36] That means that here, even if in the final analysis the intention was not historical, a biblical text is seen in a historical context (here, the persecution of Christians).

From today's perspective, to the extent that Socinianism applied reason to the question of the historicity of the Scripture, reason was seen as having an ancillary function along with Scripture, not as making critical distinctions within Scripture. Over against dogma, however, reason is a critical principle of knowledge that distinguishes between doctrines necessary for salvation and those that are merely useful.[37]

b) The Enlightenment: English Deism

Among the Socinians the newly discovered authority of reason in alliance with the Scripture led to conflicts with dogmatic theology. In the long run, the growing self-confidence of reason made it inevitable that this antidogmatic conflict would be extended to the Scripture itself. Reason now turns against the Scripture. From the perspective of the issue we are pursuing, the decisive step was taken by the English Deists, without which the historical-critical studies by Reimarus are inconceivable. The Enlightenment's discovery of autonomous reason, as in the empiricism of John Locke (1632–1704) allows it to become possible for the biblical tradition to be subjected to fundamental criticism.[38]

John Toland (1670–1722) explains, "I hold nothing as an Article of my Religion, but what the highest Evidence forc'd me to embrace."[39] Toland's contribution to the history of exegesis is especially important in that his ecclesiastical opponents also accepted his presuppositions that only the historical or literal sense is valid, and that the Scripture is to be understood as a source of information and not only as a basis for faith.[40] The "sensus historicus" ("historical

---

36. Ibid., 45: "[I]t contradicts common sense, that anyone would submit to such persecution for an untruth [the resurrection]."

37. Ibid., 46–47.

38. J. Orr, *English Deism, Its Roots and Its Fruits* (Grand Rapids: Eerdmans, 1934) 246: "The antisupernaturalism of the deists led them not only to reject the miracles of the Bible but also to reject the church doctrine of the inspiration of the Bible. Having rejected these, the deists felt the necessity for supplying some plausible theory of the natural origin of the Books and of its contents. This led to a study of the origin of the Books of the Bible, to investigations of questions of canon and authorship."

39. J. Toland, *Christianity Not Mysterious* (Facsimile Reprint of the 1730 London Edition; ed. G. Gawlick; Stuttgart: Frommann, 1964) ix.

40. R. E. Sullivan, *John Toland and the Deist Controversy. A Study in Adaptations* (HHS 101; Cambridge, Mass.: Harvard University Press, 1982) 249–50; Toland; *Christianity Not Mysterious*, 39: "Revelation was not a necessitating Motive of Assent but *a Means of Information.*"

sense") thus became the point of entry for the historical-critical method into biblical exegesis,[41] for it occasioned the possibility of reading the biblical text as a historical text. The kind of hopes attached to this new possibility is seen in this quotation from the deist Thomas Morgan (1680–1743): "[T]he biblical History has afforded more Matter of Dispute and Contention . . . than all other Books in the World. But this could never have happened, had this sacred History been read critically, and interpreted by the same Rules of natural and Rational probability and Credibility, as we read all other History."[42]

Lord Shaftesbury (1671–1713) sees the problem obviously involved, namely, that the Christian now has only a faith based on the inferences of historical study ("no more than a nicely critical historical faith").[43] The lack of personal experience of what was reported would necessarily lead to skepticism.

This problematic involved in a "historical faith" was further developed in a decisive manner by the deist Thomas Chubb (1679–1747). He made a distinction between the true gospel of Jesus Christ and what the Evangelists had made out of it on the basis of their abstruse "private opinions."[44] This basic differentiation is already found in Baruch de Spinoza (1632–1677), who played a major role in the founding of historical-critical scholarship. Although his challenge at first had only a limited response,[45] he called for a kind of biblical study that would "work out an authentic history from the Scripture, in order to derive the meaning of the biblical authors as firmly established facts and principles."[46] In order to distinguish between reliable and unreliable elements in the Jesus tradition, Chubb introduced (alongside an ethical-rationalist understanding of eternal natural law as the standard) an empirical analogical standard: "[N]ot only credibility, but also a conformity to our natural notices of things, and to the eternal rules of right and wrong in the subject, ought to be the boundaries of our faith and practice."[47] In addition, Chubb argued in a remarkable man-

---

41. U. Muhlack, *Geschichtswissenschaft im Humanismus und in der Aufklärung. Die Vorgeschichte des Historismus* (Munich: Beck, 1991) 363.

42. T. Morgan, *The Moral Philosopher* (vols. 1–3, London, 1738–1740, 1-vol. fac. reprint; ed. G. Gawlick, Stuttgart: Fromman, 1969) 3:140.

43. Lord Shaftesbury, *Characteristics of Men, Manners, Opinions, Times* (6th ed., 1738). 2:201; cited in Reventlow, *Authority of the Bible*, 314.

44. T. Chubb, *The True Gospel of Jesus Christ Asserted* (London, 1738) 49 passim.

45. Reventlow, "Wurzeln der modernen Bibelkritik," 59. Spinoza also played an important role in the mediation of the ideas of English deism to Germany (cf. Orr, *English Deism*, 190).

46. B. de Spinoza: *Tractatus Theologico-Politicus*, in *Opera/Werke, Latin and German*, Günter Gawlick and Friedrich Niewöhner, eds. (Darmstadt 1979) 1:231–33. Cited in Reventlow, "Wurzeln der modernen Bibelkritik," 60.

47. Chubb, *The True Gospel*, 78.

ner for the fundamental credibility of the existence of Jesus: "That there was such a person as Jesus Christ, and that he, in the main, did and taught as is recorded of him, appear to be probable."[48] He based this judgment on the probability of Jesus' existence on an argument from the history of effects, that is, a historical argument, namely, that the spread of Christianity cannot be understood as well on the hypothesis that the life of Jesus was an invention.

In the reflections on the history of tradition among the deists, history was found in and behind the Scripture, as well as before it. While Chubb distinguished between the teaching of Jesus and the teaching of his apostles or the evangelists and reflects on the sequence involved, in Matthew Tindal (1656–1733), an awareness of Jesus' own life setting can be perceived with particular clarity: Jesus' words were "accommodated to the then Way of speaking."[49] "However, [Tindal's] thinking did not go further at this point,"[50] but the insight into the nature of Jesus' teaching as temporally conditioned, when joined with the idea of accommodation, became very important for the later history of New Testament exegesis.

c. The Enlightenment: The Beginnings of Historical-Critical Exegesis in Germany

The development of the accommodation theory as found among the deists is an expression of the Enlightenment's discovery of the difference between "the supra-temporal truth of New Testament teaching valid for all times (as understood by the Enlightenment) and the temporally conditioned elements in which it is clothed, which are not binding on us."[51] Of interest for our question is the

---

48. Ibid., 41.

49. M. Tindal, *Christianity as old as the Creation, or, the Gospel, a Republication of the Religion of Nature*, 1730; cited by Reventlow, in *Authority of the Bible*, 382. Cf. also Morgan, *The Moral Philosopher*, 1:442: "The Books of the *New Testament . . .* ought to be read critically, with an Allowance for Persons, Circumstances, and the Situation of Things at that Time."

50. Reventlow, *Authority of the Bible*, 382. As in the case of Chubb, the eternal innate natural religion plays a determining role also in Tindal. This illustrates Reventlow's judgment that "the Enlightenment did not bring with it an authentic historical perspective. It was too fixed on timeless values to hold such a view" (Reventlow, "Wurzeln der modernen Bibelkritik," 62).

51. P. Althaus, "Akkomodation," *RGG* 1 (1957): 209. For the patristic-rhetorical origins of the thinking about accommodation and its mediation to the modern age through Erasmus, cf. P. Walter, *Theologie aus dem Geist der Rhetorik. Zur Schriftauslegung des Erasmus von Rotterdam* (TSTP 1; Mainz: Grünewald, 1991) 33–53. For the discussion of the Enlightenment period, cf. G. Hornig, *Die Anfänge der historisch-kritischen Theologie. Johann Salomo Semlers Schriftverständnis und seine Stellung zu Luther* (FSThR 8; Göttingen: Vandenhoeck & Ruprecht, 1961) 211–36. "Accommodation in the sense of the

connection between the accommodation theory and the temporally conditioned nature of the New Testament's Jesus tradition, which was referred specifically to its Jewish backdrop. The understanding of "accommodation" expressed in this context can be used in the service of biblical criticism and as an apologetic position.

The doctrine of accommodation has already been met in the Dutch Remonstrant Johannes Clericus (1657–1736), an advocate of an antiorthodox, biblical-critical position. His understanding of accommodation presupposed the inferiority of Jewish faith and thought: "But since Jesus Christ and the apostles did not come into the world in order to teach critical methodology to the Jews, one need not be surprised when they spoke in terms of commonly accepted opinions."[52] Theologically, he proceeds on the basis of the great difference between the gospel of Jesus Christ and Jewish doctrine.

The apologetic advocates of a doctrine of accommodation thought in precisely the same way. In this group belongs above all the name of J. S. Semler (1725–1791), who will be dealt with first for systematic reasons. In his view, Jesus had, so to speak, made use of the ideas of his time, despite his own better knowledge, in order to make himself understood by his contemporaries. This explanatory paradigm reflects the pedagogical interest of the Enlightenment. The hermeneutical theory of accommodation is supposed to save the authority of Jesus by distinguishing it from the dregs of Jewish faith. To be sure, on the one hand, Jesus of Nazareth was revealed as a historical figure.[53] At the same time, however, from the very beginning his being embedded in his Jewish context was perceived as a problem to be overcome, and the difference of his "own" message was emphasized. This difference was always presupposed from the outset and is bound up with a denigration of Judaism—

Enlightenment is to be distinguished from what has been called 'biblical accommodation' in the sense of adapting 'a biblical passage to a subject to which it refers neither in the literal nor typological sense, but to which it can at least be referred in terms of its wording'" (J. Schildenberger, "Biblische Akkomodation," *LTK*, 1 [1957]: 239).

52. Johannes Clericus, *Sentimens des quelques théologiens de Hollande sur L'Histoire Critique du Vieux Testament . . . par le P. Richard Simon . . .* , (Amsterdam, 1685) 126, as cited in Reventlow, "Bibelexegese als Aufklärung. Die Bibel im Denken des Johannes Clericus (1657–1736)," in Reventlow, Sparn, and Woodbridge, *Historische Kritik und biblischer Kanon*, 15. According to Clericus, it is already true for the Old Testament that God "would be compelled by his goodness to accommodate himself to Israel's coarse spirit oriented to the flesh (cited in Reventlow, "Bibelexegese als Aufklärung," 12).

53. Merk, "Anfänge neutestamentlicher Wissenschaft," 17 notes an important step made by Semler in contrast to Reimarus: "Historical reconstruction must constantly take into consideration that one factor in the reconstruction of history is the interpretation of traditional materials, instead of speaking of the disciples' and apostles' betrayal of Jesus. Such an interpretative approach can overcome the dichotomy Jesus/Apostles."

whoever denies this difference is arguing in a way that is critical of Christianity and devalues Jesus. The question as to which elements of the tradition the accommodation theory applies may be regarded as a forerunner of the CDJ. That point is valid to the extent that the distinction between "essential" and "unessential," which followed the accommodation theory in the historical reconstruction of the life of Jesus, later led to identifying "essential" with "historical." In the tradition of the CDJ the chain of identification goes still further:

| Christian | = | essential | = | historical |
| Jewish | = | unessential | = | unhistorical |

An example of the derogatory tendency toward Judaism in the accommodation theory is Semler's evaluation of future eschatology and present expectation of the near end.[54] The former he considers to be an accommodation to the hopes of contemporary Judaism. This historical assessment is bound up with a theological denigration of (Jewish) future eschatology. In contrast, Semler understands the Gospel of John as an expression of authentic Christian faith and its present eschatology as "a direct criticism of the particularism of the Jewish soteriological expectation."[55]

H. S. Reimarus (1694–1768) had comparable historical insights but applied them differently in his study of Jesus. We find in him a critical application of the accommodation doctrine. He distinguishes two kinds of material in the teaching of Jesus, that dealing with general religion and that dealing with positive religion. The former deals with the natural, reasonable element "to which Jesus, in his reformation, sought also to guide that which was positive in Judaism without wanting to abolish it.[56] The other part is from one Jew for other Jews.[57] It is thus clear for Reimarus that "[a]s the Messiah, Jesus did not want to alter the Levitical rites. . . . Everything remains within the narrow confines of Jewish customs."[58] On these grounds he rejects some of the Johannine versions of Jesus' sayings as unhistorical. Differently from Semler, Reimarus uses precisely the accommodation argument to express his view that Jesus

---

54. Cf. Hornig (*Die Anfänge*, 227–30), who also makes extensive reference to Semler.

55. Hornig, *Die Anfänge*, 228.

56. H. S. Reimarus, *Apologie oder Schutzschrift für die vernünftigen Verehrer Gottes*, G. Alexander, ed. (First complete publication, Frankfurt, 1972) 40 (§1). *Fragments from Reimarus [microfilm] Consisting of Brief Critical Remarks on the Object of Jesus and His Disciples as Seen in the New Testament.* Translated from the German of G. E. Lessing; edited by Charles Voysey (Lexington, Ky.: American Theological Library Association, Committee on Reprinting, 1962).

57. Ibid., 40–41 (§1).

58. Ibid., 2:97, 108 (heading to chapter 4 and §5).

could not have expressed himself as represented in the Gospel of John, since he could not have made himself understandable to the Jews if he had spoken in the manner of the Johannine speeches.[59]

Reimarus was strongly influenced by the English deists.[60] In particular, it is the differences that Chubb saw between Jesus and the apostles that are methodologically confirmed by Reimarus. We have before us, in a document that remained unpublished during Reimarus' own time (middle of the eighteenth century), a very early formulation of the CDC: "[T]he later system of the apostles [is oriented] not to the *factis*, but the narration of the *factorum* must be oriented to their changed thought world. Consequently one must omit everything in their story that reflects the later thought world of the apostles, and not regard it as significant for establishing the picture of Jesus himself, if one wants to know his own true meaning and intention."[61]

Reimarus is also important for methodological history because of his doctrine of human reason, in which he formulates general principles for "knowing the truth." These "Instructions on the Right Use of Reason"—as expressed in the title of his doctrine of reason—summarize quite pointedly the Enlightenment's new understanding of the world. "The describing of what in fact happened presupposes the application of the principles of non-contradiction and of sufficient evidence, i.e. the stability of the world and its resistance to miracles. . . . Accordingly, one can deal with the statements of the witnesses found in the Bible in the same manner as one deals with witnesses in the courtroom."[62] Thus Reimarus says, "It depends on the *rem facti*, what the founders

---

59. Ibid., 2:66 (§10).

60. C. H. Reventlow, "Das Arsenal der Bibelkritik des Reimarus: Die Auslegung der Bibel, insbesondere des Alten Testaments, bei den englischen Deisten," in *Hermann Samuel Reimarus (1694–1768) ein 'bekannter Unbekannter' der Aufklärung in Hamburg. Vorträge gehalten auf der Tagung der Joachim Jungius-Gesellschaft der Wissenschaften Hamburg am 12. und 13. Oktober 1972* (Göttingen: Vandenhoeck & Ruprecht, 1973). The dependence on Chubb is documented on 56–57. G. Gawlick, "Der Deismus als Grundzug der Religionsphilosophie der Aufklärung," in *Hermann Samuel Reimarus (1694–1768) ein 'bekannter Unbekannter'*, 43 n. 35: "Reimarus represents the late phase of the history of deism; he summarizes and systematizes the results of his predecessors, especially the English deists."

61. Reimarus, "Apologie," 2:172. Much less radical, since he was not oriented to the "true meaning and intention of Jesus," J. P. Gabler at the end of the eighteenth century called attention to the possible different intentions of the biblical authors (J. P. Gabler, "Von der richtigen Unterscheidung der biblischen und der dogmatischen Theologie und der echten Bestimmung ihrer beider Ziele" (1787) in G. Strecker, ed., *Das Problem der Theologie des Neuen Testaments* (WF 367; Darmstadt: Wiss. Buchges., 1975) 40.

62. W. Schmidt-Biggemann, *Theodizee und Aufklärung. Das philosophische Profil der deutschen Aufklärung* (stw 722; Frankfurt: Suhrkamp, 1988) 82.

of a new sect said and wrote, and how their works are to be understood."[63] Included in Reimarus's list of principles is the argument already found among the Socinians, that the credibility of a witness is strengthened when his testimony causes him troubles.[64] The testimony of a witness is also enhanced by the criterion of coherence that also stands behind the form of the CDC mentioned above: "A writing, or a passage in a document, is to be ascribed to the purported author . . . when the particular words and expression, as well as the opinions and facts, agree with the purported author's style, opinions, and times; and in a particular passage, when it accords with its context."[65] Reimarus also includes the criterion of multiple attestation, among others, in his collection of critical rules for determining the authenticity of a particular item of testimony.[66]

This will be illustrated by a few advocates of the Enlightenment. The methodological presuppositions for both types of the criterion of dissimilarity had already been created in the eighteenth century. Even earlier, the beginnings of source criticism had made the CDC possible at the literary level. With the deists' perception of Jesus' disciples as historical individuals, a distinction between them and Jesus was recognized and the CDC was then also applied at the historical level.

The Enlightenment's discovery of the history behind the Scripture led to a conflict between traditional dogmatics and historical insights—all the more so as historical singularity and particularity were difficult to combine with the Enlightenment's idea of a general, timeless religion. The accommodation doctrine is an attempt to defuse this conflict by different hermeneutical means, or to make it productive by other means. The basic problem here is the Jewishness of Jesus. Semler hardly conceals the theological bases for his creation of a preliminary form of the CDJ, in that he explains Jewish elements by means of an accommodation theory. In the process he also distinguishes and sets apart Jesus' "Proprium" (that which was characteristically Jesus' own) not only theologically but historically.

This preliminary form of the CDJ does not yet make the distinction between the historical and authentic on the one side from the unhistorical and inauthentic on the other, but rather the "essential" from the "temporally conditioned." However, only the one category of material is traced back to Jesus, whether designated "the essential" in the preliminary form of the CDJ or "the historical" in its later developed form. In the preliminary form as found in

---

63. Reimarus, "Apologie," 2:21.
64. Reimarus, *Vernunftlehre*, §247, 260.
65. Ibid., §252, 266–67.
66. Ibid., §252, 267.

Semler, Jesus himself made the accommodation to the Jewish world. The step to the historical-critical use of the CDJ was then made when this accommodation was ascribed to the disciples of Jesus as the transmitters of his words and deeds, and thus Jesus was relieved of the task.

1.3 Historicism

a) Introduction

Friedrich Meinecke describes historicism as "primarily nothing other than the application to historical life of the new life-principles attained in the great German movement from Leibniz to the death of Goethe."[67] In the preceding sections we have seen how in Humanism and the Enlightenment there was a step-by-step dissolution of theology and the Bible as determining authorities. Nonetheless, in this period, historical-critical research still took place in the context of normative cognitive interests—"historia magistra vitae" (history as life's teacher). The autonomy of human thinking and acting is central for the newly attained life principles named by Meinecke. When applied to history, however, they no longer bring with them a normative interest in history, but a purely descriptive interest. The background and presupposition for these new principles is the change in the way reality is experienced in view of the great upheavals that have taken place in the process by which modern Europe has been formed. A dynamic interpretation of history is the result, in which reality is seen as basically historical, fundamentally bound to human activity and formed by human hands alone.[68] History in itself, namely, history as the expression of the historicalness of human existence, becomes its own theme. In this process it also happens that historical science becomes a discipline in its own right, no longer understanding itself as an auxiliary discipline. This new historical science occupies itself with historical movements and developments, which receive a new dignity by the falling away or cutting loose from the idea of a transcendent history outside or above humanity. Thus in historicism the sharp turn to immanence makes its definitive appearance.[69]

This new independent importance assigned to historical action is to be seen in connection with the enormous personal force exercised by the actions of great charismatic figures. The place previously occupied by a transcendent

---

67. F. Meinecke, *Die Entstehung des Historismus*, (ed. C. Hinrichs; Werke Bd. 3; Munich: Oldenbourg, 1959) 2.

68. "Historicism understands history as the realization of human freedom." Muhlack, *Geschichtswissenschaft im Humanismus*, 427.

69. Ibid., 419 passim. Cf. also Muhlack, "Von der philologischen zur historischen Methode," 180.

spirit that permeated and ruled history was taken by human figures who acted in a historically recognizable way. The discovery of autonomous human thinking and acting led to a fixation on the individual personality that permitted social and economic factors at work in history largely to fade from view.

Leopold von Ranke (1795–1886) is the outstanding first advocate of historicism,[70] whose ideal it was "to make historical truth visible to the world."[71] His historicism "in the good sense," as Meinecke formulates it, encompasses the two poles of individuality and individual development.[72] Ranke regarded the recognition of historical individuality as the basic presupposition for historical knowledge. This individuality is to be held fast in its irreplaceable uniqueness, and it is the task of the historian to work out the differences between the individual historical periods. Keys to what is generally true can be found only by dealing with the individuals. Precisely on this point Ranke's view of history stands in contrast to that of Hegel, which (for Ranke in quite an unhistorical manner) is determined by a metaphysical philosophy of history. It is in this contrast to Hegel that Ranke's classic formulation of historicism is to be read: God is directly present in every epoch of history.

This immanence of God in all history gives every period its own inherent value—in the time after Ranke, "immanence" without any connection to God. On the one hand, this view of immanence motivated historical investigation to develop a clear methodology, and, on the other hand, called for a strict objectivity in order to represent what actually happened as closely as possible. By omitting an external reference point for history, historicity itself became its own standard. This is the explanation for the high value placed on the "authentic," and this is also the background in the philosophy of history for the historian's adoption of philological source analysis, which is characterized by the demand for a close connection between source analysis and the writing of history.

Both impulses, that toward a clear methodology and that toward objectivity, are Ranke's twin legacies to historical science. He caused the critical method of source analysis to be generally recognized as standard, and he called for the strictest objectivity on the part of the historian, an objectivity that has as its goal "simply to show how it really was" (*wie es eigentlich gewesen ist*).[73]

---

70. A good introduction to Ranke is presented by Helmut Berding, "Leopold von Ranke," in Hans-Ulrich Wehler, ed. *Deutsche Historiker* (Göttingen: Vandenhoeck & Ruprecht, 1971) 1:7–24.

71. L. v. Ranke, *Zur Kritik neuerer Geschichtsschreiber* (2nd ed., L. v. Ranke's Sämmtliche Werke 33/34; Leipzig: Duncker & Humblot, 1874) 150.

72. Meinecke, *Die Entstehung des Historismus*, 595.

73. L. v. Ranke, *Geschichten der romanischen und germanischen Völker von 1494 bis 1514* (L. v. Ranke's Sämmtliche Werke 33/34; 2nd ed.; Leipzig: Duncker & Humblot, 1874), Preface to first edition of 1824, vii.

The consequence of historicism in the historicization of reality eventuated in a thoroughly critical source analysis, one of the greatest achievements of the nineteenth century in this area. Since the sources themselves were understood to belong to the realm of history, that is, were subject to changes in the course of history, the concept of the history of traditions was discovered, a history from which the original report is to be distinguished.[74]

In this way historicism developed the direct methodological and material premises for the dissimilarity criterion.

b) The Ideal of "Personality" as the Category for Understanding Jesus

The manner in which Jesus research sees the figure of Jesus and fits him into some category affects the selection of its method. The theological perspective in turn participates in the philosophical thought world of its time. In the Jesus research of the nineteenth century the neoromantic admiration for the "hero" and "genius" played a significant role. This vast thematic complex cannot here be discussed as a theme in itself. It is important to call attention to one point, however: from the point of view of the philosophy of history, the dissimilarity criterion can be understood as an expression of the concept of the role of the individual in history. An inference of the doctrine of individuality is "a specifying procedure that disregards those characteristics that the event to be perceived has in common with others, in favor of such characteristics that distinguishes it from others—which does not mean, however, from *all* others."[75]

i) History-making Hero

The term "history-making hero," differently from "genius," represents the whole circle of ideas related to comprehending the historical greatness of the historic individual. Here the decisive thing is the historical effect of a powerful and effective individual[76] (and always male).

"That it is the individual—and not the general—which is the focus and goal of historical science and also determines its investigative procedures has a grand tradition especially in the German study of history."[77] This tradition is determined by the philosophical concepts of the epoch of German classical idealism.

The idea of the individuality and uniqueness of all historical phenomena belongs to the fundamental presuppositions of the historical thought of

---

74. Blanke, "Aufklärungshistorie," 173–74, in reference to Droysen's *Historik*.
75. Faber, *Theorie der Geschichtswissenschaft*, 60.
76. The exclusion of women from public life is here clearly seen.
77. Faber, *Theorie der Geschichtswissenschaft*, 45.

Johann Gottfried Herder (1744–1803) and thus was very influential. This idea is related not only to the individuality of peoples and nations, but also to the uniqueness of the individual person, whose task it is to realize the unique potential that resides only in him or her ("become what you are").[78] When one thinks of the embodiment of absolute ideas and values in the individual, one must mention above all the name of Jean Paul Friedrich Richter (1763–1825), who believed that an individual ideal image had been implanted in each human being.[79] Wilhelm von Humboldt (1767–1835), who is primarily responsible for the system of higher education that became standard in Germany in the nineteenth century (gymnasium [college prep school] and university), emphasized that nothing on earth is more important than developing the multifaceted potential of the individual's power.[80] Thus every human being should fulfill his or her own unique inner form.[81] This idea naturally pervaded the historical science of the nineteenth century, and the paradigm "individual/society" has accompanied the discussion into our own time.[82]

The idea of historical significance that accompanies this view is the notion that the general and the particular are always related in a unique manner. The classical formulation of this stance comes from the historian Jacob Burckhardt (1818–1897): "History loves from time to time to concentrate itself in one key figure to whom the world then renders obedience. These great individuals are the coincidence of the general and the extraordinary, the static and the dynamic, in a single personality."[83] Already earlier, in 1826, Schleiermacher had dealt with the theme of the "great man" in a scholarly paper: "Wherever there is a new historical development, wherever a new or renewed common life is generated, there and there alone is a great man."[84]

The epitome of the nineteenth-century philosophic ideal of the great history-making personality is Thomas Carlyle of Scotland (1795–1881), who was himself admired as a genius. As the examples from Herder to Burckhardt

---

78. Cf. K. Scholder, "Herder und die Anfänge der historischen Theologie," *EvT* 22 (1962): 428; A. Reble, *Geschichte der Pädagogik* (15th ed.; Stuttgart: Klett-Cotta, 1989) 190–91.

79. Ibid., 192–93.

80. Ibid., 193.

81. Ibid., 194.

82. One thinks of the debate about the individual and structure in the 1970s and the disputes among historians of the 1980s.

83. J. Burckhardt, "Das Individuum und das Allgemeine," in *Weltgeschichtliche Betrachtungen. Über geschichtliches Studium* (Collected Works 4; Darmstadt: Wiss. Buchges., 1956) 166.

84. D. F. E. Schleiermacher, "Über den Begriff des grossen Mannes. 24. Januar 1826," in *Werke. Auswahl in 4 Bänden,* (Leipzig: Eckardt, 1910) 1:527.

named above suggest, Carlyle enjoyed such fame because of his "view of history as the history of great men [worked effectively] as a dramatic empowerment of the most widespread opinion."[85] His most famous work, *On Heroes, Hero-Worship, and the Heroic in History*,[86] was published in 1841. Here the view that the history of the world can be written as biographies of heroes is put into practice and illustrated by examples of different types of heroes.[87] The nucleus of his widely read view is constituted by "the divine immediacy and the absolute priority of the brilliant individual."[88]

ii) Genius

Another important variant of the personality ideal of the nineteenth century is expressed in the genius cult. An adequate understanding of this genius cult requires a brief side glance at the history of the concept of the genius, since the categories that had already been developed with regard to this terminological field are important for the ways Jesus was understood in the nineteenth century.

We must begin by stating that, in ordinary linguistic practice, "genius" can refer, on the one hand, either to an individual person or to his or her intellect and talent or, on the other hand, to a superindividual pervasive spirit (e.g., the genius of a people, an era, a language). In each case, however, something unique and irreplaceable is expressed in this "genius."

The word "genius," in the form of the Latin *genius* had already entered the German language in the works of the sixteenth-century humanists.[89] Here it was understood with a clear religious connotation as the "spirit" in or alongside the person, whether as the divine voice in the person or as a separate divine being. The derivation of *genius* from *gignere* permits this divine being also to be understood as a life-generating force. In the seventeenth and eighteenth century the use of the word was extended in a more abstract direction (the genius of a time, of the human race), as well as in a more concrete usage that could refer to nature, Christ, God, and the individual human being (mostly those who were historically important). Schiller, for example, speaks of the

85. H. Kahlert, *Der Held und seine Gemeinde. Untersuchungen zum Verhältnis von Stifter-persönlichkeit und Verehrergemeinschaft in der Theologie des freien Protestantismus* (EHS.T 238; Frankfurt: Lang, 1984) 167; cf. the whole section 163–69.

86. Vol. 5 of *The Works of Thomas Carlyle* (ed. H. D. Traill; 30 vols.; London: Chapman & Hall, 1896–1901).

87. Cf. also Carlyle's essay "Biography," in *Fraser's Magazine* (April 1832) and in vol. 28 of *The Works of Thomas Carlyle*, 44ff.

88. Kahlert, *Der Held*, 141.

89. The primary source for these observations on the history of the concept is the rich article "Genie" by J. and W. Grimm in their *Deutsches Wörterbuch*, cols. 3396–450.

message of Jesus as the teaching of the heavenly genius.[90] In the following period, "genius" came to mean especially the "human spirit in its highest manifestation, at first in the realm of poetry, then expanded to all human achievement as such."[91]

The countless references in Grimm provide three associated complexes of meaning for the concept "genius:" (a) the creative, inventive, (b) the irrelevance of rules or superiority over being bound by rules, and (c) the natural, native, original, and naïve.

With regard to (a), Herder names as geniuses those who create[92] and invent[93]; v. Creuz traces the greatest changes in the world, such as new religions, back to geniuses ("in short, a new human system");[94] while Adelung distinguishes "genius" from "talent," in that the genius not only applies what is already present but also creates.[95]

With regard to (b), Schiller maintains that geniuses break the rules[96] while Gellert, Lessing, Hamann, and Goethe require that a genius be one who rebels against forms, rules, and principles.[97] In an influential series of lectures, Gellert emphasized that geniuses must free themselves from the limited value of rules.[98]

With regard to (c), Goethe associates the term "genius" with that which is native and original, just as originality is characteristic of Kant's understanding of genius.[99] Michaelis, in discussing the authenticity of New Testament writings, describes "the completely original genius" of the authors Paul and John.[100] A sense for the primitive, uncontaminated generative force is a mark of genius.[101] Schiller requires naiveté from the genius,[102] while Lessing attributes artlessness to him or her.[103] In England at the beginning of the eighteenth

---

90. Documentation in Grimm, "Genie (2f.)," col. 3402.

91. Ibid., (9), col. 3412.

92. Ibid., (9a), col. 3414.

93. Ibid., (9d), col. 3419.

94. Ibid., (9d), cols. 3418–19.

95. Ibid., (12h), col. 3449.

96. Ibid., (9a), col. 3413.

97. Ibid., (11c), cols. 3429–31.

98. Ibid., (9), cols. 3412ff.

99. Ibid., (5b), col. 3407; (9f.), cols. 3420–21; cf. also (12d), col. 3445.

100. J. D. Michaelis, *Einleitung in die göttlichen Schriften des Neuen Bundes* (2nd ed.; Göttingen, 1777) 1:47.

101. Documentation in Grimm, "Genie (11b)," col. 3429.

102. Ibid., (9a), col. 3413.

103. Ibid., (9b), col. 3415.

century also, the pure power of naturalness without artificiality or erudition is typical of genius.[104]

The religious connotation is maintained in almost all of these contexts. The genius is associated with the superhuman; the great man as genius was regarded as a demigod, god-like or divine, a god among humans.[105] Interestingly enough, Hamann describes the suffering of the genius with images from the passion story of Jesus: "[G]enius is a crown of thorns, and good taste a purple robe."[106]

iii) Jesus as History-making Hero and Genius

The models of history-making hero and genius, in which the individual plays such a special role, were adopted unproblematically into life-of-Jesus research. Since the twelfth century Jesus had emerged within the christological frame of reference as an individual, namely as the model and reference point for personal piety.[107] By the historicizing of the understanding of history itself, the central figure of Christian faith was discovered to be a historical figure, that is, he too was a great historical individual. Since the philosophical understanding of history is inevitably a factor in determining how historical research is carried on, the "historical Jesus" was necessarily thought of in such categories taken from the philosophy of history.

In both versions of the personality ideal, the "history-making hero" and the "genius," the bearer of this ideal has a special relation to the absolute. He was imbued with a mythical quality that fundamentally distinguished him from his milieu. Burckhardt designates the truly great figure as a "mysterium," which is associated with the "irreplaceable uniqueness" of the truly great.[108] The genius concept gives a name to the mystery; the genius category "explains" to a society that had become skeptical about christological dogma the historical unique and its effects in a plausible manner appropriate to the times.[109] A. Kalthoff (1850–1906) was entirely correct in his 1902 polemic: "After liberal theology no longer had the courage to confess faith in the traditional doctrines, the hero Jesus was supposed to take the same place in the consciousness of the church

---

104. Ibid., (9c), cols. 3416f.

105. Ibid., (9d), cols. 3417–19.

106. Ibid., (11g), col. 3434.

107. Cf. D. Georgi ("Leben-Jesu-Theologie/Leben-Jesu-Forschung," *TRE* 20 (1990): 566–575), who clearly points out this aspect in the course of his historical survey. The increasing importance of the individual in the second millennium is also underscored by J. Pelikan, *Jesus Through the Centuries. His Place in the History of Culture* (New Haven, Conn.: Yale University Press, 1985) 145.

108. Burckhardt, "Das Individuum und das Allgemeine," 152–53.

109. E. Grisebach critically describes the mythical character of the "genius faith" current at the beginning of the twentieth century: "This faith in the genius rests on the presupposition that an element originally present in humanity here breaks forth, an

once held by the Godman."[110] Also belonging to this context is the question of the messianic consciousness of Jesus, much discussed in the old quest of the historical Jesus, for the question not only has a psychological dimension but is also related to the philosophy of history.[111]

With reference to Jesus, a clear differentiation in the use of the concepts of "genius" and "hero" cannot be made.[112] For Bousset a prevalent aspect in the religious realm is "the unpredictability of the individual, the genius, the hero."[113] The conceptual and terminological overlapping is reflected also in Otto's ascribing to Jesus the individuality of the religious genius.[114] In the synthesis of the personality ideal, the *genius* element provided the inner foundation for the *history-making heroic personality*. The "genius" is a cipher for God, who moves world history through the ideal personality, Jesus.

Thus it is not only the ideal of personality in general, but also the honoring of Jesus as a great personality that was the widespread consensus in the nineteenth and early twentieth centuries.[115] This was true despite the fact that both Schleiermacher and Carlyle, for example, were very hesitant to classify

---

element that unites him with the universe and makes possible a 'self-transcending of life.' The genius is supposed to establish the unity between . . . the human and the divine. The genius is himself a mythical figure." E. Grisebach, *Gegenwart. Eine kritische Ethik* (Halle: Niemeyer, 1928) 97–98.

110. A. Kalthoff, *Das Christus-Problem. Grundlinien zu einer Sozialtheologie* (Leipzig: Diederichs, 1902) 20–21.

111. On the political implications of presenting Jesus as an individual, inner-personal genius, cf. the informative study by Marilyn Chapin Massey, *Christ Unmasked. The Meaning of the Life of Jesus in German Politics* (Chapel Hill, N.C.: University of North Carolina Press, 1983).

112. In his general discussions of the "great man," Schleiermacher distinguishes the great man from the genius: he is not, like the genius, entangled in life, though he has an effect on it, precisely because he is its author. But he is also limited "to that area of life to which nature has assigned him" (i.e., state or church), while the genius in his (e.g., artistic) effects has no such external limits. (Schleiermacher, "Über den Begriff des grossen Mannes," 526–29.)

113. W. Bousset: "Die Bedeutung der Person Jesu für den Glauben. Historische und rationale Grundlagen des Glaubens," in M. Fischer and F. M. Schiele, eds., *Fünfter Weltkongress für Freies Christentum und Religiösen Fortschritt (Berlin, 5.-10.8.1910). Protokoll der Verhandlungen* (Berlin: Protestant. Schriftenvertrieb, 1910) 303.

114. R. Otto, *Leben und Wirken Jesu nach historisch-kritischer Auffassung* (4th ed.; Göttingen: Vandenhoeck & Ruprecht, 1905) 62; cited in Kahlert, *Der Held*, 162.

115. Kahlert, *Der Held*, 137 and passim. A contemporary, sharp critic of Carlyle, William Thompson (later Archbishop of York) does not basically challenge "hero worship," but does object to Carlyle's selection of "heroes" and the way he describes them, and places Jesus "our great example" as the standard by which every "hero" is to be measured. (William Thomson's review in *Christian Remembrances* 6 [August 1843]: 121–43; reprinted in Jules Paul Seigel, ed., *Thomas Carlyle, The Critical Heritage* [London: Routledge & Kegan Paul, 1971] 171–92; here, 172–76.)

Jesus in the category of "great men" or "heroes."[116] This reservation was not based on their perspective of Jesus, a perspective that could not be harmonized with the personality ideal. Instead, Jesus was understood in principle as an individual of personal greatness who had to be ranked higher than all other "great men" of history.[117]

Karl Hase already saw the character of Jesus as realizing "the highest of the human spirit" who "was not merely a colorful reflection of the effects of the external world on him, but one who formed history by his own clear will."[118] According to D. F. Strauss, Jesus' own basic view of the world issued "from the innermost principle of his own heart," for in him the religious genius had become flesh.[119] In his Jesus book published in the mid-nineteenth century, Keim emphasized the role of the creative personality in world history and names Hegel, Schelling, and Schleiermacher as his authorities.[120]

Though Carlyle himself hardly categorized Jesus in this manner, German Protestant theologians were prepared to do precisely this, with explicit appeal to Carlyle. With regard to Carlyle's "clothing philosophy"[121] Baumgarten wrote in 1909: "And we would like to believe that extending hero worship to Jesus . . . , even though his authentic Scottish reserve had caused him to place Jesus outside the category of 'heroes', would give up the corresponding eccle-

---

116. On Carlyle cf. the thesis of R. Roberts, "The whole lecture on Odin [in *On Heroes, Hero-Worship and the Heroic in History*, 1840] is in fact a disguised account of the nature of Christ and of the early development of Christianity, in terms as rationalist and non-supernaturalist as those of D. F. Strauss's *Leben Jesu* (1835–1836), which was being read and reviewed by the cognoscendi in England in 1838 and 1839." R. Roberts, *The Ancient Dialect. Thomas Carlyle and Comparative Religion* (Berkeley: University of California Press, 1988) 75.

117. In Schleiermacher's discussions of the "great man," he speaks mysteriously in the subjunctive mood of the One who transcends all human standards (Schleiermacher, "Über den Begriff des grossen Mannes," 528). An extensive discussion of the understanding of the historical Jesus in Schleiermacher and Strauss in found in D. Lange, *Historischer Jesus oder mythischer Christus. Untersuchungen zu dem Gegensatz zwischen Friedrich Schleiermacher und David Friedrich Strauss* (Gütersloh: Mohn, 1975).

118. K. Hase, *Das Leben Jesu. Lehrbuch zunächst für akademische Vorlesungen* (2nd ed.; Leipzig: Breitkopf & Härtel, 1829, 1835) 23.

119. David Friedrich Strauss, *The Life of Jesus, For the People* (German 1864. London: Williams & Norgate, 1879) 1:280.

120. Th. Keim, *Geschichte Jesu von Nazara in ihrer Verkettung mit dem Gesamtleben seines Volkes* (Zürich: Orell, Füssli & Comp., 1867) 3–4.

121. According to Carlyle, clothing is symbolic and represents all that human beings think and do. Clothing, including ecclesiastical vestments, wears out in time and needs to be renewed by the creative hero who is always of the same nature, but who is absorbed into his time in a way appropriate to it, so that the hero worship of a particular society permits inferences regarding its cultural level.

siastical clothing."[122] Bousset, a great admirer of Carlyle, declared him to be a prophet,[123] and placed a citation from Carlyle at the beginning of his first Jesus book,[124] in which he characterized Jesus as a creative genius.[125] In his debate with Kalthoff, Bousset clearly affirmed: "Religion lives only in and from great personalities. . . . But the acme and midpoint . . . of all the leading bearers of the religious spirit is the person Jesus."[126] Julius Wellhausen's *Israelite and Jewish History* was clearly influenced by Carlyle, and Wellhausen also quotes him in connection with his declaration that "the religion of the Gospel is individualism."[127] Wellhausen's delineation of history culminates in the figure of Jesus, who concentrates into one burning point of light "that which is eternally valid, the divine-human, in the focussing mirror of his own individuality," for he is "the greatest example of the generating power of the individual soul."[128] Wellhausen thereby makes a comparison with Judaism: "That which the Law did not accomplish is accomplished by the individualistic model."[129] Similarly, Holtzmann designates the "religious-moral genius" as an element of Jesus that "transcends Judaism," while Messiahship belongs to his Jewish side.[130]

For Wrede too, the personality of Jesus was the decisive thing about him, the bearer of his "world view."[131] Wrede's student Weidel wants to see the

---

122. O. Baumgarten, "Carlyle, Thomas," in *RGG* (1st ed. 1909): cols. 1578–86.

123. The title of an essay by W. Bousset: "Thomas Carlyle—ein Prophet des 19. Jahrhunderts," *ChW* 11 (1897): cols. 249ff. On Bousset's reception of Carlyle, cf. Kahlert, *Der Held*, 171–202; K. Berger, *Exegese und Philosophie* (SBS 123/124; Stuttgart: Kath. Bibelwerk, 1986) 85–114, and A. F. Verhuele, *Wilhelm Bousset. Leben und Werk. Ein theologiegeschichtlicher Versuch* (Amsterdam: Ton Balland, 1973) 373–75. For extensive documentation of the high regard in which the individual genius was held by Troeltsch, including the distant influence of Carlyle, cf. Kahlert, *Der Held*, 250–67.

124. W. Bousset, *Jesu Predigt in ihrem Gegensatz zum Judentum. Ein religionsgeschichtlicher Vergleich* (Göttingen: Vandenhoeck & Ruprecht, 1892) 1. Bousset also cites from Carlyle's *Sartor Resartus* one of the rare passages in which Jesus ("our divinest symbol") is explicitly named.

125. Ibid., 79.

126. W. Bousset: *Was Wissen Wir von Jesus* (Tübingen: Mohr, 1904; 2nd ed. 1906) 72.

127. J. Wellhausen, *Israelitische und Jüdische Geschichte* (Berlin: DeGruyter; reprint of 9th ed. 1958) 360, 371. Cf. also Kahlert's arguments on Wellhausen's dependence on Carlyle in Kahlert, *Der Held*, 218–219.

128. Wellhausen, *Israelitische und Jüdische Geschichte*, 315.

129. Ibid., 315–16.

130. H. J. Holtzmann, *Das messianische Bewusstsein Jesu. Ein Beitrag zur Leben-Jesu-Forschung* (Tübingen: Mohr, 1907) 99.

131. W. Wrede, "Die Predigt Jesu vom Reiche Gottes," (1894), in W. Wrede, *Vorträge und Studien* (Tübingen: Mohr, 1907) 126: "But over all that one could call Jesus' 'worldview' stands that which inspires it, his personality."

"creative genius" in Jesus, and describes him as master of men, hero and child, prophet and reformer, absolute individualist and incomparably more.[132] Jülicher underscores the unique personality of Jesus and his importance from the perspective of the history of religions.[133] For him "whether an idea and the manner in which it is expressed is the automatic product of human society, or the sharp creation of a single towering personality"[134] is clearly recognizable.

This interpretation was of course not limited to Germany: in a 1901 article on Jesus, A. B. Bruce repeatedly describes Jesus' character and actions as "heroic" and guided by a "religious genius."[135]

The quest of the historical Jesus has always seen Jesus in connection with the Old Testament. Thus, by means of the *"theory of prophetic connection,"*[136] the idea of the role of "great men" was integrated into the history of the Old and New Testaments. Thereby the Old Testament prophets appear as a "chain of religious heroes"[137] who founded and established the religion of Israel. Interestingly enough, also in the historian Eduard Meyer is found the view that Israel's prophets were a first-rate embodiment of a "well-defined individuality as a dominant agent . . . under a religious form," so that here emerged "the first great action of individuality in the history of mankind."[138] The connection between the con-

---

132. K. Weidel, *Jesu Persönlichkeit: Eine psychologische Studie* (Halle: Marhold, 1908) 10–12.

133. A. Jülicher, "Die Religion Jesu und die Anfänge des Christentums bis zum Nicaenum," in Paul Hinneberg, ed. *Die Kultur der Gegenwart. I/4 Geschichte der christlichen Religion. Mit Einleitung* (2nd ed. Berlin: Teubner, 1909) 47, 68.

134. A. Jülicher: *Neue Linien in der Kritik der evangelischen Überlieferung* (Vorträge des Hessischen und Naussauischen theologischen Ferienkurses, H. 3; Giessen: Töpelmann, 1906) 74.

135. A. B. Bruce, "Jesus," *EncBib* 2, 1901: 2441, 2442, 2447.

136. Klaus Koch reports this view of the "prophetic connection theory:" "After a decline of five hundred years, Jesus of Nazareth—perhaps John the Baptist before him—picked up the thread of the great prophets, the series of which ended with Deutero-Isaiah." With Jesus "the God of the prophets prevails once more, truer and more human than ever before." (K. Koch, *The Rediscovery of Apocalyptic.* [Studies in Biblical Theology, Second Series 22; London: SCM Press, 1972] 37.

137. H. Gunkel, "Individualismus I. I. und Sozialismus im AT," *RGG* 3 (1st ed. 1912): cols. 493–501, 498.

138. E. Meyer, "The Development of Individuality in Ancient History," in E. Meyer, *Kleine Schriften, vol. 1, Zur Geschichtstheorie und zur wirtschaftlichen und politischen Geschichte des Altertums* (Halle: Max Niemeyer, 1910) 220. Liebeschütz compares Meyer and Jacob Burckhardt and confirms that despite all the differences, the view of the "self-discovery of the individual as the highest level of humanity" binds together these two sons of the nineteenth century (H. Liebeschütz, *Das Judentum im deutschen Geschichtsbild von Hegel bis Max Weber* [Tübingen: Mohr, 1967]) 284. Burckhardt had in any case a high opinion of the prophets and was dependent on his teacher De Wette for this evaluation (Ibid., 221–23).

cept of the great personality, the prophets, and Jesus becomes quite clear in Duhm: the prophets, leaders of humanity, have their own special genius and are to be regarded as "the men of the eternally new." The history that followed them was a decline, and finally Israel crucified Jesus, "the dangerously new One."[139] The theory of a decline after the prophetic age was presupposed as obvious in Old Testament scholarship until well into the twentieth century.[140] This formed the basis for the postulate that connected Jesus to the great prophets.

> A "theory of prophetic connection" was already found in Strauss. "Thus in later Judaism, when we compare it with the standpoint of the prophets before captivity and during it, there is no mistaking that a retrograde step has been taken. In its tendency toward the external service toward the God whom it was seeking, to multiplication of ceremonies and subtle extension of them, Judaism had gone incomparably further than the prophets who saw his presence in the mind of man, in righteousness and love of mankind." "While Jesus was forming within himself this cheerful tone of mind, identical with that of God, comprehending all men as brothers, he had realized in himself the prophetic ideal of a new covenant with the law written in the heart (Jer 31:31)."[141] So also Ernest Renan (1823–1892, famous for his 1863 *Life of Jesus*) sees Jesus as standing in the same line as the great prophets.[142] Even Kalthoff, who interpreted the Christ precisely not as a historic individual, but as "the transcendent principle of the church," stated that "the Christ of the Gospels went back centuries behind the scribalism of the Jews to resurrect the genius of the prophets."[143]

Kahlert has quite rightly seen that the "prophet-connection-theory" represents an additional facet of hero worship:[144] the prophets founded the (particularistic) religion of Israel; Jesus founded the universal religion of Christianity.

In order to mark out the continuity and discontinuity between the Jewish origin of Jesus and Jesus himself, a particular variation of the personality ideal

---

139. B. Duhm, *Israels Propheten* (Tübingen: Mohr, 1916) 4, 8. In his *Theologie der Propheten* that appeared fifty-nine years later (1875), Duhm makes explicit the presupposition of his portrayal, "namely, that the development of history is not based only on the movement of the masses, nor on the influence of external forces, but rests above all in the personality of the most outstanding of the greatest and noblest spirits." (20)

140. On this cf. "The Idea of Development in the Philosophy of History," below II. 1.4: b. ii.

141. Strauss, *The Life of Jesus, For the People*, 1:228, 281.

142. Cf. D. M. Hoffmann: *Renan und das Judentum. Die Bedeutung des Volkes Israel im Werk des 'Historien philosophe'* (Diss. Würzburg, 1988) 264, 280.

143. Kalthoff, *Das Christus-Problem*, 26, 86.

144. Kahlert, *Der Held*, 279, 280: "Hero-worship is the secret ideology of the 'prophet-connection-theory'."

was brought into play. Jesus is interpreted as the model of the transitional figure, as defined by Meinecke: "All great reforming personalities have been *transitional figures*, whose inner life was a 'battlefield between two ages.' Penetrating research often discovers that their world of ideas represents a surprising continuity with the tradition they have exploded. It is regularly the case that the new intentionally rejects only a part of the old, and never quite leaves the ground that has nourished it."[145] Burckhardt understands historical heroes as such in this same way: "In the *crises*, the old and the new (the revolution) find their culmination in the great individuals."[146] So also Kölbing places Jesus in the series of religious reformers. These reformers, "when it is a matter of expressing their religious perceptions, [make use of] the traditional forms of religious knowledge or even depend on them, in order to fill them with new content—often unnoticed by the reformers themselves."[147] Here it becomes clear how characterizing Jesus as a transitional figure allows him to be understood in a contemporizing manner as someone who had dealt with the same state of affairs that had called forth the accommodation theory one hundred years earlier—that Jesus had moved entirely in Jewish circles and expressed himself in Jewish forms. As a transitional figure or reformer, however, he must go beyond these. Thus, to be sure, Jülicher emphasized Jesus' deep roots in the Old Testament and Judaism, but he adds this qualification: "[B]ut his branches tower high above the highest that had ever grown in that forest, in regions that transcend Judaism."[148] Even more strongly than Kölbing, Ninck makes clear that the advent of Jesus was of course not completely new—as though he had fallen from heaven, but "what he took over became completely new in his hands."[149] In contrast, J. Weiss had already argued sometime earlier against "the rationalist tendency to seek Jesus' significance in the newness of his thoughts and teaching." For him it was obvious that "the new religion adopted the thought forms and means of expression available in its time."[150] When Weiss sees the decisive greatness of Jesus not in his theories but in the

---

145. F. Meinecke, "Persönlichkeit und geschichtliche Welt," in P. R. Rohden, ed., *Menschen die Geschichte machten. Viertausend Jahre Weltgeschichte in Zeit- und Lebensbildern* (2nd ed. Wien: Seidel, 1933) 1:7.

146. J. Burckhardt, "Das Individuum und das Allgemeine," 166.

147. P. Kölbing, *Die geistige Einwirkung Jesu auf Paulus. Eine historische Untersuchung* (Göttingen: Vandenhoeck & Ruprecht, 1906) 36.

148. Jülicher, "Die Religion Jesu," 54.

149. J. Ninck, *Jesus als Charakter* (1906) (3rd ed. Leipzig: Hinrich, 1925) 277; in reference to Jewish tradition: "What he does not cite is more important than what he cites."

150. J. Weiss, *Die Predigt vom Reiche Gottes* (2nd ed. Göttingen: Vandenhoeck & Ruprecht, 1900) 34–35. The substantially different first edition was translated as *Jesus' Proclamation of the Kingdom of God* (trans. & ed. Richard Hyde Hiers and David Larrimore Holland; Lives of Jesus Series; Philadelphia: Fortress Press, 1971). All citations are from the 2nd ed., translated by M. Eugene Boring.

faith he lives out, then here again his personality returns to center stage.[151] Finally, Weiss too advocates a theory of accommodation: "Even the most powerful genius also stands under the pressure of tradition, and if he wants to communicate his inner life, then he must at first express himself in words that are generally understood, a reality he is willing to live with."[152]

Alongside connecting Jesus with his Israelite heritage, there are still other points to be named for the theological relevance of particular aspects of the personality ideal: Jesus is the *great founder of a religion*. With the emphasis on Jesus' uniqueness, and precisely in reference to his role as the founder of Christianity, the absoluteness of Christianity is underscored. Jesus is considered historically as the beginning point (better: beginning personality) and nucleus of Christianity. The liberals at the end of the nineteenth century were not the first to have this view; already F. C. Baur had written, "Can one speak at all of the content and essence of Christianity without making the primary subject its founder, and without recognizing that all that Christianity consists of is due to the person of its founder?"[153] Wherever Jesus is the topic of discussion, there also Christianity must be debated.

Finally, the emphasis on personality in the concluding phase of the old quest for the historical Jesus facilitates his being approached by people who live in the modern world. The *concept of personality* receives a hermeneutical function. The failure of the attempt to write a historical biography of Jesus is acknowledged, but in the words of Jesus in the Synoptics one supposes that authentic sayings of Jesus can be found that, even without a precise knowledge of the attendant circumstances, still give an insight into his personality.[154] Personality is thereby understood as a separable and timeless entity that allows access to Jesus. Thus, on the one hand, it is affirmed that a personality can be grasped apart from its context. On the other hand, "personality" is understood to provide a bridge over the "ugly ditch" of history that connects Jesus and the modern reader. As a result of this static picture of humanity we find in the past "a person of our own flesh and blood, spirit of our spirit, personal life as we ourselves experience it."[155]

---

151. Elsewhere Weiss traces back "the origin of earliest Christianity . . . to the effect of Jesus' personality on his disciples." ("Das Problem der Entstehung des Christentums," in *ARW* 16 [1913]: 515.)

152. Ibid., 427.

153. F. C. Baur, "Das Christenthum und die christliche Kirche der drei ersten Jahrhunderte" (1853), in *Ausgewählte Werke in Einzelausgaben*, ed. K. Scholder (Stuttgart: Fromman, 1966) 3:22–23.

154. So argues Weidel, *Jesu Persönlichkeit*, 7–8.

155. E. Preuschen, "Idee oder Methode," in *ZNW* 1 (1900): 8. The analogy to many short-circuited attempts of our own time to use psychology to get nearer to the "real Jesus" is readily seen.

However, the understanding of Jesus as a great personality can also empha-size the difference between Jesus and all others. This is indicated by the theme of Jesus' "consciousness." Schleiermacher speaks of Jesus' *"self-consciousness,"* which separates him from all other human beings.[156] The theme of the—pos-sibly messianic—consciousness of Jesus in the psychological-historical sense occupied the old quest of the historical Jesus for a long time. Christological majesty could be grasped as messianic consciousness. Lührmann points to the term and concept *persona* as the christological background for "personality."[157] Once again we see the typical tendency of theological argumentation in Jesus research to transfer christological issues to the historical arena.

The examples mentioned in this section illustrate how Jesus—in a manner appropriate to the times—was thought of as a religious genius or history-making hero: as prophet, transitional person and reformer, founder of a reli-gion, and great personality. With these categories there is bound up a particular model of historical explanation of the relation of Jesus to the Judaism of his time and to early Christianity. In the following we will see how this philosophical-historical concept played a decisive role in methodology and historical reconstruction.

iv) The Ideal of "Personality" as a Presupposition for the Criterion of Dissimilarity

Whether *persona*, personality, or genius; whether "genius" was one of Jesus' qualities; or whether he was himself a "genius"—it is always a matter of trying to find the most plausible category[158] by which the uniqueness of Jesus can be expressed.

In order to arrange the following discussion into an outline, we return to the three characteristics already associated with each other in the preceding historical comments on the term "genius." These are the attributes (a) creative and inventive; (b) free from rules and/or abolishing them, and (c) natural, native, original, and naïve.

On (a), "creative and inventive": An understanding of Jesus as a creative fig-ure emphasizes his fundamental differentness over against his environment. Thereby the criterion of dissimilarity can be understood in the form of the cri-terion of underivability: that which is absolutely new cannot be derived from anything else. R. Otto sees the new religion of Jesus breaking forth "from the

---

156. F. D. E. Schleiermacher, *The Life of Jesus* (ed. Jack C. Verheyden; trans. S. Maclean Gilmour; Lives of Jesus Series; Philadelphia: Fortress Press, 1975) 102.

157. D. Lührmann, "Die Frage nach Kriterien," 61.

158. "Plausible" in the sense that there is a social consensus on the importance of this category.

depths and mystery of his religious-genius individuality: a depth and mystery that is closed off to all psychological dissection and that resists every artificial historical derivation."[159] Here it can be recognized that a basic principle of the CDJ, even in its form as the principle of underivability, is connected with the personality ideal—without however being formulated in this period as the CDJ.

The creative element thus stands in a special relation to the social environment of the great personality, when this society needs a hero in order to lead it out of a crisis.[160] In this crisis situation the great personality is recognized precisely by his or her new, creative contribution. Carlyle's philosophy of history is a variant of the basic idea of the solitary individual against the rest of the world.[161] According to Carlyle's theory, leading personalities emerge in times of human crisis and bring deliverance. In Bousset this idea is applied to the figure of Jesus within Judaism with especial clarity.[162] The leader-personality Jesus and the crisis-figure "late Judaism" are thereby posed against each other. Berger points to the twofold influence of Carlyle: "(a) Emphasis is placed [in Bousset's works] on the unconscious, creative life that is combined with the new (explicit recourse to Carlyle), and (b) pre-Jesus Judaism receives its distinguishing features from the crisis situation as portrayed by Carlyle, especially in regard to rigidity. Judaism becomes a foil for the personality of Jesus."[163]

With this historical image of Judaism as its presupposition, a clear distinction is made between Jesus and Judaism. The decisive element in Jesus is found in precisely those features that distinguish him from Judaism. Thus the CDJ is made available for the exegetical work used in the reconstruction of the historical Jesus. It is not, however, used as a criterion of authenticity, but especially

---

159. Otto, *Leben und Wirken Jesu*, 62; cited in Kahlert, *Der Held*, 162.

160. Cf. also J. Burckhardt, "Das Individuum und das Allgemeine," 166: "During a crisis the old and the new come together in great individuals in a culminating way (the revolution). Their essence remains a true mystery of world history; their relation to their time is a *hieros gamos* (sacred marriage), something that can happen almost only in terrible times, mainly times that give the only highest standard of greatness and also are the only times that need true greatness."

161. Cf. Meyer, "The Development of Individuality," 222: "the conscience of a single individuality in opposition to the whole surrounding world."

162. While "late Judaism" lacked new moral impulses, living power, and creative spirit, Jesus' preaching is supposed to be truly creative, according to Bousset, *Jesu Predigt in ihrem Gegensatz zum Judentum*, 31, 38, 41. Cf. also J. B. Heinrich, *Christus. Ein Nachweis seiner geschichtlichen Existenz und göttlichen Persönlichkeit, zugleich eine Kritik des Rationalismus, des Straussischen Mythizismus und des Lebens Jesu von Renan* (2nd ed.; Mainz: Kirchheim, 1864) 29, which speaks of the "lowest point in the history of Judaism." Examples of the claim of the decline and fall of Judaism at the time of Jesus are legion.

163. Berger, *Exegese und Philosophie*, 96.

to highlight what is decisive, essential: "From the authentic materials one must take a further step to isolate *the essential*: the essential is the new, the original. Not what Jesus shares with the people of his time, but what he possessed that went beyond them."[164]

Finally and above all, the work on the hero model (and the community of hero worshippers) in the field of the history of religions, in association with classical source criticism, leads directly to the CDC in its well-known formulation by P. W. Schmiedel: "When a profane historian finds before him a historical document which testifies to the worship of a hero unknown to other sources, he attaches first and foremost importance to those features which cannot be deduced merely from the fact of this worship, and he does so on the simple and sufficient ground that they would not be found in this source unless the author had met with them as fixed data of tradition. The same fundamental principle may be safely applied in the case of the gospels, for they also are all of them written by worshippers of Jesus."[165]

The substance of the CDC, here formulated on the basis and in the language of "hero worship," was already found in Reimarus and D. F. Strauss. The interesting thing about Schmiedel is that he clearly distances himself personally from hero worship. Just as he thought the worship of Jesus by the first Christians had gone too far, so he also rejects the Jesus cult of his contemporaries. The idea that Jesus had been an absolutely perfect model and introduced something entirely new was without religious relevance for Schmiedel. "For myself, I do not at all apply the word 'unique' to Jesus; for it either says nothing at all or can be understood as saying too much."[166] Against this background, in Schmiedel's work the CDC attains precisely the function of going against the image of Jesus based on the personality ideal. Therefore this perspective does not admit of a CDJ formulated as its parallel, which of course is directed to the distinctiveness of Jesus among his fellow human beings.

On (b), "free from rules and/or abolishing them": On the same page as the emphasis on Jesus' creative personality amidst a decrepit society stands the emphasis on his rejection of that which was seen as of central importance in that society, namely the Law, especially the "casuistry" associated with it. The description of the difference between Jesus and Judaism rests on, among other things, the claim that Jesus rejected the Law and/or "legalism." This rejection

---

164. H. Weinel, *Biblische Theologie des Neuen Testament: Die Religion Jesu und des Urchristentums* (GThW 3.2; Tübingen: Mohr, 1911) 42. Weinel thereby joins himself to Semler's chain of argument "historical-essential-Christian (see above II.1.2.c.)."

165. P. W. Schmiedel, "Gospels," *EncBib* 2 (1901): 1872.

166. P. W. Schmiedel, "Die Person Jesu im Streite der Meinungen der Gegenwart," in *PrM* 10 (1906): 280; in this regard cf. the whole discussion on 280–81.

was understood as a historical reform and/or as a return to the religion of the prophets. The Law, which Ferdinand Weber (1836–1879) was the first to disdain by associating it with "legalism" and to make it as such the essence of Jewish religion, had become under Wellhausen's powerful influence the primary distinguishing mark between Israel and Judaism.[167]

Jesus brings to the moral life a "manifold new impulse of primeval power"; with him "everything is unmediated life and act, almost nothing doctrine and theory."[168] Thus he polemicizes "against the confusing mass of regulations" and "against the multifarious laws that tear life itself to pieces."[169] The romantically colored personality ideal, which has as one of its implications the rejection of rules and principles, thus also contributes to the sharpening of the content of the criterion of dissimilarity as the CDJ. It does this alongside the primary motif of Protestant confessionalism in this regard: that of the "Law." However, the CDJ, in this theologically loaded sense, did not become important until the "New Quest" of the historical Jesus in the midst of the twentieth century.

On (c), "natural, native, original, and naïve": So also the third aspect mentioned above, the "original and simple," may be related to the criterion of dissimilarity. The CDC looks for that which has not been secondarily reformulated, for the simple, that which has not been shaped by the developing church but which was created by the original, simple power of Jesus himself. Here too the connotation is present that understanding Jesus in terms of a religious genius requires the expectation that his words can be recognized by their simple primitive power. The influence of the romantic ideal is not to be overlooked here. Bousset emphasizes the remarkable plainness of the figure of Jesus.[170] Wernle states, "The closer we come to Jesus in the traditional material, the more everything that is dogmatic and theological recedes from view."[171] Jülicher describes the charm of fresh life and makes a comparison between an original diamond and polished glass in order to illustrate the unique radiance of the real Jesus.[172] In order to function as a (mostly intuitive) criterion, this characterization of Jesus is, on the one hand, dependent on the

---

167. G. F. Moore, "Christian Writers on Judaism," *HTR* 14 (1921): 228–37. This is, of course, related to the "prophet-connection-theory" mentioned above.

168. Bousset, *Jesu Predigt in ihrem Gegensatz zum Judentum,* 51.

169. Ibid., 54.

170. Bousset, *Was wissen wir von Jesus?* 52; "The figure of Jesus is so uncomplicated that it can be painted on a flat surface, so real and impressive, that it can do without the three-dimensional representation of historical criticism, so great and masterful, that its splendor still shines forth from the mosaic."

171. P. Wernle, *Die Quellen des Lebens Jesu* (Halle: Gebauer-Schwetschke, 1904) 87.

172. Jülicher, "Die Religion Jesu," 45.

description of Judaism at the time of Jesus as decadent (e.g., the charge of legalistic sophistry), which leads it to the CDJ. On the other hand, it is dependent on a more or less critical attitude toward the church, which sees in the developing church the loss of the originally fresh impulse that came from Jesus—then it provides a foundation for the CDC.

The following three characterizations of Jesus that were inspired by the genius cult and hero worship are related to each other and, in each case, give impetus for different variations of the criterion of dissimilarity:

The genius is creative and founding (of a religion)	→ Judaism is caught in a crisis	→ CDJ
	→ the earliest Christians were epigones and "Judaizing"	→ CDC
The genius repudiates rules and principles	→ Judaism is burdened by its legalism	→ CDJ
	→ Christianity is burdened by its dogmas	→ CDC
The genius expresses him- or herself simply and with creative originality	→ in contrast to an artificial Judaism	→ CDJ
	→ in contrast to the developing church	→ CDC

In conclusion, we need only to point out that it was not only Jesus himself who was understood within the framework of the personality ideal as a "great man." His teaching too is interpreted as liberation from (Jewish) nationalism in favor of a universalistic individualism, as in the case of Bousset.[173] This contrast, bound up with the personality ideal and seen as a contrast between Judaism and Christianity, also contributes to the plausibility of the CDJ.

❧❧❧❧❧❧

Excursus: The Literary Genre "Jesus Book"

The tendencies of the philosophy of history discussed above to see Jesus as a solitary and unique personality belong to the context of the literary genre "Jesus book," in which life-of-Jesus research found its most widespread expres-

---

173. Bousset, *Jesu Predigt in ihrem Gegensatz zum Judentum*, 50; *Das Wesen der Religion. Dargestellt an ihrer Geschichte* (4th ed.; Lebensfragen 28; Tübingen: Mohr, 1903; 1920) 163.

sion. Not to be overlooked in this context is the connection between this literary form and the nineteenth-century novel, in which the "inner importance of the individual . . . attained its historical high point."[174] Both the novel and life-of-Jesus research participated in the general intellectual history of the times. To the extent that life-of-Jesus research resulted in literary expression, direct parallels of portrayals of Jesus to the characteristic features of novels in the nineteenth century are conspicuous. Of course, a historical Jesus book is to be distinguished from a fictional novel. The Jesus book cannot simply be categorized in the genre "novel." It is noticeable, however, that historical scholars in general, like the life-of-Jesus scholars of the nineteenth century, repeatedly and candidly emphasize the element of intuition and divination in historical reconstruction.[175] Every historical portrayal is at the same time a creative event in the realm of literature. The comparison between the Jesus book and the novel is therefore legitimate and reasonable.

In his classic work on the development of the novel in the late eighteenth and nineteenth century, Watt describes the intention of the author of novels to be that of giving an authentic report of factual individual experiences.[176] Originality and individuality are criteria for the genre of the novel that was being constituted, a genre that wanted to prevail over literary traditionalism. It is thus relevant to note the shift in meaning of the word "original" to which Watt calls attention: while in the Middle Ages it still meant "existing from the very beginning," it now came to mean "not derived, independent." It is in this sense that the individual experiences to be reported in the novel are unique and new.[177] We have already seen how in the realm of the philosophy of history the generally accepted personality ideal was increasingly applied to Jesus. The same is true for the literary representation of the inner life of Jesus. The emphasis on subjective experience, already documented by the flowering of the eighteenth-century novels concerned with personal development, precipitated out in the question of Jesus "consciousness" (as previously mentioned).

The genre "Jesus book" not only personalized history. At the same time it reinforced a corresponding perception within the way the figure of Jesus was understood within the philosophy of history. Thus Helmut Scheuer states in

---

174. G. Lukács, *Die Theorie des Romans. Ein geschichtsphilosophischer Versuch über die Formen der grossen Epik* (Neuwied-Berlin: Luchterhand, 1920; 2nd ed. 1974) 103.

175. Cf. R. S. Turner, "Historicism, *Kritik* and the Prussian Professoriate. 1790 to 1840," in M. Bollack et al., eds., *Philologie und Hermeneutik im 19. Jahrhundert II* (Göttingen: Vandenhoeck & Ruprecht, 1983) 474.

176. The following is based on I. Watt, *The Rise of the Novel. Studies in Defoe, Richardson and Fielding* (Harmondsworth: Penguin, 1972 [1st ed. 1957]) 9–37.

177. Cf. the English term "novel" = "new."

his studies of the literary genre of biography, "[T]he focus on the individual person is of course not only a narrative technique . . . but at the same time mediates a particular understanding of history."[178] We are thus dealing with a circular process: the heroic genius Jesus is made the theme of a Jesus book, and this manner of presentation in its turn conditions a corresponding understanding of Jesus and history.

This manner of portraying Jesus is also encouraged by a much older tradition, to which hagiography and the idea of *imitatio* belong. The emphasis on the individual that emerged at the end of the Middle Ages led, in the form of piety known as *devotio moderna*, to the understanding of Jesus as a special individual and thus to the image of Jesus as model to be imitated.[179] Within the realm of Protestantism, the christocentricity of the Reformation also placed the earthly Jesus (especially his suffering and crucifixion) at the center of interest. In the literature of edification oriented toward ethics, the picture of Jesus as a towering individual is repeatedly placed in the center of the challenge to reorient one's life to his. The slogan "following Jesus" points to the figure of Jesus as example in a way that compresses closely together the historical there-and-then and the present here-and-now. That which was said poetically in the seventeenth century—"'Follow me,' says Jesus our hero . . . 'I am the light, I shine for you with a holy and virtuous life'"[180]—in the nineteenth century is advocated by means of a historical claim. In this period a pedagogical element was added that grounded the personalizing of history in its exemplary function.[181] Finally, the readability of a popular Jesus book always lives from what Lapide has called "a basic principle of drama," according to which the hero Jesus must be sharply contrasted with his antagonists, in this case the Jews,[182] which is especially important in view of Jesus' violent death—something that calls for an explanation in any case. Through all this the difference between Jesus and Judaism came to be all the more emphasized.

178. H. Scheuer, *Biographie. Studien zur Funktion und zum Wandel einer literarischen Gattung vom 18. Jahrhundert bis zur Gegenwart* (Stuttgart: Metzler, 1979), 197. On the types of biographical study advocated by Ranke, Droysen, and Dilthey in the context of German historicism, cf. J. Oelkers, "Biographik—Überlegungen zu einer unschuldigen Gattung," in *Neue Politische Literatur* 19 (1974): 296–309.

179. So in W. Ockham. Cf. D. Georgi, " Leben-Jesu-Theologie/Leben-Jesu-Forschung" 567, who gives additional bibliography.

180. Johann Scheffler (1624–1677), Hymn 385 (*Evangelisches Gesangbuch. Ausgabe für die EKHN* [Frankfurt: Spener 1994]).

181. Scheuer, *Biographie*, 205.

182. Lapide, *Jesus in Two Perspectives*, 16.

Excursus: The Scholarly Ideal of the Solitary Original

The creative personality ideal permeated German college-prep schools and universities, especially as advocated by Humboldt, to the effect that the model to be striven for was the education of the individual. The end of the eighteenth and the beginning of the nineteenth centuries saw the advent of a new system oriented to performance that gradually replaced the dominance of the older scholarly species. At the new performance university, creative research was supposed to have the priority. The new necessity of developing a sharp profile that enables one to stand out from one's colleagues meant that originality was the presupposition for advancement in the university of the nineteenth century.

In his exalted understanding of (himself as) a scholar, Fichte demanded not only independent and creative intellectual achievement, but united this with the highest level of moral education, which was supposed to make the scholar a teacher of the human race.[183] Thus the scholar's ideal picture of his or her own professional and social class—the model of the solitary original individual—could be fused with the ideal of Jesus. There was little interest in historical lines of dependence and derivation. Even when this embeddedness was realized—the essential continued to be the new, the original, for this is what has historical significance,[184] as it also does in the life of a university scholar.

⋘⋙⋘⋙⋘⋙

c) Historicism and Authenticity

The historicism of the nineteenth century considered truth to be basically historical truth. In the theological realm the focus is on Jesus as a historical figure. The criterion of dissimilarity has as its task the determination of authentic material and the ability to distinguish between authentic, that is, original material, and later tradition. It is thus one instrument of the historical-critical method, which has as its goal "to reconstruct the 'real' past by means of critical examination of the past as it has been described."[185] "His teaching and his faith were considered the nucleus of Christianity; to the liberals he was the bringer of the absolute religion."[186] Jesus is the historical fixed star in the liberal heaven; the nearer one approaches his own truth, the more clearly his authentic figure steps forth from the fog between him and us.

---

183. According to A. Busch, *Die Geschichte des Privatdozenten. Eine soziologische Studie zur grossbetrieblichen Entwicklung der deutschen Universitäten* (Göttinger Abhandlungen zur Soziologie 5. Stuttgart: Enke, 1959) 24.

184. Cf. Weinel, *Biblische Theologie des Neuen Testaments*, 42.

185. Stöve, *Kirchengeschichte*, 13.

186. Pleitner, *Das Ende der liberalen Hermeneutik*, 7.

The Jesus books of the old "life-of-Jesus research" are historically optimistic. They consider a factually correct historical presentation of the whole life of Jesus to be possible, and proceed to carry out this claim. As the nineteenth century grew to an end, however, this early optimism was followed by a deep skepticism. In terms of the content of the historical reconstruction, dependence of the theology of the nineteenth century is all too clear. The situation with regard to sources also appears more problematic. To be sure, a consensus crystallizes with regard to Synoptic source analysis—the priority of Mark and the existence of Q—but at the same time the distance of the sources from the life of Jesus and the problem of the Gospels as *historical* sources become apparent. The resulting skepticism extends as far as to call in question the historical existence of Jesus.

Against this background, the deployment of criteria for source analysis, which has the historical reconstruction of the life of Jesus as its goal, becomes obvious. To have criteria is the proof of scientific method, that is, of reliability. It participates in the high regard inherent in the term *criticism*—"the very sum of scholarly acumen," "the aura of scrupulous precision," "strong ethical rigor and honesty."[187]

In order to confirm the historicity of the existence of Jesus and also to refute the denial of the historical figure of Jesus that emerged at the turn of the century,[188] P. W. Schmiedel formulated by means of the criterion of dissimilarity (in the form of the CDC) his "foundation pillars of a truly scientific life of Jesus."[189] They are "foundation pillars" not only because further conclusions can be based on them, but also because they themselves—in Schmiedel's view—are unshakable. They criterion on which they themselves are based embodies the ideal historical method in an excellent manner, for it places an allegedly objective and unerring guide in the hand. In view of the plethora of Jesus books with a variety of historical interpretations, it promises an objective standard—especially since it corresponds to a basic principle with which every historian complies: "Every historical scholar, it matters not in which area

---

187. Turner, *Historicism, Kritik, and the Prussian Professoriate*, 472–473.

188. Schmiedel makes this connection clear in a later publication (*Die Person Jesu*, 260). Nonetheless, Schmiedel considers his own religious faith to be independent of whether Jesus in fact ever lived—which he never doubted on historical grounds (Ibid., 281). Schmiedel formulated his foundation pillars for the first time in 1901; those who denied Jesus' historical existence wrote after him: A. Kalthoff (1902), P. Jensen (1906), K. J. Kautsky (1908), somewhat later also P. Drews (1909/II), on them cf. H. Pleitner, *Das Ende der liberalen Hermeneutik*, 124–28, 140–43.

189. Schmiedel, *Das vierte Evangelium*, 16. This German formulation from the year 1906 was preceded by an English article for the "Biblical Encyclopaedia" of 1901.

he works, observes the basic rule that in a report written to honor a hero, that which goes against such adoration is to be considered true, since it cannot have been invented."[190]

So what are Schmiedel's nine foundation pillars? (1) Jesus' relatives considered him to be deranged (Mark 3:21, 31–35). (2) Jesus had only a limited knowledge of the end of the world (Mark 13:22). (3) Jesus rejects the predicate "good" for himself, because only God is good (Mark 10:18). (4) Jesus accepts blasphemies against himself as the Son of Man (Matt 12:32). (5) Jesus cried out on the cross in despair, "My God, my God, why have you forsaken me?" (Mark 15:34). (6) Jesus refused to give signs to this "evil generation" in the sense of miraculous proofs (Mark 8:12). (7) In Nazareth Jesus could do no miracles because of the unbelief of his home town. (Mark 6:5). (8) Jesus answered John the Baptist's question as to whether he was the expected "Coming One" by simply referring to his advent as a preacher. That the blind see, the lame walk, and such, was meant in a metaphorical sense, not an appeal to miracle (Matt 11:5–6). (9) Jesus multiplied "bread" but meant thereby his teaching, which multiplied in a miraculous way. Hence he warns against the "leaven" (= the teaching) of the Pharisees and Sadducees (Matt 16:5–12). Several of these nine "foundational pillars" are still regarded as difficult to explain as secondary characteristics introduced into the tradition. The two last foundational pillars, however, rest on an allegorizing interpretation of Jesus' answer to the Baptist and a symbolic understanding of the feeding miracle, and they have rarely been adopted by other exegetes.

A. Neumann, a student of Schmiedel, regards the "foundational pillars" as "the salvation of the Synoptic Gospels, giving them a definite value as sources."[191] The criterion of dissimilarity here becomes an instrument that saves the historical credibility of the Gospels that had been threatened by "critical" work on the New Testament. That is all the more important, since for many theologians the *historical* credibility of the Scripture as such was at stake.

In Goguel's 1930 formulation of the CDC,[192] as in the case of Schmiedel himself, it was not so much a matter of the Gospels as a whole as the discovery of authentic pieces of tradition ("centers of crystallization"),[193] remnants that attain their value through the fascination with everything that is historically authentic. The heritage of historicism here lives in symbiosis with Protestantism's high regard for Scripture.

---

190. Schmiedel, *Das vierte Evangelium*, 16–17.

191. Neumann, *Jesus*, 10.

192. M. Goguel, "The Problem of Jesus," *HTR* 23 (1930): 112–13.

193. Ibid.

1.4 Backgrounds for the Criterion
of Dissimilarity's Tendencies against Church and Judaism

a) The Criterion of Dissimilarity vis-à-vis Christianity (CDC)

The CDC throws into sharp relief those features in the figure of Jesus that do not harmonize with the faith and theology of the first Christians. The decisive theological motive for the CDC is thus the critical analysis of early church history and dogma.

The struggles for emancipation from theological traditions taught as church dogma are part of the beginnings of historical-critical reading of the New Testament in the Enlightenment, in which human reason alone was accepted as the standard. To be sure, the element of contradiction when appealing to that which is old or original emerges already in early humanism. In Petrarch "*historia* [is understood as] the source of alternative conduct."[194] The affinity for the "original", that is, the "unspoiled" (see II.1.1 above) taken over from humanism placed its stamp on Protestant identity. In the debate with Rome, the Reformers had affirmed an alternative kind of continuity in order to legitimate themselves. In this view, the earliest church was contrasted with the following developments in church history, which is understood as a history of decline. On the reforming side (in the left wing, as also later by the Puritans[195]) movements emerged again and again that wanted to identify the church structures that were found in the New Testament and structure their churches only on this model.

These efforts reflect the primary reductionistic tendency to separate oneself as far as possible from later traditions. Locke called for an inner-theological reduction of christological dogmas, advocating the opinion that "only the teaching of Jesus and the apostles (in Acts!) that Jesus is the Messiah are necessary for salvation."[196] The concentration on the person of Jesus is typical. Despite all the critical analysis of church and theology by Enlightenment scholars, Jesus himself was still regarded positively. While high Christology was rejected, the person of Jesus was highly esteemed.[197]

In the course of interpretation that sought eternal and original truths, the later New Testament epistolary literature was devalued, since the letters, being occasional writings, were temporally conditioned.[198] Their interest in church

---

194. E. Kessler, *Petrarca und die Geschichte. Geschichtsschreibung, Rhetorik, Philosophie im Übergang vom Mittelalter zur Neuzeit* (Humanistische Bibliothek I/25; Munich: Fink, 1978) 38.

195. Reventlow, *Authority of the Bible*, 91–184.

196. Ibid., 270.

197. Cf. Orr, *English Deism*, 140 and passim.

198. Reventlow, *Authority of the Bible*, 270. Thereby of course a remarkable "beginnings of historical thinking" is to be noted (Ibid., 278).

order was a negative element from the point of view of liberal Protestantism, so that later the confessionally derogatory designation "early catholic" began to be applied to the post-Pauline letters.[199]

Thus both the critique of dogma, which in its free and liberal spirit preferred to base itself on reason, and the Protestant-confessional rejection of ecclesiastical traditions formed theological motives for the CDC.

b) The Criterion of Dissimilarity vis-à-vis Judaism (CDJ)

The CDJ throws into sharp relief those features in the figure of Jesus that do not harmonize with the faith and theology of the Jewish contemporaries of Jesus. The theological motive for this is anti-Judaism, which is combined with confessional and salvation-history interests.

The term "anti-Judaism" is here understood to refer to the theological rejection of the Jewish religion, expressed especially in a strongly negative portrayal of Jewish faith and life. Such a portrayal fulfills the function of a negative foil for the advent of Jesus and/or Christianity.

i) On the Term "Anti-Judaism"*

Anti-Judaism belongs within the comprehensive phenomenon of anti-Semitism.[200] In the last third of the nineteenth century, it was directed to adherents of the Jewish faith but then was transformed into a hostility against Jews based on racial biology, and thus was also directed against Jews who had been baptized. Anti-Judaism belongs to anti-Semitism but is not completely

---

199. On "early catholicism" cf. C. H. Bartsch, *'Frühkatholizismus' als Kategorie historisch-kritischer Theologie. Eine methodologische und theologiegeschichtliche Untersuchung* (SKI 3; Berlin: Selbstverlag Institut Kirche und Judentum, 1980). The term "catholic letters" was already known in the ancient church, where the phrase, of course, simply emphasized that the letters were addressed to the church as a whole. Cf. S. Neill's description of the "continental Protestant," for whom (early-) catholicism and gospel constitute irreconcilable opposites. See S. Neill and T. Wright, *The Interpretation of the New Testament, 1861–1986* (2nd ed.; Oxford: Oxford University Press, 1988) 200–1.

*Translator's note, in consultation with Dagmar Winter: In German, one can distinguish between "antijüdisch," which could be translated "anti-Jewish," and "antijudaistisch," which could be translated "anti-Judaist" or "anti-Judaistic." The former has a more contemporary ring to it, tending toward anti-Semitic. The latter term is the one generally used by Theissen and Winter when referring more to a theological objection against Judaism in the sense of Jewish theology. English does not generally make this distinction, so I have usually translated the adjective as "anti-Jewish" and the noun as "anti-Judaism," trusting that the authors' explanation and this note will make the meaning clear.

200. A good survey of anti-Semitism and anti-Judaism is found in the article "Antijudaismus" (several authors), *TRE* 3:113–168, which gives extensive additional literature. Cf. also R. Rürup, *Emanzipation und Antisemitismus. Studien zur 'Judenfrage' der bürgerlichen Gesellschaft* (KSGW 15; Göttingen: Vandenhoeck & Ruprecht, 1975), esp. 96–97.

identical with it. The way in which these two terms should be distinguished is disputed. The differentiation proposed here is not intended to separate anti-Judaism as "only" a theological matter from the terrible results of anti-Semitism in order to exculpate theology and church. It is rather the case "that anti-Semitism goes back to the centuries of anti-Jewish teaching and preaching of the Christian Church, as is widely acknowledged," despite the many questions that remain about pre-Christian anti-Semitism in antiquity.[201] At the same time, the general anti-Semitism in society (which reflects the rich tradition of churchly hostility to Jews) plays a greater or smaller role for theological anti-Judaism, even if it is only by the fact that corresponding negative images of Jews enjoy a high degree of plausibility and acceptance in society.[202]

The term anti-Judaism is thus intended to refer here to the *theological* form of anti-Semitism, and accordingly does not refer to the accusations of usury and poisoning of wells and springs, but rather to the theologically negative images of the Jewish religion (especially ancient Judaism) as legalism or as essentially a matter of rituals. This conceptual and terminological precision is also necessary in order to come to terms with the circumstance that, under the fascist reign of violence in Germany, individual anti-Judaistic theologians (and/or those who perpetuated traditional anti-Judaism) decisively rejected racial anti-Semitism.

Anti-Judaism can be traced back to the New Testament itself, found most strongly in the Gospel of John (e.g., John 8:44).[203] In the Synoptic Gospels one can see that as temporal distance increases from the life of Jesus, there is, on the one hand, an increasing tendency toward polarization, with Jesus on the one side and his (in turn increasingly undifferentiated) Jewish opponents on the other side. But also the letters, in which Christians are warned against "Judaizing" teachers, reflect the problems of a newly founded group marking off its boundaries. In search of its own "Christian" identity, the differences between the new group and the mother religion are firmed up. The resurrected Lord who stands at the center of the new faith becomes the focal point for statements about the new, the different, which he has brought into being. Discontinuity is emphasized with regard to the lines that connect the new faith to Judaism (Phil 3:2ff.).

The structure of this heritage, which in the early church and in the Middle Ages led to inhuman statements about Jews and perpetrated violence against

---

201. N. R. M. de Lange and C. Thoma, "Antisemitismus I. Begriff/Vorchristlicher Antisemitismus," in *TRE* 3 (1978) I:114.

202. Even Paul took over some ancient anti-Semitic expressions, although he always remained united to the Jewish people, whose members he calls his brothers and sisters. The question of the relation of Paul to Judaism and his theology of Israel is extraordinarily disputed, despite the presence of primary sources.

203. This is still not unambiguous, for alongside John 8:44 stands John 4:22.

them, experienced a renewed life at the Reformation. The central meaning of the figure of the Christ[204] and the Scripture led to passionate debates on the subject of the interpretation of the Old Testament. On the Reformation side, the christological interpretation of the Old Testament was advocated in a manner that left no room for other interpretations and referred the promises made to Israel only to the people of Christ. It was especially the combination of anti-Jewish tendencies in the Gospels, the Pauline theology of law and grace, and the Reformation exegesis of Scripture determined by the doctrine of *sola gratia* that resulted in presenting the Jews as theological archenemies: their supposed self-glorification collided head-on with the Reformation gospel.[205] In the Protestant consciousness there was also an analogous parallel between the Jews and the Roman Catholic Church, to the extent that they both contradicted the Reformation doctrine of grace.[206]

Although Luther in his 1538 letter "Against the Sabbatarians" sees the validity of the Mosaic Law as having been abrogated for 1500 years,[207] the Old Testament was for the most part not targeted by the Reformation's anti-Jewish criticism. In contrast, an interpretation with strongly anti-Jewish tendencies is found in Erasmus, which was also advocated by a few Baptists and Spiritualists[208] and continued in the Enlightenment.[209] The place of the Old Testament as an important constituent element of the European heritage was

---

204. Thus it was, of course, clear for Luther that for the Jews the teaching of Christ "was different, [than that] which they had heard for a thousand years" (*WA* 7, 313). At the beginning he advocated an amazingly positive attitude to Judaism. Cf. his writing "That Jesus Christ Was A Native Jew" (1523; *WA* 11:314–36).

205. This line of interpretation provides the theological basis for the fact that, and the reason that, the Jews caused the crucifixion of Jesus. This contradicts the real Reformation formulation (which of course also foresaw no salvation for the Jews apart from Christ) according to which all human beings are involved in the crucifixion of Jesus.

206. W. Mostert ("Luther" *TRE* 21 [1991]: III 580) writes, "With Pope, Turks, and spiritual fanatics they [sc. the Jews] were to him [sc. Luther] advocates of the religion of Law and thus the enemies of the Gospel." By way of qualification it needs to be said that the pejorative description of Judaism as a religion of law first originated in the nineteenth century (see below). In the question of the law in connection with Jews the decisive thing for Luther has to do with the Mosaic Law in its significance for the theological status of his Jewish contemporaries, rather than providing a definition of the essence of Judaism.

207. *WA* 50:312–37; cf. 324 and passim. Cf. also "An Instruction on How the Christians Should Resign Themselves to Moses" (1525, *WA* 16:363–93; especially 372ff).

208. Cf. Reventlow, *Authority of the Bible*, 56–72.

209. John Spencer (1630–1693), who derives the Old Testament rites from Egyptian customs, in the argument about theological meaningfulness interpreted the Jewish ceremonial law as an expression of divine accommodation. The relativizing of the Old Testament involved in this interpretation prepared the way for its rejection in a later period. Cf. Reventlow, *Authority of the Bible*, 291–92; on Erasmus, Ibid., 39–48.

denied by the radical wing of the Enlightenment.[210] This is particularly significant when one considers the larger framework for this rejection. Reventlow clearly notes two essential conceptual presuppositions for the historical-critical exegesis of the nineteenth century, both of which go back to humanism and deism: "the humanist pattern in which religion is thought to have declined from a pure and natural original form to a final form distorted by ritualism," as well as "Puritan hostility to ceremonial" and the "high value attached to the prophetic element, interpreted in anti-cultic terms."[211]

Above all, Erasmus' talk of the *superstitio* of the Jews became very important in the Enlightenment, since a sharp distinction was made between Jewish superstition and the Christian religion of reason. With few exceptions (e.g., John Toland[212]), deism was permeated by such anti-Jewish views. For Thomas Morgan (1680–1743), it was clear that Judaism and Christianity were absolutely incapable of being combined. Christianity stands for the religion of reason, which had already been corrupted by the New Testament authors, since their portrayal of the gospel was stamped by their superstitious, Judaizing prejudices and errors.[213] Thus that which here sounds like the CDC (different from the interests of Christian tradents) and the CDJ (different from Jewish ideas) ultimately corresponds only to a rationalistic CDJ (since truly Christian = reasonable, but Jewish = superstitious).

In Reimarus there is found the remarkable mixture of rationalistic anti-Jewish and confessional polemic, when he compares the Jewish religion with the "papal religion:" "They have . . . generally the same kind of defects and abuses, so far as they deviate from the religion of reason."[214]

For reconstructing the picture of Jesus in his own historical world, the formation of the separation between Israel—Judaism—church in the history of scholarship is important. This distinction combines anti-Jewish with salvation-history motifs, for which secular philosophy of history provides essential presuppositions.

---

210. H. Liebeschütz, *Das Judentum im deutschen Geschichtsbild von Hegel bis Max Weber* (Tübingen: Mohr, 1967) 1.

211. Reventlow, *Authority of the Bible*, 412; Orr, *English Deism*, 31. These ideas form especially the presupposition for the anti-Jewish "theory of prophetic connection," on which see above 1.2.c.

212. Cf. Liebeschütz, *Das Judentum im deutschen Geschichtsbild*, 3–5; as well as Reventlow, *Authority of the Bible*, 303–5.

213. T. Morgan, *The Moral Philosopher*, 1:439–441. A parallel to this idea of the Judaizing falsification of the New Testament is provided by William Whiston (1667–1752) for the Old Testament. In his "Essay Towards Restoring the True Text of the Old Testament" (1722) he advocates "the deistic contention that the Old Testament had been corrupted by the Jews" (Orr, *English Deism*, 129).

214. Reimarus, "Apologie," 38 (§10).

ii) The Idea of Development in the Philosophy of History

Despite the influence of historicism, Hegel's ideas of historical development were not destined to have a great effect. Georg Friedrich Hegel (1730–1831) also entered into direct debate with Judaism and its effect on Christianity. The Enlightenment's nostalgic longing for antiquity influenced his historical understanding, which placed Christianity in proximity to Hellenism and strongly distinguished Judaism from both. The deistic separation between Jewish superstition and reasonable Christianity is also found in Hegel, "for whom Judaism . . . represented the powers of retardation and inhibition."[215]

The basic idea of the strict separation of Judaism and Christianity stands in direct connection with Hegel's metaphysical philosophy of history and his "characteristic understanding of historical causation. In his view, the truly new and creative that emerges at a given point in history does not proceed from the achievement of the previous epoch,"[216] but from its antithesis.[217]

Hegel is important for our question primarily in regard to his effect on theologians and their understanding of history. Hegel himself does not apply his famous triadic formula (thesis–antithesis–synthesis) directly to the line of development of Judaism and Christianity, but his dialectic does exclude ancient Judaism from the further course of world history.[218]

Wilhelm Vatke (1806–1882), who called himself a Hegelian, set forth a three-level schema of the development of human consciousness, in which ancient Judaism occupies the second level, that of the antithesis,[219] since Vatke

---

215. Liebeschütz, *Das Judentum im deutschen Geschichtsbild*, 25.

216. Ibid., 39.

217. Hegel's contemporary F. D. E. Schleiermacher (1768–1834) likewise argues against the idea of a positive developmental line: there is no way that Judaism can be the forerunner of Christianity, for "every religion has in itself its own eternal necessity, and its beginning is original." Schleiermacher thereby directly rejects a historical perspective—"I hate that kind of historical reference" (*On Religion: Speeches to Its Cultured Despisers* [trans. John Oman; New York: Harper & Brothers, 1958] 238). Schleiermacher's negative image of ancient Judaism definitely supported the systematically grounded rejection of any relationship between Judaism and Christianity. This understanding intends to separate the historical from the theological and emphasizes its (theological) uniqueness. Much later this approach becomes typical of the dialectic theology of the twentieth century, where it also has an affect on theologians who do work historically, i.e., who transfer these theological ideas to the historical field. An example would be E. Schweizer in his portrayal of the historical Jesus.

218. K. Hohneisel, *Das antike Judentum in christlicher Sicht. Ein Beitrag zur neueren Forschungsgeschichte* (Studies in Oriental Religions 2; Wiesbaden: Harrassowitz, 1978) 9. For the history of the CDJ, less relevant is F. C. Baur's dialectical outline of the history of early Christianity influenced by Hegel (Petrine party–Pauline party–Johannine synthesis).

219. On this cf. Liebeschütz, *Das Judentum im deutschen Geschichtsbild*, 80–81.

here regards nature and spirit as opposed to each other. Christianity stands at the third level, which, as the final stage in the development of human self-consciousness, represents the perfect religion. Vatke is especially significant in his understanding of prophetism as the high point of the history of Israelite religion.

Against this background of the Hegelian philosophy of history, the work of Wette, Vatke, and Wellhausen led to the tripartite historical image of Israel–Judaism–Christianity, in which Judaism represented the low point in this series.[220] In Wellhausen, who built on the work of Vatke, one can observe a strongly progressive scheme of development that results in differentiating Judaism (degeneration) from Christianity (which attached itself not to Judaism but to the highest in the religion of Israel).

In the work of Hermann Gunkel (1862–1932)—despite his method based on the history of traditions, which can value new developments that emerge from their predecessors much easier than is the case with Wellhausen's source analysis—the image of the downhill slide of Judaism works very strongly to enhance that of the ascent of Christianity.[221]

Wellhausen's ideas of development are also continued by Wilhelm Bousset (1865–1920), especially in connection with Carlyle's philosophy of history (cf. II.1.3.b.i). His picture of history is determined by a series of self-perpetuating phases, in the process of which the declining forms and institutions of a society lead to a situation of revolutionary crisis. Into this situation a new leader is given, who reconstitutes order, until this too becomes rigid and declines.[222] Thus for Bousset's image of Judaism, the characterization of Jesus' time as a crisis situation was important, for it is crisis that makes the further development of history both possible and necessary. This is what Bousset sees happening in Jesus, the great leadership personality. In this variation of the prevailing philosophy of history, the difference between Jesus and Judaism is likewise a compelling implication.

The other conspicuous feature that must be noted here is that it is not an organic view of historical development that is at work, but a dialectic understanding of how history unfolds, which, for example, W. Bousset combines with the perspective of the study of the history of religions. Otherwise it would be easily conceivable to understand Jesus as the greatest flowering of Judaism.

---

220. On this cf. R. Smend, *Wilhelm Martin Leberecht de Wettes Arbeit am Alten und am Neuen Testament* (Basel: Helbing & Lichtenhahn, 1958) 101–5.

221. Cf. Hoheisel, *Das antike Judentum*, 21–24, with numerous additional references. Hoheisel also goes into Gunkel's hard-to-follow about-face, in which he gives up his previously affirmed connection of the New Testament with the Jewish milieu.

222. On this cf. the instructive diagram sketch by K. Berger, *Exegese und Philosophie* (SBS 123/124; Stuttgart: Kath. Bibelwerk, 1986) 92.

This would not only *mean* a positive attitude toward Judaism, but would also presuppose such an attitude. However, it was the widespread anti-Jewish spirit that stood in the way of precisely this kind of positive attitude toward Judaism.

Vatke's evaluation of prophetism as the high point of Israelite religion and Wellhausen's contrasting of Judaism and Christianity are the twin foundations for the "prophet-connection-theory," according to which Jesus bypassed Judaism in order to connect directly with the old prophetic tradition. It is the meaning and goal of this idea to facilitate Christianity's appropriation of the theological heritage of "Israel." Thus the "prophet-connection-theory" belongs to the broad context of the supersessionist theory, according to which it is Christianity, not Judaism, that is the theological heir of "Israel," that is, as the new "Israel" Christianity is the heir of the promises made to Old Testament Israel. Jesus attached himself to the—romantically understood—early period of Israel. In the course of this interpretation, Judaism in the time of Jesus came to be called "late Judaism." The term implies the soon end of Judaism, for which it is itself to blame, for late Judaism lacked the prophetic spirit of ancient Israel. But also the term "early Judaism" can imply that the continuity between Israel and Judaism is called in question. In any case, behind these descriptions there is a presupposed "Old Testament, yes; Judaism, no."[223]

By separating Israel and Judaism, it became possible to derive Jesus theologically from Israel, and not only to distinguish him from Judaism but to present him as underived from it.[224] This becomes clear in Wellhausen, for example: "The gospel develops hidden (!) impulses of the Old Testament, but protests against the prevailing orientation of Judaism. Jesus understands monotheism differently than his contemporary Jews."[225] This historical understanding of the gospel and, even more so, the message of Jesus historically understood emphasize their difference from Judaism.

The focus on the theme of the Law—with the corresponding confessionalist overtones—for the comparison between Judaism and Christianity did not emerge until the last third of the nineteenth century.[226] A landmark study that

---

223. H.-J. Kraus ("Das Alte Testament in der 'Bekennenden Kirche'," *KuI* 1 [1986]) shows that this stance is characteristic for great parts of the confessing church.

224. In contrast, on the basis of his theology Schleiermacher is concerned for the complete independence of Christianity from a "special inspiration or revelation from God to the Jewish people" (F. D. E. Schleiermacher, "Dr. Schleiermacher über seine Glaubenslehre an Dr. Lücke. Zweites Sendschreiben," in *Theologisch-dogmatische Abhandlungen und Gelegenheitsschriften*, H.-F. Traulsen, ed., [Krit. GA; ed. H.J. Birkner et al.; 1. Abt., Bd. 10; Berlin: de Gruyter, 1990] 353).

225. J. Wellhausen, "Abriss der Geschichte Israels und Juda's," in *Skizzen und Vorarbeiten* (Berlin: Reimer, 1884) 1:98.

226. Cf. Moore, "Christian Writers on Judaism," 242–43, 252–53.

indicated the direction of the future understanding of Judaism was the *System der altsynagogalen palästinischen Theologie* (1880) by Ferdinand Weber (1836–1879). In this book Weber characterizes the essence of Jewish religion with the theological catchword "legalism" and combines it with the idea of the infinitely distant, transcendent God in Judaism.[227] Among Weber's publications is also found a series of essays with the title "The System of Jewish Pharisaism and Roman Catholicism."[228] Here two things become clear: Weber's confessionalist motivation as well as his attempt to analyze Judaism in terms of Christian theological patterns of thought. The negative term "legalism" is extracted from Christian dogmatics and applied to Judaism. The concept expresses a typical Christian problem and a typical Christian question about the way of salvation—Judaism poses neither question in this manner.

This characterization of Judaism becomes influential in the same time as the emergence of the liberal theology that sought the essence of Christianity—with its specific difference from Judaism—in Jesus' own teaching and religious experience. Bousset's small Jesus book already illustrates this in its title, *Jesus' Message in Contrast to Judaism*. Within this framework, mutually defining opposite poles are represented by the relation of Judaism with its legal piety and distant monotheistic God, on the one hand, and the Abba-piety of Jesus on the other. The *difference* between Jesus (who represents Christianity within this framework of understanding) and Judaism becomes greater and greater, and the foundation for a CDJ as an element of scholarly preunderstanding is thereby provided: since Jesus is seen as the first "representative" of Christianity or the founder of Christianity as a whole, he can be the primary point of comparison with Judaism (seen as a whole, even as a monolith).

In accord with the historical interest of theology in this period, the genre of books called "New Testament Times" or "Background of the New Testament" emerged in the academic field of New Testament studies. The task of such books was to portray the historical background for the ministry of Jesus and the origins of Christianity. Although a trustworthy description of Judaism was intended, the main question was really about the Christianity of this time, not the understanding of Judaism on the basis of its own presuppositions. This is also seen from the fact that the historical segment dealt with had little mean-

---

227. Concerned with saving Weber's honor, Moore states that on this point Weber was favorably received: in Weber the concept of the monotheistic distant God is a reaction to the Christian doctrine of the Trinity. Consequently, it is anachronistic to have Jesus encounter this concept. Less happily, Weber is partially dependent on Andreas Eisenmenger's terribly anti-Semitic work *Entdecktes Judenthum* [Judaism Exposed] of 1700 (Moore, "Christian Writers on Judaism," 230–33.

228. Published in 1890 in the *Allgemeinen evangelisch-lutherischen Kirchenzeitung*; cf. Moore, "Christian Writers on Judaism," 228.

ing from within Judaism itself but was oriented to Christian history. Such a procedure is not reprehensible in itself, but for an understanding of Judaism and the Jewish world of Jesus it promises more than it can deliver, and so leads to false assessments of Judaism. Precisely in reference to the question of the Law, one may here name an important chapter from Schürer's compendium, §28, "Life under the Law,"[229] which further popularized the Weberian perspective on Judaism.

After World War I the problematic way in which a Christian orientation predetermined the way in which Judaism was presented reached a high point with the publication of (Strack-) Billerbeck's *Kommentar zum Neuen Testament aus Talmud und Midrasch* (1922–1928). The direct connection to the text of the New Testament sets forth, within the framework of discussion current at that time, that, for example, differences can be pointed out between the sayings of Jewish rabbis and those of Jesus. Billerbeck "develops the Pharisaic doctrine of justification as a purely negative counterpart to the splendid understanding of righteousness that Jesus is supposed to have brought to the world and is available in the Gospels."[230]

So also in Bousset it already becomes clear how strongly a confessional viewpoint permeates the charge that Judaism is "legalistic." He observes that "much of that which . . . has been presented as characteristic of legalistic religion can also be said of *certain branches of the Christian church*, just as the Greek Orthodox and the Roman Catholic church in turn manifest features of that which is essentially legalistic, ceremonial, and particularistic, from which even Protestant churches are not entirely free!"[231]

Bousset's theological opponent A. Kalthof observes,

> Previous scholarship, often enough without any awareness of doing so, is guided by a particular theological interest, namely opposition to the theology of the Roman Catholic Church. A source is sought for that presents the historical personality Jesus, in order to prove on the basis of this source that only the Protestant understanding of Christianity is correct, and that therefore the Catholic understanding represents a distortion and degeneration of Christianity. Authentic sayings of Jesus were sought, and are still sought, or their original and

---

229. Emil Schürer, *The History of the Jewish People in the Age of Jesus Christ (175 B. C.–A. D. 135)*. (New English Version rev. and ed. by G. Vermes, F. Millar, and M. Black; vol. 2; Edinburgh: T & T Clark, 1979). This section from vol. 2 is in any case one of only two sections dedicated to the religion of Judaism. Also the other, §29, "The Messianic Hope," clearly reveals its Christian interest. Sections §28 and §29 are (among others) thoroughly reworked in the revised English edition of 1979.

230. Hoheisel, *Das antike Judentum*, 43.

231. Bousset, *Das Wesen der Religion*, 105.

authentic meaning that Jesus himself intended, with the intention of providing an argument for one's own church and theology and against the church and theology of others.[232]

The combination of anti-Judaism and confessionalism has thus essentially contributed to establishing the view that Jesus and Judaism were fundamentally different.

2. THE HISTORY OF THE CRITERION OF DISSIMILARITY IN ITS SYSTEMATIC RELATIONSHIP TO THE UNDERSTANDING OF JESUS

2.1 The Liberal and History-of-Religions Quest for the Historical Jesus

a) Criteria

i) The Methodological Foundations for the Development of the Quest of the Historical Jesus from D. F. Strauss to W. Wrede

The nineteenth century's most decisive turning point in Jesus research was the publication of the *Life of Jesus* by D. F. Strauss. Since Strauss's mythical interpretation of the Gospels placed their value as historical sources fundamentally in question, Jesus research was presented with entirely new challenges. The use of the Gospels' portrayals of Jesus for historical reconstruction of the life of Jesus could no longer be assumed but now needed arguments and justification. Strauss himself did not develop his critical approach further by an analytical editing of the Gospel materials, which would have permitted an evaluation of their historical value for Jesus research. However, methods oriented to this goal were developed step-by-step in the nineteenth century: first came tendency criticism (*Tendenzkritik*) and source analysis (*Literarkritik*), and then later tradition criticism (*Traditionskritik*) and history-of-religions study (*Religionsgeschichte*).

The new foundation for Jesus research was laid by Strauss's teacher Ferdinand Christian Baur (1792–1860) by his "tendency criticism," in which he outlined the history of early Christianity as represented by the conflicts and tendencies reflected in the traditions contained in the Gospels and other New Testament writings. Baur's work essentially brought New Testament scholarship further along the path of the historical-critical method, primarily by tak-

---

232. Kalthoff, *Das Christusproblem. Grundlinien zu einer Sozialtheologie* (Leipzig: Diederichs, 1902) 12–13.

ing the impulses and ideas of historicism into theology.[233] Baur was determined "not to be guided by any other interest than the one interest in the objective historical truth, which I do not know how to separate from the true interest of the substance of Christianity itself."[234] This consistently historical point of departure[235] allowed Baur to attain two important insights with regard to our question. In the first place, he decisively placed Jesus within the historical matrix. Baur was convinced that his conviction that historical connections were fundamentally open to the cognitive approach of historical science also applied to the "wonder of wonders" of the primal beginnings of Christianity.[236] It is possible "to understand Christianity already in its earliest phase as a historically given phenomenon, and thus to understand it historically as such."[237] In the second place, he recognized that every source is historically conditioned, and he distinguished its portrayal of the event as different from "how it really was" (*wie es eigentlich gewesen ist*). From this latter insight he developed "tendency criticism," by means of which the tendency of a source or tradition itself, and not only its portrayal of the event, could be evaluated historically. In this regard one of Baur's principles shows how his drive for gaining insight into the historical course of events leads beyond an initial understanding of the falsification of history to its verification: "A tradition that for centuries had by its misleading appearance been accepted as historical truth is only then completely disproved . . . when it is not simply the case that the witnesses on which one is accustomed to rely lose their claim to historical credibility, but also turn out to be the occasion and reasons on the basis of which this misleading understanding of the tradition arose in the first place."[238] With

---

233. B. G. Niebuhr and L. v. Ranke are especially to be named here. On this topic, as well as with regard to Hegel's influence on Baur (which we cannot discuss further here), cf. K. Scholder, " Ferdinand Christian Baur als Historiker," *EvT* 21 (1961): 435–58.

234. F. C. Baur, *Die sogenannten Pastoralbriefe des Apostels Paulus aufs neue kritisch untersucht* (Stuttgart: Cotta, 1835) viii.

235. This approach opened Baur to the charge (by Bultmann among others, cf. Bultmann, *Theology of the New Testament*, 2:244) of making history as such the authority in place of the kerygma, and of contributing to the decline of research into historicism by abandoning a transcendent level of history. Nonetheless, the fruitfulness of Baur's approach remains uncontested.

236. F. C. Baur, "Das Christenthum und die christliche Kirche der drei ersten Jahrhunderte (1853)," in *Ausgewählte Werke in Einzelausgaben* (ed. K. Scholder; Stuttgart: Fromman, 1966) 3:1.

237. Ibid. VIII (Preface to the second edition).

238. F. C. Baur, "Die Christuspartei in der korinthischen Gemeinde, der Gegensatz des petrinischen und paulinischen Christentums, der Apostel Petrus in Rom," in *Tübinger Zeitschrift für Theologie* (1831, 4. Heft) 61–206; the quotation is from p. 162 in K. Scholder, "Ferdinand Christian Baur als Historiker," 445.

such reflections Baur laid the foundation for the method that explored and evaluated the history of traditions (*Traditionsgeschichte*) that would not be fully developed until the end of the nineteenth century.

In the following period New Testament study was occupied primarily with the Synoptic Problem, the issue of the sources of the Synoptic Gospels. In 1863 Heinrich Julius Holtzmann[239] gave decisive force to the theory of the priority of Mark and the two-source theory, and the work of these liberal theologians became the basis for the image of Jesus promulgated in the heyday of liberal Jesus books that followed.[240] In this period the oldest sources were often regarded as historically reliable documents. It was hoped that the methodological problems of life-of-Jesus research had been solved by means of source criticism.

However, at the end of the nineteenth century numerous voices were raised calling for a new orientation of New Testament scholarship. With regard to the doctrinal-concept method of Holtzmann,[241] William Wrede (1859–1906) formulated the issue as follows: "What are we really looking for? What we finally want to know is what the earliest Christians *believed, thought, taught, hoped, claimed, and struggled for*, not *what particular writings contain* about faith, doctrine, hope, etc."[242] In order to study this living religion of early Christianity, new methods were developed that went beyond source analysis.

Hermann Gunkel (1862–1932) carried out the assignment of the *history-of-tradition* method. The task of this method is "to investigate the pre-history of the material, which may be very complicated and extended over a considerable period of time, in order to explain the present form of the tradition."[243] The accent is here placed on the correlation of the genres and (oral) traditions with a "*Sitz im Leben*" (setting in life, a particular social and/or religious context). The same approach was followed by Albert Eichhorn (1856–1926), in which

---

239. H. J. Holtzmann, *Die synoptischen Evangelien*.

240. In view of Holtzmann's achievement, S. Neill and T. Wright make a rather harsh judgment: "For another forty years men will go on writing liberal lives of Jesus, each more subjective, more 'situation conditioned', than the last. The time for the beginning of fully scientific work on the life of Jesus had not yet come." (*The Interpretation of the New Testament 1861–1986* [2nd ed., Oxford: Oxford University Press, 1988] 120).

241. Cf. H. Pleitner, *Das Ende der liberalen Hermeneutik*, 20–21, 46–48.

242. W. Wrede, "Über Aufgabe und Methode der sogenannten Neutestamentlichen Theologie (1897)," in G. Strecker, ed. *Das Problem der Theologie des Neuen Testaments* (WF 367; Darmstadt: Wiss. Buchges., 1975) 109.

243. H. Gunkel: *Schöpfung und Chaos in Urzeit und Endzeit. Eine religionsgeschichtliche Untersuchung über Gen 1 und ApJoh 12* (Göttingen: Vandenhoeck & Ruprecht, 1895) 208.

he clearly distinguished "history" and "tradition." More sharply than Gunkel, he carried on a polemic against the "foolishness of historical criticism,"[244] that is, of source analysis: "There are really people who believe that they must identify the historical event itself with the oldest tradition available to us."[245] That perception of Synoptic texts as traditions cannot be understood as straightforward historical narratives but must be understood as having been shaped by the influence of the cultic worship within the life of the church is for Eichhorn the expression of what he called the history-of-religions method.[246] In this form it was clearly going in the direction of the CDC, which Schmiedel was to formulate only a little later.

It is inherent in the consistent application of this tradition-critical or history-of-religions method that the question of the historical backgrounds of the tradition process would be extended to the question of the historical origin of the content of the tradition itself.[247] This is the angle of vision from which the "history of religions school" approaches the issue.[248] One could consider Eichhorn the foster father of this movement, though journalistically he was less influential than some of its other members, the primary figures of which were Gunkel, Wrede, Bousset, and other Göttingen scholars.[249] They were concerned to understand early Christianity and the New Testament as integral elements of their historical context.[250] This historical context included the Hellenistic and Oriental world, on the one hand, and Judaism,

244. Also P. W. Schmiedel "Gospels," *EncBib* (1901) 2:1872, laments the unscholarly method that among other things, leads to accepting everything as (historically) true that can be traced back to a source.

245. A. Eichhorn, *Das Abendmahl im Neuen Testament* (Leipzig: Mohr, 1898) 15.

246. Ibid., 7.

247. On the lack of terminological clarity ("history of religions"—"tradition history") and its causes, cf. H. Paulsen, "Traditionsgeschichtliche Methode und religionsgeschichtliche Schule," *ZTK* 75 (1978), esp. 40–45.

248. In the following, only aspects of the history-of-religions school can be mentioned that are relevant for our question. For a concise discussion, cf. M. Rade, "Religionsgeschichte und Religionsgeschichtliche Schule," in *RGG* 1913 1st ed., 4:2183–2200; O. Merk, "Bibelwissenschaft II," in *TRE* 6 (1980): 375–409; in regard to Bousset see especially A. F. Verheule, *Wilhelm Bousset, Leben und Werk. Ein theologiegeschichtlicher Versuch* (Amsterdam: Ton Balland, 1973) 271–365.

249. The label "history-of-religions school" is misleading, since advocates of quite different points of view are subsumed under it.

250. The grand conclusion of its work reads, "The Christianity of the New Testament grew from the ground of 'syncretism.'" (M. Rade, "Religionsgeschichte," 2187.) The historical alignment, which also led to the relativizing of the canonical boundaries, allowed the members of the history of religions school to be charged with opposition to or lack of interest in the church.

on the other. The distinction between Israel and Judaism developed by Vatke and Wellhausen[251] here precipitates out in the insight that the ideas of the Old Testament were not directly effective in the world of Jesus and the New Testament, but were mediated by Judaism. The implication is also there that this Jewish thought world does not at all basically correspond to the Old Testament. The central thesis reads, "Not the Old Testament directly, but Judaism, is the history-of-religions basis of Christianity."[252] With this history-of-religions perception of Judaism, an important presupposition for the CDJ has been created. Judaism comes into view as an independent entity whose ideas are subject to criticism in a very different degree than those of the Old Testament. The Old Testament has canonical dignity and is associated with the theologically weighty "Israel," while traditionally Judaism had no theological rank—at least not in any positive sense.

Alongside this reliance on a history-of-religions approach stands the question of the tradition process that leads from Jesus to the Gospels. William Wrede's work *The Messianic Secret* (1901) indicates that considerations of the messianic consciousness of Jesus can get along without a historical foundation in Jesus himself, since the messianic theology of the earliest community shaped the tradition according to its own convictions. The problems of the Synoptic tradition appear to be so great as to prohibit any statement about the historical reliability of the tradition in its extant final form. Characteristic for this situation is Wrede's brief comment on the question of Jesus: in view of the multiple layers of tradition he rejects the claim that we have any of the *ipsissima verba Jesu* and emphasizes the openness of the situation with regard to Jesus research. Similarly, in 1904 Paul Wernle maintains, "That which we have firmly in hand is the faith of the earliest Christians."[253] At the turn of the century one could thus have the impression that all the methodological efforts in the field of Jesus research had produced no secure results. The older methods of tendency criticism and source analysis had not succeeded in reaching back to the historical Jesus. The newly developed methods of tradition criticism and history-of-religions study had allowed his profile to become vague as it receded behind myths and legends, and so made the uncertainty all the sharper.

---

251. Cf. above II, 1.4.b.ii, the excursus "The Idea of Development in the Philosophy of History."

252. So W. Wrede formulated it in "Über Aufgabe und Methode," 151. Cr. also H. Gunkel, who had already so stated in a review of Everling, *Die paulinische Angelologie und Dämonologie*, esp. 369.

253. P. Wernle, *Die Quellen des Lebens Jesu* (Halle: Gebauer-Schwetschke, 1904) 85.

ii) P. W. Schmiedel's Formulation—the Criterion
of Dissimilarity vis-à-vis Christianity (CDC)

The results of the developments sketched above provided the point of departure for the New Testament scholar Paul Wilhelm Schmiedel (1851–1935), who understood himself as a historian.[254] He sought a way out of the malaise he experienced from the fact that the answering of historical questions was dependent on a hardly solvable problem such as the source analysis of the Synoptic Gospels. He would like to establish at least a few points on which "the question as to credibility becomes independent of the synoptical question."[255] For this he did not need definitive answers to the question of the relative priority of individual layers of tradition, if only the absolute priority—"that is, the origin in real tradition"—can be determined.[256]

By means of his CDC,[257] published for the first time in 1901, Schmiedel sees himself in the position of making a detour around the synoptic problem and still able to arrive at secure historical conclusions. Source-critical considerations were not simply rejected in this process. Material that appears doubtful from this point of view is to be excluded. But from a positive perspective the decisive factor is then that "all such data, as from the nature of their contents cannot possibly on any account be regarded as inventions."[258] The criterion for this, the CDC, points to that material in the Gospels that contradicts their own perspective of hero worship. Material identified in this way can then, in a second step, be used as a material standard by which other trustworthy elements can be found. To the criterion of dissimilarity in the form of the CDC, a criterion of coherence is then attached.[259] Schmiedel thus clearly speaks out against a criterion of multiple attestation that uncritically relates the historical trustworthiness of a passage to the frequency of its appearance in various texts.

---

254. This is indicated by the repeated reference to "the historian" in presenting the required research method (Schmiedel, "Gospels," 1872–1873).

255. Ibid., 1872.

256. Ibid.

257. For the complete text of this formulation of the CDC, published for the first time in English in 1901, see the collection of such formulations in the Appendix. The German version (of 1906) follows below in the main text of this chapter.

258. Schmiedel, "Gospels," 1872.

259. A comparable combination of the CDC and the criterion of coherence is suggested by W. Heitmüller, "Jesus Christ" *RGG* 3 (1912): 361 and M. Goguel, "The Problem of Jesus" *HTR* 23 (1930): 112–13. Both are cited in the Appendix.

The German form of the CDC follows five years later, in 1906, providing the basis for the famous "foundation pillars:"

> Now the important thing is this, that they [sc. the foundation pillars for a truly scientific life of Jesus] should be selected by the same principles, those used by every historical scholar in non-theological areas. If such a scholar first gets to know a historical figure from a book that is so permeated by the intention to honor its hero as the Gospels are concerned to honor Jesus, then he considers those elements in the book to be most credible that run counter to this adoring perspective. Such a scholar says to himself that these passages could not have been invented by the author of the book within his world of thought, and yes, that they would not have been adopted by him from the material he had available if they had not had forced themselves upon him as unconditionally true.[260]

In order to identify precisely these foundational pillars that are to provide the point of departure for the study of the life of Jesus, Schmiedel sets forth a strict standard. He selects only those cases in which a form of the text available to the evangelist (as indicated by the parallel references) *has been changed in order to express his reverence for Jesus.* Such passages, which "at least from one of the three first evangelists has been omitted or changed" form Schmiedel's nine "foundation pillars."[261]

In the further discussion Schmiedel here too includes the criterion of coherence already stated in 1901: "We must also virtually establish the principle that on the basis of the 'foundation pillars' and along with them, everything in the first three Gospels deserves credibility that was appropriate to establish Jesus' significance, presupposing that it fits the image of Jesus gained on the basis of the 'foundation pillars' and raises no other doubts. The whole body of the teaching of Jesus can be placed, more or less, in this category, to the extent that it is concerned to express the religious and moral requirement placed by God on humanity and the consolation human beings may hope to receive from God."[262] Here is a reaffirmation of the interest already clearly advocated in 1901, according to which the historical reliability of the Synoptic Gospels may be maintained independently of all questions about the history of the tradition.

---

260. Schmiedel, "Die Person Jesu," 260.

261. Ibid., 260–261. Of the nine "foundation pillar" passages, five refer to Jesus' person as a whole: Mark 3:21, 31–35; 13:32; 10:18; 15:34; Matt 12:32. The other four refer to Jesus' activity as a miracle worker: Mark 6:5, 6a; 8:12; Matt 11:5; 16:5–12.

262. Schmiedel, "Die Person Jesu," 263.

Schmiedel's thought bears clearly historicist traits. Alongside his fundamentally historical orientation[263] one can name, on the one hand, his scholarly ideal of the "thoroughly disinterested historian" who can achieve by
appropriate methods these undeniable "foundation pillars," and, on the other
hand, his understanding of "historical credibility" has the overtones of the
equation "historically true" = "to be believed." Thus Schmiedel is a typical liberal: "He seeks historical knowledge about the person of Jesus, whose views
for him represent the core of Christianity."[264]

At the same time, with Schmiedel there emerges a dilemma typical for the
final phase of liberal theology. Although he works with commitment in the
field of historical Jesus research, and although as a historian he regards doubts
on the historicity of Jesus' life to be without any foundation, he negates any
significance of the *person* of Jesus for his faith.[265] The decisive element is the
teaching of Jesus, more precisely that teaching that is self-evidently true on
the basis of its religious and moral value. For Schmiedel's piety it is possible to
give up claims about the person of Jesus, his uniqueness, his testimony about
himself, his absolutely perfect example, or the newness of his teaching. What
is decisive for him and cannot be given up is the piety and morality ascribed
to Jesus, since they present "something generally human and thus eternally
valid."[266]

P. W. Schmiedel thus does in fact place himself in the ranks of liberal theologians to the extent that they emphasize the universality and general validity of the religious and ethical teaching of Jesus. At the same time, however,
he separates himself from one of the presuppositions that dominated the Jesus
research of this liberal theology: the model of the genial and heroic personality that, on the one hand, breaks through the framework of the preceding
tradition and, on the other hand, is misunderstood by its later followers and
would-be imitators. Schmiedel no longer looks for the incomparably new
in comparison to Judaism, and he also no longer assumes that the disciples
misunderstood him (perhaps due to their limited Jewish mentality). On the

---

263. On this cf. the interesting remark by H. Weinel in an apologetic-polemical article of 1910 looking back on numerous publications, in which he concedes: "[I]t seems
to me that we have worked with history in a somewhat generous manner." ("Ist unsere
Verkündigung von Jesus unhaltbar geworden?," *ZTK* 20 (1910): 111.

264. Definition by H. Pleitner, *Das Ende der liberalen Hermeneutik*, 8.

265. Cf. in contrast W. Wrede (1897), "Über Aufgabe und Methode," 135, in agreement with Holtzmann: "The message of Jesus cannot be represented simply as a specific teaching, i.e. it cannot be separated from Jesus' person and the recognizable course
of his life."

266. Schmiedel, *Die Person Jesu*, 280–82; the brief citation is from 282.

contrary, Schmiedel postulated that the model of the "heroic personality" mutatis mutandis already determined Jesus' earliest disciples. In the categories of their own time, they developed a "hero worship" for Jesus from which critical scholarship on the life of Jesus must set itself free in order to penetrate to the historical Jesus. By freeing himself methodologically from early Christian "hero worship," Schmiedel at the same time distanced himself hermeneutically from the "hero worship" of Jesus in liberal theology.

In this Schmiedel is supported by the historical understanding of precisely this liberal theology. The historical singularity of the person of Jesus, which at the beginning of the quest of the historical Jesus functioned as a historicized Christology, lost its leading, load-bearing role under the pressure of history-of-religions research. This change is clearly addressed by Johannes Weiss (1863–1914), who designates it a "rationalistic tendency" that has been overcome, a tendency "to look for the significance of Jesus in the newness of his ideas and teaching."[267] For Weiss it is obvious "that the new religion is combined with the thought forms and modes of expression of its own time. Its creative power does not lie in its theoretical constructs, but in the faith with which it is able to give them life."[268]

On the basis of such an understanding, Schmiedel also is not in a position to present the criterion of dissimilarity in the form of the CDJ. To be sure, like Weiss he obviously presupposes "the restrictive conditions of his [sc. Jesus'] thought imposed by the thought world of his time,"[269] from which his own eternally valid ideas stand out. But in all this the "cramped conditions," that is, Jesus' own time-conditionedness, his own real restriction by the history of which he is a part, is to be maintained. For Schmiedel and his contemporaries this refers above all to eschatological and apocalyptic ideas.[270] Thus for Schmiedel to have constructed from this contrast a definitive criterion of authenticity, that is, the CDJ, would be quite contrary to the tendency of critical scholarship of his time, which emphasizes precisely the strangeness of Jesus within his own context.

Emphasis is placed above all, however, on the fact that the Gospels are documents of the faith of the earliest Christian community. According to the logic of the CDC, this would only be relevant if one could proceed on the basis of strong Jewish elements in the earliest Christian community, which then could

---

267. Weiss, "Die Predigt vom Reiche Gottes," 34–35.

268. Ibid., 35. "The significance of Jesus is not that he discovered the idea of the kingdom of God, but that he lived, struggled, and suffered for this conviction."

269. Schmiedel, *Die Person Jesu*, 282.

270. The insight into the eschatological character of the message of Jesus made some difficulties for exegesis oriented to practical issues of life.

be made responsible for a "pro-Jewish" change in the tradition. The assumption of such a Jewish influence can hardly be combined, however, with the application of the CDC. Thereby an understanding of the impossibility of combining Judaism and Christianity plays an important role. The extremely influential distinction between "Israel" and "Judaism" made by Vatke and Wellhausen extends this differentiation to keep Judaism and Christianity sharply separated from each other, a process in which the image of Judaism is prejudicially negative and monolithic.

Schmiedel's criterion originated at the end of the old quest of the historical Jesus. Contrary to the hopes of their creator, his "nine foundation pillars" were denied any great influence. Only the basic idea of the CDC was preserved, and was repeatedly taken up in the phases of historical Jesus studies that were to follow.

iii) Formulation of Other Criteria

Both the effect and ineffectiveness of the "foundation pillars" are related to the dispute about the historicity of Jesus that broke out soon after the publication of the nine foundation pillars in 1901. The book most discussed by the general public was the two-volume work of the Karlsruhe professor of philosophy Arthur Drews, *Die Christusmythe* (*The Christ Myth*, 1909/1911). Drews and others who disputed the historicity of Jesus were aware of the "foundation pillars." They "devoted much effort to extensive refutations of it, and quite believed they had achieved great things by doing so."[271] Leading theologians of the time participated in the discussion, including H. Weinel, J. Weiss, A. Jülicher, and M. Dibelius. They dealt with the question of criteria only on passing.[272] Since the individual foundation pillars were undisputed, the principle on which they were based was of necessity increasingly emphasized: the demarcation of the image of Jesus from early Christianity. At that time the CDC received a form that has continued in force until the present. The formulation by H. Weinel may be taken as typical: "Only

---

271. Cf. A. Schweitzer, *The Quest of the Historical Jesus*, 431. "The Zürich theologian had given them [sc. those who contested Jesus' historicity] the occasion for cheap triumphs, for it can never be proven that certain passages cannot be invented, and besides, the nine pillars had been rather clumsily selected."

272. E. Baasland, *Theologie und Methode. Eine historiographische Analyse der Frühschriften Rudolf Bultmanns* (Wuppertal/Zürich: Brockhaus Verlag, 1992) 233, is of the opinion that the debate about criteria "became acute in 1910 in connection with the discussion about the 'Christ myth.' That is not entirely false. However, P. W. Schmiedel, who is not mentioned by E. Baasland, is the real occasion for the debate with his 1901 article in the *Encyclopaedia Biblica*. In our opinion the debate about the Christ myth only led to further clarification of something already present. Schmiedel's criterion is thus doubtless a milestone in the history of criteria, and is presented by Schmiedel as such.

those traditional features are to be considered inauthentic that could originate not from an interest of Jesus himself, but could only have originated from
the interest of the church" (1910). W. Heitmüller combined this criterion
with the criterion of coherence in his article "Jesus Christus" in the *RGG*
(1912), which gave it wide circulation. "The foundational material is that
which goes against the faith, theology, ethics, and cultus of early Christianity. . . . We can then extend this to all such material that stands in an organic
relation to this basic core."[273]

In view of the way the figure of Jesus was being derived from the collective
longings of the community and from primeval myths, it is understandable that
the reaction emphasized Jesus' individuality—also as evidence for the historicity of the figure of Jesus. But it was only as an exceptional case (Jülicher)
that "the individual" appeared as a criterion for recognizing the genuine. The
CDJ still played no role as a criterion of authenticity, and was in fact often even
intentionally denied. In the following we will discuss a series of criteria formulated in this period,[274] in order to illustrate that the CDC was present only
in an unfocused manner, and that at most only the beginnings of the CDJ can
be perceived.

In Karl Theodor Keim (1825–1878) we find the combination of ideas
(1856) that Jesus was both "the fulfillment of Judaism for the triumph over
Judaism," and the emphasis on his personal uniqueness, without formulating
this as a criterion. In the following year he made the hypothetical suggestion that a procedure could be developed in which Christian exaggerations
could be correlated with the ways in which Christian claims for Jesus were
belittled by Christianity's opponents so as to arrive at an objective mediating
statement. Thereby the same basic source-critical idea was at work in
Schmiedel, but with a different application: according to Keim, such material as corresponds to the interests of the author is to be doubted, while for
Schmiedel that which goes against the interests of the author is to be considered credible.

Apparently the same tendency in the quest for criteria is followed by Adolf
Jülicher (1857–1938) when he relates authentic Jesus material to the concept
of "that which could not have been invented" (1906). However, the criterion
for making the decision as to whether something is "the automatic product of
a human community . . . or the audacious creation of a single towering personality" remains intuitive. It is also unclear whether the indication of the
"fresh," "pointed," and "individual" refers to the contrast between Jesus and

---

273. Cf. Heitmüller, "Jesus Christus I–III," 361.
274. For the exact quotations of the formulations of criteria named in this section, with
bibliography, cf. the chronological collection of citations in the Appendix.

his Jewish contemporaries or to the formations of Christian transmitters of tradition.[275]

In 1878 August Wünsche (1839–1913) introduced a completely different criterion for authenticity, which was oriented to parallels in the Talmud. According to this criterion, a claim or saying of Jesus has a decisive claim to authenticity if it can readily be translated into the Talmudic idiom. For the Talmudist Wünsche, a CDJ would obviously be unthinkable. Twenty years later, in 1898, Gustaf Dalman (1855–1941) would bring the Aramaic original form of Jesus' sayings into the discussion, but without setting forth concrete criteria. In 1938 Leo Baeck combines the CDC with the same basic ideas advocated by Wünsche, so that a close proximity to the Jewish world of Jesus' time speaks for the historicity of the Jesus traditions. The concord of difference from Christianity on the one hand (CDC) and correspondence with Judaism on the other hand as criteria of historical authenticity is grounded in regarding the Gospels as "documents of the history of the Jewish faith."[276]

When the issue is posed once again from the history-of-religions point of view the theme of Jesus' relation to Judaism is shifted even more clearly to center stage—the theme later expressed in the CDJ. Theologians such as Johannes Weiss (1900) take it for granted that "the new religion adopted the conceptuality and language of its time." Weiss says this even though he derives this new religion directly from Jesus. Adolf Harnack (1851–1930) was more cautious in his famous lecture series of 1900 regarding Jesus' integration into contemporary Judaism.

Johannes Ninck's 1906 discussion may be taken as typical of the ambivalent attitude toward Judaism in this period. He was not able to avoid acknowledging that in Jesus' person and teaching in and of themselves there was nothing "completely new, as though it had fallen from heaven." Nevertheless, Ninck holds fast to the claim of Jesus' absolute originality and insists on a sharp contrast between Jesus' life and teaching on the one hand and Jewish life and teaching on the other. Ninck is not visibly concerned about questions of authenticity as such, but about what is essential about Jesus: "What he [sc. Jesus] does not cite is *more important* [emphasis D.W.] than what he cites."

This differentiation between "authentic" and "essential" is worked out especially by Heinrich Weinel (1874–1936). His publications of 1910 and 1911

---

275. Remarkably pointing to a completely different voice. The conservative Willibald Beyschlag (1823–1900) in 1887 expressed weighty reflections against the "*a priori* negative judgments of historical science" that did not take account of the supernatural in history. Here the attempt is made to withdraw the life of Jesus as the "divine revelation in Christ" from the realm of historical criticism.

276. As in the title of L. Baeck's book.

are a balance sheet of the previous discussion of criteria. Here is his formulation of 1910:

> Only those traditional features are to be excluded as inauthentic that could not originate from an interest of Jesus himself, but could only have originated from the interest of the church. This principle is . . . not to be extended into another, that wherever the community had an interest—but where there is no reason to believe that Jesus could not have shared this interest—the tradition as a whole is to be declared inauthentic. It is rather the case that, since it is always a matter of an exclusionary procedure, the proof must first be brought that the interest being discussed could only have emerged later. . . .
>
> What is essential" is recognized . . . by a completely different method than "what is authentic." The essential must be further distilled from the authentic, after it has been identified in the way stated above, and, in fact according to the principle that the essential is the real, the original. It is not what Jesus shared with his people and his times—that, of course, is often what is authentic in the tradition [!]—but that which distinguished Jesus from his people and his times is the essential thing about him and his message.[277]

On the one hand, for Weinel the difference between Jesus and Judaism is theologically important—one could speak of a theological CDJ—but, on the other hand, this theological evaluation is separated from the question of historical authenticity. This insight opens up the possibility that at least in part the historical integration of Jesus within Judaism would not necessarily have any theological consequences. "The essential" is an aspect of Jesus' distinctive selfhood (*Proprium*) that stands precisely in contrast to this religious-historical context.[278] In 1909 Jülicher argues similarly, when, on the one hand, he describes Jesus as rooted deeply in Jewish soil but, on the other hand, pictures Jesus as towering into "trans-Jewish heights," describing his personality as the measure of his religious-historical significance.

All these problematic evaluations of the relation of Jesus to Judaism reflect tensions within the history-of-religions school itself. The scholarly work of the group on the history of religions is oriented to the rational presentation of developments and connections, but at the same time the members of this school

---

277. Weinel, "Ist unsere Verkündigung von Jesus," 29, 35.

278. The old liberal H. J. Holtzmann, *Lehrbuch der neutestamentl. Theologie*, 408–9 (item 1911 in the collection of quotations in the Appendix), argues basically in the same way. He resolutely opposes any minimizing of the Jewish heritage, but this involvement of Jesus in Judaism has as its final goal making clear the pure fire of Jesus' independence vis-à-vis Jewish theology, messianic legends, and the eschatological perspective. Thus Holtzmann's consent to the program of an early Christian history of religion is never carried through (cf. Pleitner, *Das Ende der liberalen Hermeneutik*, 20).

were looking for the creative heroes, the shakers and movers of history. This is the reason that Jülicher, for example, goes back to nonrational modes of discovery and identification such as "intuition" in order to grasp the mystery of the great personality.[279] Thus, on the one hand, the effort of the history-of-religions school, which wanted to study Jesus as embedded in his Jewish environment, was opposed to a CDJ as a criterion of authenticity. On the other hand, however, the personality cult led to a nonrational "CDJ" that functioned in terms of theological evaluation, even if it too did not work as a criterion of authenticity. And again, the source-critical CDC declares certain passages to be authentic that manifest discontinuity between Jesus and early Christianity's reverence for Jesus. However, the element of discontinuity also plays a role for separating Jesus from Judaism when he was defined by what was "essential" about him, and here stands in tension with the customary quest within the history-of-religions school for points of contact and connecting lines.

The question of continuity and discontinuity that has thus been opened presupposes two considerations: (1) a general theory of the philosophy of history with regard to the flow of history and (2) the possibility of integrating Jesus into a historical framework (in which the christological understanding of Jesus in early Christianity is just as important as the image of Judaism). In the following section we will take a brief look at the portrayal of Jesus by Wilhelm Bousset, in which the questions and perspectives just outlined come clearly to expression.

b) The Picture of Jesus in the Work of Wilhelm Bousset (1865–1920)

Wilhelm Bousset is an important member of that group of Göttingen theologians called the "history-of-religions school" (*die religionsgeschichtliche Schule*). Two of his important books indicate the main emphases of his work—which ultimately is always concerned with the origins of Christianity within its religious setting—and at the same time a shift in the center of gravity of his work. After Bousset had composed a large work on the religion of Judaism in the New Testament period (1903), a decade later he published *Kyrios Christos*, a history of the early church's faith in Christ.[280]

Bousset himself formulated no criteria in the manner of Schmiedel and others. However, his understanding of the relation of Jesus to Christianity and especially to Judaism had produced formative basic principles that shaped the later developments of specific criteria. On the one hand, Bousset's

---

279. On the problem "tradition and individual" in the thought of the history-of-religions school, cf. Pleitner, *Das Ende der liberalen Hermeneutik*, 105–7.

280. Verheule (*Wilhelm Bousset*, 61) draws the following line of development through all of Bousset's scholarly work: "From eschatology to Judaism, from Judaism to Hellenism."

approach dealt with elements of continuity *and* discontinuity between Jesus and Christianity, and, on the other hand, with the contrast between Jesus and Judaism.

Bousset's first small Jesus book (1892) bears the programmatic title *The Preaching of Jesus Contrasted with Judaism: A History-of-religions Comparison.* The basic characteristics of Bousset's image of Jesus already emerge here.[281] In the first place, Bousset's approach stands in contrast to the method that analyzes the "concepts" in Jesus' "teaching," just as it differs from the idealistic portrayals of Jesus.[282] This stance he shares with his colleagues in the history-of-religions school. He stands apart, however, from the interpretation of Jesus in terms of thoroughgoing eschatology as advocated by Johannes Weiss. In Bousset's view, this approach needs to be supplemented.[283] A strict eschatological understanding of Jesus is problematic for Bousset's own theology, for which the ethical message of Jesus was supremely important. This was the point of departure for Bousset's approach to the figure of Jesus.

Finally, as the book's title indicates, comparison within the categories of the history of religion served to set off the distinctiveness of the figure of Jesus. The superiority of Jesus' teaching is supposed to stand out in comparison with the teaching of Judaism. A continuous line can be drawn from the nucleus of Jesus' own teaching to the nucleus of early Christianity, for the message of Jesus is Bousset's measure for what is essentially Christian. "In the preaching of Jesus the whole Gospel, in all its elements, is already present."[284]

The slightly modified view of Bousset expressed a little later reads, "[T]he nucleus and core of every religion is found in what is distinctive about it, not in what one nation or religion has adopted from another, in the original creations of great personalities, and not in what one generation hands on to another."[285] Here the emphasis on the difference from Judaism—the influence of the personality cult and Thomas Carlyle's philosophy of history[286] are obvious—stands alongside the *difference* from Christianity. In the hands of Bousset, the *analysis* of the history of traditions inspired by the "history-of-religions

---

281. On this cf. J. M. Schmidt, "Bousset, Wilhelm," in *TRE* 7 (1981): 97–101, esp. 99–100.

282. Bousset, *Jesu Predigt in ihrem Gegensatz*, 103.

283. Ibid., 6, n. 2.

284. Ibid., 78.

285. W. Bousset, *Der AntiChrist*, 10. The characteristic feature of Bousset's concern, also found in his work *Kyrios Christos*, is the intention he later describes as "to illumine the genesis of the central characteristic of the religion of ancient Christianity by means of a delineation of faith in Christ from its beginnings until the time of Irenaeus." (Bousset, *Jesus der Herr*, 2).

286. Cf. above II. 1.3.b.

method" leads to a *critique* of these traditions,[287] that is, to a critical analysis of Christian tradition, which in Bousset's view had departed from the normative nucleus of the proclamation of Jesus.

In his *The Religion of Judaism in the New Testament Period* (1st ed. 1903; 2nd ed. 1906), Bousset acknowledges his mistake "of a too one-sided emphasis on the contrast between Jewish and Christian piety," but without basically calling his procedure in question.[288] A statement in his first Jesus book makes clear that, in view of the singular figure of Jesus, he rejects the scientific ideal that claims to refrain from all value judgments.[289] In Bousset's understanding of how history works, the fundamental contrast he makes between Jesus and Judaism is an essential driving force for the forward movement of history. In this procedure, Christianity becomes the standard by which Judaism is measured; the contrast implies a denigration of elements of Jewish teaching, and this contrast becomes the basis on which historical progress from Judaism to Christianity is affirmed.[290] Moreover, for Bousset a fundamental and continuing debate comes to expression in this contrast: Jesus is "the mighty warrior against every Pharisaism in every time."[291]

Carlyle's clothing philosophy serves Bousset in the sense of an accommodation theory that enables him to handle the specifically Jewish elements that are in fact found in Jesus' teaching. Such Jewish elements were seen as "external covering," temporary husks containing eternal truths as their content: "[K]eeping himself externally entirely within the framework of Judaism, Jesus was internally directly and unselfconsciously much more free than this framework, had freed himself from it much more decisively than even his disciple Paul."[292] In his Jesus book of 1904 Bousset emphasized more strongly the aspect of adopting "the progressive ideas of later Judaism"[293] instead of the

---

287. Cf. Paulsen, "Traditionsgeschichtliche Methode," 36.

288. W. Bousset, *Die Religion des Judentums*, 58. Verheule (*Wilhelm Bousset*, 129), in our opinion, denies the problem of Bousset's portrayal of Judaism when he speaks of a "more positive evaluation of Judaism" in Bousset's later work.

289. Bousset, *Jesu Predigt in ihrem Gegensatz*, 9.

290. Hoheisel, *Das antike Judentum*, 31. Verheule (*Wilhelm Bousset*, 92) represents this state of affairs as a positive thought of Bousset, that "late Judaism had accomplished an essential preparation for the coming of Christianity."

291. W. Bousset, *Was wissen wir von Jesus*, 64. A confessional and church political controversy stands in the background here. This is seen especially the description of the Pharisees as a "security guard of the scribes among the laity, the Pietists of Jewish orthodoxy." (Bousset, *Jesus*, 32)

292. Bousset, *Jesu Predigt in ihrem Gegensatz*, 87; cf. also the comments of K. Berger, *Exegese und Philosophie*, 93.

293. Bousset, *Jesus*, 55.

purely creative activity of Jesus. Thus, in contrast to his earlier tendency, Jesus' faith in God as Father "was not entirely new," but Jesus is seen as "developer and perfecter" of something already present in Judaism.[294] Still more clearly in his later *Kyrios Christos,* Bousset distanced himself from the idea that religion was a matter of "the new and unheard-of."[295] Here too, however, he uses the "clothing philosophy's" language of eternal truth being clothed "in the colorful wrappings of temporal clothing."[296]

Bousset's occupying himself with Jesus *and* Judaism set the parameters for the research that followed. Since they have some influence on the later questions of criteria, we will here briefly summarize the contents of the theological differences between Jesus and "late Judaism" as drawn by Bousset.

Bousset's understanding of the religion of "late Judaism" may be summarized in four key words: monotheism, apocalyptic, particularism, and law. The historian of religion points out the different influences—the apocalyptic of "late Judaism," for example, is the syncretistic product of Persian ideas and Jewish messianic hope—and describes this Judaism as a contradictory structure. Its particularism, for example, contradicts the universalistic tendency of monotheism,[297] and within apocalyptic itself there is a tension between hatred for Israel's enemies and the hope for forgiveness of sins. In Bousset's view, it is the negative tendencies that dominate in each case, particularism and the hate-filled longing for God's judgment on Israel's enemies.

In Bousset's opinion, Jesus did not take over much from such a "late Judaism." In his first Jesus book of 1892 Bousset defined what was called "faith in God as Father"[298] as the center of Jesus' message. In his larger Jesus book of 1904, the idea of the kingdom of God with its eschatological message received more emphasis. Faith in God as Father and Jesus' call to repentance, with its universal and individual preaching of judgment, were traced back especially to its "ancient Israelite" origins: God as the Father of Israel, prophetic universalism, the faith of the psalmists, and the prophetic announcement of

---

294. Ibid., 51–52.

295. Bousset, *Kyrios Christos,* 117.

296. Ibid., 118.

297. Cf. R. Ruether, *Faith and Fratricide: the Theological Roots of Anti-Semitism* (New York, Seabury Press [1974]) 216–22, on the misunderstanding of this contrast between particularism and universalism, in which universalism represents an anticipation of Christian catholicity. Cf. also Hoheisel, *Das antike Judentum,* 38.

298. A. Schweitzer, *Geschichte der Leben Jesu Forschung* (9th ed.; Tübingen: J. C. B. Mohr [Paul Siebeck], 1984; unchanged reprint of 7th ed. 1966) 259 calls this word (i.e., the German term *Gottvaterglaube*) a "bastardization of theological language." The sentence is not present in the most recent English translation *Quest of the Historical Jesus* ([Minneapolis: Fortress, 2001] 204) translated from the 6th German edition of 1950.

judgment lead directly to Jesus. The "late Jewish" monotheism, which, from Bousset's perspective, in fact led to an abstract and distant deity, stands in contrast to Jesus' faith in God as Father and as near to the believer. The only element from the "late Jewish" side that became really fruitful in Jesus' own faith in God as Father is the individualistic piety of "late Judaism," which was at home in apocalyptic[299] and was paired with the older Israelite ideas of God as Father. Also formative for Jesus' preaching of judgment was the "late Jewish" concept of the universal world judgment, although this idea received a decisive modification in Jesus' own teaching. Jesus understood the judgment concept in universal terms, so that in the image of the future judgment it was not merely Israel, or one's own party among the "late Jewish" groups, that would be vindicated on the last day. In Bousset's reconstruction of Jesus and ("late") Judaism, therefore, Jesus' faith in God as Father and his universalism stand in clear contrast to this "late Judaism."

As already mentioned, Bousset formulates no concrete criterion in the manner of Schmiedel, but from time to time two elements emerge in his argumentation related to the criterion of dissimilarity. In his major Jesus book *Jesus* (1st ed. 1904; 3rd rev. ed. 1907), Bousset refers only briefly to Wernle for his methodological foundation.[300] On the issue of the origin of the messianic faith, a factor appears in the argument that appears to run directly contrary to Schmiedel's version of the CDC. His inferential procedure allows him to deduce from the earliest Christian community's faith that Jesus was the Messiah that Jesus himself must have had a messianic consciousness. This continuity is not "suspicious" but is to be counted as an argument. Otherwise, "the origin of this faith is simply unexplainable."[301] In order to support this point, Bousset also points out that faith in the Messiah could not have been a completely new development among the post-Easter disciples, "for one would then have to assume that the wonderful experiences of the Easter days had generated something

---

299. Jewish apocalyptic is cast in the role of a preliminary stage of the Christian gospel; cf. note 55.

300. Wernle, *Die Quellen des Lebens Jesu*, presented a general introduction to the Johannine question and the Synoptic problem, tracing the way back from the canonical Gospels to the oldest traditions. That these oldest traditions go back to eyewitnesses is affirmed on the basis of intuitive awareness. "But how unpretentious and unprejudiced, how fresh and joyful Mark reports everything—this speaks with a high degree of probability that here we have the pure voice of good tradition. Here we have nothing less than eyewitness report" (70). In such statements written in 1904 one can recognize an influential liberal theologian who is quite distant from a methodologically reflective determination of criteria.

301. Bousset, *Jesus*, 77. There would be no explanation, "if Jesus himself had not made himself known as Messiah to his disciples during his lifetime." Bousset thus reckoned not only with Jesus' messianic consciousness, but with a self-revelation to his disciples.

absolutely new in their souls in some purely magical manner without any psychological means. But from a strictly historical standpoint, this cannot be accepted."[302]

Obviously it presented no problems to Bousset to ascribe this creative, messianic interpretation to Jesus himself. This links up with his view of great, creative personalities who achieve something truly original. In his first Jesus book Bousset approaches the appearance of Jesus "with the awareness of standing before the most significant and amazing figure in human history."[303] Of course, Bousset himself later modified this position.[304] This reflects the tension typical of history-of-religions scholars between, on the one hand, the personality cult of the scholar's own time, and, on the other hand, the methodological approach oriented to the faith of religious communities. After 1904 Bousset's interest shifted "from the historical Jesus to the faith and cultus of the community."[305] The influence of the early Christian community's theology on the developing Synoptic tradition began to play a more important role for him. In 1916, with regard to his earlier view of the messianic consciousness of Jesus himself, he emphasized "the creative formative power of the church's faith and its capacity for reforming historical reality."[306] The quest of the historical Jesus became a more complex and difficult problem.[307] When Bousset describes the problematic of the Gospels containing a "web of church tradition and genuine words of the Master woven together in a manner than often cannot be untangled,"[308] he is expressing a consideration that lies at the base of the CDC. In *Kyrios Christos* Bousset even grounds the influence of the image of Jesus in the history of Christian piety on the "peculiar combination of the historical figure of Jesus and the proclamation of the community," which first created this image of Jesus.[309]

---

302. Ibid., 77.

303. Bousset, *Jesu Predigt in ihrem Gegensatz*, 10.

304. For a discussion of Bousset's change of perspective, cf. Verheule, *Wilhelm Bousset*, 173–182.

305. Kahlert, *Der Held*, 37.

306. Bousset, *Jesus der Herr*, 11.

307. This is seen clearly in Bousset's lecture "The Significance of the Person of Jesus" ([1910] 292–298). Bousset basically has a minimal estimate on how extensive our knowledge of the historical Jesus is, and sees "all attempts to base the confidence and content of our faith in historical knowledge to be burdened with great difficulties" (Ibid., 298).

308. Bousset, "Die Bedeutung der Person Jesu," 292.

309. Bousset, *Kyrios Christos*, 117. This illustrates the problem of liberal hermeneutics at the beginning of the twentieth century, as pointed out by Pleitner (*Das Ende der liberalen Hermeneutic*, 152): "the emphasis on the historicity of the person of Jesus as indispensable for faith and a determination of the function of this person, which in no way needs this historicity."

Here the new direction of New Testament scholarship already announces itself. With methodological reasons and with theological justification, the central theme is no longer the historical Jesus behind the text of Scripture, but the faith of the early church as expressed in the New Testament.

2.2 The Critical Method of Dialectical Theology and the Skepticism of Form Criticism

a) Effects on Jesus Research and the Quest for Criteria

A new phase of the debate about the historical figure of Jesus, which extends from the period of World War I to the beginning of the 1950s, is stamped on the theological side by *dialectical theology*[310] and on the methodological side by *form criticism*. Dialectical theology emphasizes the tension between God and revelation, on the one side, and world and history, on the other, and has a fundamentally christological orientation. The form-critical method turns to the early Christian tradition as such, analyzes its forms and genres, and evaluates it as the testimony of the faith of the early Christian community. The outstanding scholars of this epoch are, on the theological side, Karl Barth (1886–1968) and Emil Brunner (1889–1966); among New Testament scholars are Martin Dibelius (1883–1947), Karl Ludwig Schmidt (1891–1956), and, of course, Rudolf Bultmann (1884–1976).

In the phase shaped or influenced by these theologians, the foreground is occupied by the extremely sharp critical debate with the old quest of the historical Jesus. It was rejected on two complementary grounds. From the theological perspective, emphasis was placed on the inadequacy of attempting to provide a historical foundation for access to Jesus Christ. From the methodological point of view, the development of form criticism challenged the fundamental possibility of approaching the person and personality of Jesus by historical means. As the alternative to aligning Christian theology to the historical figure of Jesus, dialectical theology oriented itself to the kerygmatic witness of Scripture, and form criticism focused on the kerygmatic early Christian tradition. From their different perspectives, they each were concerned with the same subject matter, the early Christian proclamation, and represented a break with concern for reconstructing the historical Jesus.

i) The Theological Inadequacy of Life-of-Jesus Research

The expositions of the old life-of-Jesus research made clear their dependence on historicism. With dialectical theology, which undertook a fundamentally

---

310. The formative influence of dialectical theology extends beyond this phase of Jesus research into the New Quest.

new orientation for theological thought, the relation of theology to history was also completely rethought. This resulted in a different place for the historical figure of Jesus in theology, an adjustment that emerged in such a pointed manner because Christology became the new fulcrum and pivotal point for theology. This approach thus stands in direct contradiction to life-of-Jesus theology, which attempted to replace or bypass Christology by its appeal to the historical Jesus.

The decisive new approach becomes clear in Emil Brunner's Christology in *The Mediator* (1927): "[F]aith presupposes, as a matter of course, *a priori*, that the Jesus of history is not the same as the Christ of faith."[311] Dialectical theology here lays hold on the distinction made by Martin Kähler (1835–1912) in 1892 between the "so-called historical Jesus and the historic, biblical Christ:" "The risen Lord is not the historical Jesus *behind* the Gospels, but the Christ of the apostolic preaching, of the whole New Testament."[312] The bases and results of this separation of the world of faith from the world of history will be listed in the following.

The appeal to Scripture grounded in the Reformation perspective, which gave dialectical theology the reputation of the "neo-orthodox," was influenced by the form-critical approach to Scripture. Form criticism's working within the framework of the tradition's own intention emphasized the element of proclamation.[313] Dialectical theology as "theology of the Word" grasps this line of argument in order to provide authoritative evidence for the theological irrelevance of historical information. To be sure, faith is bound to a historical fact—the famous "mere 'thatness'" of the event itself[314]—but it is not based on it. The guiding question has to do with the origin of faith. Here the clear answer sounds forth: the Christ is not recognized by historical study but only by the testimony of Scripture,[315] and this recognition is the only basis for Christian faith.

At the end of the nineteenth century there was an ambivalence about the evaluation of historical data. In contrast to the attempt to establish irrefutable

---

311. E. Brunner, *The Mediator. A Study of the Central Doctrine of the Christian Faith* (trans. Olive Wyon; Philadelphia: Westminster Press, 1947) 184.

312. M. Kähler, *The So-Called Historical Jesus and the Historic, Biblical Christ* (trans. and ed. Carl E. Braaten; Seminar Editions; Philadelphia: Fortress Press, 1964) 65.

313. The problematic in the use of the Gospels as historical sources will be discussed thematically under 2.1.a.ii.

314. "The decisive thing is simply the 'That' [sc. of his historicity, not its 'What' and 'How']." R. Bultmann, "The Primitive Christian Kerygma and the Historical Jesus," in *The Historical Jesus and the Kerygmatic Christ: Essays on the New Quest of the Historical Jesus* (ed. Carl E. Braaten and Roy A. Harrisville; Nashville: Abingdon, 1964) 20.

315. Cf. Brunner, *The Mediator*, 153–160.

foundation pillars (P. W. Schmiedel), in view of the relativity of historical results, Martin Kähler, like Bultmann's teacher Wilhelm Herrmann (1864–1922), sought "to stake out a 'storm-free area' over against historical science."[316] Hermann thinks in the mode of experience, of encounter. In order to get out of range of historical research, he took recourse to the "inner life of Jesus" and called for ethical self-understanding on the part of human beings on the basis of experiencing Jesus' own messianic consciousness and ethical sovereignty. The crisis in Bultmann's own relation to the historical Jesus comes in at precisely this point, since he sees "that the person of the historical Jesus means hardly anything for my inner life, or even nothing at all."[317] The encounter between the inner life of Jesus and the inner life of the person today, so important for Hermann, is after Jesus' death no longer possible for Bultmann,[318] for the present manner of Jesus' existence is not comparable to that of a contemporary fellow human being.

The separation between the world of faith and the world of history is to be traced back above all to the great gulf between God and humanity, something that dialectical theology was very concerned to make people aware of. Human beings are located in history; they cannot be transformed into some kind of transhistorical beings.[319] So also, history itself is entirely human and immanent. Thus history, in and of itself, cannot be the bearer of divine revelation. According to Brunner, it is rather to be understood as "humanity as a whole in its need of redemption."[320] In reference to Jesus, this means that, for example, Bultmann rejects speculations about the ethical human personality of Jesus, as if one could grasp the divine in him merely by maximizing his human potential. Karl Barth turned sharply against the "abstract Jesus cult," which

---

316. H. Gerdes, "Die durch Martin Kählers Kampf gegen den 'historischen Jesus' ausgelöste Krise in der evangelischen Theologie und ihre Überwindung," *NZST* 3 (1961): 185. Cf. W. Herrmann, *Ethik* (GThW 5, vol. 2; Tübingen: Mohr, 5th ed. 1913) 101: "[W]hen they [the historians] claim that their discoveries not only serve our faith, but can rule it or destroy it, they would make us into comic figures."

317. Letter from R. Bultmann to M. Rade, 19 December 1920, in "Rudolf Bultmanns Wende von der liberalen zur dialektischen Theologie," in B. Jaspert, ed., *Rudolf Bultmanns Werk und Wirkung* (Darmstadt: Wiss. Buchges., 1984) 30.

318. R. Bultmann, "Zur Frage der Christologie" (1927), in *Glauben und Verstehen* 1:106. In this essay from 1927, pp. 101–13, Bultmann conducts his debate with his teacher, for whom he had great respect.

319. R. Bultmann, *Jesus and the Word* (trans. Louis Pettibone Smith and Erminie Huntress Lantero; New York: Charles Scribner's Sons, 1958) 8; cf. also R. Bultmann, "Geschichtliche und übergeschichtliche Religion im Christentum?" (1926), in *Glauben und Verstehen* 1, in which Bultmann attacks the concept of the transhistorical in Dibelius.

320. Brunner, *The Mediator*, 153.

gets around "the divine word by the direct glorification of the humanity of Christ as such." In the "faith" in the religious hero Jesus, Barth perceives a dangerous divinization of the creature.[321]

In all this, dialectical theology was clearly issuing a call to get down to business, a call for concentration on the present Lord who is both proclaimer and proclaimed, a call to make the intention of the Christian tradition's kerygma its own. Thus it was forbidden to go behind the kerygma "in order to construct a 'historical' Jesus with his 'Messianic consciousness,' his 'inwardness,' or his 'heroism'."[322]

Against this background, the search for "foundation pillars" in Schmiedel's sense is completely irrelevant and/or entirely inadmissible on theological grounds. The attributes described by the criterion of *dissimilarity*, namely, singularity and peculiarity in the positive sense, which life-of-Jesus theology had connected with the figure of the historical figure of Jesus, were attributed by dialectical theology to the transhistorical, nonworldly, nonhuman realm. But if something beyond history has stepped into history, "something superhistorical, unique, absolutely decisive,"[323] then this something cannot be historically verified and should not be. A historical criterion of dissimilarity is thus not a theme of dialectical theology, and in this phase no direct impulses for the development of criteria for the historical Jesus are to be expected. But since the essential theological aspect is seen in the "wholly other," a new significance for the dissimilarity criterion is seen to emerge, since the historical again becomes theologically important.

The theological irrelevance of historical research at first, however, helps historical-critical work to gain some free space in which to operate, since it no longer has the task of providing support for the absolute claim of the Christian faith. On the basis of the identification of the human with that which is historical, the assessment of the historical as theologically irrelevant receives a special quality that smacks of Reformation theology: it understands itself as the crossing-out of human self-justification in favor of the justifying grace of God.

In this segment of the history of theology one can observe an ambivalence in how history is to be evaluated. On the one hand, historical data are regarded as uncertain, and, since they are based on the relativities of historical study, they are experienced existentially as not structurally sound, not capable of bearing

---

321. K. Barth, *Church Dogmatics*, vol. 1: *The Doctrine of the Word of God*. Second Half-Volume. (ed. G. W. Bromiley and T. F. Torrance; Edinburgh: T & T Clark, 1956) 1/2:136–37.

322. R. Bultmann, "Die Bedeutung des geschichtlichen Jesus für die Theologie des Paulus" (1929), in *GuV* 1:208.

323. Brunner, *The Mediator,* 153.

the weight that must be placed on them. Schmiedel had attempted to meet this challenge of historical uncertainty with his "foundational pillars," but at the same time emphasized the theological boundaries of historical relevance. Bultmann goes resolutely forward, and is interested is dissolving the connection between piety and history, i.e., in dissolving "any connection between [faith and] historical cognition and scholarship."[324] When Brunner and Barth call for the radical risk of the life of faith severed from clear and certain historical facts, they presuppose a positivistic understanding of history that can no longer be held today. Brunner compares a historical fact with an "objective" (and theologically unfruitful) photograph.[325] In dependence on Kähler, Bultmann distinguishes history-as-*Geschichte* (the lived, personally significant story) and history-as-*Historie* (the "objective" product of historical research), understanding *Historie* as the "brute facts." By this he means the objectifiable, verifiable given facts of the past, which as such are unable to trigger any personal existential response.[326] History so understood is excluded from the realm of theological relevance.[327]

On the other hand, it is precisely the lack of absolute historical certainty about Jesus that is taken up thematically by dialectical theology. The basic lack

---

324. R. Bultmann, "Bultmann an Rade," *Briefwechsel Karl Barth—Rudolf Bultmann. 1922–1966* (Zürich: tvz, 1971) (= Karl Barth—GA V [Briefe], vol. 1, 19.12.1920, in B. Jaspert, "Rudolf Bultmanns Wende von der liberalen zur dialektischen Theologie," in B. Jaspert (ed.), *Rudolf Bultmanns Werk und Wirkung* (Darmstadt: Wiss. Buchges., 1984) 31–32.

325. Brunner, *The Mediator*, 185. He contrasts the concept of the photograph with that of the portrait, describing the Gospel of John as a portrait, and as such filled with theological content.

326. Bultmann himself is not consistent in the differentiation between the two concepts, which developed in this way in the course of the discussion. Cf. the works of G. Greshake, *Historie wird Geschichte*; W. Stegemann, *Der Denkweg Rudolf Bultmanns*, and J. Körner, *Eschatologie und Geschichte*, 117–131. The following text is a classic example of the specific meaning of "historical" (*historisch*) and "historic" (*geschichtlich*): "In its redemptive aspect the cross of Christ is no mere mythical event, but a historic (*geschichtlich*) fact originating in the historical (*historisch*) event which is the crucifixion of Jesus. The abiding significance of the cross is that it is the judgment of the world, the judgment and the deliverance of man. In the last resort mythological language is only a medium for conveying the significance of the historical (*historisch*) event. The historical (*historisch*) event of the cross has, in the significance peculiar to it, created a new historic (*geschichtlich*) situation (R. Bultmann, "New Testament and Mythology," 37).

327. The theological-philosophical motives for Bultmann's rejection of a "Jesus theology" are well summarized by Neill/Wright: "To focus attention on Jesus himself, apart from his dehistoricized preaching of the Word and his saving death on the cross would be to base faith on history and so turn it into a 'work', to 'objectivize' revelation, and to turn from the present appeal of the Gospel to the prison of the past—and thus to offend, at the same time, against the canons of Lutheranism, neo-Kantianism, and existentialism" (Neill and Wright, *The Interpretation of the New Testament*, 166).

of a guarantee for the accuracy of all historical knowledge here underscores the theological inadequacy of attempting to ground theology on historical study. "The fact of the incarnation, the 'being found in the form of a servant,' carries with it the possibility of holding Jesus to be a mere human being, and the impossibility of seeing in Him anything more than a man—apart from the gift of faith."[328]

ii) The Impossibility of Life-of-Jesus Research in Regard to Historical Method

In the work of W. Bousset, a shift in the center of gravity from the historical Jesus to Christian tradition could already be perceived. This shift becomes completely clear in K. L. Schmidt, since he portrays the particular concern of Jesus research as placing "particular stress on the investigation of this growth of the tradition, and the distinguishing of individual strata according to their degree of originality."[329] The reconstruction of a historical picture of the figure of Jesus is thereby abandoned by Schmidt as a concern even of Jesus research itself. The connection to dialectical theology is obvious.

In its concentration on the development of the tradition, form criticism took up Gunkel's considerations and point of view that he had developed in his Old Testament studies. The attempt to distinguish earlier layers of tradition within the Old Testament documents gave rise to the discipline of form criticism in New Testament scholarship as well. Tradition was separated from redaction, and the historical setting (*Sitz im Leben*) of each was sought. A landmark pointing the direction of future study is found in the insight that Bultmann cites with reference to Wellhausen: "We must recognize that a literary work or fragment of tradition is a primary source for the historical situation out of which it arose, and is only a secondary source for the historical details concerning which it gives information."[330]

The great form critic Martin Dibelius was concerned with the interpretation and illumination of *texts*, but precisely *not* in terms of historical issues. For Dibelius, as for K. L. Schmidt, the asking of historical questions was not the decisive aspect of critical Gospel studies.[331] To be sure, Dibelius sees in form criticism an aid in the making of historical judgments about the tradition, since

---

328. Brunner, *The Mediator*, 186.

329. K. L. Schmidt, "Jesus Christ" *RGG*² 3 (1959):110–51. Translated as several articles in Jaroslav Pelikan (ed.) *Twentieth Century Theology in the Making: Vol. I—Themes of Biblical Theology* (New York, Evanston, San Francisco, London: Harper & Row, Publishers, 1969) 93–168. The above quote is from 108.

330. R. Bultmann "The New Approach to the Synoptic Problem," in *Existence and Faith: Shorter Writings of Rudolf Bultmann*. Selected, translated, and introduced by Shubert M. Ogden (Meridian Books, Inc.; New York, 1960) 38.

331. M. Dibelius, *Gospel Criticism and Christology*, 45.

distinguishing between various genres of tradition can be a solid index of historical reliability.[332] But Dibelius' form criticism was ultimately oriented to a theological outcome, for "it dares to come to conclusions about the driving interests of the tradition by studying its forms. . . . It believes . . . it is able to show the significance the tradition of Jesus' words and deeds once had when they were first transmitted, and believes it is thereby able to penetrate to the earliest and normative connection between history and Christian faith."[333] The problematic of the relation of theology and history emerges clearly in this latter formulation, just as does the decisive difference between historical and theological results. The (theological) interest in the (historical-biographical) portrayal of the life of Jesus as practiced in the older life-of-Jesus research is rejected by Dibelius as alien to the intention of the early tradition. Dialectical theology's lack of interest in the results of historical study can thus appeal precisely to the early Christian tradition.

Form criticism, which distinguishes the variety of forms or genres within the early Christian tradition, from its own perspective underscores the kerygmatic character of the Gospels. The observation that the early Christian Gospels were not biographies[334] but the work of theologically engaged tradents and redactors brings the attempts to reconstruct the personality of Jesus by historical study to a decisive end. For Dibelius, the Jesus tradition's refusal to include such historical-biographical information indicates "the unworldly character of the original tradition," which cannot be categorized within the general rubrics of literature.[335]

A structural analogy to the old life-of-Jesus theology can be clearly discerned: while there Jesus as the central figure was taken out of the "normal" secular course of history, so here the Christian tradition, regarded as central, is removed from the context of general secular literature. Structurally, the lonely hero Jesus corresponds to the Gospels, which "represent a unique genre, without predecessors and without successors."[336]

---

332. M. Dibelius, *From Tradition to Gospel* (New York: Charles Scribner's Sons, 1935) 290.

333. Ibid., 295.

334. K. L. Schmidt, "Jesus Christ," 96, 100.

335. Dibelius, *Tradition to Gospel*, 301. Cf. also K. L. Schmidt, "Die Stellung der Evangelien in der allgemeinen Literaturgeschichte" (1923), in F. Hahn, ed. *Zur Formgeschichte des Evangeliums* (WF 81; Darmstadt: Wiss. Buchges., 1985) 228: "Early Christianity, taken as a whole, did not really enter into the world. This becomes clear in the study of the forms of its 'literature.' Thus the perspective of form criticism is a matter of theology."

336. P. Vielhauer, *Geschichte der urchristlichen Literatur. Einleitung in das Neue Testament, die Apokryphen und die Apostolischen Väter* (Berlin: de Gruyter, 1975) 282 (from the section on form-critical method).

In view of the criticism of dialectic theology, Dibelius wants to assign historical study to a theologically harmless field. This takes place by means of a clear delimitation of responsibilities. Since the real object of faith is transhistorical, it cannot really be grasped by means of historical study.[337] "The methods of critical historical science can indeed deal with human activities, but the act of God is not something that can be investigated by such historical methods. *Critical scholarship can thus not deal with the revelatory act of God, but only with historical events.*"[338]

For Dibelius, the history of Jesus is to be included in these historical events, which he sets forth in a small volume. Obviously, when the form-critical method raises the question of original material in the tradition, it will become an advocate of the CDC. The argument of source criticism that leads to mistrust about elements in the tradition that agree with the intentions of the tradents is radicalized in form criticism. It is basically the history that bears the tradition along that is illuminated, with the focus in this history on the role of the traditional forms, especially their "*Sitz im Leben.*" As a result of this approach, Dibelius speaks of a relative originality of the tradition when it is foreign to the forms of expression and the new conceptual world of Paul and the church after him.[339] This CDC is the dominant criterion when Dibelius emphasizes, "It is proper to speak of non-genuine sayings only where the later circumstances, conditions, or problems of the already existing Church are clearly presupposed."[340]

Dibelius expresses no further concern about the possibly secondary sayings in the Jesus tradition that may derive from the proverbial wisdom of Judaism, since they do not change the essential content of the Jesus tradition. Although Dibelius sees in Judaism and in *Christianity* "two basically different religious attitudes attaining their historical expression,"[341] he locates *Jesus* nearer to Judaism: "Jesus himself did not proclaim what could be called a new concept of God."[342] There is no CDJ in Dibelius' work.

Dibelius notes that it was first through faith that the story of Jesus became a historical factor of far-reaching significance.[343] That means that to the his-

---

337. M. Dibelius, *Wozu Theologie? Von Arbeit und Aufgabe theologischer Wissenschaft* (Leipzig: Klotz, 1941) 4, 10–11.

338. Ibid., 13.

339. M. Dibelius, *Jesus, A Study of the Gospels and an Essay on "The Motive for Social Action in the NT"* (London: SCM Press, 1963) 20–31.

340. Ibid., 22.

341. M. Dibelius, "Mensch und Gott," in *Der Jude. Sonderheft: Judentum und Christentum* 4 (1926): 22.

342. Ibid., 18.

343. Dibelius, *Jesus*, 129.

torical Jesus there belongs the kerygmatic Christ, who first gives the historical Jesus abiding significance. Dibelius thus develops further the line of thought concerning the history of Jesus' effects, as it had been expressed in Bousset's *Kyrios Christos*.

This insight regarding the history of effects can be combined with sociological reflections. At the level of tradition, K. L. Schmidt points to the mutual interaction between the figure of Jesus and the formation of the Jesus tradition by its *Sitz im Leben*.[344] In this period Rudolf Otto also argued sociologically with his reflections on the history of the effects of Jesus' life, which, however, completely contradicts the CDC. Otto sees the authenticity of Jesus' description as a charismatic as confirmed by the existence of the pneumatic-enthusiastic Christian community, which is to be traced back to the effect of the charismatic Jesus.[345] Here Otto applies a criterion based on the laws of sociology, the "criterion of coherence", namely, an agreement between Jesus tradition and early Christianity.

b) The Picture of Jesus in the Work of Rudolf Bultmann (1884–1976)

Rudolf Bultmann, the most important New Testament scholar of the twentieth century, began his work in the context of liberal theology, joined the developing school of form critics, and was attracted to dialectical theology, within which he went his own way. He had already laid the foundations for his historical judgments about the Jesus tradition in his predialectical phase. His book *The History of the Synoptic Tradition* (1921) is the ripe fruit of this phase. He was to stand by the conclusions attained in this book the rest of his life. However, his 1926 Jesus book already reflected the influence of dialectical theology. While his historical assumptions remained basically the same, his fundamental theological insights and perspectives experienced a sharp change.[346] His break with liberal theology finds clear expression in his theological evaluation of the historical Jesus.

---

344. Schmidt, "Jesus Christ," 86.

345. R. Otto, *The Kingdom of God and the Son of Man. A Study in the History of Religion*. (trans. Floyd V. Filson & Bertram Lee Woolf; London: Lutterworth Press, 1951) 344.

346. E. Baasland (*Theologie und Methode*) has thoroughly analyzed this shift (cf. his summary, pp. 462ff). In 1917–1922 Bultmann was the main advocate of the paradigm of historical-critical research then in place (463). "As a result of his encounter with the early dialectical theology, Bultmann saw that he had to revise his own systematic theology. The corresponding methodological consequences did not, however, lead to a real change of the paradigm, but only to shifting the emphases and to supplements within the paradigm of the history of religions school" (465). Because of this continuity in the historical-critical bases of his work, we will discuss first the picture of Jesus as represented in the dialectical phase, and then the question of criteria that played a role in Bultmann's predialectical phase. Despite Bultmann's "turn," both belong substantially together.

Appealing to Paul, Bultmann held that nothing more than the famous "that" of Jesus' existence is theologically important. This most minimal of historically verifiable data can only be the presupposition of Christian faith; it offers no religious nourishment; it is only a rind. This is intended entirely in Bultmann's sense of the reduction of objectifying thinking. "But in fact the Synoptics do offer *more . . .* , and since this *more* is handed on in the tradition, I consider it a matter of theological importance to be concerned for this 'more' and to present it in its own terms."[347] In this way, Bultmann justified his 1926 Jesus book, in contrast to Karl Barth. Bultmann's book *Jesus* appeared in a series called *Die Unsterblichen: Die geistigen Heroen der Menschheit in ihrem Leben und Wirken* (The Immortals: The Spiritual Heroes of Humanity in their Life and Work). By way of contrast, Bultmann writes in his Introduction, "Accordingly this book lacks all the phraseology which speaks of Jesus as great man, genius, or hero."[348]

Bultmann regarded reconstructions of Jesus' "personality" as historically unreliable. At most, Jesus' activity can be discerned. He is not interested in the "messianic consciousness of Jesus," so important for life-of-Jesus theology, especially since he regards faith in Jesus as Messiah as a post-Easter development. In this he takes up the view of W. Wrede. Entirely in the sense of dialectical theology, Bultmann rejects the effort to get behind the kerygma, "to use it as a 'source,' in order to construct a 'historical' Jesus with his 'messianic consciousness,' his 'inwardness' or 'heroic stature.'"[349] Likewise directed against the old life-of-Jesus theology is his acknowledgement "that for my own inner life, the person of the historical Jesus means little or nothing."[350]

The question of Jesus' personality thus experiences a double rejection: it cannot be answered historically, and it is completely irrelevant theologically.

Bultmann's disinterest in the personality[351] of Jesus may be contrasted with his attention to his work; "[H]is purpose can be comprehended only as teaching."[352] It corresponds to this that the *preaching* of Jesus stands at the central point of Bultmann's delineation of *Jesus*, both in his Jesus book and in his *The-*

---

347. Letter from R. Bultmann to K. Barth, 10 December 1926, in *Briefwechsel Karl Barth—Rudolf Bultmann. 1922–1966* (Karl Barth—GA V [Briefe] 1. Zürich: tvz, 1971) 65.

348. Bultmann, *Jesus and the Word*, 8.

349. R. Bultmann, "Die Bedeutung des geschichtlichen Jesus für die Theologie des Paulus," (1929), in *Glauben und Verstehen*, 1:208.

350. Letter from R. Bultmann to M. Rade, 19 December 1920, in B. Jaspert, "Rudolf Bultmanns Wende," 30.

351. R. Bultmann, "Zur Frage nach der Christologie" 101: "I do not know how it was in Jesus' heart, and do not want to know."

352. Bultmann, *Jesus and the Word*, 10.

ology of the New Testament. For Bultmann, the preaching of the historical Jesus may by no means be substituted for the kerygma, the church's proclamation of the crucified and risen Christ. Analogously, the portrayal of Jesus is not concerned to present specific Christian content. Instead, by means of presenting his own encounter with the story of Jesus, Bultmann would like to lead "the reader . . . to a highly personal *encounter* with history."[353] The goal is "a dialogue with history," in which Jesus' words "meet us with the question of how we are to interpret our own existence."[354] This dialogue with the historical Jesus explicitly has no christological quality. On the contrary, religious commitment should be freed precisely from this attachment to history.[355] In his Jesus book, Bultmann is not at all interested in depicting Jesus as the Christ.[356] "The Jesus of history is not kerygma, any more than my book was."[357] A theological-christological encounter can only occur with the Christ of the kerygma: "I am deliberately renouncing any form of encounter with a phenomenon of past history (including that of the "Christ according to the flesh"), in order to encounter the Christ proclaimed in the kerygma, which confronts me in my historic situation."[358]

While it is true enough that for Bultmann the preaching of the historical Jesus is not of direct theological relevance, he does consider it possible to reconstruct the message of Jesus with a fair degree of probability—in contrast to Jesus' personality. Bultmann himself presents his "Jesus book" project from another angle: the subject of his presentation is "this complex of ideas in the oldest layer of the synoptic tradition. . . . By the tradition Jesus is named as the bearer of the message; according to overwhelming probability he really was. Should it prove to be otherwise, that does not change in any way what is said in the record."[359] Here the procedure of form criticism (determining a layer of tradition) is combined with impulses from dialectical theology (the irrelevance of tracing things back to Jesus).

Apart from these preliminary theological considerations, Bultmann's judgments about the historical location of the figure of Jesus cannot be understood.

---

353. Ibid., 6.

354. Ibid., 11.

355. Letter from R. Bultmann to M. Rade, 19 December 1920, in Jaspert, "Rudolf Bultmanns Wende," 31.

356. Letter from R. Bultmann to K. Barth, 10 December 1926, in Jaspert, *Briefwechsel*, 65.

357. R. Bultmann. "A Reply to the Theses of J. Schniewind," in Hans Werner Bartsch (ed.) *Kerygma and Myth: A Theological Debate* (New York: Harper & Brothers, 1961) 117.

358. Ibid.

359. Bultmann, *Jesus and the Word*, 14.

For Bultmann, Jesus is *one* of the presuppositions of New Testament theology, and thus also for Christian theology.[360] He does not really belong to these later categories, and "cannot be understood from the later Hellenistic development, but only from the preceding Jewish development."[361] The real Christ myth is a creation of the later Hellenistic Christianity and cannot already be located in Palestinian Christianity.[362] "Christianity exists as a self-sufficient, religious congregation only where it has created its own myth and cult. Jesus was a Jew and the Palestinian congregation was a Jewish sect."[363] Here Bultmann appeals to Bousset, who understands the transition from the historical Jesus to the kerygmatic Christ as a process within the history of religions.

When Bultmann understands the teaching of Jesus as "nothing other than pure Judaism,"[364] he intends above all to contrast the teaching of Jesus with the Christian faith, which by his definition is dependent on the kerygma. The Christian kerygma is based on Jesus Christ, the crucified and risen one;[365] Bultmann never speaks of the life of Jesus as a component of the kerygma.

In my opinion, there is no denying a connection between the theological evaluation of the historical Jesus and his classification within Judaism. The interest of dialectical theology in maintaining for Jesus as autonomous an identity as possible, which relies entirely on Christology, leads to separating Jesus from everything that has no "real Christology, no real faith in Christ."[366]

---

360. Cf. R. Bultmann, *Primitive Christianity in its Contemporary Setting* (New York: Meridian Books, 1956), as well as his *Theology of the New Testament*, where in Part One the message of Jesus is dealt with alongside "The Kerygma of the Earliest Church" and "The Kerygma of the Hellenistic Church" under the title "Presuppositions and Motifs of New Testament Theology." The first sentence reads, "The message of Jesus is a presupposition for the theology of the New Testament rather than a part of that theology itself" (3).

361. R. Bultmann, "Ethical and Mystical Religion in Primitive Christianity," in J. M. Robinson. *The Beginnings of Dialectic Theology* (trans. Louis De Grazia and Keith R. Crim; Richmond: John Knox Press, 1968; lecture at the Wartburg, 1920). In this early essay from 1920 Bultmann identified historical-critical work with liberal theology, "within which I count myself" (230). At the same time, his critique and gradual separation from liberal theology is becoming clear. For a discussion of Bultmann's radical change of direction, cf. Jaspert, "Rudolf Bultmanns Wende," as well as M. Evang (*Rudolf Bultmann in seiner Frühzeit* [BHT 74; Tübingen: Mohr, 1988] 310, n. 85) who rejects the idea of a radical turn in Bultmann's thought.

362. Bultmann, "Ethical and Mystical Religion in Primitive Christianity," 224. Thus the title of this essay: the earliest Palestinian church is characterized as an ethical religion, Hellenistic Christianity as a mystic-cultic religion.

363. Ibid., 231.

364. R. Bultmann, "Die Christologie des Neuen Testaments" (1933), in *Glauben und Verstehen* 1:265.

365. R. Bultmann, *Theology of the New Testament*, 1:3.

366. Bultmann, "Die Christologie des Neuen Testaments," 253.

As a true member of the dialectical theology group, Bultmann emphasized the otherness and transcendence of God, which "means drawing a line through all that is human, the whole history of humanity."[367] This corresponds to Bultmann's comment expressed in similar language, according to which he consigns to the flames not only the imaginative pictures of life-of-Jesus theology, but along with them the *Christos kata sarka* (the "Christ according to the flesh" 2 Cor 5:16) as such.[368] All bridges that attempt to reach behind the kerygma are to be demolished. Against this background it becomes clear how Bultmann's classification of Jesus within Judaism makes it impossible to regard the quest for the historical Jesus as an effort to support faith with historical assurance. This procedure presupposes the clear separation between Judaism and Christianity.

In this separation, the theme "law and gospel" plays an important role. For Bultmann, the Christ of the kerygma is the end of history, a formula that he places in parallel with "the end of the law."[369] Bultmann understands "law" to be a given element of historical existence as such. Historical life under the law means remaining in the realm of hate and death while historical life under the gospel means belonging to the new age of love and the life.[370] The gospel thus presupposes the law. This view, in the sense of an existentialist understanding of history, is supported by a relativizing anthropological existentialist exegesis.[371] This is seen particularly in the treatment of Judaism. Bultmann explains that when Paul speaks specifically of Judaism, he is speaking of the specifically human.

According to Bultmann, in Jesus' message God remains "the demanding God of the Old Testament and Jewish tradition."[372] Jesus is compared to a prophet and a Jewish rabbi for whom the authority of the Old Testament law goes without saying.[373] Differently from Paul, it is by no means the case that the law is "annulled through the institution of God's salvation."[374]

---

367. R. Bultmann, "Die liberale Theologie und die jüngste theologische Bewegung" (1924), in *Glauben und Verstehen* 1:13.

368. Bultmann, "Zur Frage der Christologie," 101.

369. R. Bultmann, *History and Eschatology: The Presence of Eternity* (New York: Harper & Brothers, 1957) 43: "For history has reached its end, since Christ is the end of the law (Rom 10:4)."

370. Bultmann, "Zur Frage der Christologie," 109–10.

371. Cf. H. Thyen, "Rudolf Bultmann, Karl Barth und das Problem der 'Sachkritik'," in B. Jaspert, ed., *Rudolf Bultmanns Werk und Wirkung* (Darmstadt: Wiss. Buchges., 1984) 51: "Still under the spell of idealism, he [sc. Bultmann] thinks of the real history too much in terms of the mere form for a different, timeless content."

372. Bultmann, "Ethical and Mystical Religion in Primitive Christianity," 225.

373. Bultmann, *Jesus and the Word*, 57, 61, 106.

374. Bultmann, " Ethical and Mystical Religion in Primitive Christianity," 226.

Against this background it becomes clear why Bultmann makes such a sharp separation between the historical Jesus and the Christ of the kerygma: in this separation the distinction between law and gospel is reflected.

Typical for Bultmann's characterization of Jesus, however, is that alongside this clear contextualization of Jesus within Judaism stands an important supplementary consideration. A radicalization of Jesus' Jewish message is pointed out that, in terms of its content and language, approaches Bultmann's own theology—including his polemical points against particular theologians. On the question of the law, this means that, although Jesus shares the ethic of obedience and the love command with Judaism, he presents a different *understanding* of the law. For Bultmann, the ethic of Jesus gives up the formal authority of law and its demand in favor of God's demand, which is reasonable in principle. The result is the call for a radical obedience in which the individual human being is addressed by a demand that he or she can in principle affirm.[375] Bultmann hereby explicitly distinguishes Jesus' ethic from a moral idealism, a system of values, or a social-political program.[376] Instead, in Bultmann's delineation of Jesus, the foreground is occupied not by new ethical demands but by the absolute demand of God.[377] "In contrast to Judaism, Jesus demands not works, but genuine feelings, truthfulness and unconditional obedience to the good."[378] Here a disputed theological issue current in Bultmann's day is dealt with by referring to the historical Jesus. Bultmann charges liberal theology with "the confusion of a religiously-colored moralism with ethical religion. Only on this basis could one ascribe such a religious-moral significance to the historical Jesus; for what is really religious plays a relatively minor role in his meaning for us."[379] Thus P. Wernle criticizes Bultmann's portrayal of Jesus: "Jesus the good Jew with a few moral proverbs and a bit of faith in providence, but strictly speaking without deep religion . . ."[380]

On the issue of Jesus' image of God, Bultmann argues just as he had on the question of the law: on the one hand, Jesus is fully integrated into Judaism, on the other hand, the emphasis is on the radicalized stance of Jesus within this context. Bultmann fully agrees with Dibelius that Jesus did not teach a new concept of God.[381] One should rather say of Jesus "that he apprehends the

375. Bultmann, *Jesus and the Word*, 65–66, 72–77, 88, 113.

376. Ibid., 79, 84, 93–94, 104.

377. Ibid., 87–90.

378. Bultmann, " Ethical and Mystical Religion in Primitive Christianity," 225–26.

379. Ibid., 233.

380. Letter from Paul Wernle to M. Rade, 13 February 1921, in B. Jaspert, "Rudolf Bultmanns Wende," 34.

381. Bultmann, *Jesus and the Word*, 191; M. Dibelius, "Mensch und Gott," 18.

Jewish idea of God in its purity and consistency."[382] For Bultmann, the outstanding feature in this regard is Jesus' understanding of the kingdom of God, for "according to Jesus' thought the Kingdom is the marvelous, new, wholly other."[383] Bultmann sees human beings thereby called to decision—the principle topic of Bultmann's own theology is clearly recognizable. In his 1960 lecture Bultmann acknowledged that the preaching of Jesus had a thoroughly "kerygmatic character,"[384] and combined this with the insight that "one cannot speak of the act of God in the human being Jesus of Nazareth . . . without *at the same time* speaking of the 'significance' of this act *for me.*"[385]

Bultmann continued to hold fast to the view that Jesus belonged totally within Judaism. But still and all, Bultmann attributes to him a unique position *within* Judaism on the basis of Jesus' theological radicalizations of Judaism, of which he was the "conclusion and fulfillment" (1920), the one who "overcame" it (1960).[386]

Bultmann clearly formulated the criterion of dissimilarity for the first time in his 1921 *History of the Synoptic Tradition.*[387] His perspective on the issue is thus clearly oriented to the tradition process in early Christianity, in the manner of the other form critics, for he regards it as "essential to pose the question of Christian origins, including in regard to those materials that do not at

---

382. Bultmann, *Jesus and the Word,* 155.

383. Ibid., 158–59.

384. R. Bultmann, *Das Verhältnis der urchristlichen Christusbotschaft,* 15.

385. W. Stegemann, *Der Denkweg Rudolf Bultmanns. Darstellung der Entwicklung und der Grundlagen seiner Theologie* (Stuttgart: Kohlhammer, 1978) 144.

386. Bultmann, "Ethical and Mystical Religion in Primitive Christianity," 226: "Jesus concludes and fulfills the history of Judaism." Jesus could "radically overcome Judaism only as a Jew." He is "a unique figure within Judaism . . . as its conqueror." ("The Primitive Christian Kerygma and the Historical Jesus," 19).

387. Baasland, E. (*Theologie und Methode,* 234–35) has shown that Bultmann had already dealt with the problem of criteria in a survey of research in the *MPTh* 5 (1908): 158–59: The distinction between the real Jesus and the picture of the "Christ of the church" calls for going beyond literary-critical decisions between earlier sources and later revision to a procedure that could be called "concept history." This procedure would allow everything that could not be assigned to early Christianity to be attributed to the historical Jesus. The difference between Jesus and Judaism is not yet made into a separate theme; the connection between Judaism and early Christianity even receives a positive emphasis.

388. R. Bultmann, *The History of the Synoptic Tradition* (trans. John Marsh; New York: Harper & Row, 1963) 135 [128]). Translator's note: Theissen/Winter cite from the 1970 8th revised German edition of Bultmann's *Geschichte der Synoptischen Tradition.* The only English translation was from the 1931 3rd edition. That translation was sometimes deemed unsatisfactory. I have thus translated the text that appears in Theissen/Winter and retained the German pagination, with the corresponding page in the English translation sometimes appearing in brackets.

first suggest it of themselves."[388] The possibility of being able to get back to the historical Jesus himself lurks here in the background. The CDC is advocated on the basis of the form critics' dictum that "a connection between the figure of Jesus and the fortunes and interests of the early church"[389] points to a Christian origin. At the same time, Bultmann's evaluation of Jesus' place in Judaism means that a characteristic individualistic spirit in an element of tradition can point to its dominical origin, without here formulating an explicit CDJ.

Thus the classical form of the criterion of dual dissimilarity is found in connection with Bultmann's treatment of the parables. He speaks of the "contrast with Jewish morality and piety" and the lack of specifically Christian features, but also positively of the specific eschatological mood that points to an authentic parable of Jesus.[390] Against the background of Jesus' context in Judaism, the sharp formulation of the "contrast" is not entirely cogent and can be attributed primarily to Bultmann's own theological heritage.

E. Baasland has analyzed Bultmann's use of criteria in *The History of the Synoptic Tradition*.[391] His most important conclusion (and his decisive critique of Bultmann) is that Bultmann already presupposed a particular image of Jesus that he then used in order to evaluate the tradition. On the basis of an intuitive insight into the data as a whole, Bultmann had decided that Jesus was an eschatological prophet. This image functioned as a material criterion in conjunction with the contrast Bultmann saw between Jesus and the faith and ethic of Judaism.[392] The examples cited by Baasland indicate, however, that the contrast with Judaism is primary, and that the resulting picture of Jesus as eschatological prophet is, in fact, a result of this methodological procedure, not its presupposition. That can be briefly illustrated by the most important forms of the sayings tradition.

Among the wisdom sayings, for Bultmann those are inauthentic "that manifest few or none of the characteristics of a new and individual piety that goes beyond Judaism" (*History of the Synoptic Tradition* 108 [104]). Of the prophetic sayings, those are authentic that are stamped with the consciousness of eschatological authority, for example, some of the beatitudes: "And inasmuch as this eschatological consciousness is something new in contrast to Judaism, these beatitudes are in any case un-Jewish" (*History of the Synoptic Tradition* 133

---

389. Ibid.

390. Ibid., 205.

391. Baasland, *Theologie und Methode*, 230–61.

392. Ibid., 260: On the basis of his comprehensive picture of Jesus constructed intuitively, in his *History of the Synoptic Tradition* Bultmann can "neglect the deployment of firm criteria in his approach, and simply (sic!) base it on a particular image of Jesus" (similarly 236–37). But it is not that simple!

[126]). Among the legal sayings and community regulations the logion about purity of Mark 7:15 belongs to the terse "conflict sayings" that "parabolically express Jesus' stance to Jewish religion." Thus its authenticity is to be presumed (*History of the Synoptic Tradition* 158 [147]). Finally, for the first time in the history of New Testament exegesis, with regard to the parables Bultmann formulates a clear statement of the criterion of dissimilarity that combines the demarcation from both Judaism and early Christianity (*History of the Synoptic Tradition* 222 [205]).

It is clear that Bultmann wants to utilize a comparative method derived from the study of the history of religions to determine what is unmistakably characteristic of Jesus. For him, this means what is *recognizably* authentic—but not everything that is authentic *in itself*. He chooses a formal procedure that does not necessarily prejudice the outcome, but that can be applied in an open manner. It need not be disputed that, in fact, all academic research is always motivated by the anticipation of a particular result. Good methodology, however, consists precisely in its ability to correct such anticipations. Thus also in the case of Bultmann, his results do not simply follow automatically from the methodological premise of his (often only implicit) application of the criterion of dissimilarity. His category of the "eschatological prophet" allows him to locate Jesus squarely in Judaism (in the sense of a "theory of prophetic connection," see above 1.3.b.iii). On the other hand, he does not isolate Jesus from early Christianity, in that there too other eschatological prophets appeared. The criterion of dissimilarity is de facto "packaged" with an application that functions in terms of context and history of effects, thus our thesis that Bultmann's incidental references of the "contrast between Jesus and Jewish ethics and religion" (e.g., *History of the Synoptic Tradition*, 222 [205]) does not entirely square with his own historical work.

In the context of his form-critical work, in 1926 Bultmann once again formulated the criterion of dual dissimilarity with reference to the tradition of Jesus' sayings. In this American publication he indicated that the reconstruction of a historical picture of early Christianity is a presupposition for the reconstruction of a picture of Jesus and his message, and speaks in this regard of the Sayings Source. On the basis of his presuppositions about the history of the tradition as indicated by form criticism, Bultmann emphasizes, in dependence on Wellhausen, that the Sayings Source is permeated (only) by the spirit of Jesus, so that its words are not necessarily the ipsissima verba of Jesus. However, according to Bultmann, the distinction between specific interests of the early Christian community or expressions of Jewish religion, on the one hand, and grand original ideas, on the other, make it possible "to derive from them a

---

393. Bultmann, "New Approach," 38–39.

definite conception of the preaching of Jesus."[393] Here too, however, it becomes clear that Bultmann is not really interested in pursuing this quest behind the kerygma. This is only *one* possible critical use of the Sayings Source, which he regards primarily as a source of information about the earliest church.

We thus find in Bultmann the first clear formulation of the criterion of dual dissimilarity that combines the CDJ and CDC. However, he formulated it only with regard to particular sayings genres, whether it was for the parables in particular or for the sayings tradition as a whole. It had not yet been generalized to become a comprehensive criterion for the tradition as a whole. Perhaps it was his disinterest in the question of the historical Jesus that prohibited Bultmann from taking this step. He left this step to his students, especially E. Käsemann, who for the first time formulated the criterion of dual dissimilarity as a general criterion. This move was motivated by a new interest in the historical Jesus that had the christological imagery of early Christianity as its point of departure and that focused on the issue of the continuity between these images and the historical Jesus. Bultmann's students could appeal to Bultmann himself, who could speak uninhibitedly of an implied Christology in the message of Jesus: "Jesus' call to decision implied a Christology."[394] For Bultmann the continuity between Jesus and the early church is provided by the fact that the kerygma—not the Christ of the kerygma, who, in contrast to the kerygma itself is not a historical phenomenon[395]—takes the place of the historical Jesus.[396] Bultmann takes up a formulation of E. Käsemann in saying "that the 'once' of the historical Jesus is transformed into the 'once-for-all' of the kerygma."[397] The question remained, however, of the "what" of the historical Jesus, and how the content of this image is related to the "that" of Bultmann's "once," and this question called for scholars to turn once again to the quest of the historical Jesus.

2.3 The New Quest of the Historical Jesus

a) The Motives for the New Quest

The revival of the quest for the historical Jesus in the 1950s has been the subject of important monographs and innumerable articles.[398] Here we will only

---

394. Bultmann, *Theology of the New Testament*, 1:43.

395. Bultmann, "The Primitive Christian Kerygma and the Historical Jesus," 20, 28.

396. Ibid., 42.

397. Ibid., 40.

398. E.g., J. M. Robinson, *Kerygma und historischer Jesus* (Zürich: Zwingli, 2nd ed. 1967); W. G. Kümmel, *Dreissig Jahre Jesusforschung (1950–1980)* (BBB 60. Königstein-Bonn: Hanstein, 1985). (A collection of his bibliographical research reports).

briefly sketch the framework within which the discussion of criteria of that period was carried on. It is above all a matter of the *motives* of the quest that are relevant for reflection on methodological issues.

The so-called "New Quest" is "new" in the Bultmann school that dominated German scholarship, and is characterized by the fact that the Bultmannian concept of the kerygma was set in a relation to the historical Jesus in a way that can be precisely defined. The New Quest is thus new for those theologians who come from a "kerygma theology" and are now turning back to questions about the historical Jesus. J. M. Robinson, who gave the "New Quest" its name,[399] points out that "in the scholarly tradition carried on in French or English . . . the life-of-Jesus research of the nineteenth century has continued almost without interruption until the present (1960).[400] Similarly, H. K. McArthur presents what he calls the "British viewpoint," which had never adopted Bultmann's radical views, rejected the label "*New* Quest," and spoke instead of a Quest that had been "resumed" or "continued."[401] Not only in other countries, however, but in Germany too there had always been theologians who, alongside the dominant Bultmann school, had never given up a direct historical interest in the historical-theological relevance of the historical Jesus. Joachim Jeremias may be mentioned as the most well-known advocate of this view.[402]

The beginning of the New Quest of the historical Jesus in the Bultmann school may be dated precisely in 1953–1954. At the annual meeting of the "Old Marburgers" (Bultmann's students) Ernst Käsemann (born 1906) delivered a

---

399. Two American systematic theologians wrote energetic protests against this designation for the new phase of investigation (V. A. Harvey and S. M. Ogden, "How New is the 'New Quest for the Historical Jesus?'," in Carl E. Braaten and Roy A. Harrisville, *The Historical Jesus and the Kerygmatic Christ* (Nashville: Abingdon, 1964). Alongside methodological reflections, they consider the 'New Quest' neither new nor promising. However, the taking up of an old project in combination with the processing of new theological and methodological considerations justifies the designation "new," and also makes possible new results.

400. Robinson, *Kerygma und historischer Jesus*, 11–12.

401. H. K. McArthur, *The Quest Through the Centuries*, 124. The English New Testament scholar Reginald H. Fuller had already in 1956 expressed reservations about theological research on the continent: "Bultmann's kind of *entweder/oder* may appeal to the Germanic mind, but the practical-minded Englishman in the street, and the scholarly Englishman brought up by his classical training to believe that faith and reason cannot be thus divorced, suspect that there is a catch in it somewhere" (*The Mission and Achievement of Jesus: An Examination of the Presuppositions of New Testament Theology* [SBT 12; London: SCM Press, 1956] 15).

402. Käsemann, "Die neue Jesus-Frage," in J. Dupont, ed., *Jésus aux origines de la christologie* (BETL 40; Leuven: Leuven University Press, 1975, 2d ed., 1989) 47, speaks of Jeremias's "almost reckless historical and theological optimism."

programmatic lecture with the title "The Problem of the Historical Jesus," which was published in 1954. Käsemann pointed out what in his view was the current deficit in life-of-Jesus research, on the one hand, and in Bultmann's theology, on the other. With the Bultmannian concept of the kerygma as his point of departure, he is concerned with the dual anchor points of the kerygma: the Easter faith, on the one hand (here he sees a deficit in the life-of-Jesus theology and a correct, though one-sided, new starting point by Bultmann), and the proclamation of Jesus, on the other hand (here he sees a deficit in Bultmann's approach and a correct approach in the life-of-Jesus theology, which appealed one-sidedly to the teaching of Jesus). Käsemann combines both approaches but rejects their respective one-sidedness when he states, "The Easter faith was the foundation for the Christian kerygma, but was not the first or only source of its content."[403] A limitation is thus given to the exclusive significance of the Easter faith for the kerygma, since for Käsemann an interest in the earthly Jesus belongs essentially to the kerygma itself. The form of the Gospel as the story of the earthly Jesus is inseparable from the Christian message itself.

The renunciation of the "Old Quest" of the historical Jesus[404] is based on an identification with the Easter faith of earliest Christianity in which the kerygma is understood to be concentrated and summarized. For Käsemann it is important, however, that the earliest church did not separate the exalted Lord from the earthly Jesus. He directed this insight, on the one hand, against attempts to attribute a one-sided interest in the earthly Jesus to the earliest church. On the other hand, he makes the theological-christological character of the early Christian confession clear, in order to free himself all the more decisively from being bound by the judgment of early church: "For the deci-

---

403. Käsemann, "The Problem of the Historical Jesus," 34.

404. This renunciation is based (among other things) on a work of the nineteenth century, namely on Martin Kähler's *The So-Called Historical Jesus and the Historic, Biblical Christ*. (trans. and ed. Carl E. Braaten, Seminar Editions; Philadelphia: Fortress Press, 1892, ET 1964). The debate about the historical legitimacy of the New Quest goes directly back to Kähler. It was not without good reasons that his work was reintroduced in 1956. On the new concern with Kähler cf. H. Gerdes, "Die durch Martin Kählers Kampf gegen den 'historischen Jesus' ausgelöste Krise in der evangelischen Theologie und ihre Überwindung," in NZST 3 (1961).

405. Käsemann, "The Problem of the Historical Jesus," 24. For scholarly circles less influenced by Bultmann, the necessity of a basic interest in the earthly Jesus by early Christianity is obvious (cf. W. G. Kümmel, "Jesu Antwort an Johannes den Täufer. Ein Beispiel zum Methodenproblem in der Jesusforschung" (1974), in W. G. Kümmel, *Heilsgeschehen und Geschichte. Bd. 2. Ges. Aufs. 1965–1976* [Marburg: Elwert, 1978] 187). The debate with the Bultmannian orientation serves as the justification for his own interest in the earthly Jesus.

sion taken by primitive Christianity obviously does not permit us to choke off the question about the Jesus of history."[405]

Thus Käsemann emphasizes—along with Bultmann—his agreement with the renunciation of life-of-Jesus research, just as he emphasizes—against Bultmann—the legitimacy of the historical question of the historical Jesus. The difficulty of the sources is found in the fact that "the exalted Lord has almost entirely swallowed up the image of the earthly Lord."[406] Although the early church affirmed the identity of the two, from the historical point of view they cannot simply be exchanged. This leads Käsemann to the characteristic feature of the New Quest, the *question of continuity*: "The quest of the historical Jesus is legitimately the question of the continuity of the gospel in the discontinuity of the times and in the variation of the kerygma."

A decisive element for the New Quest's ability to assert itself is found in the perspective that Käsemann sees as destined for it. He believes that he can show that "out of the obscurity of the life story of Jesus, certain characteristic traits in his preaching stand out in sharp relief, and that primitive Christianity united its own message with these."[407]

Here is reflected what Hans von Soden had previously formulated in a different way: since "every possibility of knowledge is an obligation to fulfill this potential," the attempt to distinguish between traditional material that comes from Jesus and that which comes from the church must be undertaken.[408] Käsemann sees this as a given possibility, but his main concern is to distinguish Jesus from Judaism. Then early Christianity stands in continuity with that which has been marked off as distinctive of the historical Jesus. In this way Käsemann negotiates past the decisive stumbling block for the Bultmann school.[409] In a retrospective survey he later makes an antidocetic interest responsible for the fact that the exalted Lord may not a priori be preferred to the earthly Jesus. Important elements of Christian social ethics "cannot be grounded as such, apart from the earthly and crucified man of Nazareth."[410]

In the Bultmann school the dominant mode of argument has the structure "yes—but." On the one hand, there is consensus on the methodological and

---

406. Käsemann, "The Problem of the Historical Jesus," 46.

407. Ibid.

408. H. v. Soden, "Die synoptische Frage," in H. v. Campenhausen (ed.), *Urchristentum und Geschichte. Ges. Aufs. und Vorträge, Bd. 1, Grundsätzliches und Neutestamentliches* (Tübingen: Mohr, 1951) 211.

409. It is something of a riddle how S. P. Kealy comes to the conclusion in his survey of research ("Gospel Studies Since 1970," *IThQ* 56 [1990]: 167) that Käsemann's initiative met with little response ("attempted to get a new quest going but with little success").

410. Käsemann, "Die neue Jesus-Frage," 57.

theological renunciation of the older research's attempts to write a life of Jesus, just as, on the other hand, consensus prevails regarding the fundamental relevance of the historical Jesus. *Yes*, it is impossible to write a biography of Jesus, *but* Jesus is nonetheless of theological importance—the contrast with docetism is here repeatedly put forward as an argument. There is little unanimity, however, in defining the "how" of the newly postulated theological relevance of the historical Jesus.

The position of Ferdinand Hahn seems to me to be typical of the tendency of the New Quest. He rejects a theological *function* for the isolated portrayal of the *historical Jesus* and sees this function to be rather in the investigation of the *transition* from the historical Jesus to the preaching of the early church.[411] This leads to the following dictum: "In theology, the quest of the historical Jesus, with all its unavoidable scholarly preliminary work involving the philosophy of history as such, should finally occupy us only so that the factual-theological relevance is able to bear the weight placed upon it."[412]

In a lecture published in 1955 on the historical Jesus as a problem for both historical science and theology[413], N. A. Dahl sees himself more strongly bound to history than the vast majority of the "New Questers." In borderline cases, the question of the authenticity of a saying of Jesus can even be a standard by which its value is measured: a "saying of Jesus" can more easily be set aside "when objective historical criteria suggest that there is no authentic word of Jesus."[414]

The systematic theologian Hermann Diem in 1957 identified precisely the question of the continuity between Jesus' preaching and that of the church as

---

411. F. Hahn, "Die Frage nach dem historischen Jesus und die Eigenart der uns zur Verfügung stehenden Quellen" (1960 Lecture), in F. Hahn, W. Lohff, and G. Bornkamm, *Die Frage nach dem historischen Jesus* (EvFo 2. Göttingen: Vandenhoeck & Ruprecht, 1962) 204.

412. Ibid., 205.

413. N. A. Dahl, "Der historische Jesus als geschichtswissenschaftliches und theologisches Problem," KuD 1 (1955): 104–132. Translated as "The Problem of the Historical Jesus," in Nils Ahlstrup Dahl, *The Crucified Messiah and Other Essays* (Minneapolis: Augsburg, 1974) 48–89 and in Carl E. Braaten and Roy A. Harrisville, eds., *Kerygma and History: A Symposium on the Theology of Rudolf Bultmann* (Nashville: Abingdon, 1962) 138–171. A revised translation was published in Nils Alstrup Dahl, *Jesus the Christ: The Historical Origins of Christological Doctrine* (ed. Donald H. Juel; Minneapolis: Fortress Press, 1991) 81–111, which is cited in this book. In a remarkable parallel to Käsemann, the lecture was given in 1952 (and first published in 1953, the year of Käsemann's Marburg lecture). Dahl must therefore be given more credit than he is presently given as co-founder of the "New Quest."

414. Ibid., 108.

the decisive issue in the quest of the historical Jesus. At the same time, in a manner similar to Käsemann, Diem is concerned with identity of Jesus Christ in the variations of the kerygma.[415] A historical continuity within all the discontinuity of content is expressed by C. Burchard with his formulation of the "conserving transformation of the message of Jesus."[416]

All these statements are concerned with the essential legitimacy of Christian faith in Jesus. When seen against the background of this debate about legitimacy, the basically optimistic quest for some connection, in whatever form, between the historical Jesus and the kerygma reveals the direction in which the New Quest is looking:

1. Both the renunciation of *life*-of-Jesus research and the concept of the kerygma lead to a concentration on reconstructing the *message* of Jesus. The Jesus books of this phase of the discussion mostly confine themselves to an introductory chapter, or an introduction and conclusion, in which something is said about the course of Jesus' life, with the center of attention focused throughout on the tradition of Jesus' sayings. To be sure, one (apparent) exception deserves special mention: Ernst Fuchs steadfastly argued for more attention to Jesus' conduct and actions. In this he was especially concerned for the *connection and continuity* between Jesus' words and his deeds. The same self-orientation is to be found in Jesus' word as in his act.[417] His famous remark that "Jesus' conduct is the 'framework' of his message . . . ," is a hermeneutical statement. The 'nucleus' of Jesus' acts *is* precisely what Jesus *said*."[418] Fuchs was ultimately interested in Jesus' conduct as the event of his *word* and *speech*.

2. This concentration on the proclamation of Jesus and the church, combined with the question of continuity, permitted the difference between Jesus and Christianity (in the sense of the CDC as the basis for the image of Jesus) to slip into the background. The decisive shift vis-à-vis Bultmann lies, of course, precisely in the careful transfer of Jesus back across the line from Judaism to Christianity, and, in fact, as its beginning. While for Bultmann the line between Judaism and Christianity is not to be drawn until after the

---

415. H. Diem, "The Earthly Jesus and the Christ of Faith," in Carl E. Braaten and Roy A. Harrisville, eds. *Kerygma and History. A Symposium on the Theology of Rudolf Bultmann* (Nashville: Abingdon, 1962) 210; cf. also 197.

416. C. Burchard, "Jesus," *KP* 2 (1967): col. 1353.

417. E. Fuchs, "The Quest of the Historical Jesus," in Ernst Fuchs, *Studies of the Historical Jesus* (SBT 42; London: SCM Press, 1964), 21–22.

418. E. Fuchs, "Einleitung: Zur Frage nach dem historischen Jesus. Ein Nachwort," in *Glaube und Erfahrung. Zum christologischen Problem im Neuen Testament.* (Collected Essays, Vol. 2, 1–31. Tübingen: Mohr, 1965) 19.

ministry of Jesus, the advocates of the New Quest find Jesus "at the crossroad where Christianity and Judaism begin to separate from each other."[419] The transfer may be charted as follows:

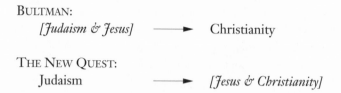

BULTMAN:

    [Judaism & Jesus]   ⟶   Christianity

THE NEW QUEST:

    Judaism   ⟶   *[Jesus & Christianity]*

In the context of the history of scholarship, the advocates of the New Quest find themselves in a situation in which they are fighting at the same time against the theological renunciation of historical-Jesus research *and* against the picture of a consistently Jewish historical Jesus. The emphasis on the difference from Judaism and the stronger coherence with Christianity is thus no surprise.

The revival of Reformation theology in dialectical theology spread abroad the negative topos of "legalism," which was easily connected with Judaism. This negative image of Judaism likewise led to separating Jesus more decisively from Judaism and, as the alternative (!), to bring him nearer to Christianity.

A negative tendency in the way Judaism is viewed can be seen especially in the work of Käsemann. From his retrospective statements in 1975, it may be concluded that a driving motive for his "new" preoccupation with Jesus is to oppose Bultmann's incorporation of the earthly Jesus within Judaism. Especially on the issue of Torah, Käsemann sees the earthly Jesus as on a different plane than the Jewish groups of his time: the break with the Torah was characteristic of Jesus and the reason he was executed. It is the message of justification that for Käsemann forms the decisive line of the gospel's continuity from the pre-Easter to the post-Easter period. "The preacher of a sharpened morality and Torah remains . . . a Jewish rabbi or prophet, and cannot be taken seriously as the means of our forgiveness."[420] Thus for Käsemann the problem of the historical Jesus touches all of Christology.

Adopting a phrase of Bultmann,[421] the New Quest speaks of an implied Christology in connection with the earthly Jesus. Even though the earthly

---

419. Dahl, "The Problem of the Historical Jesus," 95.

420. Käsemann, "Die neue Jesus-Frage," 52. Cf. the discussion of his formulation of criteria, below 2.3.b.

421. Bultmann, *Theology of the New Testament,* 1:46: "Jesus' call to decision implies a Christology." The limitation to the "call to decision" was broadened by the New Questers to include the effect of Jesus' ministry as a whole.

Jesus explicitly claimed no christological titles for himself, his preaching implies a claim to authority that, in terms of its content, corresponds to the claim to be "Messiah," "Son of God," or "Son of Man." But this implicit claim to authority did not become the explicit claim to authority of early Christian Christology until after Easter. Characteristic of the New Quest is the connection between this explicit Christology of the post-Easter kerygma and the quest for the historical Jesus, a quest that is considered necessary. A "sanctified restraint" that can and should see Jesus only with the eyes of the believing community, as E. Schweizer was still calling for in 1945, could no longer be maintained.[422] H. Conzelmann speaks of the conversion of indirect into direct Christology such that indirect Christology is the presupposition of direct Christology, and infers from this that "the kerygma itself requires a historical portrayal of the advent of Jesus and his message."[423] The other side of the mutually constitutive relationship between Jesus and the kerygma, as typically understood by the New Quest and its orientation to continuity, is directly named by J. Schneider: "The kerygma of the church, in its main features, goes back to Jesus himself."[424]

For G. Buttler also, whose approach is clearly derived from the kerygma theology, historical study of Jesus is compulsory: "The Christ of the apostolic preaching is the starting point for every quest for the 'historical Jesus.' From that point of departure, the 'historical Jesus' *must* be researched, because the proclaimed Christ is named Jesus of Nazareth."[425]

By virtue of the connection seen by the New Quest between the earthly Jesus and the exalted Lord, the uniqueness of the exalted Lord as seen from a christological perspective is transferred to the earthly, "historical" Jesus. This concept of uniqueness strengthens the tendency to draw a clear dividing line between Jesus and Judaism, since Jesus lived in Judaism among Jews. His uniqueness is made to stand out by giving the historical figure of Jesus a contrasting profile to the Judaism of his time. In his survey of life-of-Jesus theology, Georgi clearly indicates how important this uniqueness was for the New Quest: "For the ordinary individual, especially the great personality, the

---

422. E. Schweizer, in *Kirchenblatt für die reformierte Schweiz*, 1945:204–205. Cited from W. Michaelis, "Notwendigkeit und Grenze der Erörterung von Echtheitsfragen innerhalb des Neuen Testaments," *TLZ* 77 (1952): col. 398.

423. H. Conzelmann, "The Method of the Life-of-Jesus Research," in Carl. E. Braaten and Roy A. Harrisville, eds., *The Historical Jesus and the Kerygmatic Christ: Essays on the New Quest of the Historical Jesus* (Nashville: Abingdon, 1964) 68.

424. J. Schneider, "Der Beitrag der Urgemeinde zur Jesusüberlieferung im Lichte der neuesten Forschung," *TLZ* 87 (1962): 412.

425. G. Buttler, "Das Problem des 'historischen Jesus' im theologischen Gespräch der Gegenwart," *MPTh* 46 (1957): 244.

demarcation of distinctiveness is the necessary dialectical counterpart to continuity. The assertion of Jesus' uniqueness belongs here, especially its intensification by the classification procedure of the history-of-religions school. Thus the majority of non-Jewish scholars in this period still placed value on distancing Jesus from Judaism, although meanwhile the attempt has been made to eliminate the most offensive anti-Semitic remnants of this line of argument based on making Jesus as distinct from Judaism as possible."[426]

Since the New Quest is primarily shaped by the theme of the theological relevance and legitimacy, the methodological discussion did not really begin until later.[427] At the end of the 1960s, and then in the 1970s, this methodological discussion was carried on intensively both in Germany and elsewhere, long after most of the Jesus books emanating from the Bultmann school had been composed.

b) The Criteria in the Discussion

i) The Influence of Form Criticism

Form criticism plays a variety of roles in the discussion of the criterion issue. In the first place, the results of form-critical study of the tradition brought an end to the classical quest of the historical Jesus.[428] Then form criticism was credited with having recognized the authenticity of Jesus' parables.[429] Thus the form-critical method in general was adopted as a criterion for other types of traditional material.[430] But also, as argued by Martin Lehmann, the explicit formulation of criteria and the debate about them within the New Quest can be traced back to the form-critical background of this new phase of research. "The question of criteria was automatically raised by the new correspondence between 'form criticism' and 'the quest of the historical Jesus,' for form criticism—though an indispensable foundation—is not Jesus research in itself. When used in the service of Jesus research, then the necessity of criteria becomes obvious, criteria that will facilitate the separating out of authentic

---

426. D. Georgi, "Leben-Jesu-Theologie/Leben-Jesu-Forschung," 572.

427. In the early 1950s the question of authenticity was already discussed in limited circles. Cf. W. Michaelis, "Notwendigkeit und Grenze."

428. Cf. above, II.2.2.a.ii.

429. Cf. D. Lührmann, "Die Frage nach Kriterien für ursprüngliche Jesusworte. Eine Problemskizze," in *Jésus aux origines de la christologie* (ed. J. Dupont; BETL 40; Leuven: Leuven University Press, 2nd ed., 1989) 63; H. E. W. Turner, *Historicity and the Gospels. A Sketch of Historical Method and its Application to the Gospels* (London: Mowbray, 1963) 76.

430. Conzelmann, "The Method of the Life-of-Jesus Research," 56–60; cf. also P. B. Payne, "The Authenticity of the Parables of Jesus," in R. T. France / D. Wenham, eds., *Gospel Perspectives. Studies of History and Tradition in the Four Gospels*, vol. 2 (Sheffield: JSOT, 1981) 323, for whom Jesus' parables are unique and the high point of rabbinic parable tradition.

Jesus material from within church tradition."[431] However, this formulation may not be misunderstood as if the primary concern were the difference between Jesus material and church tradition. It is rather the case that a relative proximity between the authentic message of Jesus and the preaching of the earliest church was presupposed. In fact, that authentic and inauthentic Jesus tradition were so intertwined in the same stream of tradition that they could be distinguished only by stringent and disciplined methods. In any case, it is only the CDC, not the CDJ, that is here addressed.

Ernst Käsemann, whose criterion of dissimilarity will be discussed below, is himself entirely clear about the fact that his judgment on the issue of the burden of proof is conditioned by his form-critical way of thinking: "With the work of the form critics as a basis, our questioning has sharpened and widened until the obligation now laid upon us is to investigate and make credible not the possible unauthenticity of the individual unit of material but, on the contrary, its genuineness."[432] To be sure, the usefulness of form criticism in Jesus research has its limits, since it is not concerned with "historical individuality." "The only help it can give us here is that it can eliminate as unauthentic anything which must be ruled out of court because of its *Sitz-im-Leben*."[433] A form-critical determination thus results in a negative variation of the CDC: everything that has a discernable *Sitz im Leben* within the Christian community is regarded as *non*authentic.

By way of contrast, the later scholarship of the 1970s raised fundamental questions against the usefulness for Jesus research of form criticism's quest for the *Sitz im Leben*. Morna D. Hooker points out that the *Sitz im Leben* of a unit of tradition as determined by form criticism is not identical with its origin.[434] Traugott Holtz argues similarly: although the content of a tradition is only available to us in a particular form, the content existed apart from any particular form, and the resolution of purely formal questions does not mean that the question of the origin of the content has been solved.[435]

---

431. M. Lehmann, *Synoptische Quellenanalyse und die Frage nach dem historischen Jesus. Kriterien der Jesusforschung untersucht in Auseinandersetzung mit Emanuel Hirschs Frühgeschichte des Evangeliums* (BZNW 38, Berlin: de Gruyter, 1970) 205. Hans Conzelmann points explicitly to the close connection between form criticism and Jesus research when he comments "that form criticism itself originated entirely within the quest for the historical Jesus and the documentary value of the Gospels" (H. Conzelmann, "The Method of the Life-of-Jesus Research," 57).

432. Käsemann, "The Problem of the Historical Jesus," 34.

433. Ibid., 35.

434. M. D. Hooker, "On Using the Wrong Tool," 573.

435. T. Holtz, "Kenntnis von Jesus und Kenntnis Jesu. Eine Skizze zum Verhältnis zwischen historisch-philologischer Erkenntnis und historisch-theologischem Verständnis," *TLZ* 104 (1979): 4.

ii) Ernst Käsemann's Formulation of the Criterion of Dissimilarity and the Discussion of the 1950s[436]

In his pioneering lecture and article with which Ernst Käsemann rang in the New Quest on the basis of the criterion of dissimilarity, he formulated it in the dual form of the CDC and the CDJ, which was then repeatedly cited.[437]

> In only one case do we have more or less safe ground under our feet; when there are no grounds either for deriving a tradition from Judaism or for ascribing it to primitive Christianity, and especially when Jewish Christianity has mitigated or modified the received tradition, as having found it too bold for its taste.[438]

This criterion of dissimilarity is formulated positively, that is, it allows authentic (not inauthentic) material to stand out. Such an orientation of the question results from Käsemann's stance on the issue of the burden of proof: it is authenticity, not inauthenticity, that must be established.[439] Thus, on the one hand, he shares the skepticism that had been brought on by the collapse of previous life-of-Jesus research and by the insights of his exegetical work. On the other hand, the "yes—but" approach of the New Quest becomes clear in the confidence he expresses in being able to locate "authentic" material. The supplementary statement referring to Jewish Christianity is conspicuous. The CDJ, which is to be understood in the sense of the history-of-religions school ("neither derived from Judaism") and the CDC based on source analysis ("not attributed to early Christianity") now receives a supplementary CDJ based on source analysis. The CDC is at least partially defined as CDJ, for the demarcation from *Jewish* Christianity is indirectly a demarcation from Judaism. The effect is a methodologically determined intensification of the separation of Jesus from Judaism and/or from the basic elements of Jewish theology. This accent in particular is taken up by F. Hahn in his 1960 rendering of Käsemann's criterion, when he emphasizes that through Jesus the framework of Jewish

---

436. Biographical data for exegetes of the recent past and the present will no longer be given. The dates refer to the statement or quotation, and facilitate their location of the full citation in the Appendix.

437. H. Conzelmann, *Jesus* (trans. J. Raymond Lord; ed. John Reumann. Philadelphia: Fortress Press, 1973) 16. Originally "Jesus Christ," *RGG*[3] (1959): col. 623. Conzelmann's important article gave widespread circulation to this criterion of dissimilarity in Käsemann's sense and designates it as the methodological principle for the reconstruction of Jesus' *teaching*.

438. Käsemann, "The Problem of the Historical Jesus," 37.

439. This connection is clearly seen in Norman Perrin's especially important formulation of the criterion of dissimilarity for English-language readership (N. Perrin, *Rediscovering the Teaching of Jesus* [New York: Harper & Row, 1967]) 39.

thought has been decisively broken.[440] Käsemann, of course, adds a qualification to his own formulation:

> But in so doing we must realize beforehand that we shall not, from this angle of vision, gain any clear view of the connecting link between Jesus, his Palestinian environment and his later community. . . . However, it is even more important for us to gain some insight into what separated him from friends and foes alike.[441]

This final qualification makes one sit up and take notice. It could indicate that what is sought by means of the double-sided criterion of dissimilarity is not the "authentic" but the "important" (in the sense of the essential). As we have seen, at the beginning of the twentieth century a consensus congealed on the matter of criteria that said that the authentic elements in the Jesus tradition will be found in demarcating it over against early Christianity, but the essential in these authentic traditions will be found in demarcating them over against Judaism. In the middle of the century, the center of gravity shifted: the demarcation over against Judaism, the CDJ, which also overlapped the CDC in the form of a demarcation over against Jewish Christianity, became the decisive criterion of authenticity. This was possible because a hermeneutical presupposition had been changed: the model of the "genial and heroic personality," which had left its traditional context behind, was replaced by the theological concept of the kerygma that transcended the boundaries of everything human. The "genial personality" must be integrated into history; the kerygma "from above" can radically break into history: Jesus drops out of the Jewish context.

While the demarcation over against Judaism is becoming the decisive criterion of authenticity, there is a certain tendency to explain the elements of continuity with Christianity as belonging to the "essential:" the whole energy of historical Jesus research is now concentrated on finding points of contact for the "kerygmatic Christ" of early Christianity with the "historical Jesus." "Implied Christology" becomes an essential element in the message of Jesus. The first objections against the double-sided criterion of dissimilarity were thus aimed more at relativizing the demarcation over against Christianity than the contrast to Judaism. Peter Biehl, among others, objected that the criterion of dissimilarity in this dual form as formulated by Käsemann would make it impossible to understand the transition from proclaimer to proclaimed.[442] This interest of Biehl, typical of those New Questers who followed the

---

440. Hahn, "Die Frage nach dem historischen Jesus," 38.
441. Käsemann, "The Problem of the Historical Jesus," 37.
442. P. Biehl, "Zur Frage nach dem historischen Jesus," *TRu* 24 (1957/58): 56.

kerygma theology, appears to be of less importance, since he emphasizes the importance of the material that separates Jesus from both opponents and friends. However, Käsemann is also concerned with continuity, which is missed by Biehl. For the Käsemann who has been shaped by dialectical theology, this continuity of the gospel is found precisely in the character of the material discontinuity of the gospel in relation to its environment, in the sense of a connection that transcends time and the Easter event. As Jesus was discontinuous with his environment, the church was discontinuous with its environment, and this corresponding discontinuity, though with different contents, is the continuity that binds together Jesus and the church—not a material continuity, but an analogous discontinuity with their respective contexts. Thus also from a theological point of view it is less important for Käsemann to be exercised about what Jesus shared with either his Jewish context or the first Christian community.

The Scandinavian New Testament scholar Nils Alstrup Dahl adopts Käsemann's criterion of dissimilarity with still a different accent. Dahl accepts the criterion, but with the condition that the material discovered by this means represents only "a critically-assured *minimum*."[443] He identifies the historical Jesus' way to the cross as the beginning of the separation of Judaism and Christianity. He thus presupposes that Jesus was firmly embedded in his Jewish context, but at the same time, Dahl also understands the New Testament's Jesus tradition, as transformed by early Christianity, as "a *maximum* that contains everything of importance for our historical knowledge about Jesus."[444] This assertion not only emphasizes a fundamental continuity from Jesus to early Christianity; it also reflects a decidedly theological-historical approach over against an approach oriented to secular historical method.

iii) The Continuing Discussion of Criteria

The continuing debate about criteria cannot be placed in a clear chronological framework, except to note that the discussion's center of gravity is found in the 1960s and 1970s. In the 1980s a new phase of research begins with the Third Quest, but contributions to the previous discussion within the New Quest continued into the 1990s, untouched and/or unmotivated by the newer developments. In general, it can be said that the 1960s' discussion of the criterion of dissimilarity was characterized by a tendentious and critical agreement. For the most part, Käsemann's formulation served as the reference point. Only Charles F. D. Moule returned explicitly to P. W. Schmiedel's CDC

---

443. Dahl, "The Problem of the Historical Jesus," 97.
444. Ibid.

(1967).[445] Criticism intensified in the 1970s, especially in English-language publications, so that one can certainly already recognize here forerunners of the Third Quest, but energetic champions of a strict criterion of dissimilarity in its dual form also spoke out in the following years.

In the discussion that follows, we present the formulations of the criterion of dissimilarity cited in the Appendix, and conclude with a summary of the critical responses it evoked.

1. *Variations from the strictly dual form of the criterion of dissimilarity.* Frequent mention was made of the stringency or rigor of the criterion of dissimilarity, and a plea was made for a more moderate version. This was especially the case when the criterion of dissimilarity was applied negatively and understood as a "classification criterion," as by Harvey K. McArthur (1964)[446], Reginald Fuller (1965),[447] and Howard M. Teeple (1965).[448] Such a negative utilization implies a basic judgment about inauthenticity, while the positive utilization leaves open the question of whether nondistinctive elements in the tradition are authentic or not. Thus H. Schürmann was justified in his 1975 demand: "There is an urgent need for an additional investigation of the 'residue' left by the classification principle." Others see in this nonexcluding application of the criterion of dissimilarity its only legitimate utilization:[449] it is only in this limited manner that N. J. McEleney (1972) can consider the "criterion of difference"—he is speaking of the CDC—to be a tool that promises any positive results.[450] D. L. Mealand (1978) and R. Riesner (1981) reject it as a negative "classification criterion."[451] The study of D. G. A. Calvert divides all criteria into positive and negative categories, and likewise comes to the conclusion that all negative forms of the CDC are worthless.[452] He bases this conclusion on

445. C. F. D. Moule, *The Phenomenon of the New Testament. An Inquiry into the Implications of Certain Features of the New Testament* (SBT 2nd Series 1. London: SCM Press, 1967) 62.

446. H. K. McArthur, "Basic Issues. A Survey of Recent Gospel Research," *Interpretation* 18 (1964): 50.

447. R. H. Fuller, *The Foundations of New Testament Christology* (London: Lutterworth, 1965) 18.

448. For H. M. Teeple, however, coherence with the Palestinian context is also important ("The Origin of the Son of Man Christology," *JBL* 84 [1965]: 219).

449. H. Schürmann, *Jesu ureigener Tod. Exegetische Besinnungen und Ausblick* (Freiburg-Basel-Wien: Herder, 1975) 23.

450. N. J. McEleney, "Authenticating Criteria and Mark 7:1–23," *CBQ* 34 (1972): 442.

451. D. L. Mealand, "The Dissimilarity Test," *SJT* 31 (1978): 43; R. Riesner, *Jesus als Lehrer: Eine Untersuchung zum Ursprung der Evangelien-Überlieferung* (WUNT II, 7; Tübingen: Mohr, 1981) 91.

452. Calvert, "An Examination of the Criteria," 211ff.

our lack of knowledge of Judaism and the early church.[453] Of course, this argument can be applied only to the negative form of the criterion of dissimilarity in which agreement with either the early church or Judaism means classifying the tradition as inauthentic. We could evaluate differently the cases where there is difference from Judaism and church only by adopting a monolithic concept of both of the historical realities (Judaism and early Christianity) and by overestimating how completely we know each of them.

The call for the investigation of the "residue" remaining after separating out the "authentic" materials by means of the criterion of dissimilarity does not necessarily avoid the implication that the reconstruction of the historical figure of Jesus should be based on his presumably "different" characteristic features. This implication depends on the extent to which the investigation relies on that minimal stock of material separated out by the criterion of dissimilarity. Two clearly different positions are assumed in this regard by Dahl and Zahrnt: for Dahl the criterion of dissimilarity is only one means among others,[454] while for Zahrnt the minimum established by the criterion of dissimilarity becomes itself the standard by which the rest of the tradition is measured.[455]

If one rejects the criterion of dissimilarity when it functions negatively to sort out inauthentic material, there are three possible ways in which its rigor may be moderated: one can either downplay the contrast of the Jesus tradition to both sides of its context—to Judaism and Christianity—or one can one-sidedly emphasize a (greater) connection with early Christianity or a (greater) continuity with Judaism.

The first possibility is found in the work of Howard C. Kee (1979). He alleges that the criterion of dissimilarity—as formulated by E. Käsemann—is a *via negativa* on both sides of the issue and thus designates it as a weak criterion. He therefore strengthens the continuity of Jesus with both Judaism and Christianity.[456]

The second possibility is advocated by H. W. W. Turner and O. Cullmann. Turner (1963) regards the rigor of the criterion of dissimilarity to be an inherent limitation of its applicability. He reckons with overlapping interests in authentic Jesus material and its use in the church. By being able to distinguish

---

453. Cf. also R. S. Barbour, *Traditio-Historical Criticism of the Gospels. Some Comments on Current Methods* (SCC 4; London: SPCK, 1972) 7; and M. D. Hooker, "Christology and Methodology," *NTS* 17 (1970/71): 482.

454. Dahl, "The Problem of the Historical Jesus," 97.

455. H. Zahrnt, *Es begann mit Jesus von Nazareth* (Stuttgart: Kreuz, 1960) 119. On the importance of such a procedure with regard to content, see below 3 "The Problem of Historical Plausibility".

456. H. C. Kee, *Jesus in History: An Approach to the Study of the Gospels* (New York: Harcourt, 1970) 264ff.

different levels in the way the same theme is handled, he believes he is able to recognize the historical Jesus. He pleads for a refined, discriminating version of the CDC—but against the background of a basic continuity.[457] While Oskar Cullmann (1960) accepts the results of studies that operate with the criterion of dissimilarity, he warns against drawing conclusions from it that are too far-reaching. He thus reckons with the same theological concerns in the earliest church as were present in Jesus' ministry. Evidence of a "church tendency" is itself thus insufficient for a negative judgment about authenticity. Only additional evidence that a particular Jesus tradition does not fit within the framework of Jesus' own situation, or that it corresponds to the obvious general rules of legendary development, makes such a judgment of inauthenticity plausible.[458]

The third possibility of moderating the rigor of the criterion of dissimilarity consists of emphasizing the continuity between Judaism and Jesus. W. Marxsen (1960) begins by first pointing out the limitations of our ability to recognize the boundary between Jesus and the early church. He gives good reason to reflect on the fact that the criterion of dissimilarity in its dual form and positive application (he is referring to H. Conzelmann), while it can yield material that is not at home either in Judaism or in the later Christian church, may still point to material that derives not from Jesus but from the earliest Christian community.[459] Marxsen sees, at the same time, the proximity of Jesus to Judaism and criticizes a possible negative application of the CDJ, as though Jewish material could never be from Jesus. If one wanted to transform Marxsen's reflections on the problems of the criterion of dissimilarity into a formulation that represents his own criteria, it might read as follows: "That which we cannot derive from early Christianity does not necessarily come from Jesus. But if at the same time it can be derived from Judaism, then it could be from Jesus." John G. Gager (1974) presents the problematic involved in the formulation of criteria more simply. Since the Jesus tradition was transmitted by *Christians*, he rejects the CDJ and considers only the CDC as relevant (he obviously does not consider the factor of Jewish Christian tradents).[460]

---

457. H. E. W. Turner, *Historicity and the Gospels. A Sketch of Historical Method and its Application to the Gospels* (London: Mowbray, 1963) 74. (Appendix 1963).

458. O. Cullmann, "Out of Season Remarks on the 'Historical Jesus' of the Bultmann School," *USQR* 16, no. 2 (1961): 154–55.

459. W. Marxsen, *The Beginnings of Christology: A Study in its Problems* (trans. Paul J. Achtemeier; Facet Books Biblical Series 22; Philadelphia: Fortress Press, 1969) 14–15. Similarly also E. Schillebeeckx, *Jesus: An Experiment in Christology* (trans. Hubert Hoskins; New York: Crossroad, 1979) 92–93.

460. J. G. Gager, "The Gospels and Jesus: Some Doubts about Method," *JR* 54 (1974): 81.

2. Variations of the criterion of dissimilarity with regard to the burden of proof. E. Käsemann connected his formulation of the criterion of dissimilarity with an unambiguous "rule about the burden of proof." The circumstances with regard to source analysis and the state of scholarship have presumably resulted in a situation in which "the obligation now laid upon us is to investigate and make credible not the possible unauthenticity of the individual unit of material but, on the contrary, its genuineness."[461] This situation is not a matter of a general scholarly principle of scientific research that is valid independently of the concrete situation with regard to sources but of one that is directly dependent on how this state of source analysis is evaluated. Four possibilities may be distinguished: (a) If the tradition is in general to be trusted, then inauthenticity is to be proved. (b) If the tradition in general is considered untrustworthy, then authenticity must be proved. (c) If parts of the tradition are considered trustworthy, but not all, then the burden of proof can vary depending on what part of the tradition is being considered. (d) The final possibility is that we are uncertain as to whether there is any justification for a general trust or mistrust of the tradition as a whole. This uncertainty suggests a dual form of the "rule of the burden of proof": Both the authenticity and the inauthenticity require arguments before a decision can be made. In the discussion that followed Käsemann's proposal, all four positions found their advocates.

(a) The first position, which insists on a reversal of Käsemann's rule about the burden of proof, was argued in the most nuanced manner by W. G. Kümmel (1974): the Jesus tradition in general deserves "critical sympathy/support," since all historical documents require some reason for preliminary confidence in their credibility in order to interpret them properly, and in the special case of the Jesus tradition the interest of the earliest church in the historical Jesus justifies such a preliminary confidence, but in a way that does not exclude further critical investigation.[462]

(b) In contrast, the second position, advocated by Käsemann himself, struck the most responsive chord. It became almost the consensus position within German language scholarship. J. Sauer made a final emphatic plea for this position (1991): the earliest church had already created new traditional material or secondarily ascribed current materials to Jesus. Only a "healthy mistrust" can keep us from combining the historical Jesus with the image of Jesus in a particular Christian community.[463]

(c) The third position is advocated by H. K. McArthur (1970–1971). He wants to shift the burden of proof depending on which source or com-

---

461. E. Käsemann, "The Problem of the Historical Jesus," 34.

462. W. G. Kümmel, "Jesu Antwort an Johannes den Täufer," 177–200.

463. J. Sauer, *Rückkehr und Vollendung des Heils. Eine Untersuchung zu den ethischen Radikalismen Jesu* (Theorie und Forschung 133; Philosophie und Theologie 9. Regensburg: S. Roderer, 1991) 81–84.

bination of sources one is dealing with: when a motif is documented by three or four Synoptic sources, then it is the inauthenticity that must be demonstrated. That which is found in only one or two sources must be considered inauthentic unless convincing authenticity can be presented.[464] McArthur thus makes the burden of proof dependent only on the criterion of multiple attestation. One could, however, extend his suggestion to all arguments that depend on the evaluation of sources: the more that general arguments (such as age, local color, multiple attestation in independent traditions) speak for a preliminary confidence in a source or tradition, the more it is the inauthenticity and not the authenticity that must be proven.

(d) The final position probably corresponds most closely to the unclear status of contemporary research. According to M. D. Hooker (1970–1971) the burden of proof rests on whomever wants to make a case for his or her position. A pedigree must be produced for every logion, regardless of whether it is traced back to Jesus or to the early church.[465]

3. *Variations with regard to the respective goals of the criterion of dissimilarity and Jesus research.* "In the tradition of the *proclamation* of Jesus . . . the medium of transmission is identical with the medium of what is transmitted, so that the tradition *from* Jesus can preserve the word *of Jesus.*"[466] This observation of Dieter Lührmann points to the maximal goal in the application of the criterion of dissimilarity, to the goal of finding ipsissima verba of Jesus.[467] Most exegetes have backed away from this goal. Instead of thinking in terms of the alternatives "authentic" or "church formulation," Ferdinand Hahn reckons in most cases with "mixed formations."[468] For Christoph Burchard (1967), "only substantial authenticity, not authenticity in the exact form, can be proven."[469] Thus here the goal is no longer Jesus' exact words (ipsissima verba), but the "very voice" (*ipsissima vox*) of Jesus—the typical ideas, motifs, and expressions of his message. Many go even further: thus instead of the *ipsissima vox,*

---

464. H. K. McArthur, "The Burden of Proof in Historical Jesus Research," *ExpTim* 82 (1970/1): 116–19.

465. Hooker, "Christology and Methodology," 485–486; "On Using the Wrong Tool," 580. So also Barbour, *Traditio-Historical Criticism,* 11.

466. Lührmann, "Die Frage nach Kriterien," 64–65.

467. R. H. Stein ("The 'Criteria' for Authenticity," in R. T. France and D. Wenham, eds., *Gospel Perspectives. Studies of History and Tradition in the Four Gospels,* vol. 1 [Sheffield: JSOT, 1980] 244) considers the criterion of dissimilarity to be "a most valuable tool in the quest for the *ipsissima verba* or *vox* of Jesus."

468. F. Hahn, "Methodologische Überlegungen zur Rückfrage nach Jesus," in K. Kertelge, ed. *Rückfrage nach Jesus. Zur Methodik und Bedeutung der Frage nach dem historischen Jesus* (QD 63; Freiburg-Basel-Wien: Herder, 1974) 29.

469. Burchard, "Jesus," 1346.

W. Thüsing looks for the "*ipsissima intentio.*"[470] Anton Vögtle speaks incidentally of a "sense of direction of the ministry of Jesus taken as a whole."[471] Such considerations lead Heinz Schürmann to call for keeping in view the life and fate of Jesus as a whole.[472] Gerhard Dautzenberg makes a similar appeal (1979).[473] Christoph Demke (1976) formulates this appeal into a criterion: that material is most likely authentic "in which Jesus' words and his conduct go in the same direction."[474] Such a way of seeing the matter boils down to making a coherent image of the figure of Jesus as a whole into an overriding criterion. This view had already been made a supplementary criterion to the CDC by Werner Georg Kümmel in 1963 and strengthened in 1969, when he speaks of the resulting image of Jesus taken as a whole as the decisive control for the process of exclusion of inauthentic Jesus material from consideration.[475]

4. *The spectrum viewpoints in how "difference" is understood.* The criterion of dissimilarity has many names. But what constitutes "difference" (or "dissimilarity") is understood in a variety of ways. Heinz Zahrnt (1960) speaks of what is "not derivable" from the Jewish context or from early Christian thought.[476] More sharply focused on the contrast with Judaism is Eduard Lohse's formulation that speaks of that which cannot be derived from early Christian preaching or from the *presuppositions* of first-century Judaism. Strictly understood, this formulation implies a Jesus with no historical presuppositions at all, since Lohse, of course, does not locate Jesus in non-Jewish Hellenism rather than Judaism.[477] Walter Simonis (1985) describes the matter such that it is precisely

---

470. W. Thüsing, "Neutestamentliche Zugangswege zu einer transzendental-dialogischen Christologie," in K. Rahner and W. Thüsing, *Christologie—systematisch und exegetisch. Arbeitsgrundlagen für eine interdisziplinäre Vorlesung* (Freiburg: Herder, 1972) 183.

471. A. Vögtle, "Jesus von Nazareth," in A. Benoît et al., eds., *Ökumenische Kirchengeschichte*, vol. 1 *Alte Kirche und Ostkirche* (4th ed. Mainz: Grünewald und Munich: Kaiser, 1983; 1st ed., 1970) 23.

472. Schürmann, *Jesu ureigener Tod*, 25ff.

473. G. Dautzenberg, "Der Wandel der Reich-Gottes-Verkündigung in der urchristlichen Mission," in G. Dautzenberg et al., eds., *Zur Geschichte des Urchristentums* (QD 87; Freiburg: Herder, 1979) 14–15.

474. C. Demke, *Im Blickpunkt: Die Einzigartigkeit Jesu. Theologische Informationen für Nichttheologen* (Berlin: Evangelische Verlagsanstalt, 1976) 63.

475. W. G. Kümmel, "Der persönliche Anspruch Jesu und der Christusglaube der Urgemeinde (1963)," in W. G. Kümmel, *Heilsgeschehen und Geschichte. Ges. Aufs. 1933-1964* (Marburg: Elwert, 1965) 432; Kümmel, *The Theology of the New Testament. According to Its Major Witnesses, Jesus—Paul—John* (trans. John E. Steely. Nashville: Abingdon, 1973) 26.

476. H. Zahrnt, *Es begann mit Jesus von Nazareth* (Stuttgart: Kreuz, 1960) 118.

477. E. Lohse, "Die Frage nach dem historischen Jesus in der gegenwärtigen neutestamentlichen Forschung," *TLZ* 87 (1962): 168.

the task of the criterion of dissimilarity to trace out elements *"with no positive analogy"* (in Judaism or Christianity).[478] Proceeding on the basis of the exalted status of the sayings of Jesus, for the Roman Catholic New Testament scholar Klaus Gamber, "[S]ayings of Jesus . . . could not have been invented."[479]

In contrast, Norman Perrin (1970) formulates a somewhat weaker version of the goal of the criterion of dissimilarity. It is intended to reveal "what is distinctive in Judaism or the church,"[480] that is, what can be distinguished *within* Judaism as distinctive. Here another problem of the criterion of dissimilarity becomes clear, namely, the vagueness of the terms "difference," "distinctive," or "dissimilar" (assuming that radical underivability is not meant). In view of the fact that Jesus must necessarily have used human language and concepts, the question of what degree of similarity to or difference from the language and concepts of his time is necessary before one speaks of difference/distinction/similarity cannot be answered.[481]

Behind the discussion of the criterion of dissimilarity, there stands a problem of the content with which the issue is concerned: To what extent is the history of Jesus a unique phenomenon within history? Two different formulations with decisively different nuances point to the problem: Leonhard Goppelt (1975) speaks not of difference, but of specific features from the point of view of the study of the history of religions, which he explicitly does not equate with religious uniqueness.[482] For the New Testament scholar René Latourelle, everything is still illumined by the idea of uniqueness: "[T]he unique Jesus of Nazareth" is connected with the singularity of the gospel genre.[483]

This emphasis on the uniqueness of Jesus expresses a particular way of dealing with history that has been energetically advocated by some Bible scholars, including New Testament specialists. It is quite interesting that, in the course of making a general critique of the historical-critical method, claims are made from within conservative circles that ultimately correspond to a rigorous criterion of dissimilarity. Martin Hengel argues (1973) that in dealing with biblical history, one must reckon with the possibility of "events for which there is

---

478. W. Simonis, *Jesus von Nazareth. Seine Botschaft vom Reich Gottes und der Glaube der Urgemeinde. Historisch-kritische Erhellung der Ursprünge des Urchristentums* (Düsseldorf: Patmos, 1985) 26.

479. K. Gamber, *Jesus-Worte. Eine vorkanonische Logiensammlung im Lukas-Evangelium* (StPatrLtg Beiheft 9; Regensburg: Pustet, 1983) 7.

480. N. Perrin, *What is Redaction Criticism?* (Philadelphia: Fortress Press, 1969) 71.

481. Cf. Barbour, *Traditio-Historical Criticism*, 8; McArthur, "Basic Issues," 50.

482. L. Goppelt, *Theology of the New Testament*, 1:13.

483. R. Latourelle, "Critères d'authenticité historique des Évangiles," *Greg* 55 (1974): 622.

no analogy."[484] A similar defensive position toward secular historical science is taken by Gerhard Maier (1974), who also expects to find in the biblical realm "what happens *only once*—the thing that cannot be analogized."[485] It is under these presuppositions that the most rigorous formulation of the criterion of dissimilarity known to us is made, namely by the evangelical New Testament scholar R. T. France (1976): : "If anyone else in the world of the New Testament could have said the saying in question, it cannot be taken as a saying of Jesus."[486]

In this extreme position it becomes clear that already in the understanding of "dissimilarity," even before it becomes a matter of theological function, fundamental decisions about how history may be understood have been brought into play. The understanding of "difference" in the sense of "without any analogy" and "underivable" from the presuppositions of the historical context cannot be carried through with regard to a figure who is to be understood historically. This is true because historical understanding occurs by means of "correlations."[487] "The wholly unique would be totally incomprehensible."[488] Thus Dahl (1976) insists on the embedding of the criterion of dissimilarity in "historical considerations of synchronic similarity and diachronic continuity."[489] It is only in the course of the Third Quest that these initial impulses are brought fully into play.[490]

5. *The theological function of the "difference:" The uniqueness of the figure of Jesus.* The criterion of dissimilarity in its function of historical reconstruction also has a notable theological dimension. It depends on the general significance that is given to the material assembled under the heading of "dissimilar:" Is it the pivotal point for understanding Jesus, or merely one point among others? In the theological discussion, there is often an unacknowledged inclination to

---

484. M. Hengel, "Historische Methoden und theologische Auslegung des Neuen Testaments," *KuD* 19 (1973): 86.

485. G. Maier, *The End of the Historical-Critical Method* (trans. Edwin W. Leverenz and Rudolf F. Norden; St. Louis: Concordia Publishing House, 1974) 51.

486. R. T. France, "The Authenticity of Jesus' Sayings," in C. Brown, ed. *History, Criticism, and Faith* (Downer's Grove, Ill., 1976) 109.

487. H. Schürmann, "Kritische Jesuserkenntnis. Zur kritischen Handhabung des 'Unähnlichkeitskriteriums'," *BiLi* 54 (1981): 19.

488. Barbour, *Traditio-Historical Criticism*, 8.

489. N. A. Dahl, "The Early Church and Jesus," in *Jesus in the Memory of the Early Church* (Minneapolis: Augsburg, 1976) 172. Cf. also the term "evolutionary continuity" in David R. Catchpole, "Tradition History," in I. H. Marshall, ed. *New Testament Interpretation. Essays on Principles and Methods* (Exeter: Paternoster, 1977) 177.

490. E.g., (as already clear from the title) A.E. Harvey, *Jesus and the Constraints of History. The Bampton Lectures, 1980* (London: Duckworth, 1982).

identify the historically authentic with the essential, to consider the essential element in Jesus as the historically unique, and to consider the unique to be an indication of divine revelation. Eduard Lohse, in a 1961 lecture, is clear about the fact that the positive application of the criterion of dissimilarity in its dual form does not exclude the proximity of Jesus to either Judaism or Christianity. It is nonetheless the case that Lohse's goal is not so much a broad historical reconstruction, but the quest for Jesus' *own* message.[491] He is thus basically looking for the *essential* element in Jesus' message!

This position is clearly formulated more rigorously, especially in the demarcation over against Judaism, in the formulation of Kurt Niederwimmer in his Jesus book of 1968. For Niederwimmer, whatever Jesus may have shared with Judaism is a peripheral matter for understanding Jesus' own work. The specifically significant elements for understanding Jesus are rather those elements without any analogy in Judaism, namely, those that separate the church (!) from Judaism. Niederwimmer's quest for the Jesus-specific elements is oriented to conflict theory as an approach to historical effects. He regards the death of Jesus on the cross (understood as the rejection of Jesus by Judaism) and the departure of Christian groups from Judaism as the decisive historical effects to be explained.[492] The image of "difference" understood in terms of conflict thus permeates Niederwimmer's perception of the historical figure of Jesus. Therefore for him the CDJ is *the* method of distinguishing those elements of the Jesus tradition that he has decided in advance are most important and relevant. He, too, is looking for the "essential" Jesus—by which he means the Jesus who generates conflict.

A similar view was advocated by Herbert Braun in his Jesus book of the following year (1969). Like Niederwimmer, he concentrated on the CDJ and decided in advance that while a Jewish element in the Jesus tradition could be authentic, it could not be typical of Jesus—the typical element in Jesus is that which distinguishes him from Judaism. Then Braun adds an interesting nuance, in which the idea of the CDC could stand in the background: that which is not derivable from Judaism in terms of its content, but is formulated in a Jewish manner, is "with great probability" an authentic saying of Jesus.[493] This refinement of the criterion by concentrating on its content thus means that, in terms of form, the analogy of Jesus to the people of his time is conceded and that formal agreement with Judaism counts as a criterion. The decisive

---

491. E. Lohse, "Die Frage nach dem historischen Jesus in der gegenwärtigen neutestamentlichen Forschung," *TLZ* 87 (1962): 168.

492. K. Niederwimmer, *Jesus* (Göttingen: Vandenhoeck & Ruprecht, 1968) 25–26.

493. H. Braun, *Jesus of Nazareth: The Man and His Time* (trans. Everett R. Kalin. Philadelphia: Fortress Press, 1979) 29–30.

element, however, has to do with the content, and here the CDJ is applied with full force. This position becomes clear in Dietz Lange (1975): "[H]e [sc. Jesus] was not a literary person, and his originality was not a matter of form, but of content."[494] Rainer Riesner (1981) argues in the same manner when he considers *criticism* of the Torah in a semitizing linguistic form to be probably authentic.[495] Here the criterion of dissimilarity serves to distinguish form and content. Once again, this criterion is basically used to discover the "essential."

Critique of the criterion of dissimilarity has been directed primarily against this equation of "what is different" or "what is distinctive" with "typical," "essential," "characteristic," and "central."[496] In the historical quest in terms of content, an interpretation has been adopted that presupposes a historical judgment on the part of the historian: Jesus' *own* preaching, in the sense of his characteristic message, was different from the thought world of both early Christianity and Judaism. Thus R. S. Barbour (1972) thinks that the use of the criterion of dissimilarity already implies a hypothesis about the historical Jesus.[497] Strictly understood, of course, this idea is no critique of the criterion of dissimilarity itself, but of the interpretation of its results based on this historical hypothesis.[498] On its part, it rests on a particular ideal of "personality" (cf. above II.1.3.b). In this view, the appropriate access to Jesus is opened up by grasping the ingenious essence of his great historical personality. In this understanding, this essence must necessarily be uniquely different.[499] The

---

494. D. Lange, *Historischer Jesus oder mythischer Christus*, 310. This is not a matter of his own original exegetical work, but Lange here expresses—perhaps all the more clearly—a principle adopted from New Testament scholarship.

495. Riesner, *Jesus als Lehrer*, 91. For W. Trilling, in contrast, Jesus' style as a whole "could not have been invented" and was "without parallel"(*Fragen zur Geschichtlichkeit Jesu* [Düsseldorf: Patmos, 1966]). Latourelle, "Critères d'authenticité" (1974), 622, describes this style as unique and inimitable.

496. The tendency to make this equation has been criticized with particular clarity and sharpness by M. D. Hooker, "On Using the Wrong Tool," 574–575. Cf. also J. Gager, "The Gospels and Jesus" (1974), 257; Catchpole, "Tradition History" (1977), 174; F. Mussner, et al., "Methodologie der Frage nach dem historischen Jesus," in Kertelge, ed., *Rückfrage nach Jesus. Zur Methodik und Bedeutung der Frage nach dem historischen Jesus*, 132.

497. Barbour, *Traditio-Historical Criticism*, 19.

498. It was only in the course of the Third Quest that a consistent change of direction was made on the matter of criteriology, in which correspondence with Judaism forms the direct anticriterion of the criterion of dissimilarity.

499. Academic discussion among secular historians has ridiculed such a procedure that seeks after the most specific indications of individuality possible: according to Max Weber, even in the case of Bismarck—the typical example of a "great personality"—such an indication is merely the thumbprint (cited according to K.-G. Faber, *Theorie der Geschichtswissenschaft* (2nd ed.; Munich: Beck, 1972) 60.

connection between the criterion of dissimilarity and the ideal of "personality" comes to light here once again. In their critique of the criterion of dissimilarity, Luise Schottroff and Wolfgang Stegemann (1978) thus rightly refer to the "lonely pedestal of the heroic genius" as the result of the application of the criterion of dissimilarity.[500]

Independently of this historically conditioned personality ideal, however, it is also true that the quest for what was "essential" about Jesus has its own way of posing the question: that which is described as characteristic for Jesus' preaching is also that which is considered important for the present. The quest for "Jesus" is clearly bound up with the quest for the *uniqueness* of the Christian faith and becomes "the question of what Christianity originally and essentially is."[501]

The uniqueness of Jesus serves to bring him nearer to *us* by the emphasis on his distance to the worlds of Judaism and early Christianity that are foreign to *us*.[502] In addition, the presumed discontinuity of Jesus to the history that preceded him and his foreignness in the world suggest the individualistic-existentialist "understanding of existence"[503] of the theology of the Bultmann school. And finally, the assertion of Jesus' uniqueness historicizes the christological dogma of the singularity of Jesus Christ.[504] This also then serves as a self-justification of critical exegesis (with its tradition of criticism of dogma!) in response to ecclesiastical questions.

6. *Summary of the critique of the criterion of dissimilarity.* Criticism of the criterion of dissimilarity has concentrated on the following points:

1. The term "difference" ("dissimilarity," "inderivability," "inconceivability") is not clear.
2. The use of the criterion of dissimilarity is burdened with the idea of the unique personality adopted from the philosophy of history. Thus *distinctive* material is sometimes confused with that which is *typical* and *essential* for understanding the historical figure of Jesus.
3. In view of the fact that the Jesus tradition is a *Christian* tradition, the CDJ cannot be made plausible.
4. Our lack of knowledge about Judaism and early Christianity makes any comparative judgment about "dissimilarity" more difficult.

---

500. L. Schottroff and W. Stegemann, *Jesus and the Hope of the Poor.* (trans. Matthew J. O'Connell. Maryknoll, N. Y.: Orbis Books, 1986) 2.

501. Lührmann, "Die Frage nach Kriterien," 72; cf. also Koch, *The Rediscovery of Apocalyptic*, 117–18, 127–29.

502. Cf. also Dahl, "The Early Church and Jesus," 168.

503. Cf. Barbour, *Traditio-Historical Criticism*, 15.

504. Similarly Barbour, Ibid., 34, who speaks of a historical and metaphysical grounding of the kerygma by means of the criterion of dissimilarity.

5. The criterion of dissimilarity per se conflicts with the double demand for locating the historical Jesus within the Judaism of his day and for locating the effects of his life within the history of the beginning of Christianity. Wherever this demand is made, we are already among the forerunners of the Third Quest.

c) The Criterion of Dissimilarity and the Picture of Jesus in the Work of Günther Bornkamm (1905–1990)

In the preceding section on the motives and criteria of the New Quest, we see clear tendencies toward emphasizing the continuity between Jesus and Christianity while at the same time emphasizing the discontinuity between Jesus and Judaism. These tendencies can also be seen, for example, in the Jesus books of Herbert Braun, Heinz Zahrnt, and Kurt Niederwimmer. We now turn to the work of Günther Bornkamm in order to investigate more precisely the use and function of the criterion of dissimilarity in the question of how authentic materials are determined and the way Jesus is portrayed. While it is true that Bornkamm did not address the question of criteria directly, his Jesus book is the outstanding example of the New Quest within the Bultmann school. *Jesus of Nazareth*, which appeared in 1956, belonged to the standard works on Jesus for three decades both within the world of theologians and among the general public, and it was also widely circulated in non-German-speaking lands.[505]

Five years before the appearance of his Jesus book, Bornkamm made a critical contribution against Bultmann to the discussion of demythologization: "Jesus Christ has become the mere saving event, and has ceased to be a person. He himself no longer has a history."[506] Bornkamm's Jesus book wants to realize the equation formulated in the first chapter: "Jesus Christ—no other than the rabbi from Nazareth, whose earthly history began in Galilee...."[507] Because it is a matter of this earthly history taken as a whole, his Jesus book does not concentrate on the message of Jesus alone. With sections on Jesus' disciples and Jesus' way to Jerusalem, he also goes into the life of Jesus and is indebted to the Gospel narratives (and not just the sayings tradition).

Bornkamm is concerned with history, because of his concern with *this* Jesus of Nazareth—thus the title of the book. His goal is not the historical legitimization of the kerygma, but an understanding of the historical side of the

---

505. Fourteen editions in Germany, translations in ten languages. In the following, when citations occur that correspond to the English translation of the third edition (*Jesus of Nazareth*. [trans. Irene and Fraser McLuskey with James M. Robinson; New York: Harper & Row, 1960]), the wording of that translation is followed. When later editions are cited, the translation is by M. Eugene Boring.

506. G. Bornkamm, "Evangelium und Mythos," *ZdZ* 5 (1951): 9.

507. G. Bornkamm, *Jesus of Nazareth*, 16.

kerygma. The task to which his book is addressed is to find the history *in* the kerygma of the Gospels and the kerygma in this history: "If we are asked to differentiate between the two, that is only for the purpose of revealing more clearly their interconnection and inter-penetration."[508] Thus Bornkamm completely typifies that primary interest of the New Quest that J. M. Robinson has located in the overlap of Jesus and the kerygma.[509] The "quest for the material convergence of the story of Jesus and the message of the Christ" is central for Bornkamm.[510] Thereby the contradiction to Bultmann becomes clear, since the history of Jesus is taken into the midst of New Testament theology and no longer regarded as a preliminary.

The mutual interpenetration of the earthly Jesus and the kerygma finds its point of crystallization in the way the figure of Jesus is understood: "Jesus belongs to this world. Yet in midst of it he is of unmistakable otherness."[511] This point makes it possible to bridge the gap to the Christian kerygma that is more than simply the confessional language of the church, for that unmistakable otherness of Jesus is within the realm of the historically verifiable. In the Afterword to the tenth edition of *Jesus of Nazareth*, Bornkamm speaks of the historian's ability to call attention to the *demonstrable* characteristics of Jesus' claim to authority.[512] By this procedure the continuity between the historical Jesus and the Christian message can be made transparent. Here is illustrated the fundamental combination of history and kerygma at the basis of the New Quest.

Bornkamm's concept of history shimmers between "history" in the sense of the result of the historian's work and "history as occurrence and event."[513] It is the latter understanding that quickens the heart of Bornkamm the theologian, for it is in this sense that the Gospels let "the historical person of Jesus [become visible to us] with the utmost vividness."[514] As an example, Bornkamm is skeptical about the historical factuality of the Gethsemane scene but nonetheless understands it as a "historical document in a higher sense."[515]

Based on this inseparable interweaving of kerygma and history, Bornkamm consistently resists rigid commitments and criteria with regard to authenticity.

---

508. Ibid., 21.
509. J. M. Robinson, *Kerygma und historischer Jesus* (2nd ed.; Zürich: Zwingli, 1967) 185.
510. Bornkamm, *Jesus von Nazareth*, 10th ed., 206.
511. Bornkamm, *Jesus of Nazareth*, 56.
512. Bornkamm, *Jesus von Nazareth*, 10th ed., 209.
513. Ibid., 25.
514. Ibid., 24.
515. Ibid., 162.

"Should we reduce the tradition to that which cannot be doubted on historical grounds, we should be left ultimately with a mere torso."[516] Thus the indisputable facts about Jesus, which Bornkamm does later list, are in themselves ultimately "barren."[517]

Bornkamm's critique of such a reductionistic procedure becomes concrete in his taking a clear position against that form of the CDC that basically infers the inauthenticity of any unit of tradition that has been given a Christian stamp: "It is . . . not apparent why a word or story which was first formulated by the church should not in content possess a historical genuineness."[518] A reductionistic procedure oriented to the CDC would contradict that mutual interpenetration of history and kerygma, especially—and here Bornkamm breaks with Bultmann— since the pre-Gospel tradition itself already attests a considerable interest in the pre-Easter history of Jesus.[519] The close connection between Jesus and the tradition is reflected in Bornkamm's view that "Jesus himself, his history and his person . . . imposed themselves on the transmitters of the earliest traditions and compelled them to shape their portrayals of him in particular ways."[520]

Moreover, Bornkamm avoids any formulation of criteria. In his thorough analysis of Bornkamm's Jesus book, which Bornkamm himself deals with in the Afterword from the tenth edition on, Leander E. Keck describes Bornkamm's ambivalence in regard to historical reconstruction: Bornkamm wants to have it both ways, both critical reconstruction and results that are in continuity with the kerygmatic texts of the Gospels.[521]

A more careful look, however, makes clear that this fluctuation between critical reconstruction and the quest for historical authenticity, on the one side, and a (rather more likely) uncontrolled, wholesale acceptance of material as authentic, on the other, is not divided between these two sides.

In connection with the passion story, Bornkamm addresses the issue of historicity several times: the historical reliability of the Gospel of John is denied; the legendary element is emphasized[522]; and "the historical authenticity of the passion-and-resurrection predictions [are doubtful] as to their details."[523]

---

516. Ibid., 15.

517. Ibid., 55.

518. Ibid., 11.

519. Ibid., 22.

520. G. Bornkamm, "Die Bedeutung des historischen Jesus für den Glauben," in *Die Frage nach dem historischen Jesus. Beiträge von F. Hahn / W. Lohff / G. Bornkamm* (EvFo 2; Göttingen: Vandenhoeck & Ruprecht, 1962) 63.

521. L. E. Keck, "Bornkamm's *Jesus of Nazareth* Revisited," *JR* 49 (1969): 6.

522. Bornkamm, *Jesus von Nazareth*, 10th ed., 137.

523. Ibid., 136.

Although Bornkamm acknowledges that "we have little certain knowledge in the proper historical sense about the last chapter in the life of Jesus,"[524] this does not place the basic historicity of the accounts as a whole in question.

In regard to the Last Supper, Bornkamm applies the CDC without any explanation: Mark 14:25 has found no place in the eucharistic liturgy. If it were a church formation, that is where it would have had its *Sitz im Leben*, so it can be inferred from this otherwise unmotivated tradition that it must be authentic.[525]

The discussion of (in-)authenticity becomes confused on the issue of whether Jesus' last meal was a Passover. Bornkamm traces this interpretation back to the theology of the earliest church and concludes it is historically incorrect—which corresponds to the rule of the CDC. In terms of its content, however, this finding converges with the tendency of the CDJ, as long as a Jewish practice or interpretation by Jesus is *not* adjusted to the Jewish context: Jesus' act is "without analogy" in the Passover celebration.[526]

The CDC is applied with regard to christological titles: Bornkamm regards "Son of God" as a title for the pre-Easter Jesus as unhistorical because it derives from Christian confession.[527] In principal, the CDC is also brought into play in the question of the historicity of the title "Messiah."[528]

In contrast, Bornkamm is essentially more generous on the question of authenticity when it is not a matter of a central theme of Christian faith, but deals with the way Judaism is portrayed as the backdrop for the contrasting picture of Jesus.

For Bornkamm, the identity of Jesus is determined essentially by his unmistakable otherness in the midst of this world. It is concerned with the question "of the outlines of his historical person seen in the setting of his own world."[529] The spotlight is on the distinction. This comes to expression, for example, in Bornkamm's intention "to make clear Jesus' understanding of the will of God:"[530] this can be derived by means of Jesus' *critique* of casuistry and such, even when Bornkamm concedes that what Jesus objected to and characterized in his own critical perspective did not do justice to the way his opponents understood themselves. Nonetheless, Bornkamm emphasized in this connection, "To what extent the sayings of Jesus here referred to are authentic in their

---

524. Bornkamm, *Jesus of Nazareth*, 157.
525. Ibid., 160.
526. Ibid., 161.
527. Bornkamm, *Jesus von Nazareth*, 10th ed., 144.
528. Bornkamm, *Jesus of Nazareth*, 169–78.
529. Ibid., 55.
530. Bornkamm, *Jesus von Nazareth*, 10th ed., 210.

details can safely remain out of consideration."[531] It thus happens that whole-sale negative comments about Judaism remain unchanged, even in the different revisions of Bornkamm's Jesus book. This applies to the formalizing of law and obedience in Judaism,[532] or to the supposition that that which was considered shocking and offensive in Judaism was actually liberating and cause for joy and celebration.[533] Not the least of the ways in which Bornkamm makes clear the important differences between Jesus and the Judaism of his time is the key concept of immediacy by which Bornkamm characterizes Jesus' teaching (called the *authority* of Jesus in the Gospels).[534] For "according to the Jewish faith the immediate present is practically non-existent,"[535] since, according to Bornkamm, for Judaism the presence of God was only a matter of the past and future. In contrast, the "character of unmediated presence" embodied in Jesus means the " making-present of the reality of God . . . the end of the world in which it takes place."[536]

The significant changes Bornkamm made in the revised tenth edition of *Jesus of Nazareth* (1975) should not go unmentioned here. The revisions concern especially his statements about Judaism. Thus for instance in chapter 2 ("Period and Environment"), the Pharisees are portrayed in a less negative light. Quite revealing is a small change that Bornkamm made in connection with his discussion of the concept of reward. While in the older editions Jesus was still set off in an ethically positive way in "contrast to Jewish thought," in the revised edition Bornkamm speaks of the "contrast to popular thought."[537] Here Bornkamm himself seems clearly to have become aware of how he had previously misused Judaism as the foil and opposing picture for Jesus.

Günther Bornkamm is a typical advocate of the New Quest who is interested in the history that stands behind the text of our Gospels and who wants to combine this with the theology of the kerygma. He thus focuses his historical gaze on the newly discovered historical Jesus, who is now seen to be relevant for the Christian faith. In this process of historical reconstruction, forms of the CDC are applied. This historical approach leads to a historicizing of Jesus' uniqueness, and the distinction between Jesus and Judaism becomes clear on the historical plane of the description of Judaism. To be sure,

---

531. Ibid., 92.

532. Ibid., 70.

533. Ibid.

534. Bornkamm, *Jesus of Nazareth*, 55. Cf. also p. 100, "the immediate presence of the divine will."

535. Ibid., 55.

536. Ibid., 62.

537. Bornkamm, *Jesus von Nazareth*, 125.

Bornkamm had no particular historical interest in Judaism as such. A negative historical rough sketch of Judaism is by no means intended. With regard to Judaism, the spotlight is focused not on Judaism itself, but on a description of his own position attained from the perspective of the Jesus tradition. The question of the extent to which this position vis-à-vis Judaism does not coincide with the Judaism of Jesus' day—or with modern Judaism, for that matter—completely misses Bornkamm's intention.

The continuity between Jesus and Christianity appears to be in the discontinuity with Jewish content. In terms of content, this corresponds to the tendency of the CDJ. However, Bornkamm never directly addresses the issue of criteria.

2.4 The "Third Quest" of the Historical Jesus

a) "Third Quest"—A New Phase of Jesus Research

i) Designation and Brief Characterization of the "Third Quest"

"Third Quest" is an English designation, for this phase of scholarship originated and has its center of gravity outside Germany in Anglo-Saxon territory, especially in Great Britain and the United States. In Great Britain, the term "Third Quest" was introduced by N. T. Wright in his continuation and expansion of S. Neill's history of New Testament scholarship.[538] Without mentioning its origin, Graham Stanton also used the phrase in a 1990 article on the historical Jesus.[539]

This same movement in the history of scholarship, which began about 1980, is called "Jesus Research" by the American New Testament scholar J. H. Charlesworth (1986).[540] Charlesworth speaks decidedly against using the word "quest" for this new phase of scholarship: "It suggests we are in a dark room, fumbling about trying to find the door. . . . We are not on a quest. We are compelled to raise historical questions because of what is now placed so graphically before us."[541] In his Jesus book (1988) Charlesworth describes this new "Jesus research" as representing a paradigm shift.[542] Interestingly enough,

---

538. Neill and Wright, *The Interpretation of the New Testament*, 379.

539. G. Stanton, "Historical Jesus," in R. J. Coggins and J. L. Houlden, eds. *A Dictionary of Biblical Interpretation* (London-Philadelphia: SCM/Trinity, 1990) 289.

540. Charlesworth, "From Barren Mazes" 221. I. Batdorf's survey of interpretations of Jesus is still worth reading, but had appeared already in 1984, when the great movement of the 1980s was not yet recognizable.

541. J. H. Charlesworth, *Jesus Within Judaism. New Light from Exciting Archaeological Discoveries* (New York: Doubleday, 1988) 9.

542. Ibid., 2.

he introduces Leonhard Goppelt's *Theology of the New Testament*—relatively little noticed in Germany—as documentation for this turn of New Testament scholarship toward attributing more importance to the historical Jesus. Quite apart from the possibly greater influence of Goppelt in the United States, it appears to us that the rediscovery of the theological significance of the historical Jesus for theology is not the real paradigm shift, since the theological importance or unimportance of the historical figure of Jesus has been a disputed point on various fronts for a long time. What appears new to us is rather the ecumenical-academic preoccupation with the historical Jesus.

A third designation for the new interest in Jesus research is found in the work of M. J. Borg. He spoke in 1988 of a *"Renaissance"* in Jesus research. Behind this term also stands his critique of a minimalist portrayal of the figure of Jesus in the "New Quest."[543]

In the following, this new phase of concentration on the historical Jesus will be called (pace Charlesworth) the *Third Quest* or the *Third Phase*.[544] The designation "Jesus Research" is indeed programmatic but, in German-language scholarship, not precise enough in its direct translation "Jesusforschung," which is also used in a more general sense.

What is this new phase of the academic study of the historical Jesus all about? Actually, it is concerned with something not all that new. In 1930 Maurice Goguel commented critically, "There has been more interest in showing that things did not happen exactly as the gospels state than in discovering the real course of events."[545] In the New Quest that followed, the center of gravity was placed in the positive connection between the Gospels and the historical Jesus. But "discovering the real course of events," detached as much as possible from the issue of the normative function of the New Testament, is an essential concern of the Third Quest. If the New Quest had wanted to bring theology and history together (in a new way)—and if the value of history was thereby upgraded by showing its connection with theology—in the Third Quest these two realms were strictly separated, and attention was directed exclusively to history. Four interrelated impulses characterize the Third Quest:

1. To be named first is, as already suggested, the (re-)emancipation of the historical quest for Jesus from the field of theology and Christology.[546] His-

---

543. M. J. Borg, "A Renaissance of Jesus Studies," TToday 45 (1988): 282.

544. In the United States, the Third Quest movement found its institutional expression in 1983 in the formation of "The Historical Jesus Section of the SBL (Society of Biblical Literature)," and then in 1985 in the founding of the Jesus Seminar by Robert Funk.

545. M. Goguel, "The Problem of Jesus," HTR 23 (1930): 106.

546. It is in this sense that the survey article by J. P. Meier of 1986 bears the appropriate title, "Jesus Among the Historians."

torical research about Jesus serves neither to legitimize nor delegitimize Christology. This emphatically *secular-historical* impetus is connected in some advocates of the Third Quest with a negative emotional feeling about German theology and is to that extent an emancipation of Anglo-Saxon theology over against the earlier dominance of German-language theology. The placing of a low theological value on the debate about historical issues as such was never deeply shared outside Germany and now is given its proper due. Thus a more open discussion of Jesus' identity goes hand in hand with the Third Quest. J. H. Charlesworth points out the multiplicity of perspectives shared by the Third Questers. The spectrum ranges from somewhat conservative scholars to liberal or secular advocates, and includes Catholics, Protestants, and Jews.[547]

2. This (secular) historical impulse cannot be separated from the growing recognition of, as well as an increasing sense of the importance of, the fields of sociology and, especially, *social history* for the field of historical studies. In this sense, there has been talk of an "interdisciplinary quest for the historical Jesus."[548] This designation suggests a stronger sense that this historical figure must be seen as belonging to a social group in a particular social-political context. In contrast, the individual "Jesus" loses some of his importance; moreover, the christological dignity of Jesus is strongly relativized. As a representative of the change of direction, one might mention the reception given to a sociopolitical way of looking at Jesus as found in S. G. F. Brandon's 1967 *Jesus and the Zealots*. His basic approach could not find much of a hearing in the scholarly atmosphere of that time, quite apart from the weakness of his concrete theses.[549]

3. The third impulse has to do finally with *Judaism*, though this comes to expression in several different ways. This impulse, in turn, goes hand in hand with the significance of the historical context (cf. the first two points). For one thing, in the ten to twenty years before the Third Quest, important Jewish publications about Jesus appeared that received much attention and furthered the perception of Jesus as a Jew.[550] In the theological-dogmatic realm Don Cupitt had already stated in 1979, "Jesus

---

547. Charlesworth, "From Barren Mazes," 225. Cf. also M. Eugene Boring, "The 'Third Quest' and the Apostolic Faith," in *Interpretation* 50/4 (October 1996): 341ff.

548. Bernard Brandon Scott, an oral comment cited by M. J. Borg, "A Renaissance of Jesus Studies," 284.

549. The weakness of his particular theses were evaluated as pointing to the weakness in principle of his sociopolitical approach. To the extent that this approach (and Brandon's contribution) are today taken seriously in academic circles, a change has taken place. Cf. E. Bammel, "The revolution theory from Reimarus to Brandon," in E. Bammel and C. F. D. Moule, eds., *Jesus and the Politics of His Day* (Cambridge: Cambridge University Press, 1984).

550. See below II.2.4.a.ii 1. Obviously there had already been previous Jewish publications about Jesus—Shalom Ben-Chorin speaks of the effort that had lasted 150 years "to bring Jesus home to his own people" (S. Ben-Chorin, *Jesus im Judentum* [SCJB 4; Wuppertal: Brockhaus, 1970] 7)—but in their time they could not produce any comparable response.

the Jew has now outlived the cosmic Christ Almighty."[551] As a second point, during this period knowledge had increased about the intertestamental literature as well as about Judaism and Palestine of the first century. In Charlesworth's words, prior to 1980 "scholars were *searching* for Jesus. Now, scholars find themselves *bumping into* pre-seventy Palestinian phenomena."[552] And a third point: the growing perception of theological anti-Judaism and criticism of it both made possible and encouraged New Testament scholarship's occupation with a Jewish Jesus.

4. A fourth characteristic is the consideration of noncanonical sources. On the one hand, increasing attention was directed to the Q source of Jesus' sayings reconstructed from the canonical Gospels, and, on the other hand, the *Gospel of Thomas* that had been (re-)discovered in 1945. Scholars broke free from what had been overstated as "the tyranny of the Synoptic Jesus,"[553] in order to investigate what could be learned of Jesus from apocryphal and "heretical" traditions.

It is probably already clear how strongly these four impulses are interwoven. In summary we may say that this Third Phase of Jesus scholarship seeks the Jewish Jesus in his historical context. It seeks a "contextual Jesus."

ii) The Genesis of the Third Quest—a Brief Sketch

1. *The impulse of Jewish research on the historical Jesus.* As previously suggested, Jewish research on the historical Jesus[554] played an important role in paving the way for the Third Quest.[555] The essential impulse consists in the positive, even sympathetic, portrayal of Jesus that emerges when he is consistently incorporated into the context of Judaism.

Very important in this regard is the beginning that was made by Joseph Klausner. His 1907 book in Hebrew was intended to give a Jewish readership "a truer idea of the *historic* Jesus," that is,

---

551. D. Cupitt, *Explorations in Theology 6* (London: SCM Press, 197) 68, cited from P. Botha, "Probleme van die vraag na die historiese Jesus. 'n Pleidooi vir meer demokrasie in die Nuwe-Testamentiese wetenskap" *ThEv*(SA) 20 (1987): 7.

552. Charlesworth, "From Barren Mazes," 224.

553. Cf. C. W. Hedrick, "The Tyranny of the Synoptic Jesus," *Semeia* 44 (1988): 1ff.

554. J. Maier ("Gewundene Wege der Rezeption. Zur neueren jüdischen Jesusforschung," *HerKorr* 30 [1976]: 313) has rightly pointed to the problematic involved in such a "Jewish" (or "Christian") research. Nonetheless, it is obvious that there are publications that resolutely, or more likely unconsciously, advocate a particular standpoint. From this point of view, that Jesus research of the "New Quest," for example, can be described as "Christian" Jesus research is clear.

555. For a thorough survey of Jewish research on the historical Jesus, cf. since 1970 the following authors: 1970, S. Ben-Chorin, *Jesus in Judaism*, 7–39; 1976, J. Maier, "Gewundeene Wege der Rezeption"; 1984, D. A. Hagner, "The Jewish Reclamation of Jesus" (a respectful, but critical evangelical position); 1988, W. Vogler, *Jüdische Jesusinterpretation in christlicher Sicht* (Weimar: H. Böhlaus Nachf.) (Vogler systematizes from a Christian point of view).

an idea which shall be alike far from that of Christian or Jewish dogma, which shall be objective and scientific in every possible way, which shall also give some conception of a teaching akin to Judaism and yet at the same time far removed from it, and some conception of the civil, economic and spiritual environment of the Jews in the days of the Second Temple, an environment which made possible this historical scene and his new teaching—then I shall know that I have filled in a blank page (from the point of view of Hebrew writers) in the history of Israel which has so far been written upon almost solely by Christians.[556]

This initiative reaches far beyond its own time and points to the concerns that will be championed in the Third Quest.[557]

Moreover, the "recapture of Jesus" for Judaism plays a large role in Klausner's work,[558] an event called by Shalom Ben-Chorin "bringing Jesus back home to his people."[559] It is also found in Leo Baeck's 1938 publication, *Das Evangelium als Urkunde der jüdischen Glaubensgeschichte* (*The Gospel as a Document of the History of Jewish Faith*). This work was not destined to have a great effect on Christian theology. Baeck understands "the Gospel as a piece of Jewish history," "as a witness of Jewish faith," and this approach to the Jesus tradition is for him the presupposition for a *life of Jesus*.[560] This view corresponds to a fundamental change of perspectives: it is not the dissimilarity, but the agreement with Judaism that is important. Thus Jesus' originality and individuality recedes.

A milestone in Jewish work on the historical Jesus since World War II is provided by the publications of Samuel Sandmel, which had a deep effect on the academic community far beyond the Jewish readership to which they were primarily directed.[561] He describes matter-of-factly[562] the problematic involved in attempting to place the historical figure of Jesus, about whom our knowledge is only indefinite, into his historical context, about which our knowledge is likewise indefinite—as is characteristic for much Jesus

---

556. J. Klausner, *Jesus of Nazareth: His Life, Times, and Teaching* (trans. Herbert Danby; New York: Macmillan Co., 1925) 11. (The book was quickly translated into English, and in 1934 a German translation appeared.)

557. Cf. the reference by E. P. Sanders to Klausner, *Jesus and Judaism*, 18.

558. Klausner, *Jesus of Nazareth*, 363. "Jesus of Nazareth was the product of Palestine alone, unaffected by any foreign mixture." This is a clear contradiction of statements for which the Jewish element in Jesus amounts to an unwanted additive.

559. Ben-Chorin, *Jesus im Judentum*, 7.

560. L. Baeck, *Das Evangelium als Urkunde der jüdischen Glaubensgeschichte* (Berlin: Schocken, 1938) 5; cf. also 70.

561. S. Sandmel, *A Jewish Understanding of the New Testament* (Cincinnati: Hebrew Union College, 1957); *We Jews and Jesus* (London: Goolancz, 1965).

562. Cf. Maier, "Gewundene Wege der Rezeption," 318.

research.[563] His debate on the theme of the uniqueness of Jesus is worthy of note, and pointed the way to the future: "Jesus was not unique in any one isolated way. He was unique, however, in that combination of attributes which made him a person of marked individuality."[564]

The popular Jesus books of David Flusser and Shalom Ben-Chorin appeared in the late 1960s, but without immediately influencing Jesus research or the portrayals of Jesus in Germany. In his *Jesus* (1968), D. Flusser wants to show that it is possible to write a life of Jesus.[565] He is thus concerned with the historical value of the Gospels, a concern that shows his relationship with the impulses at work in the New Quest. His interest, however, is directed not toward bridges between Jesus and the Christian faith, but toward bridges that connect Jesus with contemporary human beings as such. Thus the ethical and psychological aspects of Jesus' ministry play the primary role. It is remarkable how obvious Flusser considers it to be that Jesus should be portrayed as a Jew who was faithful to the Law, while at the same time being able to point to features of Jesus' person that made him different.[566]

S. Ben-Chorin emphasizes Jesus' humanity and speaks, in dependence on Martin Buber, of "brother Jesus"[567]—as in the title of his 1967 book. His concern to relativize the figure of Jesus over against his exaltation in dogmatic theology corresponds to a characteristic of the Third Quest. The relativizing approach applies to his own portrayal of Jesus (*a* Jewish view, not *the* Jewish view; "from the perspective of my own existence, which happens to be Jewish"). This reflects a difference from the approach of the Third Quest, which is concerned to produce a reconstruction that is as historically objective as possible.

This difference becomes especially clear in comparison with the important publications of Geza Vermes.[568] His first Jesus book (1973) was called *Jesus the Jew. A Historian's Reading of the Gospels*.[569] This title already basically includes

---

563. Sandmel, *A Jewish Understanding*, 201.

564. Ibid., 284.

565. D. Flusser, *Jesus, in Selbstzeugnissen und Bilddokumenten dargestellt* (RoMo 140; Hamburg: Rowohlt, 1968) 7.

566. Thus for Flusser Jesus is "the only ancient Jew known to us" who announced at the same time the end time and the beginning of the time of salvation (*Jesus*, 87).

567. Ben-Chorin, *Bruder Jesus. Der Nazarener in jüdischer Sicht* (Munich: dtv, 1967; 6th ed. 1983) 10–11.

568. Here it is not a matter of comparing the Jesus books on the basis of their popular or more strictly academic character, for alongside *these* distinctions, other distinctions can be recognized that do not necessarily follow.

569. This book appeared in 1993 in a German translation. Included in the volume are also the Riddell Memorial Lectures of 1981 ("The Gospel of Jesus the Jew") in German translation.

all the main characteristics of the Third Quest: (1) Jesus is perceived fundamentally as a Jew. (2) Research on the historical Jesus proceeds with neither a
Christian nor a Jewish perspective, but is an academic historical enterprise.
Vermes is moved by the "single-minded and devout search for fact and reality."[570] With this approach, Vermes belongs to the more notable forerunners
of the Third Quest, which was to begin in the 1980s. With *Jesus and the World
of Judaism* (1983),[571] he became himself an important advocate of this third
phase of research.

In the mid-1980s, embedded in the Third Quest, Harvey Falk's *Jesus the
Pharisee* represented yet another type of Jewish Jesus book. Its background and
point of departure is the Holocaust and the anti-Jewish history connected with
it. Falk pursues a twofold goal[572]: In the first place he advocates the old historical thesis that Jesus had been a Hillelite and that the anti-Jewish texts in
the New Testament were directed against the Shammaites. In the second
place, Falk combines a contemporary concern, namely, pointing to the common foundation of Judaism and Christianity: the Judaism of today follows the
school of Hillel, and Christianity is based on a Hillelite, Jesus. This Jewish
Jesus book by Rabbi Falk, with its historical theses, is thus clearly at the same
time a *direct* contribution to Jewish-Christian dialogue and mutual understanding in our own times.

2. *Some advocates of the Third Quest since the 1980s.*[573] A brilliant beginning
was made by John Riches' *Jesus and the Transformation of Judaism* (1980) and
Anthony E. Harvey's *Jesus and the Constraints of History* (1980, published 1982).
While they received a strong echo in the English-speaking world, Kümmel
rightly notes with regard to both books that they were not noticed on the
Continent.[574] John Riches rejects the false alternative of supposing that Jesus
can either be fully integrated into Judaism or that he was a religious genius
standing completely apart from his context. His guiding question has to do
with the intention of Jesus—a question that he understands in a decidedly historical manner. He believes the proper answer to this question is that Jesus
intended the transformation of Judaism. For Riches, this transformation must

---

570. Vermes, *Jesus the Jew*, 17.
571. The Riddell-Memorial-Lectures (1981) are also included.
572. For the central theses, cf. H. Falk, *Jesus the Pharisee: A New Look at the Jewishness
of Jesus* (New York: Paulist Press, 1985) 9, 113, 115.
573. An excellent survey of the trends and the advocates of Jesus research in the years
1980–1984 is provided by J. H. Charlesworth, *Jesus Within Judaism*, Appendix 5,
187–205. Thorough information on the different positions within the Third Quest
(with discussion) until 1986 is also provided by Neill and Wright, *The Interpretation of
the New Testament*, 379–403.
574. W. G. Kümmel, "Jesusforschung seit 1981 II," *TRu* 54 (1989): 14,17.

proceed from the conventions of his society, including its given linguistic conventions. That is, Riches is interested in Jesus as a reformer of Jewish conventions and basic assumptions, as an alternative Jewish reaction to Hellenism. A. E. Harvey has a similar concern with regard to the necessary adaptation of Jesus' way of expressing himself to the "constraints," the limitations of his culture.

The widespread response to E. P. Sanders's *Jesus and Judaism* (1985)[575] first brought the Third Quest to the attention of German scholars.[576] Sanders does not understand himself as a theologian and thus directs his efforts to the often-cited liberation of "history and exegesis from the control of theology."[577] Sanders's work searches for the intention of Jesus and its connection to his Jewish contemporaries. This way of asking the question is placed in a broader historical context that is concerned with the historical reasons for the death of Jesus and the beginning of Christianity. It is against this background that Sanders deals with the criterion of dissimilarity and the problem of Jesus' uniqueness. He sees this especially in the historical effects of Jesus, independently of Jesus' actual intention.[578] Although Sanders and Davies name and use the criterion of dissimilarity in their workbook on the Synoptic Gospels, they are aware of the problem in equating "unique" and "authentic." They point to the anti-Jewish tendency of this equation, and its tendency toward exclusivism, for "'non-unique' does not prove 'inauthentic',"[579] so that also continuity with Judaism—instead of dissimilarity with it—increases the probability of authenticity.[580] As further criteria they name multiple attestation, agreement in the negative and positive images of Jesus, as well as elements in the tradition that go against the tendencies of the tradition.[581] Sanders is basically no different from Riches and Harvey in placing Jesus within the framework of the thought world of first-century Judaism. In the process, he assigns Jesus to a stream of nonmilitant Jewish

---

575. His nontechnical Jesus book *The Historical Figure of Jesus* followed in 1993 (Harmondsworth: Allen Lane, 1993).

576. Cf. also Kümmel, "Jesusforschung seit 1981 II," 27. Nevertheless, it is amazing how little the Third Quest has been noticed in Germany.

577. Sanders, *Jesus and Judaism*, 331, 333–34. Cf. also his *The Historical Figure of Jesus*, 2.

578. Sanders, *Jesus and Judaism*, 240; cf. e.g., 220: "Jesus started a movement *which came to see the Gentile mission as a logical extension of itself*" (emphasis in original). Cf. also his *The Question of the Uniqueness of the Teaching of Jesus. The Ethel M. Wood Lecture 1990* (London: University of London, 1990).

579. Sanders and Davies, *Studying the Synoptic Gospels*, 322.

580. Ibid., 322–23.

581. Ibid., 323–33.

eschatology that strove for and expected the restoration of Israel ("restoration eschatology").[582]

Two other important publications, each of which illuminates different aspects of the Jewish life and work of Jesus, and which have been discussed especially in the United States, are John D. Crossan's *The Historical Jesus* (1991) and John P. Meier's *A Marginal Jew: Rethinking the Historical Jesus* (vol. 1, 1991; vol. 2, 1994).

The approach adopted by Meier is virtually a classic example of the central theme of the Third Quest: Meier explains the plan of his book in terms of an imaginary nonpapal conclave composed of a Catholic, a Protestant, a Jew, and an agnostic. They are locked in a first-class library and given the assignment of producing a consensus statement on the historical form and intention of Jesus of Nazareth, using only historical sources and historical arguments. The result would be a "non-religious formula of concord," that would contain no Roman Catholic or Protestant tenets of faith and would be open to general verification. Meier's horizon is thus that of the dialogue between Christians and Jews, Christians of different confessions, believers and nonbelievers, historians and theologians. "Such a limited consensus statement, which does not claim to act as a substitute for the Christ of faith, is the modest goal of the present work."[583] Meier's work is reserved in its historical criticism. He sorts carefully through previous research and comes to relative "conservative results," which he advocates with a rigorous scholarly ethos.

In contrast, J. D. Crossan writes a lively, somewhat racy book that breaks new ground in the choice of sources, in its methodology, and in its results. Alongside the canonical Gospels, he bases his work especially on apocryphal traditions that he often considers historically superior. With the help of social-anthropological findings, Crossan shows how Jesus breaks through the general social mechanisms of honor/shame and patron/client. Here, in relation to antiquity as a whole, Jesus is seen in contrast to his environment. At the same time, with the help of information and insights from the social world of his times, Jesus is related to the various renewal and protest movements of his contemporary Judaism. In regard to Judaism, Jesus is thus given a predominately positive relation to his environment, in that Crossan differentiates between inclusive Judaism and exclusive Judaism. Jesus is assigned to

---

582. Unfortunately Sanders does not debate with M. J. Borg's theses on Jesus' eschatology, which he had been working on since the beginning of the 1970s before he published them in 1984 under the title *Conflict, Holiness and Politics in the Teaching of Jesus* (SBEC 5; New York: E. Mellen, 1984).

583. J. P. Meier, *A Marginal Jew. Rethinking the Historical Jesus*. Vol. 1: *The Roots of the Problem and the Person* (New York: Doubleday, 1991) 1–2; the quotation is from 2.

"inclusive Judaism," which is open to the Gentile world. This openness is manifested in Jesus in a way that places him in a certain nearness to the Cynics. Thus for Crossan, Jesus is a *Jewish Cynic*. For the issue of criteria investigated in this book, it is important to note that Crossan decidedly renounces the criterion of dissimilarity in all its forms as a means of reconstructing authentic Jesus tradition. His criterion is that of multiple attestation, in the use of which he enlarges the number of independent witnesses by including apocryphal Jesus traditions (especially by including the *Gospel of Thomas*). His results often deviate from the traditional consensus. He sketches the picture of a noneschatological Jesus who advocates a paradoxical practical wisdom for everyday life. What does not fit this picture is excised by means of historical criticism.

J. P. Meier and J. D. Crossan represent two cognitively different styles of grappling with the problem of the historical Jesus. Each in his own way advocates an emphatically *historical* approach. Both are Roman Catholics. Between the poles they represent are found other works of Catholic exegetes for whom a connection between historical questions and theological interests is characteristic.

Here one must first mention the work of Ben F. Meyer with the title *The Aims of Jesus*, which had already appeared in 1979. Meyer's concern is already clear from the title—he is interested in more than historical factuality. Bernard J. Lee, in *The Galilean Jewishness of Jesus* (1988), wants to remove the figure of Jesus from its christological frame but ultimately still aims at a *Christian* understanding of the Jewish Jesus.[584] With the question of continuity and discontinuity as his point of departure, he wants to do justice to the Jewish element in Jesus as much as he wants to do justice to the Christian faith.[585] His reflections are characterized by the perspectives of process philosophy and process theology. Finally, D. Georgen is a systematic theologian who understands Jesus research as a necessary prolegomenon to Christology. His book *The Mission and Ministry of Jesus* (1986) is to be assigned to the Third Quest since it is concerned with Jesus as a Jew.[586]

The Jesus Seminar founded by Robert W. Funk is a particularly American project. This is seen in the first place by its debate with biblical fundamentalism: Funk argues on the plane of the *ipsissima verba Jesu*—"what he really said"[587]—and, in his edition of the Gospels, it is not the words of Jesus as such that are

---

584. B. J. Lee, *The Galilean Jewishness of Jesus: Retrieving the Jewish Origins of Christianity*. Vol. 1: *Conversation on the Road Not Taken* (New York: Paulist Press, 1988) 4: "The Christian retrieval of Jesus' Jewishness."

585. Ibid., 18.

586. D. Goergen, *A Theology of Jesus*. Vol. 1: *The Mission and Ministry of Jesus* (Wilmington, Del.: Michael Glazier, 1986) 206.

587. R. W. Funk, "The Issue of Jesus," *Foundations and Facets Forum* 1 (1985): 7; cf. also Funk and Hoover, *The Five Gospels*, ix.

printed in red, but the *verba Jesu* that can be evaluated as sufficiently authentic. In the second place, there is an "anti-Europe" motive embedded in the work of the Jesus Seminar: it is supposed to demonstrate the end of European dominance in theology.[588] The Jesus Seminar voted on the level of authenticity to be assigned to each purported saying of Jesus. The procedure of voting by means of colored marbles bears the features of public opinion polls, very much in the sense of a break with the "religious establishment" and coming out of the "academic closet."[589] Probably in terminological dependence on Schmiedel's "foundation pillars," the working procedures of the Jesus Seminar are based on seven "pillars" of scholarly wisdom that summarize the results of previous research on the Gospels. The concluding eighth rule, "Beware of finding a Jesus entirely congenial to you"—implies a kind of criterion of dissimilarity that critically challenges the intention of Jesus research itself.[590]

On the German scene, it has been especially Gerd Theissen, with his sociological studies of the Jesus movement, who has prepared the way for the Third Quest. With his semi-fictional Jesus book (*The Shadow of the Galilean. The Quest of the Historical Jesus in Narrative Form* [London: SCM, 1986]) he himself joined the Third Quest.[591] Meanwhile, he coauthored a textbook with Annette Merz, *The Historical Jesus* (1996). The 1987 essay on Jesus by Christoph Burchard, along with his "Aufbesserung der Quellenlage durch Zeitgeschichte" ("Improving the Source Base by Studying Contemporary History") is also to be counted as part of the Third Quest.[592] Also to be mentioned is Klaus Berger, since a number of his works attempt to correct the distorted pictures of Judaism found in Christian literature, including the New Testament.[593] His Jesus book, *Wer war Jesus wirklich?* (1995), sketches a very original portrayal of Jesus that combines historical considerations with meditative elements.

Among Roman Catholic works, Joachim Gnilka's *Jesus of Nazareth* (1995) must be mentioned. His 1993 article oriented to the history of research[594] is representative of the scholarship of both Catholics and Protestants in Germany: he

---

588. Funk, "The Issue of Jesus," 8–9.

589. Ibid., 8, 10; Funk and Hoover, *The Five Gospels*, 34–35. Typical of the tendency of the Third Quest is the Jesus Seminar's edition of the Gospels (that includes the *Gospel of Thomas*) "free of ecclesiastical and religious control." (Ibid., xviii).

590. Ibid., 5. The Jesus Seminar is now working on the question "What did Jesus really do?" (Ibid., x).

591. Cf. Neill and Wright, *The Interpretation of the New Testament*, 396.

592. C. Burchard, "Jesus von Nazareth," in *Die Anfänge des Christentums. Alte Welt und neue Hoffnung* (Stuttgart: Kohlhammer, 1987) 12.

593. Cf., e.g., K. Berger, "Jesus als Pharisäer und frühe Christen als Pharisäer," *NovT* 30 (1988): 231–62.

594. J. Gnilka, "Zur Frage nach dem historischen Jesus," *MThZ* 44 (1993): 1–12.

treats impulses from the Third Quest, without noticing this new phase in the history of scholarship as such. His Protestant counterpart is Jürgen Becker's text-book *Jesus of Nazareth* (1995), which places Jesus in the context of early Judaism and thereby makes contact with the Third Quest, but as a whole cautiously continues the main tradition of German-language scholarship. Martin Hengel's important historical works are also to be named here, since their results are discussed in the sphere of the Third Quest. Hengel himself, however, does not belong to the Third Quest except in a broad sense of the term, since he regards himself as more strongly committed to a claim for the uniqueness of Jesus.[595]

Hand in hand with the Third Quest, and given momentum by the Jewish-Christian dialogue, we may here somewhat tangentially refer to the new movement in systematic theology, a movement that likewise began in the United States and is concerned with a "Christian confession of Jesus the Jew."[596] Since the 1980s, this conciliatory stance has also found expression in Germany in appropriate ecclesiastical statements regarding Judaism.[597]

The new developments have, of course, lead to countless popular publications that place Jesus in the context of Judaism. These publications, which continue to be produced at a rapid rate, are written by nonscholarly authors and are of varying quality. In this setting, the conscious distance from theology that characterizes the Third Quest has fit in well with the anti-church interests of many publishers. The debates about the Qumran documents have further promoted public interest in such issues, so that fortunately publications at the popular level have also emanated from scholarly circles.[598]

---

595. Most clearly, however, in one of his older works, *The Charismatic Leader and His Followers* (New York: Crossroads, 1981; German original *Nachfolge und Charisma*, 1968), which speaks of breaking through all the analogies posed from the point of view of the history-of-religions approach (69, 84–88). See also *Zur urchristlichen Geschichtsschreibung* (Stuttgart: Calwer, 1979).

596. So in the title of the Christology by F.-W. Marquardt, *Das christliche Bekenntnis zu Jesus, dem Juden. Eine Christologie* (Vol. 1; Munich: Kaiser, 1990). For the discussion see vol. 51, no. 5 of *Evangelische Theologie* (1991), on the theme of Jewish-Christian conversation about the Bible, and the protest from E. Käsemann in *EvT* 52 (1992): 177–78.

597. Cf. U. Schwemer, ed., *Christen und Juden. Dokumente der Annäherung* (GTB 790; Gütersloh: Mohn, 1991).

598. Cf., e.g., on Qumran, K. Berger: *Qumran und Jesus. Wahrheit unter Verschluss?* (Stuttgart: Klett, 1993); H. Stegemann, *Die Essener, Qumran, Johannes der Täufer und Jesus. Ein Sachbuch* (2nd ed.; Freiburg: Herder, 1993). On the more strongly psychologically oriented Jesus publications, cf. F. Hahn, "Umstrittenes Jesusbild? Problematische neuere Veröffentlichungen zur Geschichte und Gestalt Jesu von Nazaret" (Lecture on Bavarian Radio and elsewhere), in *MThZ* 44 (1993). For a comprehensive presentation of the historical Jesus written for the general public, see especially G. Theissen, *The Shadow of the Galilean*. Very readable is the Jesus book by E. P. Sanders written for the general public, *The Historical Figure of Jesus*.

b) The Criterion of Dissimilarity in the Discussion

The discussion during the 1970s, especially its critique of the CDJ, is fundamental. The critical points were often repeated in the publications of the Third Quest and need not be repeated here. Instead, we should like to indicate the new approaches to criteriology that emerged in the Third Quest on the basis of these critical points. In the process of this discussion it will become clear that the criteria themselves are a constituent part of the particular research hypotheses being pursued, rather than universally valid, objective foundations for research in general.[599]

In 1977 D. R. Catchpole published an excellent summary of the critique of the criterion of dissimilarity and developed it further in the sense of the Third Quest.[600] He posed the question of what the decisive impulse within Judaism could have been that generated a new movement from which Christianity could have originated, and he came to the conclusion that "the most probable answer to that question is Jesus."[601] With this historical way of posing the question, Catchpole preserves an important aspect of the CDJ, without presupposing a priori a basic dissimilarity between Jesus and Judaism. Instead, it is this historical way of looking at the issue that only secondarily suggests certain "differences" between Jesus and his Jewish environment. *This* concept of "difference" is necessarily embedded within a concept of continuity, that is, in a correspondence between the historical figure of Jesus and his environment. Catchpole speaks of "evolutionary continuity."[602] His position marks out two points to which the discussion of the criterion of dissimilarity in the Third Quest is oriented. The historical embedding of Jesus is undertaken with regard both to the time of his ministry and to its effects in the time following his death. That implies a critique of both the CDJ and the CDC, which had focused on historical dissimilarity in a manner precisely the opposite of interest in the historical connections of Jesus to both Judaism and the church. In accordance with this, the Third Quest sees the primary danger of a consistent orientation of the image of Jesus to the criterion of dissimilarity as producing an "unhistorical Jesus."[603]

---

599. So F. G. Downing, "Criteria," in R. J. Coggins and J. L. Houlden, *A Dictionary of Biblical Interpretation* (London-Philadelphia: SCM Press/Trinity Press International, 1990) 153. The article presents a summary of classical criteria and the critiques they have evoked.

600. Catchpole, "Tradition History," 174–178.

601. Ibid., 177.

602. Ibid.

603. Charlesworth, *Jesus Within Judaism*, 167 criticizes the criterion of dissimilarity in that it presents Jesus as a non-Jew and as a leader without followers. C. C. Caragounis, *The Son of Man. Vision and Interpretation* (WUNT 38; Tübingen: Mohr, 1986) 157: the Jesus of the criterion of dissimilarity is not the "Jesus of history."

This is also the sense of Schürmann's argument when he speaks of the *correlation* of Jesus both to his environment and to the history of his effects.[604] Wilder names this state of affairs the interlocking of Jesus with history.[605]

The aspect of the embedding of Jesus in his Jewish context is emphasized by A. E. Harvey with his approach that emphases "the constraints imposed . . . by culture"[606] for a necessary correspondence of Jesus to his environment— otherwise he could not have communicated with his own time and setting. This approach necessarily rejects at least that form of the criterion of dissimilarity that postulates a fundamental contrast between Jesus and his environment as characteristic. By "communication," Harvey understands the way Jesus both spoke and acted, his course of life that led to his death. These actions must have taken place within a common framework of communication with his environment, otherwise they would have never been understood—thus Harvey's perspective on the matter. To be noted is Harvey's presupposition that Jesus' intention was to communicate directly.[607] So also, Jesus' resolute path toward death occurred for the disciples "in a manner of which they could make some sense."[608] On the other side, this concept of "constraints" corresponds to this assumed deeper intention of Jesus: even when Harvey's "constraints" apply equally to Jesus and his environment, the idea that Jesus adapted to the "constraints" might suggest that he did this consciously and somewhat unwillingly. It is not, however, a matter of a complete adaptation. Harvey presupposes that it was possible to operate within the given communications frame with some creativity, and thus that originality was also possible. Here is the limited place for the CDJ and CDC, which he applies in the sense of the *lectio difficilior* rule taken over from text criticism: that which has no parallel must, because of its peculiarity, be at least an echo of a historical event.[609] In this procedure he is aware that the limitations of our historical knowledge relativize such decisions with regard to authenticity. Thus in Harvey's view the criterion of dissimilarity may never be applied in isolation.

---

604. Schürmann, "Kritische Jesuserkenntnis," 19.

605. A. N. Wilder, "The Historical Jesus in a New Focus: A Review Article of *The Silence of Jesus*, by James Breech (Philadelphia 1983)," *USQR* 39, no. 3 (1984): 234.

606. Harvey, *Jesus and the Constraints of History*, 6.

607. Cf. Gnilka, who in a similar argument compares Jesus with a missionary to China whose task would be impossible if he or she refused to speak Chinese (*Jesus of Nazareth: Message and History* [Peabody, Mass.: Hendricksen, 1997] 20). Such a comparison implies the problematic idea in the background, that Jesus was not really at home in his Jewish environment.

608. Harvey, *Jesus and the Constraints of History*, 7.

609. Ibid., 8.

At first J. Riches and A. Millar proceed from the same point of departure as Harvey, that Jesus' form of speech much have fit in with that of his time and place in order to have had any effect at all. They distinguish the content of Jesus' message from the form of his speech, however, so that the result is a criterion that combines (linguistic) correspondence with (material) dissimilarity.[610]

How strongly it is possible within the Third Quest to proceed on the basis of Jesus' correspondence to his (Jewish) environment is clearly seen in the suggestion of C. Burchard, who wants to supplement the fragmentary situation with regard to sources with other data from the history of the times.[611]

With the concepts of correlation, correspondence, constraints, and history of effects, a historical approach is suggested that contradicts a view of Jesus based entirely on dissimilarity. That does not mean, however, an absolute rejection of dissimilarity as a *criterion*. In a modified form it continues to be used by advocates of the Third Quest as also by other scholars.

J. Gnilka can be included in the Third Quest only in a limited sense. He describes the criterion of dissimilarity in its negative form (only what cannot be derived from Judaism or attributed to Christianity is from Jesus) as "a helpful, but sharp sword."[612] With it, too much is severed from Jesus. Moreover, he sees the connection between the originality called for by the double form of the criterion of dissimilarity and a particular Christology.

J. Becker argues with a bit more subtlety. He concedes that the criterion of dissimilarity is often rightly criticized but thinks that this critique only properly applies to the misuse of the criterion in an exclusive and excluding manner: "The criterion is by far without peer when we understand that its goal is to find an unmistakable nucleus of Jesus material that is at one and the same time an expression of his Jewish context and an antecedent that stands in continuity with primitive Christianity."[613] When one compares this formulation of the criterion of dissimilarity with its classic formulation by E. Käsemann, it becomes clear: it has experienced a decisive change as a result of the criticism it has received. A criterion of dissimilarity that combines considerations of Jesus' historical context and his later affects is approaching the criterion of historical plausibility as advocated in this book, even if it cannot be combined with a *deliberate attempt* to discover the unmistakably unique characteristic(s) of Jesus.

---

610. J. Riches and A. Millar, "Conceptual Change in the Synoptic Tradition," in A. E. Harvey, ed. *Alternative Approaches to New Testament Study* (London: SPCK, 1985) 46, 57.

611. Burchard, "Jesus von Nazareth," 12.

612. Gnilka, *Jesus of Nazareth*, 20.

613. J. Becker, *Jesus of Nazareth* (trans. James E. Crouch. Berlin: de Gruyter, 1998) 14.

This refined judgment presented by J. Becker has by no means become the common understanding. This can be seen in two examples in which the line of argument with regard to "dissimilarity" is related in terms of form, but with completely different results.

R. Riesner's 1981 publication *Jesus als Lehrer* (*Jesus as Teacher*) is not to be counted within the Third Quest. He proceeds on the basis of an Aramaic-speaking early Christianity that was conservative with regard to Torah observance. Thus when tradition critical of the Torah is under consideration, the CDJ causes authentic Jesus material to stand out. When one regards early Christianity as Torah-true, material critical of the Torah in the traditions it handed on can only come from Jesus himself.[614] P. van Buren exhibits the reverse procedure: he focuses his view especially on the Gentile Christian traditions contemporary with the evangelists, so that when the criterion of dissimilarity is applied, those elements in the tradition that speak with and for Israel are probably from Jesus.[615]

Both cases of the application of this criterion deal with the same issue, namely, source criticism and/or tradition criticism. The only difference is how the group handing on the tradition is perceived, whether it is thought of as representing Jewish Christianity or Gentile Christianity. The following statements about the question of criteria are in this sense all "source critical." So also the history-of-religions comparison of Jesus with his Jewish environment as a rule deals with material that is in tension with the tendency of the (Christian) sources.

In this sense the pure form of the CDC is found in the 1986 publication of A. F. Segal, who understands the criterion of dissimilarity exclusively as CDC.[616] According to Segal, apocalyptic elements were characteristic of Jesus and his contemporaries, which were rejected by the tradents of the early Christian community. Apocalyptic tradition is accordingly ascribed to Jesus himself.

J. P. Meier makes use of the CDC in a general sense, which he calls the "criterion of embarrassment," which refers to those deeds and sayings of Jesus that were difficult or scandalous to the early church.[617] Meier adds the qualifying

---

614. Riesner, *Jesus als Lehrer*, 91.

615. P. M. Van Buren, *A Theology of the Jewish-Christian Reality*. Part 3: *Christ in Context* (San Francisco: Harper & Row, 1988) 63. While van Buren is not a New Testament scholar, we are concerned here with the structure of the argument, which represents the mirror image of Käsemann's evaluation of Jewish and Gentile Christianity in contrast to Jesus.

616. A. F. Segal, *Rebecca's Children. Judaism and Christianity in the Roman World* (Cambridge, Mass.: Harvard University Press, 1986) 68–69: "The historicity of the teachings ascribed to Jesus can confidently be asserted only when they conflict with the teachings of the church that followed him."

617. J. P. Meier, *A Marginal Jew. Rethinking the Historical Jesus*. Vol. 1: *The Roots of the Problem and the Person* (New York: Doubleday, 1991) 168.

comment, however, that we today cannot know exactly what would have been objectionable to the early church.[618] He discusses the CDC and CDJ as the criterion of discontinuity. He rehabilitates the CDJ inasmuch as he rejects its radical reversal (everything that breaks with things Jewish cannot be assumed to come from Jesus).[619] Jesus was for him a "marginal Jew," a Jew who stands on the edge of Judaism.

In a virtually classical manner, it is important for J. H. Charlesworth to affirm correspondence with Judaism (rejection of the CDJ) while holding on to the CDC. Between *this* correspondence and dissimilarity he sees a material connection: "that . . . which is discontinuous with the needs and concerns of the earliest Christians places Jesus squarely in the midst of early Judaism."[620]

A methodologically similar but differently structured line of thought in terms of its content is pursued by F. W. Horn (1990), who made no further contributions to the Third Quest. He concludes that we have original Jesus material "wherever in the Gospels there are still objections against Jesus from the Jewish environment." The criterion is grounded in source analysis and/or form criticism to the extent that Horn argues with little interest in the identity of the tradents themselves and thus raises the question of the *Sitz im Leben*. That stance is problematic, for a statement about the *Sitz im Leben* does not necessarily imply a statement about origin or originality.[621] His procedure is also problematic with regard to content, since he links his criterion with the idea of a "normative Judaism" at the time of Jesus.[622]

In most of the recent contributions to the discussion, the criterion of dissimilarity is relativized by relating it to historical context and history of effects. Within the Third Quest, this relativizing occasionally raises the question of the uniqueness of Jesus. Once again E. P. Sanders, in his Ethel Wood Lecture of 1990, has taken a basic stand on this issue. He shows that, in principle, it is methodologically impossible to establish uniqueness, just as it is in the fatal alteration and mixture of uniqueness and superiority. In this sense, J. P. Meier suggests that instead of "unique" it would be preferable to speak of "what is strikingly characteristic" or "unusual."[623] Sanders concludes that—with many

---

618. Ibid., 170.

619. Ibid., 173; hereby he also criticizes E. P. Sanders.

620. Charlesworth, *Jesus Within Judaism*, 6.

621. Cf. A. P. Winton, *The Proverbs of Jesus. Issues of History and Rhetoric* (JSNTS 35; Sheffield: JSOT, 1990) 110.

622. F. W. Horn:, "Diakonische Leitlinien Jesu," in G. K. Schäfer and Th. Strohm, eds. *Diakonie-biblische Grundlagen und Orientierungen. Ein Arbeitsbuch zur theologischen Verständigung über den diakonischen Auftrag* (Heidelberg: HVA, 1990) 116.

623. Meier, *A Marginal Jew*, 174.

parallels to his environment in the details of his message—when Jesus' work is taken as a whole it is obviously unique.[624] His life, however, is in no way different from the lives of other human beings, for no two human beings are totally alike.[625] B. J. Lee traces the question of the uniqueness or remarkableness of Jesus back to the question of Christian identity. This identity is constituted, however, only in part by the historical figure of Jesus; the other part is the history of Christianity. Lee has thus achieved a theological unburdening of the quest for the historical Jesus, in that he does not let the question of Christian identity depend only on this historical quest.

The Jesus research of the Third Quest has, of course, been concerned with other criteriological issues than that of the criterion of dissimilarity. In the following, only a few main points regarding the other criteria will be noted: (1) the criterion of multiple attestation, (2) the criterion of material coherence, (3) the criterion of contextual plausibility, (4) the criterion of the plausibility of historical effects, and (5) an attempt to introduce a new "criterion of data analysis."

1. *The criterion of multiple attestation.* J. D. Crossan's 1988 work begins directly with the variety of ways that Jesus is understood within the early Christian traditions. From this point of departure he moves back in quest of the words and deeds of Jesus that could have generated this plurality of understandings. This search leads him to a criterion that he formulates as an alternative to the criterion of dissimilarity: the original is that which best explains the variety within the tradition.[626] In his Jesus book of 1991, Crossan uses this criterion within a larger methodological context. For him the Jesus tradition consists of three layers: (1) authentic Jesus materials; (2) expanded, modified, and adapted materials; and, finally, (3) materials that have been secondarily created, including the combining of complexes of traditions.[627] Crossan considers his primary task to be a careful delineation of the stratigraphy of this tradition, a procedure in which he intentionally adopts this concept from geology and archaeology and applies it to the temporal strata of the tradition. He compares the methodology of Jesus research in the present to that of archaeology in the nineteenth century, thus criticizing the arbitrary use of elements of the material according to the interests of the researcher or in order to con-

---

624. Ibid., 174.

625. E. P. Sanders, "The Question of Uniqueness in the Teaching of Jesus" (The Ethel M. Wood Lecture 1990; London: University of London, 1990) 6, 24–26. Cf. also Sanders and Davies, *Studying the Synoptic Gospels,* 316–23.

626. J. D. Crossan, "Divine Immediacy and Human Immediacy: Toward a New First Principle in Historical Jesus Research," *Semeia* 44 (1988): 125.

627. Crossan, *The Historical Jesus,* xxxi.

firm his or her own position, without regard to which layer of the tradition they may be found. Although Crossan keeps in mind the larger picture of Jesus' times, he clearly focuses on the stratification of the tradition itself. His decisive criterion is that of "multiple attestation" (see above). In all this he is concerned with the reconstruction of the historical figure of Jesus, not with the exegesis of New Testament texts.[628]

2. *The criterion of material coherence.* T. Holtz rejects the old version of the criterion of dissimilarity in its dual form and emphasizes the necessity of proving the inauthenticity of a tradition (not only the authenticity), and formulates as his criterion the "coherence of the material one is searching for" (1989).[629] He thus does not use the "coherence" terminology to refer to the coherence of elements of the tradition with those materials that have already been established as authentic. By "coherence" he points instead to a historical portrayal of Jesus as a whole—typical for the horizon of the Third Quest, which is not primarily concerned with the verification or falsification of the authenticity of particular biblical texts.

3. *The criterion of contextual plausibility.* This shift in the perspective from which the question is asked becomes clear in discussions by Winton, who asks how the Jew Jesus understood himself as the founder of a renewal movement in his own time. Thus Winton has little interest in showing distinctions and dissimilarities between Jesus and Judaism, but concentrates instead on their continuity, and Jesus' modification of traditional Jewish ideas.[630] In this sense J. P. Meier names two criteria that are concerned to make it understandable how Jesus could be rejected and killed in his Jewish context.[631]

4. *The criterion of the plausibility of historical effects.* E. P. Sanders focuses his attention on inner-historical relationships and connects the idea of Jesus' correspondence to his environment with a criterion of historical effects that relates Jesus to the later movement that appealed to Jesus as its founder. Those traditions are authentic that correspond to a twofold standard: "making Jesus a believable figure in first-century Palestine and the founder of a movement which eventuated in the church."[632] G. Theissen argues in a similar manner when he makes it a condition for the authenticity of Jesus traditions that they be historically possible within the framework of the Judaism of his time and that they make possible the development of early Christianity.[633]

---

628. Ibid., xxiii.
629. T. Holtz, "Jesus," *EKL* 2 (1989): 825.
630. Winton, *The Proverbs of Jesus*, 110.
631. Meier, *A Marginal Jew*, 177, 180.
632. Sanders, *Jesus and Judaism*, 167.
633. Theissen, *The Shadow of the Galilean*, 141.

This history-of-effects criterion is deepened and extended by S. Fowl (1989), who relates it to the issue of the burden of proof: when the historical hypothesis used by a scholar to explain the materials contradicts that of the evangelists, the scholar must also be able to explain how the incorrect explanation given by the evangelists came about.[634] Of course, Fowl relates this criterion to another plane, that is, not on the level of the trustworthiness or authenticity of *tradition* but on the level of the trustworthiness or plausibility of *theses of scholarly research*. He clearly is aiming at the historical reconstruction of the Third Quest.

For this historical reconstruction, Winton in 1990 formulated three convincing test questions that summarize what has been said so far: In the first place, Jesus must be credibly presented within the Jewish context of his time. Second, his execution by the Romans must be explainable. And in the third place, how the Christian communities came into being must be at least illuminated—even if not totally explained.[635]

From a methodological point of view, the most thoroughly thought-through recent catalogue of criteria is that of E. Baasland (1992), for it clearly highlights the importance of the history of effects (*Wirkungsgeschichte*). Baasland distinguishes three perspectives from which the questions reflected in the different criteria are posed: (1) the criterion of dissimilarity or discrepancy derives from the question of the *original*, (2) the criteria of coherence and cross-section perspective derive from the question of *internal connections*, and (3) the criteria of longitudinal perspective and consequences derive from the question of the *effects* of Jesus' life.[636] He sees the following alternative: *Either* one combines the quest for the original with that of the internal connections— a combination that results in the criterion of dissimilarity that dominates exegetical studies. *Or* one combines the quest for the effects with that of the internal connections—this combination then opens new ways for research to proceed: "For a truly historical understanding the principles of coherence and consequences must have priority over the theologically-oriented criterion of discrepancy."[637] The question is then, What is it that can make understandable Jesus' death; his effect on his disciples, Jews and Romans; the origin of the early church and its mission; as well as the origin of the Jesus tradition itself. The results discovered by this method should then once again be examined within the framework of a "comprehensive historical picture" by means of

---

634. S. Fowl, "Reconstructing and Deconstructing the Quest of the Historical Jesus," *SJT* 42 (1989): 327.

635. Winton, "The Proverbs of Jesus," 123.

636. Baasland, *Theologie und Methode*, 260.

637. Ibid., 261.

three criteria. The first regards how they fit into their purported Jewish context. Do they really fit into Jesus' historical milieu? Second, with regard to their interrelatedness, do Jesus' sayings fit together with each other and with Jesus' actions into an understandable whole? And finally must be asked, What seems exceptional within this complex of interconnections? Can a plausible explanation be found even for the dark and difficult elements in the tradition? These reflections bring Baasland into the proximity of our criterion of plausibility, but with two differences: the criterion of dissimilarity is not adopted even in its corrected form (in the sense of a quest for the contextual individuality of Jesus). This is understandable as a reaction to its overrated status, but it is a material deficit. In addition, the history-of-effects is overemphasized. In his program, the elements in the tradition that go against its flow or even contradict it play at most a corrective role and only at the third stage (in the explaining of dark sayings). In the background stands the hypothesis, widespread in Scandinavia, according to which there was an amazing continuity and stability in the Jesus tradition. Baasland appeals to general studies in folklore in support of this understanding of the Jesus tradition. Independently of this critique, however, one can say that Baasland has presented one of the most important contributions to the new formulation of criteria.[638]

5. *The criterion of data analysis.* Parallel to the present book appeared the Habilitationsschrift of A. Scriba, which referred to our own work (*Kriterien der Jesus-Forschung. Darstellung und Kritik mit einer neuen Rekonstruktion des Wirkens Jesu* [1998; now published as *Echtheitskriterien der Jesus Forschung: Kritische Revisionen und konstruktiver Neuansatz.* BWANT 2000]). A. Scriba shares our critique of the traditional criteria and rightly sees that our fourfold specification of the criterion of dissimilarity adopts some of the earlier criteria. He thinks, however, that precisely by so doing their weaknesses are taken over as well, especially because he thinks of early post-Easter Christianity as more creative and pluralistic than do we, and because he reckons with more direct continuity between Judaism and Christianity than do we—a continuity not mediated by Jesus. Nonetheless, he accepts our criterion of plausibility—not so much to establish the authenticity of particular texts, but more as a "means of getting a rough idea of the factors that shaped Jesus' life and work" (220). He uses this criterion in his original and astute reconstruction of Jesus' work: on the one hand, he denies to Jesus the message of judgment, though this is often attributed to him in the texts, and, on the other hand, he attributes to

---

638. The work by E. Baasland was a Norwegian dissertation essentially finished in 1979 but thoroughly revised for the German translation (1992). It thus appeared as a methodological study about the same time as the beginning of the "Third Quest." Especially to be emphasized is the intensive debate with secular historical scholarship.

him an eschatological expectation focused on a very specific date (Passover eve of the year 28 C.E.), which is never documented in the texts. In order to be able to make such concrete reconstructions and statements, it is clear that he had to go beyond "getting a rough idea" of what was historical! How is that possible? He proposes a new criterion of "data analysis" and explains programmatically that he will use this criterion "and avoid the other criteria as much as possible" (3). Many data are indisputable, such as the baptism of Jesus by John the Baptist, the crucifixion, and the Easter appearances. With them as a point of departure, the historian can proceed to reconstruct connections, whether on the basis of parallels within the history of the tradition, or on the basis of the horizon of his experience as a historian. Since A. Scriba presents no precise summary formulation of his new criterion, we will cite an extensive section:

> For historical data that are only handed on in an isolated manner or have been displaced from their original context and placed in another, one can reconstruct the complex of actions and thought world to which they originally belonged by comparing the history of traditions of similar data whose original context is still recognizable. An illuminating example, repeatedly discussed, is provided by the execution of Jesus on the cross: however political Jesus may have intended his own words and deeds to be, one can conclude from the manner in which he was put to death that he was dealt with by Pilate as a political agitator.
>
> When parallels in tradition history that can be directly analyzed are not available, a broader constructive procedure can be applied, if done so with care. To be sure, in the data handed on there must be nuanced reports, and the ways in which they are connected must be at least partially recognized. From these, within the framework of the historian's own experienced horizon, the different effects of the transmitted data in different sets of circumstances can be projected and the respective probability of each can be evaluated. Parallels from current history of traditions can provide support for this procedure.
>
> In historical Jesus research, these insights raise the following questions: Which events in the life of Jesus can be made historically probable? What can still be perceived of their context? What does the internal structure of these events look like, and what range of possible functions would they fit? (93)

We would like to make only one point in regard to this new criterion: It is not a criterion, but an application of different criteria. The named "data" are not simply "self-evident givens," but are evidently authentic because they are documented as elements that resist the tendencies of the traditions in which they are embedded (e.g., the baptism of Jesus by John); also because they are found in several potentially independent streams of tradition; and because they possess a high degree of contextual plausibility. In our judgment the criterion of data analysis stands on the same level as the "indications of dissimilarity" and the "argument from evaluating the sources" as subcriteria dependent on the primary criteria. As a whole, the attempt of A. Scriba is reminiscent of P. W. Schmiedel's quest for "foundational pillars" for the reconstruction of the historical Jesus at the beginning of the twentieth century, except that Schmiedel wanted to assemble a list of authentic texts while Scriba wants to find particular data in (and behind) the texts. While E. Baasland is a "conservative" voice in the discussion, A. Scriba represents a "critical" voice that wants to reconstruct the historical Jesus even "against the text"—without doubt one of the most important contributions to the issue of criteria in recent years.

Despite their differences from earlier Jesus research, the authors of the Third Quest are in one regard very similar to their predecessors: they are not concerned, in any degree worth mentioning, with the issues and methods of (secular) historical scholarship (with the notable exceptions of E. Baasland and A. Scriba). The discussion of criteriological questions mostly runs along internal theological lines.[639]

c) The Picture of Jesus in the Work of James H. Charlesworth

When James H. Charlesworth writes his Jesus book, he can already recognize the Third Quest as a new period of scholarship, to which he had already referred in earlier essays on the history of Jesus research.[640] The 1985 Gunning Lecture in Edinburgh was the basis of his 1988 book *Jesus within Judaism*. More strongly than is the case in Sander's work, for example, Charlesworth is interested in writing in a way understandable by the general public.[641] The series in which Charlesworth's book appeared, The Anchor Bible Reference Library, also has this commitment.

The prevailing approach of the book is to see Jesus as a historical figure within Judaism, that is, as an insider to the Jewish community. This is already clear in the pointed title, *Jesus within Judaism*. Illustrated contributions from archaeology are an integral element in his presentation.

Charlesworth is fascinated by the wealth of Jewish sources and archaeological finds from the time of Jesus. The subtitle makes clear that he sees here an important impulse for research: "New Light from Exciting Archaeological Discoveries." In his excitement for such historical material, Charlesworth is close to the Old Quest for the historical Jesus. An outstanding example of this

---

639. A work of interest in this context is that of J. Vansina, *Oral Tradition as History* (Madison: University of Wisconsin Press, 1985), a completely revised version of *Oral Tradition: A Study in Historical Methodology* (Chicago: Aldine Publishing Co., 1965).

640. See above under II.2.4.a.i; cf. also Appendix 5 of his Jesus book.

641. Charlesworth, *Jesus Within Judaism*, ix.

interest is his engaged discussion of determining the location of Peter's house in Capernaum.[642]

The structure of the book reflects the intent of its content: the middle four of the six chapters are occupied with the relation of Jesus to the Old Testament Pseudepigrapha, to the Dead Sea Scrolls, to the Nag Hammadi codices, and to Josephus, as well as to archaeological discoveries. With much more precision than in the New Quest, he deals with Judaism (but also with apocryphal Christian traditions such as the *Gospel of Thomas*) and brings them into relation to Jesus. The framework is provided by an introductory chapter on Jesus research in the 1980s and a concluding chapter on Jesus' self-understanding and his understanding of God. The former is central for Charlesworth's own understanding of Jesus.

Typically for the Third Quest, Charlesworth intentionally brackets theological questions posed from a clearly Christian position (although he personally identifies himself unhesitatingly with such a position[643]), and concentrates on issues raised by a purely historical perspective. Commentaries oriented to matters of Christian faith are considered "intrusive."[644] To be sure, Charlesworth considers a biography of Jesus, for example, in the sense of presenting a novelistic portrayal of the development of his personality, to be impossible because of inadequate information in the primary sources. In emphatic contrast to Bultmann, however, he considers it crucial to affirm more than the undeniable "thatness" of Jesus existence. Charlesworth is interested in relatively sure knowledge we may obtain about Jesus' intention,[645] so that for him Jesus research is no more prolegomenon for a theology of the New Testament.[646]

Charlesworth repeatedly emphasizes that Jesus research has become necessary because of the flood of new knowledge about Jesus' environment,[647] even though there is no *theological* necessity for scholarly study of the historical Jesus. This grounding in scholarly historical study rather than theological considerations is typical of the approach of the Third Quest. Charlesworth notes, however, that theological objection to Jesus research has disappeared, and he sees the function of Jesus research and archaeology as serving the Christian faith.[648] However, the theological relevance of historical study of

---

642. Ibid., 112.

643. This becomes clear in the discussion of the evaluation of the Qumran discoveries, cf. Charlesworth, *Jesus within Judaism*, 57, 74–75.

644. Ibid., xi.

645. Ibid., 132.

646. Ibid., 21.

647. Ibid., 6, 9, 13, 26–27.

648. Ibid., 27, 127, 156.

Jesus, and/or the *theological* guidelines for the appropriation of such study remains unclear.

It is of fundamental importance for Charlesworth that Jesus can only be understood from within Judaism.[649] Precisely on this point the problematic of the criterion of dissimilarity becomes virulent for Charlesworth; it is a problem to which he points from the very beginning: Jesus speaks as a Jew within Jewish culture and tradition, and he cannot possibly be understood if the authenticity of Jewish sayings and deeds is methodologically excluded at the beginning.[650]

In discussing the theme "Sin and Forgiveness," Charlesworth points out the anti-Jewish history of Christianity and its portrayal of Jesus as the contrasting picture to Judaism.[651] In the course of this discussion, he emphasizes the Jewish piety of Jesus and traces his religious brilliance back to its roots in Jewish theology.[652]

In Charlesworth's portrayal of Jesus, the Pseudepigrapha plays an important role. Even if Jesus is not to be counted directly among the apocalyptists, the influence of apocalyptic streams of thought (Daniel, Enoch) is still noticeable.[653]

In regard to the question of the relation of Jesus to the Essenes, Charlesworth advocates an intermediate position. He does not identify Jesus as an Essene, but neither does he consider it plausible that Jesus was strictly separated from them. The important thing for him is that the Qumran scrolls enlarge our knowledge of Judaism in the time of Jesus, and that the Essene community and Jesus shared the same ancient traditions, the same land, the same time and place.[654] This position that incorporates Jesus into the apocalyptic stream and relates him to the Essenes implies a criterion of correspondence with Judaism.

In order to confirm the influence of the Essenes on Jesus, Charlesworth names two criteria. The first criterion aims at the most trustworthy Jesus material we can recover, and thus seeks sayings of Jesus that show no traces of the post-Easter time or the evangelists. It is thus a form of the CDC. The second criterion determines material expressed in specifically Essene forms of thought not otherwise present in contemporary Judaism.[655] Charlesworth finds Essene influence in both the negative and positive senses: Mark 2:27

---

649. Ibid., 169.
650. Ibid., 166–77.
651. Ibid., 45–51.
652. Ibid., 50.
653. Ibid., 38, 42.
654. Ibid., 59.
655. Ibid., 54.

serves as an example for distinguishing Jesus from the Essenes, while Matt 5:3 serves as an example for the possible sympathy of Jesus with Essene points of view, for they describe themselves as "poor in Spirit."[656]

Charlesworth concludes that the Essene movement was one of several Jewish streams that contributed to the formation of early Christianity. He names Jesus as the founder of Christianity,[657] later restricted to the Palestinian Jesus movement.[658]

In the discussion of the *Gospel of Thomas*, to which he attributes considerable importance,[659] he uses the criterion of coherence, understood in the sense of coherence with material already considered authentic on other grounds.[660]

Charlesworth is especially interested in Jesus' self-understanding, and here too he betrays a certain affinity with the nineteenth-century studies of the historical Jesus. The beginning point for Charlesworth is Jesus' understanding of God.[661] For this he depends heavily on Joachim Jeremias's studies of Jesus' use of "Abba." While he decidedly rejects the claim that Jesus was absolutely unique in his use of "Abba," he still holds that Jesus' *emphasis* on "Abba" was indeed unique.[662] This view means, of course, a repetition in weakened form of the old argument about the distant God of Judaism and the near God of Jesus, in the background of which stands an anti-Jewish tradition.[663]

Central for Charlesworth's understanding of Jesus is Jesus' own understanding of himself and his intention. He explicitly disclaims the attempt to make statements about Jesus' self-consciousness, as though Jesus proclaimed himself. While Charlesworth associates Jesus' *self-consciousness* with a psychoanalytic or a nineteenth-century romanticized approach to Jesus for which there is no justification in the statements of the biblical tradition, with Jesus' *self-understanding* he means the intention of Jesus' life and work as derived from our available sources.[664]

---

656. Ibid., 65–67, 68–71.

657. Ibid., 75.

658. Ibid., 167.

659. Ibid., 90.

660. Ibid., 86, 88.

661. Ibid., 132.

662. This idea is to be accepted despite the problem involved in the argument from silence, of which Charlesworth is aware.

663. Charlesworth, *Jesus Within Judaism*, 133–34.

664. Ibid., 135–36; Charlesworth expresses the matter thus: "An attempt to comprehend Jesus' self-understanding must be kept distinct from, although it is somewhat analogous to, an attempt to understand Jesus' self-consciousness." (Ibid., 135).

Three New Testament traditions are decisive for Charlesworth's portrayal of Jesus' self-understanding: Jesus' choice of twelve disciples (this implies, if authentic, the possibility of a messianic self-understanding of Jesus), the entrance into Jerusalem, and the parable of the Wicked Vineyard Keepers. Charlesworth uses social-history exegesis, among other methods, to argue that the basic form of the parable comes from Jesus, and he infers from this parable Jesus' self-understanding as the "Son."

Charlesworth consistently advocates the criterion of correspondence with Judaism.[665] For example, he applies this criterion when he argues that the Jewish use of the term "Son of God" in Jesus' time implies that Jesus also used it.[666]

Charlesworth is to be classified with that wing of the Third Quest that has its roots in a tradition of Jesus research that did not let itself be influenced by the rejection of the quest for the historical Jesus on theological grounds. The name to be mentioned as standard-bearer of this movement is Joachim Jeremias. An unmistakable Christian motivation drives Charlesworth to historical studies of Jesus, but he is concerned to keep this motivation separate from historical method itself.[667] He is thus a typical representative of the Third Quest, just as he is with his newly sharpened perspective on Judaism and its subtly nuanced streams, within which he perceives Jesus. Jesus' being a Jew and his effects on Jews and Gentiles are for Charlesworth the fundamental data for a historical image of Jesus.[668]

2.5 Concluding Comments: The Historicity of Jesus and the Criterion of Dissimilarity

The criterion of dissimilarity and the motives that stand behind it run like a red thread through the various phases of Jesus research. We have shown that what has been called the "criterion of dissimilarity" deals with two distinguishable criteria, with which two different interests are often associated: the source-critical CDC, which is especially motivated by criticism of church and dogma; and the CDJ, associated with the history of religions and comparative religions approach, which is characterized by anti-Jewish perspectives and materials as well as the thought world of the history of philosophy. The idea of the "great man," the personality who shapes history, plays a role here, just as does Protestant confessionalism, which identified Judaism with Roman Catholic traditionalism.

---

665. Ibid., 168.
666. Ibid., 152.
667. Cf. Ibid., 168, which speaks of "disinterested scientific historical research."
668. Ibid., 167.

For the Old Quest of the historical Jesus, a critical stance toward church and dogma was especially important, and it precipitated out methodologically in the CDC. In addition, anti-Judaism—in tandem with a positive valuation of "ancient Israel," understood as antithetic to Judaism—leads to a frequently implicitly presupposed CDJ, which was used in this phase of Jesus research less as a means of determining the "authentic" as of determining the "essential."

In the New Quest the center of gravity shifted in the direction of the CDJ. The CDJ is explicitly formulated and aggressively advocated. In contrast, the CDC recedes under the ecclesiastical pressure of critical biblical scholarly methodology and is applied in a more regulated manner.

However, behind both forms of the criterion of dissimilarity, behind the CDC as behind the CDJ, stands a common inclination toward the ahistorical. Since the historicity of Jesus also implies his relativity, it is perceived as problematic. This relativity has two levels. On the one level, "history is necessarily an imprecise science because of the nature of the subject matter."[669] Therefore the results of historical work can "only" obtain various levels of plausibility, and the results are always revisable.[670] While dialectic theology saw the radical decision necessary for the life of faith as endangered by the indisputable "facts" of history, it is also true that the fear that faith would become dependent on the changeable results of historical study played a role. The second level of the relativity of the "historical" Jesus refers to his being brought within a realm where he can be compared with other historical figures and phenomena. The historical perspective relates Jesus to his preceding history, his environment, and the history of his effects.

Here the criterion of dissimilarity in both of its forms is an attempt to overcome the historicity of Jesus—and that means also his relativity. The criterion of dissimilarity—resting on identifiable historical methodology—is supposed to soften the effect of this relativizing historical methodology, that is, to subdue the effect of historical work with its own weapons. In practice, the criterion of dissimilarity is supposed to overcome the historical relativizing of Jesus, or to compensate for it, by showing that on particular points Jesus is unrelated to his own historical context. To state it in an oversimplified manner, Jesus was incomparable in his environment, without historical antecedents (CDJ), and/or after him there were only pale epigones captive to their own structures, thus no continuing effect on history (CDC).

---

669. C. Murray, "History and Faith," in A. Cameron, ed., *History as Text. The Writing of Ancient History* (London: Duckworth, 1989) 179.

670. This is seen also in the procedure of the Jesus Seminar, where marbles of different colors are used for different degrees of probability.

The postulate of the uniqueness of Jesus that stands behind all this has its origin in dogmatic theology. This postulates outlines an essential problem of the criterion of dissimilarity: the category of the historical individuality of Jesus is transformed into a historicized Christology. This leads to the difficulties that E. P. Sanders has splendidly described in his Ethel Wood Lecture: more and more details are sought in order to strengthen faith in Jesus' uniqueness.[671]

For the Christian religion that has its own origin in history, the question of the uniqueness of Jesus is a question of its own identity. This question is also discussed in other fields of theological study. One can think of the debate in the theology of pastoral care about the "proprium" of Christian pastoral care in contrast to psychotherapy. Identity is sought by marking itself off over against its "environment," and this uniqueness or "proprium" is to be located in particular identifiable elements. However, one can only meaningfully speak about historical uniqueness by speaking of historical individuality that keeps the person as a whole in view (and this includes the person's environment, antecedent history, and later effects). Lee is entirely right in his statement that specific details about the person of Jesus are only one step in approaching the specific identity of Christianity—the following developments of Christian groups in the two generations after Jesus are just as important.[672] It is particularly difficult for Protestant theology to see this history as on the same plane with the history of Jesus. The canon within the canon of the *sola scriptura* is from time to time a *sola historia Jesu*.

With regard to the "dissimilarity" and uniqueness of Jesus, the Third Quest differs from both the original Quest of the Historical Jesus and the New Quest. In the Third Quest, the CDJ is fundamentally rejected—with the help of a critical perception of the anti-Jewish element in the history of Christian theology, and the CDC is applied in a controlled manner. Above all, however, a change takes place in contrast to the earlier phases of Jesus research, a change that transcends a shift in the way the CDJ and CDC are evaluated. In the "Third Quest" it is no longer principally a matter of showing the dissimilarity and historical uniqueness and distinctiveness of Jesus. Questions of Christian and ecclesiological identity recede into the background in favor of a variety of individual religious approaches independent of normative prescriptions.

The alignment to the historical question, not bound to exposition of the Bible as Christian Scripture, allows confessional boundaries to fade away, and doubtless one of the most important elements in the Third Quest is the conversation about Jesus between scholars of Christian and Jewish background.

---

671. Sanders, "The Question of Uniqueness," esp. 23.
672. Lee, *The Galilean Jewishness of Jesus*, 96.

The change in climate is clear: "dissimilarities" are not as zealously sought as are common elements. Along with this, the insight is present that uniqueness or distinctiveness does not necessarily mean better or having a higher claim to truth. Thus even where the CDC is still applied in moderate form, the criterion of dissimilarity in the Third Quest as a whole has lost its determinative function because it has lost its function as a landmark that points the way. It continues to be a desideratum that other criteria in the Third Quest's Jesus research will become as clear as this one has.

The development of Jesus research within the Third Quest has produced a sharp cleft between interest in the "historical Jesus" and exposition of the Scripture. However welcome the autonomy of study of the historical Jesus from ecclesiastical interest may be, New Testament scholarship does not do well to concentrate on exegesis and to let historical questions about Jesus fade into the background. The whole mountain of popular publications about Jesus shows that the task of New Testament study cannot be limited to handling New Testament texts within the framework of a nonhistorical literary criticism that considers itself bound only to the text itself. The fact of Jesus' historicity broadens the perspective beyond understanding the evangelists merely as reflections of early Christianity; it presents them also as windows through which the events that lie behind them may be seen.

Studies of the historical Jesus and exegesis of the New Testament are overlapping fields that mutually supplement and stimulate each other. Jesus research alone, with its historically plausible results, cannot bring religious truths to light. All the less can it deliver a historical guarantee for religious truths. The motif of providing a fundamentally positive evaluation of Jesus that runs through the Old Quest into the Third Quest may not mislead us into combining historical portrayals with pseudoreligious claims. This fact is what distinguishes the serious literature of the Third Quest from the innumerable other publications on the historical Jesus that come from the same period.

The task of theology is that of further work on the relation of history and faith in regard to Christologies that take Jesus seriously as a historical person. In this process it is important that the commonplace of the "Jewishness of Jesus" be nuanced, so that the picture of a monolithic Judaism, in itself already to some extent anti-Jewish, is not subtly strengthened. In the sense of this book's own scholarly interest in pointing out anti-Jewish structures of thought, it is to be hoped that such historical insights will work themselves into a wide range of churchly praxis and general public awareness.

The historicity of Jesus is a *locus inevitabilis* for theology and church. Even when they have sometimes shown little interest in the "historical Jesus," he has radiated a strong attractive power. People who have long been alienated from church and Christianity are concerned about Jesus as a historical figure.

Opportunities for dialogue on this point should not be missed. But the historicity of Jesus is also a *locus inevitabilis* inasmuch as it does not relieve one of normative decisions. It does not absolve us from responsibility of conducting ourselves with critical regard to that which we know about Jesus historically. And finally, the historicity of Jesus is a *via inevitabilis*. It encourages us, in the reality of the historical present with all its complexity, contradictions, and ambiguities, to dare to follow the footsteps of Jesus through history.

III

The Criterion of Historical Plausibility as a Correction of the Criterion of Dissimilarity

Methodological Aspects of the Quest for Criteria

The criterion of dissimilarity has played an important role in all phases of the research on the life of Jesus. However, the preceding survey of research has also shown that in its double-sided form as a strategy of marking Jesus off from both Judaism and Christianity, the criterion of dissimilarity has only been advocated programmatically during the period of the "New Quest" (from ca. 1953 to 1980). Here it was applied only weakly with regard to Christianity, since there was a conscious effort to develop a continuity between the historical Jesus and earliest Christianity. In contrast, its application intensified with regard to Judaism, since it was supposed that Jesus himself had already made an exodus from Judaism. It was in this exodus that the New Quest saw a continuity between Jesus and Christianity. In the meanwhile, reservations about the criterion of dissimilarity had become increasingly louder. Scholarly research had developed in another direction by locating Jesus solidly within Judaism and by making a clear methodological distinction between study of the historical Jesus and the problems of legitimizing Christian theology. It is therefore time to replace the criterion of dissimilarity with a new criterion, in the process keeping its legitimate elements and correcting its distortions and one-sidedness.

In a first section we will formulate our suggestion for a new criterion, which we call "the criterion of historical plausibility." It has a connection to the traditional criterion of dissimilarity in that this criterion is also two-sided: in regard to Judaism we speak of contextual plausibility; in regard to Christianity, of the plausibility of historical effects. In the two following sections we reflect on the historical use of this criterion with its subcriteria in two directions. First, we ask what we are really looking for when we formulate criteria of authenticity: What do we understand under "authenticity"? Then we discuss the degree of probability of the results of a historical investigation of Jesus. In other words, we ask, What does "historical plausibility" mean in this context? We thus deal with three themes: (1) the criterion and its subcriteria, (2) the authenticity of the tradition we are seeking, and (3) the plausibility of the results and of the portrayal of Jesus as a whole.

1. THE CRITERION OF HISTORICAL PLAUSIBILITY AND ITS SUBCRITERIA

The double-sided criterion of dissimilarity—with a one-sided delimitation of Jesus over against Judaism—cannot be maintained in its traditional form. For a historian, the study of Jesus cannot be only a matter of "demarcation," drawing contrasting dividing lines. The historian is interested in determining the material relation of Jesus to his context and to the history of his effects, in which there will be both points in common and points of disagreement, both lines of continuity and gaps of discontinuity. Both are important for a reconstruction of the "historical Jesus"; that is methodologically understandable. Moreover, every historian will insist that justice be done to both sides of the criterion: the determination of the relation of the Jesus tradition to Judaism as well as to early Christianity. In this process the latter is to be given a certain priority in matters of authenticity, since we have relevant Jesus tradition almost exclusively in the form of Christian traditions. We must always first "subtract" specifically Christian perspectives, clear post-Easter expressions of Christian faith, and material reflecting church tendencies in order to precipitate out those traditions that we can make the basis of a reconstruction of the historical Jesus. When in these remaining traditions, though they have been transmitted and shaped by a community with Christian convictions and ecclesiastical necessities, we discover clearly Jewish elements that cannot be explained as Jewish Christian reactions against the tendencies of Gentile Christianity that were already present, then we are probably close to the historical Jesus. In any case, we can identify such Jewish elements in the tradition by bracketing out the Christian character of the sources—that is, by being sensitive to the difference of the Jesus traditions in contrast to early Christianity. We thus begin with a new formulation of this side of the criterion of dissimilarity.

1.1 The Plausibility of Historical Effects and the Criterion of Dissimilarity vis-à-vis Christianity (CDC)

The Christian sources that derive from Jesus are a part of his historical effect, even when they cannot be traced back to Jesus in a monocausal manner. There were other factors that determined the history of his own effects. In a source-critical investigation of the Jesus tradition, the important thing is precisely to distinguish all these different factors and to be able to assess how much and which parts of the tradition derive from Jesus. We may thus examine the extant sources in terms of the history of Jesus' affects under a twofold aspect. On the one hand, this history has carried the tradition further and further from Jesus. Thus we must search for remnants of the historical Jesus that have been preserved despite those tendencies in the history of Jesus' effects that have generated this increasing distancing from Jesus. On the other hand, this history of effects was set in motion by Jesus himself. This history is what connects early Christianity to him. We can thus also look for traits and distinctive marks in this history that connects it lastingly to Jesus.

a) Opposition to Traditional Bias as the First Aspect of the Plausibility of Historical Effects

When we look for those elements in the history of Jesus' effects that have been preserved despite all the other tendencies at work in the tradition, then we can make renewed use of the criterion of dissimilarity in its positive function (that is, its confirming function and not its negative, excluding function). This corresponds to the line of argument practiced everywhere in source-critical historical scholarship: historical credibility belongs accordingly to the "remnants," that is, to unintentional evidence that is not influenced by the tendency of the source. Such remnants are either in some tension with the tradition or even explicitly contrary to it. We thus suggest the criterion of "opposition to traditional bias" as the means of separating such elements in the tradition. The presupposition of this criterion is that the continuing effects of Jesus were reformulated in early Christianity in a "tendentious" manner—among other ways, by the Easter faith, the formation of the church, the acceptance of Gentiles, as well as the increasing adoration of Jesus as a divine figure. That which contradicts such clearly demonstrable tendencies (or at least is in tension with them) has a claim to authenticity. We may illustrate by three examples where such tradition-resistant elements in the tradition can be found. (Additional examples for the individual criteria may be found in the final chapter.) The three examples are as follows:

> 1. Early Christianity rather quickly distanced itself from Judaism and polemically distinguished itself from it. The Pharisees and scribes became the stereotypical opponents of Jesus. When, contrary to this tendency, in Mark 12:28ff. a "reasonable" scribe appears and agrees with Jesus that the double commandment of love for God and love for neighbor is the most important of all the commandments, even more important than the sacrificial cult, then this is against the flow of the tradition.

2. Moreover, early Christianity developed a positive ethos with regard to the family. Contrary to this tendency, however, it preserved the memory of a conflict between Jesus and his family. According to Mark 3:21, Jesus' "own" come to Jesus and want to seize him as though he were out of his mind. This can not possibly have been invented! After Easter, members of Jesus' family belonged to the early Christian community and were disciples of Jesus.

3. Early Christianity always numbered Judas Iscariot among the twelve disciples and had simply scorned and condemned him as the one who betrayed Jesus. When nevertheless the Jesus tradition preserves a promise that the twelve (and not the "eleven"!) disciples will exercise future rule over the restored Israel (Matt 19:28/Luke 22:28–30), there can be no doubt that this is a saying that has withstood the tendencies of the tradition.

It is certainly possible to express doubts as to whether such resistance to the tendencies of the tradition is sufficient to claim that a particular saying or story can be traced back to Jesus. In each case material that is detected by this criterion should be subjected to further tests (1) by investigating its tradition history up to its reception in a written source and (2) by a comparison of Jesus materials that have a related content in other strands of the tradition. Two problems arise here:

First, is it conceivable that in early Christianity traditions were handed on without being connected to the purpose of some short-term historical situation in a particular phase of its transmission, a phase that can no longer be perceived or reconstructed, so that the traditions shaped by it must now appear to us as relics?[1] In other words, could it be that elements in tension with or opposed to the tendencies of the tradition are not a reflection of the life of Jesus, but relics of one of the earliest phases of Christian history? To return to one of our examples, Might the amicable discussion between a scribe and Jesus about the double commandment of love go back to an early phase in the life of the church in which Christians still understood themselves as a part of Judaism, and were also so understood by others? Or, to take another example, in Mark 10:17–18, when Jesus rejects the address "good teacher" and then contrasts himself with the only God, who "alone is good," this is certainly an element contrary to the tendencies of the developing tradition. Here Jesus is intentionally distinguished from God, whereas elsewhere we find the tendency to revere Jesus as a divine being. But could it not be that here we have a relic of an early stage of reverence for Jesus that presents him as an exemplary and consistent advocate of Jewish monotheism? So also in the temptation story in

---

1. Thus the reflections of W. Marxsen, *The Beginnings of Christology: A Study in its Problems* (trans. Paul J. Achtemeier; Facet Books Biblical Series 22; Philadelphia: Fortress Press, 1969) 14–15; E. Schillebeeckx, *Jesus*, 92–93.

the Sayings Source, Jesus appears as a Jew who consistently rejects the divine honors offered him and holds fast to the worship of the one God alone. But hardly anyone would argue that the temptation story is the report of a historical event. In its present form it bears the imprint of the post-Easter church. Thus does Mark 10:17–18 also derive from a milieu comparable to that in which the temptation story was formed?

A second problem results from the internal plurality of early Christianity, which very early had already split into different branches. We find different images of Jesus in the Sayings Source, in the Gospel of Mark, in the Johannine tradition, in the *Gospel of Thomas*. Each of these images of Jesus is a well-rounded, finished product, independent of the others, even if the sources in which they are preserved reveal traces of mutual interdependence. Thus if very early there were already independent streams of Christian tradition, we might find in these complexes of tradition elements in tension with the tradition that are not relics of the historical Jesus, but that represent the influence of some other stream of tradition.[2] Here too we may present an example. In the Sayings Source, Matt 11:27 is almost always noted as a "Johannine logion," an erratic foreign body that has somehow gotten lodged in the Sayings Source:

> All things have been handed over to me by my Father;
> and no one knows the Son except the Father,
> and no one knows the Father except the Son
> and anyone to whom the Son chooses to reveal him.

Here one immediately perceives the Johannine atmosphere. In Q, this saying might perhaps be called "in tension with the tradition," but that does not make it a saying of the historical Jesus. On the contrary, it more likely bears the marks of the Easter experiences of the church. We are reminded of the words of the risen Jesus in Matt 28:18: "All authority in heaven and on earth has been given to me . . . ," even if the same expression probably designates something different in each case. Matt 11:27 most likely refers to the delivery of knowledge of divine revelation; Matt 28:18, to the investiture with divine authority.

The basic problem is repeatedly the same: the history of the effects of Jesus' message and deeds do not form a unity, an organic whole, that as a unit can be distinguished from the message and ministry of Jesus himself. Within this his-

---

2. This objection is found in G. Schille, "Prolegomena zur Jesusfrage," *TLZ* 93 (1968): 481ff.: The dissonance between Jesus and early Christianity does not explain everything. "If one were to take the other alternative and proceed on the assumption that the secondary constructions of the church after Easter had several roots, one could derive the dissonance from the contrast between two different stances of post-Easter faith, even if they are interpreted more radically than previously."

tory of Jesus' effects, we find different phases and a number of different streams of tradition. Does this then mean that it is not really possible to locate elements in the sources that are contrary to the tradition, as generally practiced in historical studies? Hardly! In the Sayings Source we can clearly designate the elements that are "contrary to the tradition" and fit in with the Johannine style, which are different from the style of the Jesus tradition elsewhere, and which do not go back to Jesus. And in the other cases in which the influence of early Christianity could be perceived, at least so much can be said: we stand nearer to Jesus here than elsewhere. But especially with the awareness of the internal plurality of the history of Jesus' effects, another possibility of knowledge is opened that complements that of locating the more original elements in the tradition by their tensions and contrasts with the general tendencies of the tradition: the more numerous and more independent from each other the sources are, the better we can evaluate the historicity of the event to which they testify! With this we come to the second aspect of the criterion, "the plausibility of historical effects:"

b) Coherence of Sources as the Second Aspect of the Plausibility of Historical Effects

When sources independently of each other testify to the same event, the prospect that we are dealing with authentic material is enhanced. This presupposes that the sources are sufficiently different from each other to assume that they are mutually independent, and still sufficiently similar to each other to assume that they refer to the same event or saying. The increasing awareness of the plurality of early Christianity and its Jesus traditions is thus an opportunity for Jesus research. When particular characteristics of Jesus' words and deeds have survived in most of the complexes of tradition, we could then have the effects of Jesus himself. This is all the more likely when these recurring characteristics are contrary to the other tendencies that we have recognized by the diachronic investigation of the history of the tradition. With this subcriterion of "coherence of sources," we are no doubt joining forces with the traditional criterion of "coherence," but we are providing a new basis for it in the history of Jesus' effects, and we formulate it independently of a "criterion of dissimilarity" that has already been applied. Previously, the criterion of "coherence" was applied to supplement traditions that had been identified as authentic by means of the criterion of dissimilarity. The only criterion was agreement in terms of content with a nucleus of traditions previously so identified—independently of the number of witnesses in independent sources and traditions. We, however, are basing our criterion on the indisputable facts of the diversity of Jesus traditions. With the help of the criterion of "coherence of sources" we lay hold of the elements in these sources that recur repeatedly and thus may represent the effect of the historical Jesus. This also means that the criterion of the coherence of sources may be brought into play in a variety of ways.

The *"cross-section" evidence*[3] refers to recurring items of content, or formal motifs and structures in different streams of tradition. For example, on the basis of such cross-section evidence we are quite certain that Jesus spoke in parables and metaphors. The typical well-known parabolic forms are transmitted to us independently and documented in Q; Mark; the materials peculiar to Matthew and Luke, respectively; the *Gospel of Thomas*; and even the Gospel of John. In John, Jesus speaks in metaphorical "I am" sayings and in allegorical discourses, but here, too, we find, in the analogies of the shepherd and the door in John 10:1–5, similes that have been secondarily adapted to the Johannine allegorical imagery. The specifically Johannine forms of verbal imagery are clearly a further development of the Synoptic parable forms. The Synoptics themselves already have secondary allegorical elements (such as Matt 22:7) and allegorical explanations (such as Mark 4:13–20) that can be distinguished from the original parables. We can thus document the presence (synchronically) of recurring parabolic forms that cannot be traced back to a tendency in early Christianity, and which at the same time (diachronically) confirm a tendency to deviate from them, that is, to transmit them with nonparabolic elaborations. We may therefore be certain that Jesus really did speak in parables.

A further variant of the coherence of sources consists in the quest for features and motifs that have maintained themselves in different genres, a subcriterion for which we suggest the designation *"genre-constancy."*[4] That which is found independently in different forms and genres probably goes back to the historical Jesus. Thus the motif of "seeking the lost" is found not only in the famous parables of the lost (Luke 15:1–32), but also in apophthegms, when Jesus turns to publicans and sinners (Mark 2:15–17), or in sayings in which he speaks of the lost sheep of the house of Israel to whom he is sent (Matt 15:24). The motif is so well documented and present in such different genres that nothing speaks against its attribution to the historical Jesus.

---

3. This subcriterion is found for the first time with the designation "cross-section method" in Dahl, "The Problem of the Historical Jesus," 95: "Words and reports in different forms and genres, transmitted within different traditions and layers of tradition, mutually illuminate one another and provide a comprehensive picture in which something characteristic of Jesus becomes visible." G. Schille, "Ein neuer Zugang zu Jesus?: Das traditionsgeschichtliche Kriterium," *ZdZ* 40 (1986): 250, advocates substantially the same procedure for locating authentic material, which he calls the "history-of-tradition criterion." The term "cross-section evidence" is used by F. Mussner, et al., "Methodologie der Frage nach dem historischen Jesus," 134ff.

4. Different forms of the criterion of multiple attestation are used especially by C. H. Dodd, *History and the Gospel* (London: Nisbet & Co., 1938) 91ff.

As the final variant of the criterion of "coherence of sources" we may name the *multiple attestation* of traditions. In distinction to the recurring forms and motifs in different streams of tradition or genres, here it is a matter of the same traditions that are documented in variants independent from each other. The parable of the Mustard Seed may serve as an example: it is found in Mark 4:30–32, but independently also in the Sayings Source, as shown by the Minor Agreements between Matt 13:31–32 and Luke 13:18–19. Moreover, it is also found in *Gospel of Thomas* 20, so that one can speak of three independent instances—presupposing that the *Gospel of Thomas* represents an autonomous tradition that was only secondarily adjusted to the Synoptic tradition. The parable of the Mustard Seed is thus so well attested that it has a good claim to authenticity.

Our preliminary summary is that the two aspects of the criterion of the plausibility of historical effects take up two traditional criteria (or three, depending on one's categories): on the one hand, the "criterion of dissimilarity" in its application to early Christianity (here called "resistance to tendencies of the tradition"), and, on the other hand, aspects of the criteria of "coherence" and "multiple attestation" (here combined under the heading "coherence of sources"). We have seen that the source-critical criterion of "resistance to tendencies of the tradition" can become a problem in view of the plurality and history of the Jesus tradition. Nonetheless, it remains an important criterion. The more one wants to limit its validity by referring to the multiple phases and streams in early Christianity, all the more weight must one grant to the complementary criterion of "coherence of sources." "Resistance to tendencies of the tradition" and "coherence of sources" grasp different aspects of the history of the effects of Jesus' life and work. The criterion of resistance to tendencies of the tradition considers this history of effects under the aspect that the tradition has deviated from Jesus' original words and deeds, so that relics of his effects are especially to be found in elements that can be detected as "against the stream." The criterion of coherence of sources looks at this history of effects under the aspect that it reflects and preserves the influence of Jesus in such a manner that some of his characteristics have been preserved independently in different realms of the tradition, different genres, and in variant forms of the traditional elements.

1.2 The Plausibility of Historical Context and the Criterion of Dissimilarity vis-à-vis Judaism (CDJ)

All the results attained by means of the criteria based on the history of effects, namely, "resistance to tendencies of the tradition" and "coherence of sources," can be further examined with regard to their contextual plausibility. Contextual plausibility seeks to discuss, on the one hand, whether or not they fit into the Jewish context in which the Jew Jesus of Nazareth lived, and, on the other hand, whether they point to a particular individual within this context—to a person who evokes both respect and offense, and who polarizes his hearers into disciples or opponents. Accordingly, the criterion of contextual plausibility has two sides: it looks for points of correspondence with the context as well as distinctive features within this context—that is, for something that is individual and clearly defined enough to make tensions and conflicts understandable.

a) Contextual Appropriateness as the First Aspect of Contextual Plausibility

When we adopt correspondence to the Jewish context as a criterion of historical Jesus research, we stand the traditional criterion of dissimilarity on its head. According to it, only that which cannot be derived from Judaism is authentic. In contrast, according to the criterion of contextual appropriateness, only that which can be derived from the context can be authentic. Or formulated more precisely, the better a tradition fits into the concrete Jewish context of Palestine and Galilee, the more claim it has to authenticity. Of course, this criterion, applied in isolation, has its limits: that which fits well into the Jewish context can also sometimes fit well into the context of (earliest) Christianity. Thus the other aspect of the criterion of contextual plausibility must always be kept in mind: that which in this Jewish context has an independent profile more likely comes from Jesus than from one of his Jewish followers. While with this aspect of the criterion of contextual plausibility, we take up a concern of the traditional criterion of dissimilarity, at the same time we also correct it through the subcriterion of contextual appropriateness.

Against such a criterion of contextual appropriateness, one might pose the legitimate question, Did Jesus not, in some points, fundamentally break with his Jewish setting? Did he not break the Sabbath? Did he not challenge the purity laws (Mark 7:15)? Did he not encourage the violation of the command to honor father and mother when he said to a would-be follower that he should let the dead bury the dead and not be concerned with the burial of his own father (Matt 8:21–22)? And finally, did he not fundamentally criticize the temple cult? We must first emphasize that the fact that Jesus evoked conflicts *in* Judaism is indisputable. But it can be well disputed whether these were conflicts *with* Judaism. There is nothing un-Jewish about charismatic figures whose messages evoke conflict with their environment. On the contrary, the chain of prophets is documentation for the fact that they were deeply rooted in Judaism. Jesus belonged to Judaism no less than did Amos and Hosea, Isaiah and Micah, Judas the Galilean and John the Baptist. This is also indicated by the points of conflict named above, which can be mentioned only briefly and not adequately appreciated within the framework of a methodological study such as this.

Jesus certainly did break the Sabbath when he healed people on the holy seventh day. At least, this is clearly presented in the tradition as violation of the Sabbath. But he basically only extended the rules that were already in place, rules that provided for exceptions to the Sabbath rest when it was a matter of saving lives to cases of enhancing life. When it was lawful on the Sabbath to save the life of a stranger and even to kill in self-defense, was it not consistent to consider it lawful to heal people? Jesus' liberal observance of the Sabbath may go beyond that which other Jewish teachers considered lawful—but he only extended tendencies that were already present in Judaism.[5]

Jesus certainly did express a fundamental skepticism about the distinction between clean and unclean things (Mark 7:15). That he only placed internal purity above external purity, without fundamentally disputing the latter, cannot be said on the basis of Mark 7:15. But the decisive thing is that this general statement formulated in the indicative has no corresponding directions for conduct formulated in the imperative. One can have consistent reservations in principle with regard to an objectively based distinction between clean and unclean things—and nonetheless observe the purity rules, whether as a matter of accommodation, out of respect for valid traditions, or because one interprets them spiritually. In Judaism the decisive thing is not what ideas one has in principle, but what one concretely does![6]

Jesus certainly did call for the man to leave his father behind unburied! But he certainly did not intend to make a general rule out of this. It was a matter of an enacted prophetic sign that he demanded from one of his followers.[7] Hosea was called to marry a prostitute and adulteress, but this does not mean he intended to legitimize prostitution and adultery. It was a matter of delivering a message through a provocative act. In the case of Hosea, the message was the charge that the people of Israel had been unfaithful to God; in the case of Jesus, the message was that now the time is breaking in which even the pious respect due to one's father becomes unimportant in view of the coming kingdom of God.

---

5. On the problematic involved cf. S. O. Back, *Jesus of Nazareth and the Sabbath Commandment* (Åbo: Åbo Akademi University Press, 1995).

6. It is characteristic for early Christianity that the debate about purity was decided, among other ways, by narrating a vision of Peter that contained a clear imperative to eat unclean animals (cf. Acts 11:7). In addition, cf. on the question of purity G. Theissen and A. Merz, *The Historical Jesus: A Comprehensive Guide* (Minneapolis: Fortress Press, 1998) 365–367.

7. W. D. Davies and D. C. Allison, *The Gospel According to Saint Matthew* (2 vols.; Edinburgh: T & T Clark, 1988/1991) 2:57, compare Matt 8:21–22 with the symbolic acts of the prophets.

The prediction of the destruction of the temple is probably not a fundamental attack against the cult. On the contrary, it promises a new temple in place of the present one. It thereby betrays a deep inner bond to the Jerusalem cult. Moreover, there was at that time in Judaism a plethora of traditions and ideas critical of the temple. With his critique of the temple, Jesus does not stand as an isolated figure in his own time.[8] There is a good criterion on the issue of whether someone within belongs within the framework of a particular religion: the attitude one has to the rituals of this religion. People may have very different ideas in their heads about their religion, ideas that may be more or less heretical. But the decisive thing is whether or not they participate in its public rituals. In the case of Jesus, it is precisely these that never become problematic. The Essenes boycotted the temple. For them, their own community was a living substitute temple for the one in Jerusalem. John the Baptist preached baptism for the forgiveness of sins—a vote of no confidence in the atonement rites of the temple, which had become inaccessible and obviously were in themselves no longer adequate for the present situation. But no one uses these data as grounds for doubting that the Essenes and the Baptist belong within Judaism. Compared with them, in fact, Jesus stands much closer to the everyday life of Judaism. To be sure, he adopts John the Baptist's call to repentance (cf. Luke 13:1ff.), but he never demands that people be baptized, even though he highly values the baptism of John. For Jesus, God offers salvation without any ritual act, which distinguishes his followers from all other Jews. Nor does Jesus withdraw into the desert as did John and the Essenes who lived at Qumran. He worked in the midst of the inhabited land. He belongs in the midst of Judaism.

But independently of this judgment about the historical figure of Jesus is to be said that every historical figure is to be understood fundamentally within the context of his or her world. Anything else would be an unhistorical procedure. This is the way the criterion of contextual appropriateness everywhere functions in historical investigation. If someone appears to us to be such a foreign body within his time and environment as not really to belong to it, then a historian would more likely suppose that we do not know enough about his time and environment. Correspondingly, it is valid to say with regard to Jesus that, if on the basis of some words and deeds Jesus appears in the eyes of many theologians to have left the world of Judaism, it more likely means that theological scholarship does not yet know this world well enough to judge what was or was not possible and conceivable within it. What we do know from this

---

8. Cf. H. Mödritzer, *Stigma und Charisma im Neuen Testament und seiner Umwelt* (NTOA 28; Freiburg-Göttingen: Universitätsverlag Freiburg Schweiz/Vandenhoeck & Ruprecht, 1994) 144–56.

world, however, is the basis for a valuable subcriterion for the detection of authentic Jesus traditions. With its help we can make at least one thing plausible: The more an image of Jesus can be made understandable on the basis of its Jewish context as a product of Jewish history, the less we can assume it to be the product of early Christian history and imagination. In the following we provide a few examples of the application of the criterion of contextual appropriateness.

The saying about divorce is well documented through multiple attestation (Mark 10:10–12 par.; Matt 5:32; 1 Cor 7:10–11). It fits into a Jewish context, for we also find tendencies among the Essenes to make pronouncements about the illegitimacy of divorce. Moreover, there was a currently relevant problem: the divorce of Herodias from her first husband had been noticed among her Jewish contemporaries. The initiative for this divorce had come from Herodias although, according to the dominant legal tradition in Judaism, only the man could initiate a divorce. The general criticism among the people of this deviation from Jewish traditions had become vocal in John the Baptist. It is thus no surprise that Jesus, too, took a position on this problem—exceptionally so in that it was even in the form of a halakah, that is, a legally valid statement of law, while otherwise his ethical teaching consists of basic wisdom maxims and admonitions. The context sketched here may also explain why the divorce rule formulated by Jesus has a double-sided form: not only the man, but also the woman, is prohibited from divorce (or more precisely: from remarrying after divorce). Moreover, alongside the dominant tradition that granted the right of divorce only to the man, there was possibly a minority tradition that granted this right to both partners.[9] From whatever side one looks at it, the saying fits very well in the concrete context of the life of Jesus.

The scandalous saying "Let the dead bury the dead" (Luke 9:60) is attributed to Jesus mostly because of its provocative character. Here Jesus tests the degree of loyalty a particular man has to him by calling for a crass act of impiety with regard to the dead. If one asks whether something like that could even have been imagined in Jesus' time, one comes across the ruler of Jesus' own land. In 19 C.E. Herod Antipas transferred his capital from Sepphoris to Tiberias. Tiberias, however, was built on the site of a cemetery. The city was ritually unclean; its founding was an act of impiety with regard to the dead (cf. Josephus, *Ant.* 18:36–38). Everyone who moved into this city thus was subject to a loyalty test: they had to value their commitment to the ruler of

---

9. On the divorce logion and the variety within the Jewish legal tradition on this point cf. M. Fander, *Die Stellung der Frau im Markusevangelium. Unter besonderer Berücksichtigung kultur- und religionsgeschichtlicher Hintergründe* (MThA 8; Altenberge: Telos, 1989) 200–57.

their country over their commitment to holy Jewish traditions. Antipas possibly intended it so. At least he could be sure that he had assembled a population with a personal loyalty to him. Of course, Jesus did not have Herod's conduct directly before his eyes as a model when he called for an act of impiety with regard to the dead. But there probably was a latent contextual connection between these two kinds of loyalty tests.

Similarly, the paradoxical admonition not to resist evil and to respond without a murmur to a blow on the cheek with a demonstrative offer of the other (Matt 5:39) is also contextually plausible.[10] Pilate—probably at the beginning of his term of office—had attempted secretly to bring images of the emperor or shields with the emperor's monogram to Jerusalem—certainly also a kind of test of whether the Jewish population was politically loyal enough to back off from the local prohibition of images in order to show their loyalty to the emperor. When the matter became known, it generated vehement protests. Pilate attempted to intimidate the crowds of protesters by confronting them with soldiers with drawn swords. But the Jews immediately threw themselves to the ground and bared their necks, showing their willingness to die rather than to allow their laws to be violated. Pilate then abandoned his plan (cf. Josephus, *J.W.* 2.169ff.; *Ant.* 18.35ff.).

Numerous other examples could be given. All have in common the manifestation of not only contextual appropriateness but also individual traits that make them stand out within their context. Apart from such individual traits, the Jesus traditions would not be recognizable as traditions of a distinct figure—they would rather be seen as an accidental collection of general wisdom sayings and common-sense convictions. But that is precisely what they are not. Their individual stamp leads to a further subcriterion.

b) Contextual Distinctiveness as the Second Aspect of Contextual Plausibility

The traditional criterion of dissimilarity attempted to find elements of the tradition that were underivable and without analogy—one could even say, unimaginable elements—and thus burdened research with an impossible assignment, namely, the task (1) of proving global statements about the factual absence of particular ideas and motifs in Judaism and, even beyond that, (2) the underivability of ideas from other ideas, traditions, and convictions of Judaism (by which traditions with no analogies were supposed to be isolated from the rest). Sometimes—even outdoing the previous claims—(3) a third

---

10. Cf. G. Theissen, "Gewaltverzicht und Feindesliebe (Mt 5,38–48/Lk 6,27–38) und deren sozialgeschichtlicher Hintergrund," in *Studien zur Soziologie des Urchristentums* (WUNT 19; 3rd ed.; Tübingen: Mohr, 1989) 191ff.

task was assumed, requiring the claim that particular ideas and motifs were in principal inconceivable in Judaism, which would be a claim about the potential of historical reality. Such demands involve postulation of hybrid claims, which reasonable historians cannot accept. They will register two objections. (1) The first concerns the situation with regard to sources. The sources available to us always represent only fragments of what was actually thought, said, and experienced. Thus no one can say that this or that in a particular culture is really without analogy. At the most, one can only suppose that this is so. By contrast, on the basis of available sources one can sometimes show concrete contradictions between one tradition and other traditions, positive relationships between particular traditions and other traditions, in which "relationships" can include both similarities and differences. In short, no statement is valid except in relation to the given limitations of the available sources. (2) In addition to the argument on the basis of the incomplete state of the available sources, there is another fundamental objection to the quest for elements that are without analogy, underivable, and unimaginable. This methodological regulation betrays that one is surreptitiously looking for a Jesus who dwells in some realm beyond history. This Jesus does not merely have individuality, as all human beings have. He has not only a distinctive profile, as all historically significant human beings have. He fundamentally transcends the human sphere. Now, it is not to be excluded that in the case of Jesus such an incursion from another world, in fact, happened. What is certain is that historical study of Jesus can never confirm this. It can only confirm that people of that time reckoned with such an incursion from another world and that they interpreted Jesus in this way. And historical study can make this faith and this interpretation understandable—again by means of analogies to such a faith and its interpretations.

Precisely because it is on the basis of hidden theological claims that the expectations of Jesus' "singularity" are raised above the historical plane, it must be emphasized that the quest for distinctive individual traits of the historical Jesus is not thereby discredited. It is only necessary to hold fast to this methodological principle: this quest is bound to a historical context. We are looking for distinctive individual traits of Jesus within the framework of the Judaism of his own time—not for singular elements that transcend any historical context. We may sketch three ways of ascertaining such distinctive individual characteristics: constructing a comparative profile, searching for evidence of distinctive features, and establishing individual complexity.

First, we can compare Jesus with charismatic figures of his environment: with the Teacher of Righteousness, Judas the Galilean, John the Baptist, and the Jewish sign-prophets. Moreover, one can determine the relation of such a *comparative profile* to different groups and streams in Judaism, that is, to

Pharisees, Sadducees, and Essenes.[11] Within the framework of a book devoted to critical analysis of methodology, we can only sketch such comparisons very briefly:

The Baptist lived within an eschatological expectation of the immediate end: the ax is already laid at the root of the tree (Matt 3:10). There was simply no time left in which those who professed to repent could demonstrate their seriousness by their deeds (that is, through the "fruits of repentance"). In this situation the Baptist offered baptism in water as a symbolic act that God would accept as a sign of authentic repentance. By contrast, in Jesus God again gives humanity time. If people do not immediately bring forth the "fruits of repentance," there is still some time in which this might yet happen (Luke 13:6–9). The gift of time is the expression of God's grace.

The Baptist called on all to be baptized. By contrast, Jesus did not baptize— at least not during the historically decisive period of his own public ministry.

The Baptist threatened all with the "wrath of God," but offered deliverance from it for those who repented. By contrast, at the center of Jesus' message stood the announcement of the kingdom of God, which means salvation precisely for the weak, the poor, the underprivileged.

The Baptist lived an ascetic life. He lived in the desert, wore primitive clothing. Much in his conduct had the character of a protest-asceticism. Jesus' own contemporaries already noticed that on these points Jesus was different from his master: he was considered a glutton and a winebibber (cf. Matt 11:18–19).

The Baptist announced a mightier one to come, who would baptize with fire and wind/Spirit. He is clearly a different figure than John himself. By contrast, Jesus spoke in a mysterious way of a "Son of Man"—and until this very day there is uncertainty over the question of whether he referred to himself or to someone else.

As we have already said, several such comparisons could be carried out: Jesus shares with Judas the Galilean a radical theocratic seriousness. But for him the radical theocratic alternative between God and idols is not a choice between God and the emperor (cf. Mark 12:13ff.) but the alternative "God or Mammon" (Matt 6:24). With the Pharisees, Jesus shares faith in the resurrection and distinguishes himself from the Sadducees precisely on this point (Mark 12:18ff.). However, with the Sadducees he shares the rejection of oral tradition and cites the Torah against such traditions (Mark 7:1ff.), actions that in turn distinguish him from the Pharisees. He is related to the Essenes by his sharpening of the marriage laws, but is different from them by his open-

---

11. Cf. Theissen and Merz, *The Historical Jesus*, esp. 140, 208ff., 225ff.

ness to sinners—including those sinners who do not live by the marriage laws. Here we are not attempting to construct a definitive comparative profile, but only to illustrate a methodological procedure. What such a procedure makes clear is that such comparative profiles can be constructed without making indefensible statements about Judaism in general, but rather by making concrete observations. Here there is no quest for the "singularity" that transcends any historical context, but the characteristic features of a particular individual in that historical context, features that associate him with some and separate him with others.

A second way in which the characteristic individual features of Jesus may be identified is the quest for *evidence for such features* as already outlined in chapter 1. Thus to date no one has discovered a real parallel for an initial nonresponsorial *amen*. Quite soon in the early church this was already perceived as a distinctive element in Jesus' own speech. This initial *amen* thus found its way into sayings from which it was originally absent. It is therefore in itself no indication of the authenticity of any particular saying. But there can be no doubt that it was an authentic characteristic of the *vox Jesu*. While a comparative profile can be constructed especially by the methods of history-of-religions studies, the establishment of evidence for such features is primarily on the observation of Jesus' specific expressions. These can then be corroborated by further comparison with Jewish texts. Here we often arrive at relatively certain judgments in regard to the historical figure of Jesus as a whole.

Third, the establishing of *individual complexity* does not proceed on the basis of individual distinctive marks and particular Jesus traditions, but on the basis of their combination. We will see below, on the basis of further methodological and hermeneutical considerations, why the course we adopt here is particularly productive. But we can already emphasize that individuality is found in the combination of different elements. As individual features they may have many analogies, but the particular combination of even a relative few elements is unlikely. We thus get an impression (often intuitively) of a person as a whole. And that is again a basis for the judgment that this or that does or does not fit the person as a whole. By working out the individual complexity of Jesus, we thus take up the traditional "criterion of coherence" in a manner that it does not appeal to the agreement between different sources (streams of tradition, genres, traditional variants), but to material coherence.

The concrete examples show that, as a rule, in historical work several criteria work together. It is precisely the quest for Jesus' individuality that illustrates the connection between contextual and history-of-effects ways of posing the question. On the one hand, Jesus' extraordinary effects on later history are introduced to document Jesus' distinctive individuality, while, on the other hand, appeal is made to his place within the Judaism of his time. The conviction of Jesus' distinctiveness thus does not recur only in the history of his effects (after Jesus' death), but also in the history of his life (before his death). We will thus in conclusion consider the whole ensemble of criteria once again under this aspect, namely, the combination of history-of-effects and contextual plausibility, which is especially important for a "verification" of the picture of Jesus as a whole and for describing his "characteristic features." We can speak here of a "comprehensive historical plausibility" of those results we have obtained in detail by investigating their plausibility in terms of history-of-effects and contextual plausibility.

1.3 Comprehensive Historical Plausibility as the Combination of the Plausibility of Historical Effects and the Plausibility of Historical Context— and the Distinctiveness of the Historical Figure of Jesus

Behind the line of argument that combines history of effects and the distinctiveness of the historical figure of Jesus is sometimes found a monocausal conclusion, as though Jesus were the only factor that could explain the history of effects found in early Christianity. This procedure gives Jesus a clear profile that shows how distinctive he is by contrasting him with his context. Behind this procedure there often stands a break in the line of argument that would lead to definite conclusions, as though Jesus, in his own distinctive individuality, were not himself the product of a variety of causal complexes that all turn back into Judaism. Both lines of argument are problematic. Comprehensive historical plausibility does not construct a picture of Jesus until it has first surveyed the whole scheme of things that includes context and history of effects.

Changes in history are always explained in the form of "derivations,"[12] for every time and every human being stand in a "network of continuities."[13] Only so is Jesus to be understood—in derivation from and in continuity with Judaism. Many factors in Judaism brought forth this one figure. Early Christianity, as a product of the history of effects of the figure "Jesus," also stands within a network of derivations and continuities. Just as Jesus may not be postulated a priori to have lived and acted as an isolated "distinctive" being, neither can the origin of early Christianity be interpreted as the effect of Jesus alone. This may be represented in a simplified chart:

---

12. K. Hübner, *Kritik der wissenschaftlichen Vernunft* (3rd ed.; Freiburg: Alber, 1986) 334–37.

13. T. Nipperdey, "Kann Geschichte objektiv sein?," in *Nachdenken über die deutsche Geschichte. Essays* (Munich: Beck, 1986) 231.

Instead of:

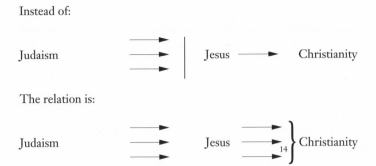

We will first look at the influence of the historical context on Jesus, that is, his being embedded in the history of Judaism. That which applies to every other human being applies also to Jesus: he comes forth from of a long biological and historical prehistory. Because of the complexity of this prehistory, like every other individual he is biologically and historically an "absurd borderline case of improbability."[15] The dictum also applies to him that "the individual is not . . . a social atom . . . [but] a complex synthesis of social elements."[16] The concern of the CDJ to show the uniqueness of Jesus can thus be accepted if we relativize his uniqueness as that of a historical figure like the uniqueness of *every* human being, and if we realize that such individuality does not consist in every detail of a person's life being distinct from his or her environment and later history, but in the unique combination of these elements drawn from the rich treasure of historical circumstances and possibilities.[17] The question that then arises for Jesus research is, Which combination of elements common to his environment constitutes the individual Jesus of Nazareth, and how are they related to one another so that the combination is unmistakably Jesus? We seek a "historical" comprehensive picture of him that embraces his context as well—and not just as a negative foil. It is rather a matter of the individuality of Jesus *in* Judaism, thus of contextual individuality, not of absolute singularity.

---

14. Among the other factors (in addition to the historical Jesus) influencing the formation of early Christianity, one has in mind such elements as the effects of the Easter faith, the Gentile mission, the work of Paul, and the further growth of Christianity.

15. M. Lintzel, "Voraussetzungen des Individuums," 173.

16. F. Ferrarotti, "Biography and the Social Sciences," *Social Research* 50 (1983): 79.

17. Here once again it becomes clear how a uniform picture of Judaism and the idea that Jesus was different from all his surroundings support each other: without dissimilarity from his environment Jesus could no longer be identified among his contemporaries, and without the uniformity of Judaism the dissimilarity of Jesus would be more difficult to maintain.

Against the background of these relativizing considerations regarding contextual individuality, the question of the distinctiveness of the individual Jesus of Nazareth, seen from the perspective of the history of his effects, is a legitimate question, that is, a quest for those impulses that went out from Jesus into early Christianity in which something "unmistakable" comes to expression. For "[p]eople are not like molecules in a gas. Some are different from others and some have more effect upon society than others. It is still a good question whether without Lenin there would have been the October Revolution."[18] It must accordingly be asked, Would Christianity be conceivable without Jesus? Is their a causal connection between the historical Jesus and post-Easter Christianity? And what importance does this connection have? E. P. Sanders says in the opening chapter of his Jesus book, "[T]hat there is no causal thread between his [i.e., Jesus'] life, his death and the Christian movement . . . is possible, but it is not satisfying historically."[19]

We thus have two bases for the distinctiveness of Jesus when his life is viewed as a whole: contextually, he is an individual combination of elements that he shares with his Jewish world; in terms of the history of effects, he is the cause of a historical sequence of events that lead beyond the boundary of Judaism. To test this comprehensive picture of Jesus for its distinctiveness, both aspects of the criterion of historical plausibility are necessary. For this purpose, both aspects of the criterion may be summarized in the following formulation: *The combination of different elements in the life of Jesus, who represents a unique constellation in the context of Judaism and at the same time permits the recognition of a meaningful conjunction with the origin of early Christian faith that is in the process of separating from Judaism—and to that extent is also "unique"—is a criterion for historicity. We speak of comprehensive historical plausibility.*[20] The uniqueness and individuality of the figure of Jesus as a whole is thus not contrasted with his environment (differently than in the traditional criterion of dissimilarity), but embedded within it. Because of its greater complexity, such a contextually bound individuality (or "dissimilarity") of Jesus, when his person is regarded as a whole, can be made more probable than can individual say-

---

18. M. Brodbeck, " Methodological Individualism," 327.

19. Sanders, *Jesus and Judaism*, 22. This "criterion," i.e., whether or not something is historically satisfying, has been often criticized—possibly on good grounds, to the extent that a continuity cannot be presupposed a priori. Finally, however, this critique does not really hit Sanders, since for him it depends on whether "the evidence shows that there was a causal connection." Sanders rightly emphasizes, "This is far more important than *a priori* suppositions."

20. Formally, even though he also has a different material focus, this way of posing the question corresponds to that of Klausner (*Jesus of Nazareth*, 9: "Christianity was born within Israel, but Israel as a people rejected it utterly. Why?").

ings of Jesus. It remains to be shown that this dissimilarity is fundamentally based on the individuality of every human being (i.e., on the difference between any human being and all others) and does not contradict the principle of analogy. In this sense J. Riches rightly characterizes Jesus' vision and message as "a distinctive yet analogous response"[21] to the surrounding reality in which he lived.

2. THE PROBLEM OF HISTORICAL AUTHENTICITY

The quest for the "distinctive" in Jesus in the era of the criterion of dissimilarity was closely connected to the quest for the "authentic;" one could say these were identical. But what is authenticity? The answer at first seems easy: Jesus research has available to it in the Christian tradition[22] reports about the life of Jesus. His words and deeds are narrated, along with the events of the last days of his life. Historical criticism investigates the genuineness and authenticity of these purported expressions of Jesus' life—that is, whether they really come from Jesus. Often, however, more than this appears to be meant. And therein lies the problem.

2.1 The Problematic Involved in Applying the Concept of "Authenticity" to the Sayings of Jesus

A brief look at the history of the word "authentic" shows how problematic it is to speak of "authenticity" in connection with New Testament texts. The Greek word αὐθεντικός designates that which was there at the beginning, the original. In the Middle Ages "authentic" was used for a document that bore a seal attesting its unmodified originality, as well as for the documents that guaranteed relics to be genuine (*authenticum instrumentum*). On the basis of these documents, the relics could be accepted as genuine. The "authenticity" of the Holy Scripture was understood to refer to its normative status, resting on inspiration and canonicity.[23] Thus when the term "authenticity" is used in studies of the historical Jesus, the term brings much baggage with it.

---

21. J. Riches, *The World of Jesus. First-Century Judaism in Crisis* (Understanding Jesus Today. Cambridge: Cambridge University Press, 1990) 9.
22. The canonical Gospels are our primary sources, but restricting ourselves to them and excluding the noncanonical Gospels would be "unhistorical" (cf. H. Koester, *Die ausserkanonischen Herrenworte*, 236.
23. Cf. F. Hauck and G. Schwinge, "Authentie," *Theologisches Fach- und Fremdwörterbuch* (6th ed.; Göttingen: Vandenhoeck & Ruprecht, 1987) 30–31.

For one thing, in the question of the authenticity of the Scripture there is a supernatural element involved that is inappropriate for the pursuit of historical questions.[24] This supernatural element refers not only to the "authentic" content but to the certainty of its authenticity. This misunderstanding leads to the expectation that Jesus research might produce results, that is, historical evidence, that can overcome the crisis of faith, results that are "faith-crisis resistant." Accordingly, historical knowledge is supposed to be exactly as "certain" for the believer as the existence of God—and conversely, the existence of God as "certain" as the historical facts. The concept "historical authenticity" turns out to be subject to the suspicion that it wants to deal with absolute truth. Harvey expresses the better alternative: "What we have to ask is not whether a given statement is true with a kind of supernatural certainty but whether the fact which it reports may be regarded as at least as well established as any other fact which comes down to us from antiquity."[25]

Another element in the "baggage" associated with the word "authenticity" is that in the history of Jesus research the term has been applied mostly to Jesus' sayings—but the genuineness of a relic and the authenticity of a saying of Jesus cannot be placed on the same level for comparison. A relic can be absolutely genuine, that is, it is possible that a particular bone, in fact, is a fragment of the dead body of a particular person revered as a saint. This would then be an isolated fact established as genuine. Analogously, it at first seems possible to speak theoretically of an authentic saying of Jesus. But the comparison ends here, since the difference between the authentic "content" in each case makes all the difference. In order to determine authenticity, one must be able to make the object of such a determination absolutely clear. A relic or an *authenticum* are material objects, while a saying of Jesus is a linguistic event. Thus in the case of a saying of Jesus, the content must first be understood. This content, however, is not unequivocal, for it is not a matter of a material object but of a meaning, not a matter of a *brutum factum*, such as a fragment of papyrus containing a few words that must be investigated to determine its date of composition or the source of the ink.[26] It follows that the quest for an authentic saying of Jesus involves an essentially more complex problem than trying to determine the authenticity of a relic or its certifying document. In the case of a relic, the material object itself is the decisive thing, even when it is embedded in a sacred legend that gives it its importance. By contrast, in the case of a saying of Jesus the material substratum

---

24. Historical study as such cannot deal with the category of "inspiration," for it cannot perceive unhistorical or transhistorical realities.

25. Harvey, *Jesus and the Constraints*, 5.

26. Cf. Riches and Millar, "Conceptual Change" 37: " . . . from an epistemological point of view the *senses* possessed by the expressions occurring in a text are not *hard data*—they have to be inferred."

(consisting of manuscripts and printed matter) is unimportant and exchange-able—in comparison with the meaning that is "transported" through it. Thus one can say that, while a relic in a certain sense is a self-contained object (and can thus stand independently alongside other mortal remains of the same Saint), an "authentic" saying of Jesus is always connected to a whole complex of sayings that first makes possible the understanding of each individual saying. Even more, "determining the sense of the expressions in a text or spoken discourse involves the identification of a network of beliefs which are systematically related to one another, which are anchored, however loosely, in experience. . . ."[27] Historical understanding of an "authentic" saying of Jesus requires knowledge of the whole historical context. This knowledge is the only way to clarify what it is that is to be determined as authentic or inauthentic.

This brings the question of the authenticity of any particular saying of Jesus into a difficult situation. To this historical context belongs the context in which the saying originated. The question of the originator of the saying is itself a part of the context. The resolution of this issue contributes to determining the object being investigated. But this question of the author is itself the question that must be settled with regard to authenticity! Inasmuch as the author belongs to the context, the object being investigated changes with the identity of the author. In other words, a saying attributed to Jesus in the tradition changes its meaning according to whether it is attributed to Jesus himself or to one of his later followers. The intended narrated time in Jesus sayings remains the same in each case. But the narrative time would be different depending on authenticity or inauthenticity. We thus find ourselves in a circle in which the question of authenticity is bound up with the understanding of the meaning of a saying, and vice versa.

This set of circumstances may be illustrated by the interpretation of Mark 8:34, "If any want to become my followers, let them deny themselves and take up their cross and follow me." At first glance, the saying seems to presuppose the crucifixion of Jesus. This would mean it originated after Easter. It would then quickly have come into conflict with the fact that only a few of Jesus followers suffered martyrdom. Such martyrdoms were the exception. But the saying itself formulates it as the rule. One would expect that in reflecting on the *imitatio Christi*, Jesus' followers would have been challenged to take up "his cross" (i.e., the cross of Jesus) and not their own. If one wants to ascribe the saying to Jesus, there are three possibilities of interpretation: a realistic, a spiritual, and a ritual interpretation. The *realistic* interpretation says that Jesus reckoned not only with his own execution at the hands of the Romans, but with the execution of his followers. Discipleship was for him the path to execution. This saying would have been modified only slightly, if Jesus had taken over such a saying from the

---

27. Ibid.

freedom fighters of the Jewish resistance movement. In any case, one would have to attribute to him a much clearer expectation of conflict than is usually the case. Jesus, too, knew that in his own way he was practicing "resistance." The *spiritual* interpretation understands "taking up one's cross" to be a general image for "suffer." There is no documentation for this meaning in the historical context, however. The *ritual* interpretation assumes that Jesus tattooed the sign of the cross on the forehead of his followers—that is, that he marked them with a seal that was to protect them from the danger and distress of the endtime (cf. Ezek 9:4–6). However one decides the interpretation of this saying, the important thing here is that the interpretation and a judgment about a sayings' authenticity mutually condition each other. The saying must have a different meaning if it is judged to be authentic than if judged to be inauthentic. And conversely, according to the meaning ascribed to it, it can be judged authentic or inauthentic.[28]

2.2 The Problematic Involved in Applying the Concept of "Authenticity" to the "Facts" and Events of the Life of Jesus

The problem of the lack of unequivocal interpretation of the sayings of Jesus due to the double plane of communication (namely, that of the time narrated and the time of the narration) is present in exactly the same fashion in all the other data from the life of Jesus. Only "nuclear facts" about pure chronicles[29] provide information that (like relics) is not subject to change. Hübner calls attention to the many possible interrelationships between an event and the changes that it brings about: "[W]ith the passing of time, the events [are] seen in their manifold relation to other events, increasingly numerous and increasingly later. . . . Thus the details assume more and more relation to each other, and thereby not only does their significance undergo change, but also their function and even their content."[30] The historical object itself compels us

> in the course of development to alter our understanding of what was
> important or unimportant about it, what belongs with it or is to be

---

28. Cf. U. Luz (*Matthew 1–7: A Commentary* [Minneapolis: Augsburg Fortress, 1989] 164–72) on the different exegetical possibilities.

29. Cf. H. White on the distinction between history and chronicle: "Histories gain part of their explanatory effect by their success in making stories out of mere chronicles; and stories in turn are made out of chronicles by an operation that I have elsewhere called 'emplotment'. By emplotment I mean simply the encoding of the facts contained in the chronicle as components of specific kinds of plot-structures." ("The Historical Text as Literary Artifact," in R. H. Canary and H. Kozicki, eds., *The Writing of History. Literary Form and Historical Understanding* [Madison: University of Wisconsin Press, 1978] 46).

30. Hübner, *Kritik der wissenschaftlichen Vernunft*, 346.

kept separate from it, what is bad or good about it. . . . "The object changes" thus means nothing else but that it emerges in new relationships with later events. . . . From then on it presents the historian with a new hermeneutical potential that must be reckoned with.[31]

And thus also a "saying of Jesus" or a "deed of Jesus" receives a different content if it is judged not to derive directly from Jesus, a content that we cannot see apart from the interpretative framework of the two thousand years of Christian history that followed him.[32] Thus, "interpretation always becomes an *internal* part of a 'fact'. Interpretation enters into the construction of fact. . . . If there is some free construction, it is also true that our interpretation is never simply arbitrary, for it is based on and limited by what our experience receives, i.e., by the object of experience."[33]

Now, it contradicts our everyday common sense that, in making judgments about the facticity of events, such a great role should be played by their interpretation—especially that the meaning to be interpreted changes in the course of historical development. We will thus sketch out one example as an illustration: the "cleansing of the temple" (Mark 11:15–19). Since the time that the historicity of the Jesus traditions has been disputed, whether or not they have been considered historical has depended largely on their interpretation.

Wherever Jesus has been interpreted politically, this text has been regarded as a key to the historical understanding of his work. Does not this conflict with the temple show that Jesus had planned a revolt, which was betrayed by Judas and thus lamentably was defeated? Was not the disruption of the temple business an intentional attack on the political elite of this small temple state? Within the framework of such a political interpretation of the life of Jesus, the purification of the temple was naturally considered to be historical.[34]

---

31. Ibid., 356.

32. A contemporary historian would, of course, have seen the events very differently. Cf. Tacitus's famous note, *Histories* 9: "Sub Tiberio quies," "under Tiberius all was quiet," or even "under Tiberius nothing much happened."

33. Lee, *The Galilean Jewishness of Jesus*, 41. Here he appeals especially to W. Dean. Cf. also Humphreys: "Documents can be regarded not merely as a sum composed of the separate pieces included within it, but as a representation—hence as a description—of some larger reality external to the documents as such." (R. S. Humphreys, "The Historian, His Documents, and the Elementary Modes of Historical Thought," *HTh* 19 (1980): 9.

34. A classic presentation of Jesus as a political rebel is R. Eisler, *IHSOUS BASILEUS OU BASILEUSAS: messianische Unabhängigkeitsbewegung vom Auftreten Johannes des Täufers bis zum Untergang Jakobs des Gerechten nach der neuerschlossenen Eroberung von Jerusalem des Flavius Josephus und den christlichen Quellen* (Religionswissenschaftliche Bibliothek 9; Heidelberg: Carl Winters Universitätsbuchhandlung; vol. 1, 1929; vol. 2, 1930). The title means "Jesus—A King Who Never Reigned."

If one regarded Jesus especially as a religious-ethical preacher who in the Sermon on the Mount had admonished his followers to renounce violence and to love their enemies, then this use of violence against things and people contradicts the center of Jesus' own teaching. What is more understandable than to point out the inherent improbability of this incident? With his small band of disciples, how is Jesus supposed to have brought the enormous forecourt of the temple under his own control and prohibited the sale of sacrificial animals? Is it not unhistorical imagination at work here?[35]

Finally, if Jesus is understood as an eschatological prophet who announced the restoration of Israel, then the expectation of a new temple shifts back to the center of Jesus' message: the renewal of Israel comes to expression in the renewal of its central institution! Thus to the extent that eschatological expectation plays a role, Jesus' action in the temple could be interpreted as a prophetic symbolic act. Its significance does not lie in its actual effects on the business carried on in the forecourt of the temple, but in the message about the temple—it is soon to be destroyed, in order to give place to a better temple![36]

It is not impossible to combine these different political, ethical, and eschatological interpretative approaches. Prophecy about the temple and purification of the temple belong together as prophetic message and prophetic symbolic act. Their eschatological interpretation is in accord with the message of Jesus as a whole. So too, the "political" interpretation is not without justification. Prophetic preaching in Israel was often connected with social and political tensions. Jesus' opposition to the existing temple was only a variation of a widespread opposition to the temple in the Judaism of his time. It is an expression of the built-in conflict between rural and urban.[37] Moreover, it can be shown that, precisely in the time of Jesus, political conflicts were often acted out in the form of symbolic actions.[38] They were thus also thereby defused. An example for such a politically symbolic overcoming of conflicts on a small scale is the disputation over tribute (Mark 12:13–17). In it Jesus himself does not directly take a position on whether tribute is to be paid to

---

35. Something like this is argued by E. Haenchen, *Der Weg Jesu: Eine Erklärung des Markus-Evangeliums und der kanonischen Parallelen* (2nd ed.; Berlin: de Gruyter, 1968) 382–389: "Between the Jesus who with his disciples introduces a 'new order' in the temple, and the Jesus of the parables, there exists a great gulf" (387).

36. E. P. Sanders interprets the passage in this sense (*Jesus and Judaism*, 61–76). It is developed further by Mödritzer (*Stigma und Charisma* 144–56).

37. Cf. G. Theissen, "Die Tempelweissagung Jesu. Prophetie im Spannungsfeld von Stadt und Land," in *Studien zur Soziologie des Urchristentums* (3rd ed.; Tübingen: Mohr, 1989) 142ff.

38. Cf. G. Theissen, Jesus und die symbolpolitischen Konflikte seiner Zeit. Sozialgeschichlice Aspekte der Jesusforschung." *EvT* 57, no. 5 (1997): 378–400.

the emperor. He avoids a clear stance toward the campaign against imperial taxes that had been going on since 6 C.E. At first he shifts the medium to non-verbal language. He calls for an imperial coin and asks for its inscription to be pondered. From the religious and moral point of view, return of imperial property to the emperor is no cause for concern. The issue of the legitimacy of paying taxes to the emperor is thereby relativized, especially since Jesus in his verbal (and not only symbolic) answer adds, "and give to God what belongs to God." We can find similar politically symbolic actions in Jesus' time, both from the side of the rulers and from the side of prophets among the people. The use of a symbolic medium is thus also an indication of a relatively peaceful time. Symbolic actions can replace militant actions—or at least delay them. Such actions can thus be combined with the message of nonviolence and love of enemies.

The example illustrates that, also in the case of an "event," the question is not exclusively whether it is historical or unhistorical but in what sense it must be understood in order to consider it either historical or unhistorical. The interpretation of its meaning decides the issue of its facticity. According to how one interprets it, it fits better in the Jewish history of Jesus' own times or in the post-Easter context of the history of early Christian effects and traditions. It is thus immediately obvious that, in interpreting the "cleansing of the temple," the interpreter's general perspectives on the connections between religion and society, church and politics, scholarship and social action, play a role, and that such perspectives are dependent on the situation and biography of the scholar. Accordingly, we can thus state a methodological summary of our reflections: In investigating and making judgments about the words and deeds of Jesus' life presented by the traditions, we must consider their distinct contents and meanings when regarded as coming from different origins (i.e., Jesus or various post-Easter origins) and within the framework of different hermeneutical perspectives. Then, with the help of the criteria developed above, a decision can be made about the historical plausibility of attributing the material to Jesus.

2.3 The Authentic "Object"

How far back can this material be traced, that is, what can be regarded as "authentic?" So far we have only spoken of individual sayings and deeds of Jesus. Nowadays, however, Jesus research reserves the predicate "authentic" not only for the *ipsissima verba* (the "very words" spoken by Jesus), but also uses the term for the *ipsissima vox* (the "very voice" of Jesus, not bound to his literal words). To qualify as *ipsissima vox*, it is sufficient that the saying manifests the general characteristics of Jesus' message and his linguistic forms, the items we have called "evidence of distinctiveness." This methodological shift is to be welcomed. Authenticity in the sense of verbal authorship could only be claimed in any meaningful sense if we had documents composed (or dictated) by Jesus himself. Due to the history of the tradition, however, all serious attempts to determine the literal *verba Jesu* result in no more than an absolute minimum burdened with imponderable difficulties.[39] Such attempts have often been motivated by the theological concern of establishing a canon within the canon consisting of Jesus' own words.[40]

For many scholars however, even concentrating on the *ipsissima vox* goes too far. In 1959 J. M. Robinson had already aimed at a concept of authenticity that referred to historical significance, not on word-for-word authenticity.[41] Vögtle brought into play the somewhat broader concept of the "orientation of the work of Jesus as a whole,"[42] and Thüsing suggested that we speak of the "*ipsissima intentio Jesu*" (Jesus' "very intention").[43] Unless the attempt is to establish Jesus' words as a canon within the canon, it is essentially more interesting to attempt to understand the direction of Jesus' life as a whole rather than trying to determine which words he actually spoke. The concept and terminology of "intention" is itself problematic, however, if it means the internal will of Jesus. It is rather the case that we are limited to the "external"

---

39. Among the reasons that Harvey gives for abandoning the *ipsissima*-approach to posing the question is the following: "There is virtually no single report of any of the words and deeds of Jesus of which we can be certain, and there is indeed quite a large number of them which are likely to be either fictitious or fashioned by the tradition into something very different from the original." (Harvey, *Jesus and the Constraints*, 4). Hahn rejects the alternative "authentic or secondary church formulation" and proceeds on the basis that in most cases we are dealing with "mixed formulations." (Hahn, "Methodologische Überlegungen," 29.

40. That was already the intention of the service rendered by Th.Chubb at the beginning of the eighteenth century. How such a canon can serve theological interests even today is made clear, for example, in Gamber's comment in the Foreword to his collection of sayings of Jesus: "In the present time, in which Jesus as a historical figure and his message are misrepresented, so that not a few see in the man of Nazareth primarily a social reformer, it appears to us to be especially important that what Jesus in fact taught be set forth ever anew." (Gamber, *Jesus-Worte*, 3).

41. J. M. Robinson, *A New Quest of the Historical Jesus* (London: SCM, 1959) 99, n. 3.

42. A. Vögtle, "Jesus von Nazareth," 23.

43. W. Thüsing, "Neutestamentliche Zugangswege zu einer transzendental-dialogischen Christologie," in K. Rahner and W. Thüsing, *Christologie—systematisch und exegetisch. Arbeitsgrundlagen für eine interdisziplinäre Vorlesung* (QD 55; Freiburg: Herder, 1972) 183: "Thus here 'intentio' may not be understood in the narrow and superficial sense of the identifiable internal consciousness, but means the sense of direction for his life and work as a whole that arises from the depths of this singular human being Jesus—*and from there* is also expressed in individual concrete cases."

expressions of Jesus' life, to words and deeds that can be examined, that is, to that which Jesus in fact communicated to others.[44]

The abandonment of the goal of recovering the *ipsissima verba* or *vox* of Jesus goes even further in that Jesus research no longer is to be limited to the "sayings of Jesus." In order to illuminate the meaning of these sayings, one already needs some knowledge of the life of Jesus as a whole. From this point of view, Jesus research—especially among Protestant scholars—should make a fundamental break with its concentration on establishing Jesus' authentic words and make its main theme the work of Jesus as a whole. Thus Harvey's backing off from the question of "authenticity" rightly points to the whole tradition as the way to the historical Jesus: "Attention . . . is now directed more towards the impression made by the narrative as a whole."[45]

This discussion about the boundaries of the question of authenticity points to a fundamental problem in Jesus research, namely, to the relation between the picture of Jesus as a whole and judgments about the many individual traditions of his words and deeds.

2.4 Authenticity and the Comprehensive Historical Picture

The approach of the criterion of dissimilarity, like that of many other criteria, seeks to establish the "authenticity" of individual expressions or characteristics of Jesus. These are awarded great importance, but their tendency has already been established by the nature of the criterion itself. The criterion of dissimilarity, for example, already prejudices the image of Jesus as a whole, namely, by only portraying him in contrast both to his Jewish contemporaries and to the earliest Christian communities. Thus in formulating judgments about the authenticity of individual traditions the image of Jesus as a whole held by the particular scholar already plays a role. A specific comprehensive picture of Jesus is also found in each source in which authentic material is sought. The Christian tradition had already undergone a process of selection, so that it already offered a tendentious selection.[46] And not everything that

---

44. It is thus questionable when Charlesworth identifies the significance of Jesus' words with his inner intention: "My concern is not with the sound of his own voice (*ipsissima vox*), but with the meaning he poured forth through the words that appeared when he intended to communicate something to someone." (Charlesworth, *Jesus within Judaism*, 166).

45. Harvey, *Jesus and the Constraints*, 5.

46. This is not a moralistic objection, but the old and important insight of form criticism, which understands texts first on the basis of the time in which they are composed, not on the basis of the time they narrate. It is to be emphasized, however, that this insight applies not only to New Testament texts, as though as kerygmatic texts they are

found entrance in early Christian writings was preserved for us in the canonizing process. Many such compositions were lost. This insight makes clear that authentic material extracted only from these sources cannot lead to a complete or representative picture of the historical Jesus. Thus all attempts to get back to the "historical Jesus" by a process of subtraction limited to the New Testament tradition can have only a limited success. This applies to the traditional use of the criterion of dissimilarity, as well as to all the ideas of finding a pure, uncontaminated "authentic" Jesus by removing all "secondary" materials.[47]

The interest in establishing the authenticity of individual traditions is often more an exegetical than a historical interest. Historical Jesus research, whose goal is not the exposition of New Testament texts but a comprehensive picture of the person of Jesus, should thus not want to make its central issue the determination of the authenticity of particular texts. In making such a procedural proposal, it is only suggested that this not be the *first* pivotal point, since it already presupposes some comprehensive picture of Jesus. However, a comprehensive historical picture of Jesus goes quantitatively and qualitatively beyond the individual traditions preserved in the canonical Jesus tradition.[48]

We may thus say in summary that indiscriminate talk of authenticity is exegetically problematic and of little help historically. We must instead distinguish between the authenticity of individual sayings, general characteristics of Jesus' teaching, and the direction in which his life as a whole is oriented, that is, between *verba ipsissima*, *vox ipsissima*, and *intentio ipsissima*. As this approach is carried through it will become clear that we are more certain about general statements about Jesus' life and teaching than about judgments on many individual items. When we say about the *ipsissima intentio Jesu* that in his preaching he attached great importance to the coming of the kingdom of God,

---

different from all other texts, but to all sources. In the words of a historian of a previous generation, the sources are at the same time "relics" of the present in which they originated (Droysen, *Historik*, 37; also 65: "As the sources are themselves interpretations, they contain a double moment, the time that is interpreted and the time in which the interpretation is made"). Furthermore, it is fundamentally true that "the unique and unrepeatable is that which is worthy of being remembered and repeated." —and this is especially relevant in regard to the application of the criterion of dissimilarity to the Christian tradition. (R. Bubner, *Geschichtsprozesse und Handlungsnormen. Untersuchungen zur praktischen Philosophie* [stw 463; Frankfurt: Suhrkamp, 1984] 132.)

47. As stated, e.g., by E. Floris, *Sous le Christ, Jésus: Méthode d'analyse référentielle appliquée aux Évangiles* (Paris: Flammarion, 1987) 13: "It was possible to separate the Christ from Jesus, as in a fresco one separates the surface picture from what is beneath it."

48. This is to be maintained against Dahl, who sees the Jesus tradition as "a *maximum* in which everything important for our historical knowledge of Jesus is contained." (Dahl, "The Problem of the Historical Jesus," 97).

this statement is more resistant to objections than the claim regarding his *vox ipsissima*, that he spoke of this coming kingdom of God in the terminology of the *olam-ha-ba* (the Age to Come). And this claim is easier to support than the concrete evaluation of the authenticity of the logion "Truly I tell you, whoever does not receive the kingdom of God as a little child will never enter it" (Mark 10:15). Probably we have here an *ipsissimum verbum*, but we are not clear about the original wording (cf. the variation in Matt 18:3). Judgments about authenticity are thus of varying degrees of plausibility in different spheres—but even this is not a general rule: in some particular sayings, we are amazingly sure that Jesus said (the gist of) this or that saying!

This problem of degrees of plausibility is also related to a second result of our reflections. Methodologically, judgments about the authenticity of individual traditions by no means stand at the beginning of the effort to reconstruct a historical picture of Jesus, as though we could then inductively piece together a comprehensive picture. It is rather the case that judgments about individual traditions are dependent on a comprehensive picture of Jesus, however vague and open this picture may be. To a great extent, historical Jesus research consists of the testing and refining of such preliminary comprehensive images. It thus is quite a happy circumstance that in many regards we can make general statements about Jesus (i.e., about the "comprehensive picture") with relatively great probability. We can thus speak of a hermeneutical circle between the plausibility of a comprehensive picture of Jesus and the plausibility of evaluations about details of his ministry and message.

Both problems together—the varying degrees of probability in general and concrete statements in Jesus research, and the circle that connects the preliminary comprehensive picture of Jesus and judgments about individual traditions—allow us now to inquire about the status of our knowledge resulting from studies of the historical Jesus. It is precisely for this reason that we have designated our criterion "the criterion of historical plausibility." But then, what is "plausibility?"

3. THE PROBLEM OF HISTORICAL PLAUSIBILITY

We will never know "how it really was" (Ranke), nor can we ever be able to slip into the role of an eyewitness of that time, whether or not this would seem to be a desirable or meaningful possibility. An accurate and comprehensive picture is an ideal, a horizon that can be approached only as a matter of plausibility. Plausible judgments are relative judgments. Their relativity is indicated by three signs: they are intersubjective; they are a matter of probability; and they are unrepeatable.

The first sign may be illustrated with the help of etymology: *Plausible*, from the Latin *plausibilis* (also related to the English word "applause") means "deserving applause" and may be defined or paraphrased by the English words "illuminating, understandable, credible, sound, well-founded, convincing."[49] A criterion for historical plausibility[50] can accordingly only be a criterion for research. "We perceive from the past that which *we* have understood from the transmitted content of the documents *and consider to be true*."[51] But for us to "consider it to be true" and thus for it to be imparted intersubjectively, it must be plausible.[52] It is a matter of the credibility and persuasive power of research theses.[53] By describing our criterion as the "criterion of plausibility," we thus are including the subjectivity of the scholar and the intersubjectivity of the scholarly community (and that means what can be accepted there) in our methodology.

Moreover, the concept of plausibility contains a *probability* factor. It implies that judgments about probability are involved. Probability is based on a comparison of different possibilities. When something is probable, then it is always "more probable" than something else. Decisions are made by carefully weighing greater and lesser probabilities, in our case about historical plausibility. The basically greater degree of plausibility may be objectively based, but the *degree* of plausibility is dependent on an individual assessment. When particular items of evidence point to a particular conclusion as plausible and make it appear probable, personal evaluations on *how* plausible and probable it is can vary.

---

49. Theissen and Winter cite the standard German dictionary, *Duden*, vol. 5, *Fremdwörterbuch*, (Mannheim, 1974) 568. Cf. the standard comprehensive English dictionaries.

50. The term "criterion of plausibility" is also used by K. Berger, who thereby intends the coherence of a comprehensive historical picture or course of events (cf. K. Berger, *Einführung in die Formgeschichte* (UTB 1444; Tübingen: Francke, 1987) 184–85. In his discussion pleading for the adoption of such a historical method of working, "plausibility" is understood as a synonym for "consistency": "The criterion is thus the consistency and plausibility of this picture as a whole" (Ibid., 184).

51. H.-I. Marrou, *Über die historische Erkenntnis. Welches ist der richtige Gebrauch der Vernunft, wenn sie sich historisch betätigt?* (frz 1954; Freiburg: Karl Alber, 1973) 157.

52. Of course, one must agree with Marrou that historical knowledge "finally [rests] on an act of faith," since to be sure, "no historical truth is really indisputably compelling in the strict sense of the word." (Marrou, *Über die historische Erkenntnis*, 160). But he also rightly acknowledges that every historical assertion considered "worthy of belief" (here referring directly to sources) must also be grounded on a reasonable judgment (Ibid.).

53. Cf. the simple statement of A. Cameron: "It is after all part of a historian's job to convince his audience" (in A. Cameron, ed. *History as Text: The Writing of Ancient History* [London: Duckworth, 1989] 207).

A third aspect of the concept of plausibility (alongside intersubjectivity and probability) is that a judgment about plausibility is open and can be modified. "The weight of a plausible argument may be extremely important [at the time it is made], but such importance is provisional, ephemeral, transient."[54] In other words, a judgment about plausibility can be falsified, and progress in academic knowledge may make it obsolete. A naïve "falsificationism" would be satisfied with evidence of the inauthenticity of individual Jesus traditions and would suppose that such evidence had refuted the picture of Jesus that presumes the disputed traditions to be authentic. In contrast to this, we plead for an intelligent falsificationism ("sophisticated falsificationism"): "Contrary to naive falsificationism, *no experiment, experimental report, observation statement or well-corroborated low-level falsifying hypothesis alone can lead to falsification. There is no falsification before the emergence of a better theory.*"[55] This double demand of an intelligent falsificationism can be adopted by Jesus research at two levels: the level of the comprehensive picture of Jesus and the level of concrete individual traditions.

A comprehensive picture of the work of Jesus cannot be shaken by evidence that details of its construction are inauthentic or unhistorical. Rather, we cannot speak of a conclusive "falsification" until an alternative picture of Jesus can be outlined within which the falsified elements no longer play a role. For example, in order to refute the eschatological model of Jesus (in our opinion, the correct picture), it is not enough to show that individual eschatological sayings attributed to Jesus are probably not authentic. The model of a "non-eschatological Jesus" first becomes plausible when one can present a credible alternative for the traditional image of the eschatological Jesus: the picture of a Jewish Cynic who teaches paradoxical wisdom for a living. If one can make it probable that such a Jewish Cynic is conceivable in first-century Galilee, then the denial of futuristic eschatological sayings becomes more credible. But even then the necessary work on these inauthentic traditions would not yet be done, for one must also show how early Christianity could develop a futuristic-apocalyptic eschatology for which it found no example in Jesus. In short, one must also make the "inauthentic sayings" understandable in their (different)

---

54. G. Pólya, *Mathematics and Plausible Reasoning* (Princeton, N.J., Princeton University Press, 1954) 2:138.

55. I. Lakatos, "Falsification and the Methodology of Scientific Research Programmes," in I. Lakatos and A. Musgrave, eds. *Criticism and the Growth of Knowledge* (Cambridge: Cambridge University Press, 1970) 119. Droysen had already demanded that in cases of disputed authenticity, "it belongs to a real proof of inauthenticity to show the real origin of that which has been falsely attributed to someone else, including the time and the goal of the forgery." (J. G. Droysen, *Historik. Vorlesungen über Enzyklopädie und Methodologie der Geschichte* (ed. R. Hübner; Darmstadt: Wiss. Buchgesellschaft, 1974) (= unchanged reprint of the 7th ed. of 1937) 100.

context, namely, from within the comprehensive context of early Christianity and its history. With this we move to the second level to which intelligent falsificationism can be applied: the plane of individual traditions. If sayings are judged to be inauthentic, a new historical homeland must be sought where they can be plausibly relocated.

The double demand of an intelligent falsificationism has here practically already prevailed in the dispute about burden of proof that has long played a major role in the discussion of Jesus material. Until about the middle of the twentieth century, the burden of proof rested on those who argued that a particular saying of Jesus was inauthentic; then the situation experienced an abrupt about-face. Meanwhile, some scholars (e.g., Hooker[56] and Sanders[57]) advocated the view that any claim, for or against authenticity, bore the burden of proof. That is a reasonable demand, since such claims are always a matter of probabilities.

Thus historical research is not faced with the simple alternative "authentic" or "inauthentic," but with the question of how the extant tradition may receive the most satisfactory historical explanation, whether this is by tracing it back to Jesus or explaining it from some other historical context. There are three possibilities to which the traditions attributed to Jesus may be traced: to Jews, to Jesus, to Christians. The logic of research means that tracing a tradition back to Jews has a different relative importance in the sense of the double demand of an intelligent falsificationism than does tracing a tradition back to early Christianity.

3.1 Jesus among Jews (Contextual Plausibility)

The threefold alternative, Jews—Jesus—Christians, is problematic in that it obviously sets Jesus apart from Judaism and puts his distinguishability from his Jewish contemporaries on the same level with that of later Christians. A. E. Harvey has attempted to grasp the relationship of Jesus to his Jewish context with the concept "constraints of history," which he adopted from J. Bowker and applied to Jesus.[58] "No individual, if he wishes to influence others, is

---

56. Hooker, "On Using the Wrong Tool," 580.

57. Sanders, *Jesus and Judaism*, 13.

58. J. Bowker, *The Sense of God: Sociological, Anthropological and Psychological Approaches to the Origin of the Sense of God* (Oxford: Clarendon, 1973) 61: "[I]t is . . . illuminating to look at the whole range or repertory of possible eventualities, and then to ask what has constrained this particular item into its actual expression." Ibid., 86: "If religion is seen as the attempt to organize meaning and action in relation to particular compounds of limitation, it can be seen that as goal-seeking behavior it will operate within particular constraints." Elsewhere Bowker explicitly applies this approach to Jesus: " If Jesus had not stayed so obviously within the boundary condition of Israel, then his unique

totally free to choose his own style of action and persuasion: he is subject to constraints imposed by the culture in which he finds himself. If communication is to take place, there must be constraints which are recognized by both the speaker and his listeners."[59] The involvement of Jesus in the patterns of life and language of his environment must not, of course, be misunderstood in a docetic manner, as though it were a matter of historical conditions that Jesus had voluntarily adopted for the sake of his "limited" contemporaries with whom he wanted to communicate.[60] A further difficulty consists in Harvey's elaboration of this approach, in which he wants to establish by means of the *constraints* the possibilities that Jesus had available.[61] The attempt to work out the profile of the historical Jesus derives its life from the presupposed ideas of Jesus' actual conduct, and all too easily becomes circular reasoning. The approach in terms of historical options is thus vigorously criticized by Ben Meyer in his review of Harvey's Jesus book:

> The systematic effort to determine what "options" were "available" to Jesus is sometimes misleading. Historical inference moves not from possibility to actuality (as Harvey's procedure implies), but simply from the known to the unknown. Often we have better knowledge of what the subject actually did than of what range of options had been open to him. Moreover, history is full of surprises, regularly bringing to light the realization of options that no one could know—or even after the fact could independently establish—to have been "available". Having judgments of fact hinge on our antecedent knowledge of "available options" makes for tame history.[62]

Harvey acknowledges this criticism to a certain degree: like every creative person Jesus was able to subject the *constraints* of his time to his own goals.[63] One can say against Meyer's objection, however, that it is precisely through social-historical research that general options (not necessarily options for a particular individual) can be made transparent, options that are important for a historical judgment about a particular period of the past.

---

configuration of teaching would not have been so disruptively problematic" (*The Religious Imagination and the Sense of God* [Oxford: Clarendon, 1978] 129).

59. Harvey, *Jesus and the Constraints*, 6.

60. So in the accommodations-theory of Reimarus and Semler. Cf. G. Hornig, "Akkomodation," *HWP* 1 (1971): 125–26. In this connection the word "constraint" has an unfortunate undertone of compulsion.

61. Harvey, *Jesus and the Constraints*, 7: "These constraints . . . allow us to establish the options which were open to a person such as we believe Jesus to have been."

62. B. F. Meyer, "Review of A. E. Harvey, *Jesus and the Constraints of History*," *JBL* 103 (1984): 654.

63. Harvey, *Jesus and the Constraints*, 7.

The social-historical approach requires that for an adequate understanding of the historical figure of Jesus we must make everything that we can find out about his time the object of our research.[64] On this basis Banks wants to broaden the framework within which historical Jesus research is carried on. In this connection he designates three areas that he would like to see included, namely, the contemporary milieu and behavior as well as psychological and sociological aspects.[65] He formulates his goal as follows: "The consequence of such research would, I believe, be a Jesus more firmly located in his immediate social and historical context, more broadly related to the popular attitudes and ethical ideals of his times and more precisely understood at a psychological and sociological level."[66] Lee argues similarly: "While we cannot enter into the subjectivity of Jesus, if we can ascertain with some security, as I think we can, what his assumptive world was like, we stand a better chance of authentically hearing the basic proclamation of the Good News."[67] In terms of a theory of criteria, it leads to Stein's "criterion of Palestinian environmental phenomena."[68]

Thus, for us, the idea of the involvement of Jesus in his environment and the Jewish character of a purported saying of Jesus implies no loss of plausibility in attributing it to the historical Jesus. This is even less the case in view of the facts that the New Testament tradition was transmitted and edited by Christians, and that the relationship between Jews and the growing Christian movement quickly deteriorated. Thus our criterion of "tension with the tradition" (and thus a correction of the CDC) goes against the CDJ in the traditional sense, which means that the latter must be corrected. What is plausibly "Jewish" enjoys a high degree of historical plausibility in being traced back to the historical Jesus. At the least, "authentic" Jesus material must be material that in the broadest sense can be integrated into the multi-sided picture of the Judaism of his time. This is what we call "*Jewish contextual plausibility*." It is not possible on the basis of the "Christian" tradition to attribute an element within it that has been influenced by Judaism to a Jewish contemporary of Jesus and to deny it to Jesus himself.

At the most, this would be possible in one case: the Judaism of Jesus' time is not a homogeneous unity but is comprised of numerous streams, some con-

---

64. In this regard cf. the essay by W. Stenger, "Sozialgeschichtliche Wende und historischer Jesus," who provides extensive bibliographical references.

65. R. J. Banks, "Setting 'The Quest for the Historical Jesus' in a Broader Framework," in R. T. France and D. Wenham, eds. *Gospel Perspectives. Studies of History and Tradition in the Four Gospels*, vol. 2 (Sheffield: JSOT, 1981) 62.

66. Ibid., 72.

67. Lee, *The Galilean Jewishness of Jesus*, 55.

68. Stein, "The 'Criteria,'" 236–38.

tradicting the others. If one could classify a Jesus tradition within a Judaism that was clearly different from the Judaism of Jesus, and if one could make it probable that such a Judaism distinct from Jesus was present in early Christianity and had influenced the transmission, selection, and formation of sayings of Jesus, then one could regard such a purported saying of Jesus as inauthentic. Thus in our opinion, in those places where a post-Easter Jewish Christianity already resists post-Easter Gentile Christian tendencies, one could reckon with a secondary formulation of the church. The statement that Jesus has not come in order to destroy the law and the prophets, but to fulfill them (Matt 5:17), could be explained in this way. Our line of argument shows, however, that we have not here declared a saying of Jesus to be inauthentic because it belongs to Judaism but because it represents a particular variation of post-Easter Christianity.

To summarize: In the sense of the double demand of an intelligent falsificationism, showing that a purported saying of Jesus corresponds to a Jewish context is not an alternative to claiming it as an authentic saying of Jesus. On the contrary, correspondence with its Jewish context is a necessary (though not a sufficient) condition for the recognition and identification of sayings as authentic sayings of Jesus.

3.2 Jesus and Christians (Plausibility of Effects)

On the basis of the Christian tradition and its self-legitimizing appeal to Jesus, a purported saying of Jesus that does not make particularly good "Christian" sense, and thus cannot plausibly be seen as a Christian creation, can plausibly be regarded as coming from Jesus. This is the argument of the plausibility of historical effects, inasmuch as it looks for elements in the tradition that are in tension with or contrary to the tradition itself. Conversely, an explanation of sayings of Jesus within the framework of early Christianity would fulfill the double demand of an intelligent falsificationism, according to which a saying must not only be explained as inauthentic but must show how the saying in question can be better explained from within an alternative historical context.

But here too, three qualifications must be made. First and foremost, we must remember the discussion in the preceding section about the changing object being examined for its authenticity. It is possible for a saying that has a plausible Christian sense to receive a different plausible meaning if it can be traced back to Jesus. Thus, in declaring a tradition to be inauthentic, we must always also test whether the saying, in a different meaning, cannot also be understood as a saying of the historical Jesus. Fitting well into the context of post-Easter Christianity does not exclude the possibility that it also fits well into the context of Jesus' ministry.

Moreover, it cannot be denied that the theological interpretative tendencies of the New Testament writings "potentially [provide] a *heuristic function* for the discovery of the 'early' theology of Jesus."[69] The texts of the New Testament, our primary sources, are a part of the history of Jesus' own effects, and thereby point back to the historical Jesus.[70] In the sense of an intelligent falsificationism, Fowl formulates a criterion: "If one's explanatory hypothesis flatly contradicts someone else's explanation (in this case, the Gospel writers') one should be able to give a reasonable account of how that explanation came to be so comprehensively misguided."[71]

In the third place, we are to remember once again our criterion of "coherence of sources." A consistently recurring characteristic in early Christian sources, a saying independently documented several times, can be authentic. This criterion too has been formulated with increasing clarity as we have become more aware of the internal plurality of early Christianity. Meanwhile, as the "criterion of multiple attestation," it has become a standard item in the catalogue of criteria. Schille has suggested a more precise criterion of the history of tradition: "[T]hat which was considered to be from Jesus within several of the different kerygmatic types of the earliest post-Easter time may in fact come from Jesus' own words and deeds."[72] The emphasis here lies on the *different* kerygmatic types. This emphasis is the basis of Crossan's similar "criterion of adequacy: *that is original which best explains the multiplicity engendered in the tradition.* What original datum from the historical Jesus must we envisage to explain adequately the full spectrum of primitive Christian response?"[73] Attribution to Jesus is plausible when elements from different strands of tradition result in a coherent picture. Here one may also attend to the coherence between the tradition of Jesus' sayings and that of his

---

69. W. Thüsing, "Neutestamentliche Zugangswege zu einer transzendental-dialogischen Christologie," in K. Rahner and W. Thüsing, *Christologie-systematisch und exegetisch. Arbeitsgrundlagen für eine interdisziplinäre Vorlesung* (QD 55. Freiburg: Herder, 1972) 116. Cf. the argument of Dahl: "The fact that these words and occurrences found a place within the tradition about Jesus indicate that they agreed with the total picture as it existed within the circle of the disciples." (Dahl, "The Problem of the Historical Jesus," 95). Here one must ask *what* this proves, for the circle of disciples that preached Jesus is inconceivable apart from the Easter experiences.

70. Under III.1.2 above we made clear that Christianity cannot be explained as the effect of Jesus in a *mono*-causal manner.

71. Fowl, "Reconstructing and Deconstructing," 327.

72. Schille, "Ein neuer Zugang zu Jesus?" 250.

73. Crossan, "Materials and Methods," 11. In this connection Hooker's call for a "genealogy" of the traditional sayings of Jesus should be considered.

deeds.[74] In order to be able to evaluate plausibility, one must be concerned with the history of the tradition, with the different transmitters of the tradition and their respective interests.[75] In this way one can decide about the *Christian traditional plausibility.*

In determining the relation of Jesus traditions to early Christianity, the double demand of the intelligent falsificationism thus begins to take effect: individual traditions that do not fit into our (so far reconstructed) picture of Jesus and his Jewish context but, on the positive side, can be well explained from the history of early Christianity are to be regarded as inauthentic. Conversely, an authentic tradition is one that does fit into our (so far reconstructed) picture of Jesus and his Jewish context but is in tension with the tendencies of early Christianity, or is repeatedly found despite the variety of tendencies in the different streams of early Christianity.

3.3 A Historically Plausible Comprehensive Picture (Comprehensive Plausibility)

Our reflections thus far have made clear that plausibility is evoked primarily by coherence. A comprehensive picture must manifest a minimal amount of coherence in order to be plausible.[76] In the context of our concerns, it is thus not only a matter of coherence in the sayings and deeds of Jesus and the like, but, beyond that, it concerns the coherence of the picture of Jesus as a whole within the context of Judaism and early Christianity. Such a picture includes incoherent elements within the message of Jesus and does not demand a system of his theology that is free of contradictions. The comprehensive picture may not set itself up as an independent criterion that would then function by excluding particular items of content that do not seem to fit. This danger is near when one supposes that an "assured" comprehensive picture has been attained.[77] It is precisely this

---

74. Such a "positive criterion of authenticity" is proposed by Demke: "We stand on relatively sure ground in those places where Jesus' sayings and his conduct go in the same direction in such a way that they mutually explain each other." (Demke, *Im Blickpunkt*, 63). So also Mussner, "Methodologie der Frage nach dem historischen Jesus," 128).

75. Under III.1.1.a. we have already alluded to the problem that "Christian" interests can change quickly according to the concrete historical situation of the bearers of the tradition.

76. Schürmann, *Jesu ureigener Tod*, 25. Schürmann designates this evidence "that the different observations and perceptions . . . come together into a coherent *comprehensive picture* . . . [the] evidence of convergence."

77. Schürmann ("Kritische Jesuserkenntnis," 21), though he formulates the matter cautiously, tends in the direction of utilizing the comprehensive picture as a criterion rather than regarding it as a goal to be attained.

"comprehensive picture so far reconstructed" that must constantly be checked. Thus what we are calling "comprehensive plausibility" is not an independent supplementary criterion in addition to contextual plausibility and the plausibility of the history of effects, but rather a "regulative concept" that is effective in evaluating particular historical evidence. The plausibility of our comprehensive picture thus increases with its reference points in historical evidence, while without this historical support the plausibility of an increasingly detailed comprehensive picture declines.[78]

4. SUMMARY: A NEW FORMULATION
OF THE CRITERIA FOR HISTORICAL JESUS RESEARCH

Historical Jesus research should not follow theological objectives.[79] History and doctrine are to be kept separated, which means that historical scholarship cannot deal with supernatural events and events that are without analogy. The traditions from and about Jesus must be studied with the research tools of general historical scholarship.[80] Exegesis and literary analysis may be applied. The Jesus traditions can also be used as source material for historical purposes. There is no reason why they may not be evaluated historically.

Historical Jesus scholarship is not interested in word-for-word reconstruction of Jesus' preaching or parts thereof, nor is it able to do so. It is rather a matter of grasping the essential contents of what Jesus wanted to communicate, within the framework of his person as a whole. Historical Jesus scholarship thus weighs probabilities in order to make judgments about the historical plausibility of tracing particular elements back to Jesus. Criteria are necessary for this. The more these criteria are fulfilled, the greater is the degree of plausibility.

Real criteria of authenticity are to be distinguished from arguments about the evaluation of sources and indicators of distinctiveness: arguments evaluat-

---

78. Cf. Marrou, *Über die historische Erkenntnis*, 170: "[I]n historical study it is often the case that accuracy [grows] at the expense of certainty."

79. Cf. E. P. Sanders' " . . . effort to free history and exegesis from the control of theology" (*Jesus and Judaism*, 333–34). The demarcation of historical study over against a theological goal set in advance understands "theological" in a narrow, ideological sense, with the intention of justifying faith in Jesus as the revealer objectively. In a broader sense, it is our opinion that it is altogether in the interest of "theology" to promote historical Jesus research, since it is a Christian conviction that Jesus was a historical figure.

80. Humphreys, "The Historian," 8: "[H]istorians regard documents not as the ultimate end of their work but as evidence; they use them to get at the ideas, actions, and pattern of behavior which they record and imply." Cf. also Marrou, *Über die historische Erkenntnis*, 144: "We study a document not for its own sake, but in order to reach through it to the past."

ing sources fix the age, location, and degree of independence of traditions and thus the general likelihood of finding historical and authentic material in them. They are already presupposed when criteria of authenticity are applied. In contrast, the indicators of distinctiveness that grasp the special features of Jesus' language and deeds already presuppose the application of criteria of authenticity. To determine authenticity, we have formulated a criterion of historical plausibility with two subcriteria: the criterion of contextual plausibility and the criterion of the plausibility of effects.

1. The criterion of (Jewish) contextual plausibility includes two aspects: contextual appropriateness and contextual distinctiveness. The first requirement is "contextual appropriateness:" *What Jesus intended and said must be compatible with the Judaism of the first half of the first century in Galilee.* The quest for "contextual distinctiveness" supplements and complements this: *What Jesus intended and did must be recognizable as that of an individual figure within the framework of the Judaism of that time.* Historical Jesus study that perceives Jesus as a historical figure in his own time begins with his Jewish and Galilean world of the first century. As a figure with a particular social identity, Jesus was able to communicate with his contemporaries. Thus general possibility and individual recognizability are not contradictory.

2. In contrast, the criterion of plausibility of effects refers to the later effects of Jesus in early Christianity. Here too, two aspects may be distinguished: resistance to the general tendencies of early Christianity and the coherence of enduring features that persisted despite the variety of tendencies at work within pluralistic early Christianity. The first place is held by the quest for elements that resist the tendencies of the tradition. *Those elements within the Jesus tradition that contrast with the interests of the early Christian sources, but are handed on in their tradition, can claim varying degrees of historical plausibility.* The two subcriteria of our criterion of historical plausibility represent two different strategies of evaluating coherence and incoherence, continuity and discontinuity, agreement and disagreement—in view of Judaism, on the one hand, then in view of early Christianity. We thus arrive at the following system of our four subcriteria.

	Evaluation of agreements	Evaluation of disagreements
Contextual plausibility	Contextual appropriateness	Contextual distinctiveness
Plausibility of effects	Source coherence	Resistance to tendencies of the tradition.

All judgments about the authenticity or inauthenticity of individual Jesus traditions are determined by more or less explicit comprehensive pictures of the life of Jesus, which are examined in the course of every individual decision.

These comprehensive pictures derive in part from the sources, in part from the history of research, in part from prescholarly engagement with the Christian tradition. Such comprehensive pictures underlie as a whole the same combination of criteria as individual traditions of Jesus' sayings, deeds, and fate: *What we know of Jesus as a whole must allow him to be recognized within his contemporary Jewish context and must be compatible with the Christian (canonical and noncanonical) history of his effects.* We do not regard this formulation of a criterion of comprehensive historical plausibility as a supplementary (third) criterion alongside contextual plausibility and plausibility of effects, but a regulative concept effective in all criteria, source-evaluation arguments, and indicators of distinctiveness. We always begin our research with an anticipation of a "comprehensively plausible" picture, however vague it may be, so that we can repeatedly test, refine, and correct it. And at the end we reexamine all individual results as to whether they fit into a consistent, well-rounded whole.

❦❦❦❦❦

5. *EXCURSUS*: ANALOGIES TO THE QUEST FOR CRITERIA IN JESUS RESEARCH: THE EXAMPLE OF SAYINGS OF MONTANIST PROPHETS

The quality of being "without analogy," which has been adopted as a criterion for the authenticity of Jesus' sayings, was often claimed as an element of the a priori methodological reflections that formulated this criterion. For the most part, this happened without surveying analogous problems in research. To be sure, one wanted to proceed on the basis of generally accepted historical-critical methods, but at the same time so emphasized the uniqueness of the early Christian sources that only criteria indigenous to Jesus research itself were considered. Something about this, in fact, rings true. But the question is, Where else in history do we find charismatics who left no written sources behind, of whose message and works we know about only through reports written long after their death? Where do we find something analogous to the singular consciousness of the tradents and composers of these reports that bear witness to someone who was not only a figure of the past but also the Risen One who is the living source of authority and inspiration in the present? Where elsewhere do we find such a mixture of authentic and inauthentic sayings? The singularity of the New Testament kerygma appears to make the survey of analogous problems superfluous—especially when one assumes that this led to a unique literary form, the Gospels. But we do find comparable problems in other areas. Here we think especially of prophetic figures—both in the history of Israel and in early Christianity.[81]

As a rule, the prophets of Israel left behind no written documents. Here, too, it was their disciples who handed on their sayings and later wrote them down. Here, too, there came into being a mixture of authentic prophetic sayings of the master and imitative sayings of their disciples, thus a combination of authentic and inauthentic sayings that have been analyzed by critical scholarship only in modern times. Here we have a predominately self-critical confidence in the scholarly ability to distinguish between authentic and inauthentic, even if it is done with different degrees of probability. A comparison between scholarly study of the Old Testament prophets and Jesus research by New Testament scholars would, from the point of view of the methodology involved, be worth a study in itself. Here we will only point out that Old Testament scholars also work with the criterion of contextual plausibility in determining authentic sayings of the prophets: that is authentic which fits the historical situation that can be reconstructed from other sources and from the prophetic sayings themselves. That which can be interpreted against the background of a later situation is considered inauthentic. When, for example, the later (Deuteronomic) picture of the prophets regards them as preachers of repentance, then all those features of the preexilic prophets that appear to presuppose only a message of unconditional judgment become candidates for authenticity.

The prophets of early Christianity, however, are also comparable in several respects, especially the so-called "New Prophecy"[82] that probably emerged in Phrygia about the middle of the second century C.E. (ca. 157; according to Eusebius not until ca. 172), and then very quickly spread beyond its local boundaries.[83] According to the oldest reports, three figures stood at the center

---

81. An informative comparison between Jesus tradition and prophetic tradition is found in M. Sato, *Q und Prophetie*, especially comparing the Sayings Source Q with the Old Testament prophetic books.

82. The term "New Prophecy" most likely corresponds to the self-understanding of the Montanist movement itself. Their supporter Tertullian speaks of the "new prophets" (*Pud.* 21.7). In the oldest sources they are mostly known to outsiders as the "Phrygians," the "Kataphrygians," of the "sect named after the Phrygians" (as in the oldest sources found in Eusebius, *Hist. Eccl.* 6.16.1). The term "Montanists" is not found until relatively late in the sources of the fourth century, in Cyril of Jerusalem (*Catechesis*, 16). The impetus for this excursus on Montanism derives from a team-taught seminar by A. M. Ritter and G. Theissen on "Orthodoxy and Heresy in Early Christianity."

83. The sources for Montanism have been collected in a helpful manner by P. de Labriolle (*Les sources de l'histoire du Montanisme*, Paris 1913 [with a French translation]) and by R. E. Heine (*The Montanist Oracles and Testimonia*, Macon, Ga.: 1989 [with an

of the movement: the prophet Montanus and two female prophets named Maximilla and Prisca.[84] The center of the movement was located between two small
Phrygian towns, Pepuza and Thymion, to which they gave the name "Jerusalem." Their message and work can be characterized by four aspects:

1. The *charismatic* aspect: The new prophets prophesied in a manner unusual
   for that time, namely, in ecstasy, in which they understood themselves to
   be the inspired instruments of the Holy Spirit—in particular as instruments of the Paraclete promised in the Fourth Gospel. They combined
   the charisma of prophecy with that of glossolalia—two spiritual gifts that
   for Paul obviously belonged to the life of the church.
2. The *ethical* aspect: They advocated a rigorous morality. They carried sex-
   ual asceticism so far as to call for the dissolution of existing marriages.
   Maximilla and Priscilla are supposed to have left their husbands. In addition they practiced dietary asceticism, new forms of fasting, which perhaps
   served as preparation for the reception of visions and auditions. They
   reportedly placed a high value on martyrdom. All this, however, did not
   lead them beyond the boundaries of the church. Although they were
   attacked as false prophets, they were not so much criticized for their ethical acts (their fruits), but primarily for the manner in which they received
   their revelations, in a form of ecstasy in which reason was switched off.[85]
3. The *ecclesiological* aspect: The New Prophecy developed an amazing orga-
   nizational ability. It won many adherents, organized assemblies in the
   "Jerusalem" cities of Pepuza and Thymion, collected donations from its

---

English translation]). In the following the sources are cited according to R. E. Heine.
From the literature we name here only a few comprehensive works: P. de Labriolle, *La
crise montaniste*, Paris 1913; K. Aland, "Bemerkungen zum Montanismus und zur
frühchristlichen Eschatologie," in *Kirchengeschichtliche Entwürfe* (Gütersloh: Mohn,
1960) 105–48; A. Jensen, *God's Self-confident Daughters: Early Christianity and the Liberation of Women* (trans. O. C. Dean, Jr.; Louisville, Ky.: Westminster John Knox Press,
1996) 133–188; C. H. Trevett, *Montanism: Gender, Authority and the New Prophecy*
(Cambridge: Cambridge University Press, 1996). For survey articles, see R. E. Heine,
"Montanus, Montanism," *ABD* 4 (1992): 898–902; W. H. C. Frend, "Montanismus,"
TRE 23 (1994): 271–79. The latter article provides a German translation of the extant
prophetic sayings and a comprehensive bibliography.

84. The name "Prisca" is also found in the sources in the diminutive form "Priscilla."
It is disputed whether Montanus was in fact the "founder" of the movement. A. Jensen,
God's Self-confident Daughters, 133ff., would like to see him as only the organizer of the
movement, only the "Paraclete" of the female prophets. The correct view, however, is
that the Paraclete spoke through all the prophets in the same manner. The female
prophets were indeed more independent of Montanus than depicted in the sources, but
Montanus was more than the organizer. Cf. Trevett, *Montanism*, 160–62.

85. An attempt to judge them according to their "fruits" is found in Eusebius' second
source: they are criticized for accepting gifts (Eusebius, *Hist. eccl.* 5.2). The Montanists
had in fact developed an effective "financial system." But other churches were also
doing this.

members, and paid regular salaries to its teachers. Especially notable is that they won many women to their movement. They were regarded as equal to men, for, after all, women were seized by the Spirit just as readily as were men.

4. The *eschatological* aspect: the New Prophecy probably brought with it a revival of near expectation of the end. Maximilla proclaimed that she was the last prophet to come before the end; after Maximilla comes the end (Epiphanius, *Pan.* 48.2.4 = Heine, no. 6).[86] It was not, however, a matter of a purely future eschatology: in the fellowship of the new prophets, the New Jerusalem was experienced as already present. That could be combined with the expectation that the New Jerusalem was expected to descend at Pepuza—a message probably to be associated with the emergence of a later Montanist prophet called Quintilla (Epiphanius, *Pan.* 49.1).[87] The expectation of a new world and a New Jerusalem that remained a living hope in Asia Minor (cf. Rev 21:1ff.) was, in any case, most likely alive in the "New Prophecy" from the very beginning.

---

86. Alternative interpretations have been proposed for this saying, e.g., that originally it only intended to claim that after prophecy comes complete knowledge, in the sense of 1 Cor 13:8ff. The saying was later transformed into a comforting saying in order to contest the view that prophecy ended with Maximilla (so, *God's Self-confident Daughters*, 144–45, 178–79). Or it has been understood as hedging the validity of the Montanist tradition for the time after the death of Maximilla: the sayings of the founding figures will have canonical validity until the end (so G. Schöllgen, "'Tempus in collecto est:' Tertullian, der frühe Montanismus und die Naherwartung ihrer Zeit," *JAC* 27/28 (1985): 87–88. But (1) The vocabulary speaks in favor of a near expectation of the end: συντέλεια alludes to Matt 28:20. Thus the meaning is precisely not that there will be no more prophets until the end of the world, but that what comes after me is not more prophets, but the end. (2) The saying is understood in the sources in the sense of near expectation of the end (cf. Epiphanius, *Pan.* 48.4ff. = Heine, no. 26, pp. 28ff.). (3) It is bound to a single context: the death of Montanus and Prisca are presupposed. Only Maximilla is still alive. It is also true that the Montanist prophecy did not finally die out, as the anti-Montanist author in Epiphanius, *Pan.* 48.2.1ff. claims. Epiphanius himself (*Pan.* 49.1) presupposes in all probability that "Quintilla" first began to prophesy after the demise of the original prophetic founders of the movement (cf. Trevett, *Montanism*, 167ff.). A latent near-expectation was in any case present among many Christians, and besides, the Montanist eschatology had traits of present, realized eschatology. The New Jerusalem was already present in their churches in Phrygia. Prophecy is an eschatological gift. It already makes present the perfected "knowledge of God" (so Maximilla in Epiphanius, *Pan.* 48.13 = Heine, no. 8). Montanism is less a revival of early Christian near-expectation than a revival of early Christian spiritual enthusiasm, which could always be motivated eschatologically.

87. Quintilla could well be a later Montanist prophet. A saying is attributed to her that is also attributed to Prisca: "Christ came to me in the appearance of a woman in shining garments, gave me wisdom, and revealed to me that this place (sc. Pepuza) is holy and that here Jerusalem will descend from heaven" (Epiphanius, *Pan.* 49:1.3 = Heine, no. 11). Tertullian knows nothing of the localizing of the appearance of the New Jerusalem in Pepuza. So also the early anti-Montanist authors have nothing to say

The important element is that the "New Prophecy" appeared in the oldest sources as an orthodox charismatic movement. Tertullian joined it with the intention of realizing what he had always intended as an orthodox Christian. Only later was the "New Prophecy" branded as heresy.

The situation with regard to sources is complex, but manageable, if one arranges them according to the three geographical regions in which Montanism emerged in the first two generations: Asia Minor, Rome, and North Africa.[88]

For Asia Minor, we have reports from Eusebius (ca. 260/5–339/40 C.E.) and Epiphanius (ca. 315–403 C.E.). Both depend on older sources. Eusebius gives excerpts from two anti-Montanist sources. The first comes from an anonymous author who wrote in the fourteenth year after the death of the prophet Maximilla—probably around 190 C.E. (Eusebius *Hist. eccl.* 5.16–17 = Heine, no. 23). The second source goes back to a certain Apollonius, composed ca. forty years after the advent of Montanus (*Hist. eccl.* 5.18 = Heine, no. 24). Epiphanius too claims to depend on older sources, which could go back as early as 200 and probably originated in Asia Minor (Epiphanius, *Pan.* 48.1–13 = Heine, no. 26). The most important sources for the arrival of Montanism in Rome are, alongside Eusebius' notes on Gaius, the opponent of this new movement (*Hist. eccl.* 2.25.5–7; 6.20.3 = Heine, nos. 28, 29), the statements of the heresy fighter Hippolytus in the first half of the third century (Hippolytus, *Haer.* 8.19; 10.25–26 = Heine, nos. 32, 33). The North African sources are distinguished by the fact that here we not only have statements from the opponents of the Montanists but traditions from the Montanists themselves: *The Passion of St Perpetua and St Felicity* and the writings of Tertullian from his Montanist phase (= Heine, nos. 35, 36–70).

The question is thus, Are the traditions of the "New Prophecy" in fact comparable to those from and about Jesus? With all the differences, one can still point to the following structural similarities:

---

about this. Since the "Quintillianists" later appear as a distinct group among the Montanists, and Epiphanius explicitly says that they permitted women to become priests and bishops, which they appear to support on the basis of this vision (Epiphanius, *Pan.* 49:1–3; Heine, no. 94), there is much to be said for ascribing the saying to Quintilla. It probably represents Quintilla's call vision: Christ appears to her in the form of "Lady Wisdom," and authorizes her to teach by conferring wisdom on her. The previously general expectation of a New Jerusalem is localized in Pepuza on the basis of this vision—perhaps as a means of coming to terms with the delay of the Parousia: even if the endtime is postponed in time, at least one is at the decisive point in space. On the ascription of the oracle to Quintilla, cf. Trevett, *Montanism*, 167ff. On the other hand, Jensen (*God's Self-confident Daughters*, 164, 189, 227–28) would like to regard the call vision of Prisca as the prophetic saying cited above, the vision that set the whole movement in motion.

88. Cf. the surveys in Heine, "Montanus," 4:898ff. and Trevett, *Montanism*, 46–76.

1. In both cases we are dealing with a charismatic movement. Both have their forerunners. The advent of Jesus was preceded by that of John the Baptist. The "New Prophecy" in Asia Minor was preceded by numerous Christian prophets: the seer John to whom we owe the Apocalypse; Philip and his prophet daughters in Hierapolis (Eusebius, *Hist. eccl.* 3.31.3; 3.39.9); the prophet Ammia in Philadelphia (Eusebius, *Hist. eccl.* 5.17.3); as well as Quadratus, who was associated with both the daughters of Philip (*Hist. eccl.* 3.17.1) and with Ammia (*Hist. eccl.* 5.17.2). The emergence of prophets in Asia Minor is thus easy to imagine. It is "contextually plausible"—especially since in the sayings of the New Prophecy we can detect the later outworking of Asia Minor traditions (such as the Revelation of John and the Paraclete concept of the Fourth Gospel).

2. At the beginning of both movements, oral tradition was the medium by which the tradition was transmitted. To be sure, we also have reports of writings of the three founding prophets. The oldest sources, however, know nothing of this: the anonymous anti-Montanist author (in Eusebius, *Hist. eccl.* 5.16–17) knows the Montanists from conversations in Ancyra (5.16.4). He cites an oracle of Maximilla (5.16–17)—which, however, he takes from a book of Asterius Urbanus; this means that about fourteen years after her death there were written copies of the originally oral oracles. These documents, however, did not come from the prophets themselves. The second source that goes back to Apollonius never refers to a writing of the prophets, but does know of the letter of one of their followers, Themison (Eusebius, *Hist. eccl.* 5.18.5). Even Epiphanius quotes no written document of Montanus, Priscilla, or Maximilla, though he cites the most prophetic sayings, always introduced with *verba dicendi*—he thus treats them as (originally) oral tradition (Epiphanius, *Pan.* 48.1–13). We do not meet books of the three founding figures until we get to Rome, where Hippolytus speaks against them (*Haer.* 8.19.1, 5). Gaius polemicizes there against their "audacious, misleading propagation of new Scriptures" (*Hist. eccl.* 6.20.3). The much later dialogue between a Montanist and an orthodox Christian (Heine, no. 89) sees in the fact that Priscilla and Maximilla composed books a violation of 1 Tim 2:12, according to which women are not to teach or have authority over men.[89] The findings are probably to be understood in the sense that the originally oral prophetic sayings have been secondarily reduced to writing—not by the prophets themselves, but by their followers. It is possible that collections of these sayings were later attributed directly to Montanus, Priscilla, and Maximilla. In any case, in the Jesus tradition, as in the

---

89. The polemic against the authorial activity of the Montanist prophets is found in Heine, no. 89, 124–25. On other writings of the Montanists, cf. K. Aland, *Bemerkungen*, 105–06, n. 3.

sayings of the New Prophecy, oral tradition was only secondarily reduced to writing.

3. Is the unique significance of the Risen One for the present perhaps a special characteristic of the Jesus tradition? Is there any parallel to the continuing effect of Jesus as the Risen One? One can at least point to the fact that in the "New Prophecy" too the Paraclete was considered the real author of the sayings. Tertullian transmits three Montanist prophetic sayings that he ascribes to none of the three founding figures but to the Paraclete himself (Tert., *Pud.* 21.7; *An.* 55.5 = Heine, no. 12, 14) or to the Spirit (*Fug.* 9.4 = Heine, no. 13). To be sure, a saying of Maximilla has been preserved according to which she is the last prophet (Epiph., *Pan.* 48.2.4). But it is demonstrable that there were prophets after her—the prophet Quintilla, from whom Epiphanius reports a vision of Christ in female form (*Pan.* 49.1), as well as a prophet of whom Firmilian reports (in Epistles of Cyprian in Ante-Nicean Fathers 75.7).[90]

4. There are comparable occurrences also in the written sources. Several potentially independent complexes of traditions and documents are available. The three ancient sources that come from Asia Minor are probably independent of each other. Apollonius, who wrote forty years after the advent of Montanus could, of course, be dependent on the anonymous author who wrote fourteen years after the death of Maximilla—both refer to the measures taken by Bishop Zoticus against the "New Prophecy" (Eusebius, *Hist. eccl.* 5.16.17; 5.18.13); but there are also differences. In the older anonymous author the ecstatic character of the New Prophecy plays a prominent role; the later Apollonius emphasizes the effective organization—and pillories the financial arrangements of the "New Prophecy" and its adherents: "[Montanus] appointed collectors of money, who organized the receiving of gifts under the name of offerings, who provided salaries for those who preached his doctrine in order that its teaching might prevail through gluttony" (Eusebius, *Hist. eccl.* 5.18.2). Do we here see indications of a development from charismatic beginnings to institutional structures? Or are they both simply interested in different aspects of the same movement? The North African sources are also partly independent of the Roman sources. Tertullian was not only informed about the "New Prophecy" via Rome.[91] With regard to the kind of sources available,

---

90. Epiphanius's source objects against the Montanists that after Montanus, Priscilla, and Maximilla, no more prophets appeared among them (Epiphanius, *Pan.* 48.2.1 = Heine, no. 26). But his argument that Maximilla, by saying that no prophets were to come after her, "destroys" the existence of the charisma among the Montanists, presupposes that the claim to possess the Spirit continued. This is the only way that the anti-Montanist author can see here a contradiction among the Montanists themselves.

91. Cf. Trevett, *Montanism*, 64.

the difference between Montanism and the Jesus movement is found above all in the fact that in the case of Jesus our sources come almost entirely from his disciples, but for Montanism the sources are primarily from opponents. In both cases the sources are tendentious. And thus in each case one may ask, Are there elements in the traditions that are in tension with their respective traditions, or even contrary to them?

With all that, the difference between the Jesus movement and the New Prophecy, between the tradition of Jesus' sayings and the sayings of the Montanist prophets, should not be denied. Comparable features—but that does not mean identical features—are that in both cases we have the charismatic origin of a movement, the beginnings of the formation of a tradition in oral speech, the present significance of the Spirit after the death of the founding figures, and the plurality of sources. These comparable features also apply to the methodological questions with regard to criteria of authenticity. Which criteria may form the basis of judgments as to authentic and inauthentic sayings?

One criterion clearly applies: that which can only be understood within the framework of a later situation is inauthentic. Thus for example some terminological expressions are clearly connected with particular theological conflicts. A model example is a fragment from the "Odes of Montanus" (Heine, no. 17):

> Christ has one nature (φύσις) and one energy (ἐνέργειαν) both before the flesh (i.e. the incarnation) and after the flesh (i.e. in his existence as the Risen One), in order that he himself would not be different when he does different and various things.

This is the language of a much later time: the dispute about the one nature was a fifth-century argument, that about the unity of the "energy" took place in the seventh century. Montanus cannot possibly have so spoken.

More complicated is the question of the authenticity in a series of sayings attributed to Montanus that have a Trinitarian formulation. He is supposed to have said, "I am the Father and the Son and the Holy Spirit (or the Paraclete)" (cf. Heine, nos. 15, 16). On the one hand, one can understand this Trinitarian self-understanding in the sense of a modalistic monarchianism—and so as the expression of a doctrine discussed in Rome contemporaneous with Montanus, namely that God revealed himself successively under the different forms of Father, Son, and Holy Spirit. On the other hand, one could regard this self-understanding as a hybrid self-apotheosis. And this is a topic that especially interested the opponents of the "New Prophecy:" since they could not charge the Montanists with any "heretical" views about God and Christ, they directed their critique especially against the ecstatic form of prophecy and the purported self-exaltation of the prophet that thereby came to expression. While we assume that after Jesus' death his followers placed him alongside God in order to worship him as a divine being, we find among the opponents of the New Prophecy a tendency to ascribe to the Montanist prophets after the fact a self-understanding that placed them in proximity to God—in order the more easily to condemn them as heretics. Thus the sayings of Montanus expressing his self-understanding with a Trinitarian formula could be inappropriate allegations of anti-Montanist opponents. They are not found until relatively late sources—in a discussion between an orthodox Christian and a Montanist and in Didymus of Alexandria in the fourth century (Heine, nos. 89, 103). It could also be a matter of one-sided reporting of authentic oracles (or of their introductory formulae), originally understood in the sense of a consciousness of inspiration: the historical Montanus certainly did not identify himself with the Trinitarian God but could well have understood himself to be the mouthpiece of God, the risen Jesus, or the Holy Spirit.[92]

In other cases there are good reasons to dismiss the suspicions regarding the authenticity of Montanist oracles. As an example, we will select the appeal to the "Paraclete." This is found only in the prophetic sayings reported by Tertullian—but not in the oldest sources from Asia Minor. Did the Montanist prophets then only appeal to the "Spirit" but without naming him the "Paraclete"? Was it only later that an appeal to the Paraclete of the Gospel of John was made, when it became necessary to support the new revelations of the Spirit with biblical texts and terminology? Was this combination of prophetic Spirit and Paraclete perhaps first made in Rome, where it is presupposed by Hippolytus (ref. 8.19) and Ps-Tertullian (Adv. Haer. 7)?[93] And is Tertullian dependent on this Roman tradition?

When one asks, What arguments can be presented against such a skepticism about the originality of the Paraclete motif in Montanist tradition, then one comes across the argument that has now become familiar to us, that of plausibility of effects and plausibility of context, even though this terminology

---

92. As an analogy one could name the Christian (?) prophets of Syria cited by Celsus who identified themselves in first-person speech with God, a Son of God, or a divine Spirit (cf. Origen, *Contra Celsus* 7.9 = Heine, no. 18). The connection with the three divine authorities is here made with "or." Even if the reference here is not to a Montanist prophet, it is still probably Christian prophets that are intended: the "trinitarian" style, the apocalyptic expectation, transition from intelligible speech to unintelligible (= glossolalia)—all this is most easily understood in terms of Christian tradition.

93. Thus according to the thesis of R. E. Heine ("The Role of the Gospel of John in the Montanist Controversy," *The Second Century* 6 [1987]: 1–19); so also "The Gospel of John and the Montanist Debate at Rome," in E. A. Livingstone, ed., *Studia Patristica XXI* (Leuven, Berlin: Akademie Verlag, 1989) 95–100. Trevett, *Montanism*, 62–66 argues against this thesis, in our opinion with persuasive evidence.

is not used. In order to illustrate that, we now apply the criteria developed for the Jesus tradition to the problem of the authenticity of Montanist prophetic sayings—with a certain concentration on the Paraclete motif.

1. *Plausibility of effects:* That is authentic which can be plausibly understood as the effect of the historical Montanist prophets, whether because it is found in several potentially independent complexes of tradition, or because it is in tension with the tendencies of the tradition (or at least neutral in regard to these tendencies), and thus is not derivable from the interests of the later tradents.

a) *Coherence with regard to sources:* It is not the case that an identification of the Spirit with the Paraclete is first found in the Roman sources of Hippolytus and Ps.-Tertullian. Epiphanius too, who edited traditions that probably came from Asia Minor, speaks of the Paraclete—not as part of a Montanist oracle transmitted by him, but in his own response to the Montanists: Montanus glorified himself, but the promised Paraclete will glorify Christ (according to John 16:14). Thus Montanus's claim is false (Epiphanius, *Pan.* 48.11.4). This objection of Epiphanius could be an echo of a claim made by the Montanists.[94] In addition, Irenaeus too speaks of the Paraclete in his rejection of the (anti-Montanist) opponents of the prophetic charisma (cf. *Adv. Haer.* 3.1.12 = Heine, no. 27). Does not this mean that he must have known the claim of the Montanist prophets that the Paraclete speaks through them? If one also takes into consideration that Tertullian need not at all have been dependent only on Roman sources and information, but in North Africa probably learned about the Montanists in other ways as well, then it is very unlikely that the Paraclete motif was only a secondary addition to the tradition. It is found (possibly) independently in the Asia Minor source used by Epiphanius, in Irenaeus in Lyon, in Hippolytus in Rome, and Tertullian in Carthage. It is probably original.

b) *Resistance to the tendencies of the tradition:* It is worthwhile to examine more closely the prophetic sayings that are attributed explicitly to the Paraclete, in order to ask whether a particular tendency is expressed in the Paraclete motif:

> Tertullian, *Res.* 11.2 = Heine, no. 9: "The Paraclete says through the prophet Prisca: "They are flesh and they (still) hate the flesh."
>
> Tertullian, *Pud.* 21.7 = Heine, no. 12: "This I recognize and want it even more (than you), for I have the Paraclete himself, who says in the New Prophecy: the church can forgive sins, but I am not willing to do it, so that they do not commit even more sins."
>
> Tertullian, *An.* 55.5 = Heine, no. 14: "If you thus want to die for God, as the Paraclete teaches, than not in a fever, asleep in bed, but as a martyr: if you take up your own cross and follow the Lord, as he himself commanded, then his blood is the whole key to Paradise."

---

94. So Trevett, *Montanism,* 64.

There is really no basis in the Gospel of John and its Paraclete sayings to attribute precisely these sayings and no others to the Paraclete. The saying about the flesh attacks Docetism, since the docetic teachers are themselves flesh but deny the coming of the Lord in the flesh and reject the flesh as such. According to the Gospel of John, however, the flesh is useless in comparison with the life-giving Spirit (John 6:63). The plural σάρκες in the Montanist saying is more reminiscent of the Apocalypse of John, where it is found three times (Rev 17:16; 19:18, 21), than of the Gospel of John.

The refusal to forgive sins is directly contradictory to the Johannine statements about the Spirit. The conferral of the Spirit by the Risen One authorizes them to forgive sins (John 20:22–23). The First Letter of John, however, knows of unforgivable sins—alongside sins that can be forgiven (1 John 5:16–17).

The saying about martyrdom is directed especially to women. A parallel passage in Tertullian (*Fug* 9.4) speaks of the delivery of a baby and refers to dying at childbirth. This parallel saying is attributed to the "Spirit" and not specifically to the "Paraclete." And in fact, there are connections between the Paraclete tradition in the Fourth Gospel and martyrdom (John 15:26–16:2), but the Montanist theology of martyrdom as such is not anticipated in the Gospel of John.

Our summary: The connection of the Paraclete with individual sayings by Tertullian is hardly motivated by the content itself.[95] When he designates a few sayings as under the authority of the Paraclete, there is no recognizable tendency in the background. It would be much more natural to explain the appearance of the Paraclete in these sayings if the Paraclete had always been considered the authority in Montanism. Thus the formula can be combined with a variety of contents. It is to be acknowledged, however, that this is only a weak argument for the authenticity of the sayings; it is, however, an argument that the appeal to the Paraclete was already in the tradition prior to Tertullian.

2. *Contextual plausibility:* That is authentic which is plausible within the situation in Asia Minor of the second century C.E., in which Montanist prophecy originated, whether because it agrees with this context, or because it is within this context that it stands out as a particular phenomenon.

---

95. The general sayings attributed to the "Paraclete" or the "Spirit" in Tertullian correspond so closely to the rigorous ethic and the mentality of Tertullian that one can ask with Jensen (*God's Self-confident Daughters,* 143–153) whether they did not originate in North Africa. Does Tertullian place his own opinions under the authority of the Paraclete—or does he select from the Montanist tradition that which fits his rigorous ethic? For our question of whether the Paraclete conception originally belonged in Montanism, the result here is that only if Tertullian considered the Paraclete as a given authority in the tradition could he have secondarily ascribed sayings to it.

a) *Correspondence to the context:* A charismatic movement that appeals to the Johannine Paraclete and claims its authority for its oral proclamation fits with all that we know about Christianity in Asia Minor (and especially in the environs of Phrygia). In the first half of the second century, Papias of Hierapolis valued oral tradition more highly than the written Gospels known to him. He certainly knew Matthew and Mark, and possibly John, which he perhaps had in mind as the standard when he lamented the defective "order" of Mark (Eusebius, *Hist. eccl.* 3.19.15). He speaks of the oral tradition using an expression with a Johannine ring, the "living and abiding voice" (Eusebius, *Hist. eccl.* 3.39.4). In addition, he was a Chiliast—and probably dreamed the concrete apocalyptic dreams that were revived in Montanism a generation after him. This area of Christendom was well endowed with prophets: John on Patmos, Philip and his daughters in Hierapolis, Ammia in Philadelphia, and Quadratus may be named here. The Montanists appear to have placed themselves in this succession of the prophets (Eusebius, *Hist. eccl.* 5.17.3). If one further takes into consideration that the Johannine writings had a huge aftereffect in Asia Minor, then it is plausible (whether correct or not) to think that precisely in this region a rebirth of early Christian prophecy would have been experienced and interpreted as an activity of the Paraclete. This interpretation must have been so obvious in this milieu that it did not need to be emphasized.

b) *Contextual individuality:* By and large, Montanist prophecy can be "derived" from the traditions of early Christian prophecy. The sayings are replete with biblical allusions; the topoi have biblical roots.[96] Yet the New Prophecy was experienced as something unusual. One could attribute this to the fact that the time of charismatic prophets was already over. That which in the beginning phase of Christianity belonged to the "normal" workings of the Spirit would have to remain a foreign body within a church in the process of institutionalization: alongside canon, tradition, and ecclesiastical office, there was no longer a place for living revelation. But perhaps that idea is too simple, for it was precisely in Asia Minor that a prophetic "tradition" existed. One should thus take seriously the new element in Montanist prophecy. People of the time saw this new element in the ecstatic state in which revelation was received and proclaimed. Already the anonymous reporter emphasizes that in Phrygia "they say that a recent convert called Montanus . . . in the unbounded lust of his soul for leadership gave access to himself to the Adversary, became obsessed, and suddenly fell into frenzy and convulsions. He began to be ecstatic and to speak and

---

96. Cf. Epiphanius, *Pan.* 48.11 = Heine, no. 2: "Then this poor little man Montanus says: 'Neither an angel nor a messenger, but I, the Lord God, the Father, have come.'" Here Isa 63:9 is cited almost verbatim. Cf. Trevett, *Montanism,* 81ff., where other examples are given.

to talk strangely, prophesying contrary to the custom which belongs to the tradition and succession of the church from the beginning." (Eusebius, *Hist. eccl.*
5.16.17). It was accordingly not the content of what he said that violated church
tradition but the form of his preaching. Several prophetic sayings are probably
already shaped by the fact that they knew this new form of prophecy must be
defended. Alongside biblical images, it is not accidental that here we receive a
new picture. In one of his most well-known utterances, Montanus says,

> Behold, man is like a lyre
> And I rush thereon like a plectrum.
> Man sleeps and I awake.
> Behold, the Lord is he who arouses the hearts of men,
> And gives a heart to men.
>   (Epiphanius, *Pan.* 48.4.1 = Heine, no. 3)

The image of the (new) heart that God gives to human beings is a biblical
image. It takes up Ezek 11:19–20; 18:31; 36:26, and Jer 31:31. The "man" who
falls into a deep sleep is reminiscent of Gen 2:12ff. The image of the lyre and
plectrum is new, however. It comes from pagan tradition. The lyre and plectrum are attributes of the god Apollo. The third Homeric hymn describes the
arrival of the god in Pythos: "There the lyre gives a love-blessed sound when
struck by the golden plectrum" (*Hom. Hymn.* 3.184–185). So is there after all
something to the tradition that Montanus was a recent convert, which had
been claimed by the oldest sources (Eusebius, *Hist. eccl.* 5.16.7)? That he had
previously been a priest of Apollo could have been added to the tradition later,
on the basis of the image of the lyre and plectrum.[97] However that may be, the
image of the lyre brings a new element into the language of prophecy.[98] Here
Montanus affirms the complete passivity of the human being during the reception of revelation, probably in order to ward off the objection that his prophecy
did not come from God. Thus only the first half of the saying would belong
to the prophetic revelatory saying. Here God speaks in the first person
through the mouth of the prophet. Then follows the interpretation, in which
God is spoken of in the third person. The commentary emphasizes the decisive element: it is God who is responsible for ecstasy. Behind the statement

---

97. So in the "Dialogue of a Montanist with an Orthodox Christian" (Heine, no. 89,
122–123).

98. This image is also documented elsewhere in early Christianity. Cf. *Odes of Solomon*
6.1–2, "As the hand [or: wind] moves through the harp and the strings speak, so the
Spirit of the Lord speaks in my members, and I speak in his love." One also finds the
image of the flute, that gives its sound by means of the breath (the pneuma) (Athenago-
ras, *Plea* 9.1). Cf. other parallels in Trevett, *Montanism*, 83.

that God arouses the hearts of human beings there lurks the phenomenon of ecstasy, so common for Montanism. References to the new element in Montanist prophecy may well be authentic.

We may conclude with this: It would be worthwhile to investigate the Montanist sayings further—both for their inherent value and on methodological grounds. In the framework of our discussion we only need to show enough to illustrate that the methodological criteria for Jesus research are general criteria in questions of authenticity, criteria that can be applied to comparable historical phenomena that have analogous source problems. One may come to quite different results in making concrete judgments in the case of Jesus' sayings and the Montanist oracles, but in each case one will inquire into a contextual plausibility and a plausibility of effects. This means asking in each case whether the sayings can be understood from their concrete historical context and whether they in turn can make their own historical effects understandable, that is, whether the data in the sources are most plausibly understood as the effect of the purported event itself or from a later situation. For us it is especially important to recognize that in the case of the Montanist sayings no one requires that they be "underivable" from their environment or from the (later) Montanist movement.[99] There is no application of a criterion of dissimilarity. Instead, contextually plausible derivability from Asia Minor Christianity and a connection with the later Montanist movement (including its opponents) with regard to the plausibility of effects form the framework for that which potentially can be considered authentic. Within this framework, that which stands out as something distinct is then, in fact, for us recognizably authentic, which means that such judgments about authenticity are always judgments about plausibility.

---

99. Jensen, *God's Self-confident Daughters*, 164, argues with reference to Epiphanius *Pan.* 49.1 on the basis that a particular idea is without parallel, but less in order to establish it as authentic as to evaluate it as the decisive impetus for Montanism: "It is quite possible that Prisca herself is here reporting the beginning of her prophetic inspiration and her authority as the or a leader of the movement. . . . The vision of Christ in the form of a woman is unusual and bold: there is no direct parallel in early Christian literature."

IV

Criteria in Jesus Research and the "Wide Ugly Ditch" of History

Hermeneutical Aspects of the Criteria Issue

1. LESSING'S PROBLEM: FAITH AND HISTORY

The preceding chapter on the methodology of historical Jesus research introduced the criterion of plausibility as a purely historical criterion. The designation "criterion of *historical* plausibility" should already emphasize its strictly historical-scientific character, just as the terminological distinction of the two subcriteria, "*contextual* plausibility" and "plausibility of *historical effects*" make this same emphasis. The embedding of events in their context and the explanation of sources on the basis of the history of their effects are part of the task of every writing of history. So also the term "plausibility" is intentionally chosen as a secular term. Plausibility is a matter of probability that illuminates in various degrees; it is not religious certainty. That which is plausible is always only relatively plausible. And precisely here a fundamental hermeneutical problem emerges from the theological use of texts and the theological appeal to history. This final chapter is devoted to that problem.[1]

Understood broadly, the term "hermeneutics" would also include methodology, inasmuch as hermeneutics is thought of as scholarly theoretical reflections on all the methods used in the liberal arts and historical sciences. We will

---

1. This chapter is based on a guest lecture on 1 January 1990 at the University of Glasgow. Reworked versions were also (in part) presented at the University of Cambridge, 8 June 1994, at the Lutheran School of Theology in Chicago on 10 October 1994, and at the University of Helsinki on 12 September 1995. Here I would like to thank all those colleagues whose stimulation contributed to the working out of these ideas. An earlier version was dedicated to Chr. Burchard and published as "Historical Skepticism and the Criteria of Jesus Research or My Attempt to Leap Across Lessing's Yawning Gulf," *SJT* 49 (1996): 147–76.

thus in the following chapter discuss once again the four methodological criteria (in each case with different examples). But the perspective from which we are now interested in them is something new. Historical methodology developed and established procedures that we can consciously place at our disposal. These procedures become a hermeneutic when they also reflect the presuppositions of historical knowledge that are not at our disposal—the historical preunderstanding, our life-relation to the subject matter, the connection with its effects, or the strangeness of the Wholly Other. So also the criteria we have developed for historical Jesus research are bound to presuppositions that we cannot place at our disposal methodologically, namely, the presuppositions of the historical consciousness that has developed since the Enlightenment. We will thus attempt to develop our criteria as the expression of axiomatic convictions that are at work in the modern historical consciousness.

Hermeneutics also include a second aspect that goes beyond reflection on the presuppositions of understanding not at our disposal. Hermeneutical work begins above all at the point where traditions considered to be normative—classical literary texts, traditional laws, and religious revelations—lose their immediate and direct normativity through changing times. In a situation of growing historical distance from the source of the original tradition, people assure themselves through hermeneutical endeavors of that which still is normative despite the changes brought about by the passing of time. Thus hermeneutical reflection has a double aspect: on the one hand, it makes us aware of the inevitable change in our relation to the past brought about by our modern consciousness. On the other hand, it poses the question of what remains valid despite our relativizing historical consciousness.

The general hermeneutical problem of the lasting validity of traditions receives a particularly sharp form in theology. The axiomatic convictions of modern historical consciousness stand in tension with the certainty of religious faith. Faith is unconditional certainty, a courage to live and die that rests on the person of Jesus and is formed by this person. But everything we know about Jesus is mediated to us by historical sources, whose interpretation is uncertain and will always be uncertain. All knowledge of Jesus is thus more or less hypothetical. It is, in the best case, "plausible." With regard to historical reconstruction, one can always say, "It could be some other way." But faith says apodictically, "This is the way it is." The problem is, How can conditional historical knowledge provide the basis for an unconditional certainty?

This was also Lessing's problem, when in 1777 he wrote his small essay "Über den Beweis des Geistes und der Kraft" ("On the Proof of the Spirit and Power"). In the historical evaluation of the Jesus traditions, Lessing was not a radical skeptic. He knew, however, that, in the realm of the historical sciences, there are no necessary decisions about what happened but only "the accidental truths of history"—truths that always stand under the qualification that they could have been otherwise. His time knew unconditional certainty only in the form of "the necessary truths of reason." Between these two he saw a great chasm: "The accidental truths of history can never be the proof for the necessary truths of reason." In view of this chasm he declared, "That, that is the wide ugly ditch, over which I cannot come, however often and earnestly I have tried to make the leap. If anyone can help me over, please do it. I ask, I implore him. He would deserve a heavenly reward for my sake."[2]

After more than two hundred years of historical-critical research, the ditch has become deeper, longer, and wider. In the following, it will be presented as it is seen today, in these three dimensions. The chapter will thus have three parts.

1. The ditch has become deeper. Historical criticism of the sources has become more radical. Whoever enters into the realm of historical-critical research knows that all sources about Jesus are created by human beings and are one-sided, tendentious, possibly unhistorical in many respects. We will never have the opportunity to check them by the events themselves. We will always only be able to compare them with other sources, which in turn are tendentious and one-sided. All historical knowledge is thus a reconstruction subject to error based on sources that are subject to error. It is always a matter of what is more or less plausible.

2. The ditch has become longer, with more branches. Let us assume that we possess an accurate picture of the historical Jesus—the problem of historical criticism of the sources would be solved and we would know that this is the way it was, and not otherwise. But this would only produce a second problem: everything we know about Jesus is derivable; it has analogies and genealogies. Everything is relative, embedded in a historical context; nothing is absolute. The problem of historical relativism threatens to dissolve Jesus' uniqueness. The ditch that leads to him has not only become longer,

---

2. Cf. G. E. Lessing, "On the Proof of the Spirit and Power," in K. Wölfel, ed., *Lessings Werke III, Schriften II* (Frankfurt: Insel, 1967) 307–12, along with the commentary by K. Beyschlag, 638–640. Two overlapping distinctions are found in Lessing's thought: the rationalistic distinction between the necessary truths of reason and the accidental truths of history, which goes back to Leibniz's distinction between vérités de fait and vérités de raison. The other distinction concerns only the factual truths that lie between these polarities and comes from an empirical tradition, namely, the distinction between facts that we can immediately experience and those that we can know only as they are mediated to us by witnesses and sources. Lessing would be satisfied if facts mediated through witnesses could be confirmed by factual analogies that could be directly experienced in the present, e.g., if miracles were not only reported for the time of Jesus, but were also still to be found in our contemporary world. The tension between the rationalistic and empiricist pattern of thought is emphasized by L. P. Wessel (*Lessing's Theology. A Reinterpretation* [The Hague/Paris: Mouton, 1977] 106ff, 119ff). A short sketch of Lessing's theology is presented by A. Schilson (*Lessings Christentum* [KVR 1463; Göttingen: Vandenhoeck & Ruprecht, 1980]).

it leads into a labyrinth of ditches, in which everything is connected to everything else, but the way to the exit remains hidden.
3. The ditch has become wider. Here also we may conduct a mental experiment: Let us assume that the problem of historical relativism could be solved, that is, that we had recognized in the traditions about Jesus something that was unmistakable, underivable, and singular—then the problem of historical distance remains. Jesus the exorcist and prophet of the end of the world belongs to a submerged world of antiquity, a world that every day inexorably recedes further from our own world. The ability to acknowledge the strangeness of this world belongs to the scholarly ethos of every historian. He or she fears nothing so much as the reproach of having modernized Jesus and having interpreted him according to this motto: Jesus, rightly understood, has basically always already spoken my own opinion. We must acknowledge the strangeness and difference of the historical Jesus.

The three problems sketched above—the problems of source criticism, of historical relativism, and historical distance—are the reasons that no one can jump over Lessing's ditch. In this remarkable theological discipline in which we are engaged, no one so far has won what could be called the "Broad Jump over Lessing's Ditch." Despite numerous attempts, so far all have failed. Even the best broad jumpers landed in the middle of the ditch. But in the process, they have made an important discovery: the ditch is full of water, and it is a lot of fun to swim around in it. This is just what we would like to invite readers to do at the end of this book: to jump with us into the ditch, into the cold water. We will reach the other side not as broad jumpers, but rather as swimmers, even if we will perhaps need someone there who can pull us onto dry land.

This imagery basically already says all that we wish to develop in this chapter. But still a few "footnotes" to this picture might be useful. At first we must ask, What are we really looking for when we try to jump over the ditch? The answer is, assurance about a historical figure, in order to be able responsibly to ground our faith, that is, our interpretation of the meaning of life and our living out this interpretation. The sought-after historical assurance would then be only the necessary, not the sufficient, condition for the grounding of religious faith. This faith, to be sure, proceeds on the basis of historical assurance, but it reaches beyond it—and it would be vulnerable if the historical data turned out to be very different than previously thought. Or, said more carefully, it would then have to understand itself differently, and make appropriate corrections.

We will take another look at Lessing's solution. For Lessing, the sought-after personal assurance could only be provided by the agreement between the accidental historical circumstances and the "necessary truths of reason"—that is, from the truths that the reader brings to the sources. Such an illuminating truth of reason was, in his understanding, the love commandment. He found it persuasive even in the entirely unhistorical legend from the testament of John, which is supposed to have consisted of only five words: "Little children, love one another."[3] Lessing's solution cannot be ours—if only because we doubt that there are any "necessary truths of reason," apart from formal and tautological statements. Nevertheless, our solution makes contact with his and develops it in a different direction. We will summarize our theoretical presuppositions in three points:

1. Certainty never comes exclusively by means of external data (whether empirical data or historical sources), but always only through the agreement of axiomatic internal convictions with more or less accidental external data. Axiomatic convictions (or ideas) are all those statements that one sees no obligation to ground but that rather serve as the basis for other statements—because, in our eyes, they are never false. The experience of certainty occurs when existing certainties are "confirmed" by external data.[4]

2. In the realm of history, axiomatic convictions that generate certainty are not innate but are themselves historical products. It is these convictions that constitute modern historical consciousness, as they have been developed since the Enlightenment, and that let the historical "ditch" appear so impassable. The problem is represented especially by the three convictions sketched above, that all our sources are produced by fallible human beings, that all events are embedded in analogies and genealogies, and that history withdraws from anachronistic retrojections. We today do not derive these convictions on the basis of concrete work with the sources, but we bring them to the sources as ideas we already have, by means of which we analyze the sources. And they are repeatedly confirmed. They are tried-and-true convictions, empirically tested ideas.

3. We cannot arbitrarily declare that the axioms of historical consciousness are no longer in force and thus make it possible to postulate, against this modern historical consciousness, that there are infallible (inspired) sources, that there are events with no historical analogies, or that there are eternal truths. If we are to find any certainty in our studies of the historical Jesus, it cannot be against our axiomatic convictions but, instead, with them. In the following, we shall thus show how the three axioms discussed above contain an internal dialectic. If one thinks them through consistently, they also contain the opposite of their own claim; they thus open

---

3. G. E. Lessing, "Das Testament Johannis" (1777), in Wölfel, *Lessings Worke III, Schriften II*, 313–18.

4. Valuable reflections on axiomatic convictions are found in D. Ritschl, "Die Erfahrung der Wahrheit. Die Steuerung von Denken und Handeln durch implizite Axiome," in D. Ritschl, *Konzepte. Ökumene, Medizin, Ethik, Gesammelte Aufsätze* (Munich: Kaiser, 1986) 147ff. These are further developed in G. Theissen, L'herméneutique biblique et la recherche de la vérité religieuse, *RThP* 122 (1990): 485–503.

up the possibility of a self-limitation to historical skepticism, historical relativism, and historical strangeness. They do not by this means establish religious certainty, but they do not block the way to it. Not by leaping over them, but by immersing ourselves in them as in cold water, do we attain the assurance available to us.

The thesis developed in the following pages is that the three axioms of modern historical research sketched above are related to the criteria of Jesus research. To be sure, these criteria do not constitute a bridge by means of which we can walk over Lessing's ugly ditch with dry feet, but they provide a kind of life preserver that keeps us from drowning as we swim across the ditch.

We remind ourselves once again of the main headings in the quest for criteria of previous research: the criterion of dissimilarity provides a minimum of historical and authentic material by means of a comparison with Judaism and early Christianity. The amount of material thus gained is enhanced by means of the criterion of coherence, which affirms as authentic all the traditions whose contents fit in with this assured minimum. A supplementary test can then be made that collects all the traditions independently attested in more than one source and thus adds further increments to the historical material. Our investigation does not have as its goal the replacement of these criteria by entirely new ones. We want rather to rearrange and supplement the elements of this catalog of criteria. In the following, it is our task to show that our reformulation of the criterion of dissimilarity corresponds to the axiomatic convictions of modern (secular) historical research. We provide in advance a brief sketch of the most important theses:

The idea of human imperfection and fallibility finds its appropriate expression in the criterion of "the plausibility of effects." It is the responsibility of historical research to interpret texts so that they can be perceived as the effects of the history they report (or the history of their authors). In other words, historical research not only has the assignment of narrating the events but of narrating them in such a way that the sources generated by them can be understood as the effects of these events (or, in the case of unreliable sources, that they are not understandable in these terms). This means that in Jesus research we must explain and interpret the historical effect of Jesus as presented to us in the form of the sources generated by him. Because of human imperfection and fallibility, we never have in these sources a completely coherent picture of events, but we also rarely have a completely incoherent picture. Instead, we find both and must therefore explain both: coherence and incoherence. Incoherent elements are valuable items of evidence for us: to the extent that they are in tension with the dominant tendencies in the Christian sources, they are a key to historical memory. This is the old criterion of difference to early Christianity, which we have designated

"Opposition to Traditional Bias" (as a subcriterion of the plausibility of historical effects). The other subcriterion consists of the evaluation of the coherence of the picture of Jesus in different sources, to the extent that these are independent of each other. The effects of the original history can also be seen in such persistent traits manifest in cross-sections that cut through different sources.

The second axiomatic basic conviction of modern historical research, the idea of the relativity of all events, comes to expression in the criterion of contextual plausibility. We must historically relativize all Jesus traditions, that is, place them in their Jewish context and thereby investigate both agreements and differences, coherence and incoherence, in regard to this context. We thus take up the traditional criterion of dissimilarity vis-à-vis Judaism and reformulate it as a criterion of contextual historical individuality—as the first subcriterion of contextual plausibility. It is in turn supplemented and complemented by a second subcriterion that looks for agreements with the Jewish context, thus the quest for contextual appropriateness. For only that which can be "derived" from the concrete first-century Jewish context and is comprehensible within it can be ascribed to the historical Jesus. This Jesus does not stand as an "absolute" within history but is interwoven into history—and that means into the concrete history of the Judaism of his own time. It is precisely in this fact that his "relativity" consists. And it is affirmed by the basic idea of historical relativism for every historical event in reference to its particular context.

The third modern basic conviction of historical research remains to be discussed: the a priori conviction of the strangeness of all events, a strangeness that means that even those cases that appear to violate our own convictions must be evaluated independently, in their own terms. This fundamental conviction has not been precipitated out in specific criteria. Thus one can by no means claim that the more alien a tradition is to our own convictions, the more claim it has to historical authenticity. The independence and integrity of history consist in the fact that we can reconstruct it neither as the positive counterpart to our historical world nor as its negative counterimage. In neither case would it be evaluated in its own terms. The independence of history first becomes accessible when we create for ourselves the possibility, by means of intentional methodological procedures, of disentangling ourselves from our own prejudices. In short, the third fundamental conviction of historical consciousness finds its concrete expression when we constantly seek for new criteria of what is historical and seek to improve and refine them.

This is our attempt to sketch out in advance how Lessing's ugly ditch may be crossed: we will jump into it, but not drown, if we can orient ourselves by methodological criteria.

2. THE PROBLEM OF HISTORICAL SOURCE CRITICISM

All source criticism is based on an implicit anthropological axiom: all human beings are fallible creatures. They never simply transmit the historical truth "in itself" (to the extent that there is any such thing), but they always transmit history as the reflection of their own interests, tendencies, and intentions. Thus the many contradictions between the sources. Thus also the necessity to regard all sources critically and to interpret them first as an expression of the situation in which they originated before we evaluate them as sources for the events and contents they portray. Although we must address our sources, even the best and most reliable, with a disciplined methodological mistrust, there are doubtless historical certainties. No one doubts that Caesar or Luther lived and affected history. Indeed, no one even doubts the existence of Pontius Pilate. Where does this certainty come from? And where, then, does the idea come from that all historical knowledge is relative and uncertain?

In the attempts to leap over Lessing's ditch, one often comes across an interesting dialectic: the conviction that all human beings are fallible—the axiomatic basis of all historical criticism—at the same time preserves us from a total skepticism. For if people are too imperfect to transmit the historical truth "in itself," then they are also imperfect enough to create perfect delusions about historical circumstances, either consciously or unconsciously.[5]

Even if there had existed in the first century a "Commission for the Misleading of Later Historians" and a conspiracy to leave behind a fictitious picture of the Palestine of that time and the events that transpired in it, even the most powerful commission would not have been able to control all the sources and historical remains and to have impressed on them a particular view of things. Should we imagine that such a commission would have agreed to have hidden different coins minted by Pilate in the ground and arranged for an inscription about him that later would be preserved in the staircase in the theater at Caesarea, unnoticed by the later generations? Should we imagine that Philo, Josephus, and Tacitus (or those who copied their writings) agreed to sprinkle references to Pilate throughout their documents? Should we imagine that someone put the evangelists up to reporting about Pilate in a way that, while their reports do not contradict the scattered references elsewhere, cannot be derived from them? Utterly impossible! Every historian will decide that, in dealing with the sources about Pilate that have been preserved entirely by accident, there arises an intuitive certainty that we are dealing with a concrete historical person. No one doubts the historicity of Pilate.

---

5. Some of the following thoughts are inspired by M. Bloch, *Apologie der Geschichte oder Der Beruf des Historikers* (Anmerkungen und Argumente 9; Stuttgart: Klett, 1974).

The imperfection of human beings, that is, their inability to transmit the historical truth without error, also means the imperfection of their ability to color everything totally with their own interests and intentions. Since we today are axiomatically convinced of human fallibility before we have studied a single concrete source, we are also a priori, that is, through the same axiom, protected from the suspicion that everything these sources report is imaginary, to the extent that we at all have an adequate complex of source material.

With this, however, we come to a new evaluation of Lessing's problem. Lessing saw, in the nature of the sources dealing with the "accidents of history," the cause of the shock wave that shattered the assurance of faith. Every tradition says to the critical reader, It could also have been different. Against this, we have confirmed: to the extent that there is historical certainty at all, it is based on the accidental character of the tradition. The more persuaded we are of this accidental character, all the more the intuitive certainty is generated within us: we are dealing with real history. It is, of course, true that the accidental truths of history cannot establish the necessary truths of reason (the existence of which is doubtful anyway). The accidental truths of history are, however, the only possible basis of historical certainty—and we cannot demand more than this kind of historical certainty when dealing with historical matters. This is precisely what we mean when we say that we must jump into the middle of the ditch of the accidents of historical reality, and we can feel good about this—for it is in the midst of the accidental nature of human history that we come to historical assurance.

To jump into the water of the accidental nature of historical reality means to deal with sources that have been accidentally preserved. Only when these sources are sufficiently complex can we bring into play both sides of the axiom of the limited capability of human beings for either the total truth or total falsehood. Our thesis is then as follows: The inability of human beings for total truth in itself is seen in the many contradictions and disagreements of the historical sources. In turn, the inability of human beings to falsify the historical truth totally is seen in the fact that such incoherent elements can in many cases be interpreted in a coherent manner. Incoherent elements that can be coherently interpreted are the best evidence that we are getting close to the historical truth. In the following we will have a look at both: the contradictions and their coherent interpretation.

To be sure, we can never compare our sources with the historical realities that stand behind them; we can only compare one source with another. In this process, contradictions always come to light. These are productive, when they can be interpreted in such a manner that source A is independent of source B, so that we have a twofold access to historical reality—so to speak, two windows through which to look at them. In Jesus research, the situation with regard to sources is not bad in this regard: even if one leaves the Gospel of John and the *Gospel of Thomas* out of consideration,[6] according to the present state of source analysis, we still have two independent ancient sources: the Gospel of Mark and the Sayings Source, and, in addition, two complexes of tradition independent of each other: the special materials in Matthew and Luke. Classical form criticism increases the number of sources still more, in that it regards every small unit of tradition as, at least potentially, an isolatable tradition—and it ascribes a specific perspective to each genre. We thus have much data at our disposable, among which minor tensions can be observed. If from this network of incoherent data composed of rounded-off, self-contained traditions, a coherent picture of Jesus can still be produced—and every Jesus book does this—then the source situation cannot be altogether unfavorable.

These considerations reinforce the necessity for us to reformulate the traditional criterion of coherence. The term "coherence" itself is already misleading. As we have seen, the criterion functions only because the sources contain a mixture of coherent *and* incoherent elements. We can either examine the coherent characteristics against the background of the incoherent elements and interpret the former as pointing to the historical reality, or we can highlight the incoherent elements against the background of the relative coherent tendencies in the sources and precisely in these awkward elements see the remnants of a history that lies behind the sources. In other words, we can make our analysis either in terms of the coherence of our sources or of the elements that resist the tendencies of the tradition. Each of the subcriteria is dependent on the other.

2.1 The Criterion of Source Coherence

Agreements among our sources[7] can undoubtedly point to the historical reality, especially when the sources are independent of each other and when their tendencies that deviate from each other can be interpreted as the idiosyncrasies of the respective sources (e.g., the typically Johannine features). When

---

6. We should distinguish between "autonomy" and "independence." The *Gospel of Thomas* is in any case an autonomous tradition, whose distinctiveness can be explained apart from the canonical Gospels. That does not exclude that the canonical Gospels have played a secondary role on the traditions in *Thomas* or on its textual history. Cf. the handling of the problem by S. J. Patterson, *The Gospel of Thomas and Jesus* (Sonoma: Polebridge Press, 1993).

7. "Agreement" and "coherence" are not timeless standards of measurement. That which we consider coherent is perhaps incoherent for others, and vice versa. The letters of Paul are full of contradictions. Yet when one thinks of the Letter to the Romans, Paul is to be classified among the "systematic thinkers" among the New Testament

we take up the traditional criterion of coherence, we are also reminded once again of an important distinction: the criterion of coherence was logically dependent on the criterion of dissimilarity. Our criterion of the coherence of sources, however, can be applied to sources without having to assume that authentic and inauthentic elements in them have already been distinguished (by means of the criterion of dissimilarity).

First, that applies to the so-called "*cross-section evidence*," which looks for recurring topoi, forms, and elements of content in the different streams of tradition. The differences found in these streams of tradition reflect the "imperfection" of human beings, their inability to transmit the historical truth in a coherent picture (which is a very creative imperfection, in that it has produced a plethora of "poetic" images of Jesus). Precisely this imperfection, however, provides us an opportunity: when, despite all distortions and tendencies pointing in various directions, persistent characteristics of Jesus repeatedly recur in the sources, then these features, compared with the various tendencies, represent historical remnants. Thus wherever we find agreements in Matthew and Luke's special material, in the Sayings Source, and in Mark, John, and the *Gospel of Thomas*, they probably have roots in the history of Jesus himself. Thus in all these streams of tradition we find the concept of the "kingdom of God" (in Matthew, the "kingdom of heaven"). There can be no doubt that here we have a central element of the message of Jesus himself. Except for John and the *Gospel of Thomas*, all our other sources speak of the kingdom of God in apocalyptic colors, that is, of a wonderful new state of affairs in which the whole world will be transformed and which transcends what is immanent in history—for the dead patriarchs will also be found in the kingdom of God (Matt 8:10–11). When John and the *Gospel of Thomas* differ from the other sources by speaking the kingdom of God as a present reality or (as does the *Gospel of Thomas*) make it into a cipher for the true, heavenly self of human beings, then what we have is a one-sided development of the present aspect of Jesus' preaching of the kingdom, partly as the effect of gnostic tendencies that have transformed the picture of the historical Jesus. Thus we are quite sure that Jesus proclaimed the kingdom within the framework of an apocalyptically tinted thought world, which he,

---

authors. Thus figures who think less systematically, including Jesus, probably have at least as many contradictions in their utterances as does Paul, if not more. We must thus develop a historical sense for what a particular author in a particular situation would have considered "consistent" and what he would have perceived as contradictory. Comparisons between the two historical works of Josephus (*Jewish Wars* and *Antiquities*) show what amazing divergences can be found in the same author in reporting the same events, using the same sources and traditions!

of course, also transcended when he proclaimed the future reign of God as already present.[8]

Also in the case of the *elements that remain constant in various genres*, we reckon with the imperfection of human ability either to transmit the truth perfectly or to pervert it completely: when different genres and forms contain comparable and mutually coherent elements, these can be historical or authentic. We thus hear, for example, of Jesus' miracles both in the form of miracle stories (i.e., a narrative genre) and in the form of Jesus' statements (i.e., in the genre of the sayings tradition). Miracles are portrayed differently in these two genres. The miracle stories lack those characteristics typical of the sayings tradition: the proclamation of the kingdom of God, the call to repentance, the idea of discipleship. But we can well explain this incoherence:[9] already in Jesus' lifetime people told stories of Jesus' miracles—independently of whether they followed his call to repentance in view of the nearness of the kingdom. Thus Jesus also meets us in some folksy stories as a miracle worker in the light of the general ancient faith in wonder workers, stories without specifically Christian traits. The matter is different with the sayings tradition. It was handed on by Jesus' followers, that is, disciples who shared his own lifestyle. Like Jesus, they were homeless, had often left their families, and were poor. They handed on the sayings that fit this lifestyle, sayings that spoke of the imminent transformation of the whole world, of the necessity of repentance for all and the call to discipleship for some. Miracles too belonged to this message. They thus appear in the sayings tradition in connection with the preaching of the kingdom (Matt 11:28par.), with the call to repentance (Matt 11:20ff.), and with the decision for or against Jesus (Matt 11:2ff.). Since their own lifestyle corresponded to that of Jesus, there was no reason for Jesus' disciples in the narrower sense, that is, the "wandering charismatics," to change Jesus' words radically and to reinterpret them in the light of a very different mentality. There is thus a good chance that the sayings of Jesus were transmitted by them in the sense and spirit Jesus himself had intended them. We may say even more: that the sayings tradition confirms that Jesus' miracles were also available to those who did not join themselves to his group of disciples (Matt 11:20–24; 12:22ff.). His opponents too knew of his miracles. On the basis of the sayings tradition, we may therefore suppose that stories of Jesus' miracles

---

8. We are aware of the tendency in some contemporary American exegesis to deny the apocalyptic and cosmic aspects of Jesus' eschatology. Cf. M. J. Borg, *Jesus in Contemporary Scholarship* (Valley Forge, Pa.: Trinity Press International, 1994) 47–68, 69–96.

9. On the following cf. G. Theissen, *Lokalkolorit und Zeitgeschichte in den Evangelien. Ein Beitrag zur Geschichte der synoptischen Tradition* (NTOA 8; Freiburg [Schweiz]/Göttingen: Universitätsverlag Fribourg/Vandenhoeck & Ruprecht, 1989) 119ff.

were not only told by Jesus' close disciples. Such references make plausible the formation of a tradition of Jesus' miracles that was not specifically Christian. Our results are thus: a historical-critical reconstruction of Jesus' ministry can explain the formation of two different source complexes, that of the miracle stories that penetrated into the population at large, and that of the sayings tradition that continued to be limited to his circle of disciples. Jesus was experienced differently by the population in general and by his own disciples. If one takes this into consideration, then one can offer a coherent explanation of the incoherent aspects of the tradition of Jesus miracles as transmitted in different genres. In this case, we do not proceed on the basis that each of our sources is equidistant from the history itself; instead, we take into consideration that the miracle stories that circulated among the population in general departed more quickly from the historical reality than did the sayings tradition.

The principle of interpreting incoherent elements in the sources as a pointer to a coherent history that lies behind them is also the basis of the traditional *criterion of multiple attestation*, which forms the almost exclusive basis for J. D. Crossan's book. When one bases the picture of Jesus exclusively on multiple-attested traditions in canonical and noncanonical texts, one makes oneself dependent on two things: first, on the accidental preservation of a few words and deeds on papyrus fragments, and second, on the tendentious selection of sayings of Jesus in the *Gospel of Thomas*. Since the *Gospel of Thomas* contains the picture of the "noneschatological Jesus," one will almost automatically end up with a picture of the historical Jesus that is noneschatological (in the apocalyptic sense). Moreover, it is a matter of fundamental importance that the criterion of multiple attestation is a weaker criterion than that of cross-section evidence and persistence in genre variation, since multiple attestation only permits inferences regarding the historical reality when we can explain the different references to one and the same traditional element not as variations of a single tradition, but only as two independent windows into historical reality—in other words, only if they can be traced back ultimately to two different eye witnesses.[10] This possibility can never be excluded, but it can hardly be proven. On the other hand, in the case of materially and formally related elements in different streams of tradition and in different genres (i.e., in the cross-section evidence and persistence in various genres) it is a priori more likely that

---

10. Cf. the same reservation in N. Perrin, *Rediscovering the Teaching of Jesus* (New York: Harper & Row, 1967) 46. The criterion of multiple attestation was especially used by T. W. Manson, who presupposed the Two-Source Hypothesis, both sources in his view having been composed by eyewitnesses. For him, the authority of Peter stood behind the Gospel of Mark, and behind the Sayings Source stood the apostle Matthew. Given these presuppositions, multiple attestation would of course be an excellent criterion of authenticity. But today hardly anyone shares these presuppositions.

several mutually independent "contacts" are based on historical reality. The criteria of cross-section evidence and persistence in various genres results only in general characteristics that can be attributed to Jesus (e.g., the motif of seeking the lost). Here the possibility is great that the motif goes back to Jesus himself, but it is difficult to establish concrete instances. In the case of the multiple attestation of a concrete individual tradition, the degree of probability for a judgment about authenticity is often less, but the result sounds more convincing because it deals with concrete stories or sayings.

2.2 The Criterion of Resistance to Tendencies of the Tradition

The criterion of resistance to tendencies of the tradition[11] illustrates especially well why it is that the historical-critical quest for truth benefits from the imperfections of human dealing with historical truth: although human beings are determined by their own tendentiousness in all their narratives and reports, they still cannot prevent some elements that are resistant to these tendencies from being preserved in the tradition. Thus the general rule applies: That which contradicts the general and prevailing tendencies in early Christian sources can be historical. For purposes of illustration we name once again a few elements that resisted these tendencies:

The baptism of Jesus resists the tendency of early Christianity to worship Jesus as a divine being, since baptism presupposes a confession of sin, which Jesus, too, probably made. At the very least, hearers and readers of the story of Jesus' baptism could readily think of this related idea. The early Christian tradition here exercised a kind of damage control. The Gospel of John, for instance, concedes that Jesus was a bearer of sins when he came to be baptized, but it does so only to emphasize that it was the sins of the world, not his own sins, that he bore (John 1:29). In this Gospel, the story of Jesus' baptism is changed into the story of an encounter between the Baptist and Jesus.

The reported criticisms of Jesus go against the tendencies of the tradition, whether it is the criticisms of his opponents, who charge him with being in league with Satan (Matt 12:24), or the criticism of the people, who see him as a glutton and drunkard (Matt 11:19). Another element contrary to the tradition is the fear of Herod Antipas that Jesus was the resurrected John the Baptist

---

11. The "pillars" on which P. W. Schmiedel wanted to base historical Jesus studies are such texts that oppose the tendencies of the tradition ("Gospels" in *EncBib*, and *Das vierte Evangelium gegenüber den drei ersten*). In Sanders and Davies, *Studying the Synoptic Gospels*, 304ff., this criterion is found under the heading, "Strongly against the grain; too much with the grain." The underlying principle according to which the *lectio difficilior* is the more probable is familiar to us from text criticism.

(Mark 6:14). This rumor presupposes a high evaluation of the Baptist and an understanding of resurrection as a return to this life, neither of which is likely to have been devised after Easter.

Above all, Jesus' death by crucifixion is to be named in this regard. It contradicts every tendency of religious reverence for Jesus. It was not easy to interpret Jesus' execution as a criminal as the destiny of the redeemer. Early Christianity was well aware of the fact that the cross was a scandal (1 Cor 1:18ff.).

An especially good example of "resistance to the tendencies of the tradition" is found where we have available two statements with opposite tendencies, but where agreements are still to be found. Where friend and foe proceed on the basis of the same facts, they are likely to be historical. Thus Jesus' exorcisms were interpreted by his followers as signs of the inbreaking kingdom of God (Matt 12:28), by his opponents as the effects of demonic power (Matt 12:24). Both sides thus presuppose the reality of Jesus' exorcisms. To be sure, we reckon in each case with the enormous tendency to present things in a one-sided and distorted manner—that is, with human imperfection in regard to handing on the truth—but precisely for this reason such agreements weigh all the more heavily.

The final example illustrates how the quest for elements resistant to the tradition and agreements within the traditions often occur together. Of course, this may at first have the opposite effect, so that either the agreements or the disagreements would serve as the point of departure for a historical reconstruction. In fact, however, both are mostly interrelated. The baptism of Jesus corresponds both to the criterion of "coherence of sources" and to the "criterion of resistance to tendencies of the tradition." It is independently documented several times (Mark 1:1–9par.; *Gos. Heb.* 2; John 1:32ff.). It is mentioned in several different genres: in the Synoptic narratives as in a summary in Acts (Acts 10:37; cf. 1:22). This results in a certain "coherence of the tradition." At the same time, however, there are aspects of the baptism story that are emphatically resistant to the tendencies of the tradition, such as Jesus' dependence on the Baptist, which is secondarily moderated in Matt 3:14, or the confession of sin presupposed by baptism, which is consciously denied by parts of the tradition (*Gospel of the Nazarenes*, frg. 2). In concrete historical work, we thus apply both subcriteria together. And there is no logical contradiction between them: that which is found in sources with clearly different tendencies is in these sources at least neutral with regard to their respective traditions. It cannot in each case be interpreted as expressing the particular perspectives of each source. And the converse also applies: that which remains in the sources against the prevailing tendencies will then be especially evaluated as historical when it corresponds to other "remnants" of this sort.

It is thus legitimate to understand both criteria as subcriteria of a single criterion. Both are based on the plausibility of effects. When we interpret the incoherent elements in the sources in terms of a coherent history behind them, then we are interpreting the history of its effects (to which also the sources themselves belong) as a distancing from Jesus in which awkward historical remnants were preserved despite the general tendencies of the tradition. We reckon with a "distancing" from the historical truth with regard to the history of effects, but a distancing that was never completely carried out. When we interpret agreements in different (independent) sources as pointers to the historical Jesus, we are considering the history of Jesus' effects and the sources that belong to it as a continuum that connects us with its origin in the life of Jesus. We are reckoning with a history of effects that resulted in a "preservation" of the historical truth but is never perfect. The branching out of the history of Jesus' effects but into several streams of tradition speaks clearly against any unbroken preservation of his memory. Both tendencies are present in every history of Jesus' effects but in different mixtures: a tendency away from the origins and another tendency in which the origin continues to have its effect. "Coherence of sources" and "resistance to the tendencies of the tradition" are each partial aspects of "the plausibility of historical effects." This criterion, in both of its aspects, thus presupposes the idea of human fallibility. To be sure, human imperfection in transmitting the truth separates us from the truth, but human imperfection in the "fabrication" of untruth preserves us in most cases from a complete falsification of history that we could not later uncover.

The criterion of plausibility of effects, however, is not adequate. The question remains: How can we be certain that the religious imagination of early Christianity after Easter did not create an image of Jesus that has been preserved in different strands of tradition and sources? Who can tell us that we have found the historical reality of Jesus, instead of the historical reality of an early image of him? Are not all sources fundamentally colored by the religious convictions of early Christianity, convictions that have radically transformed the memory of the historical Jesus in the light of the Easter experiences? This consideration shows that a second criterion is necessary: the criterion of contextual plausibility.[12] The more convincingly we can uncover the connections of Jesus to his Jewish context, the more certain we will be that we are penetrating behind the post-Easter Christian pictures of Jesus in order to find the historical reality prior to Easter, and that Jesus is not a product of the history of early Christianity, but of Judaism. This presupposes that everything about him is "relative"—relative namely to his concrete Jewish context. We must

---

12. The criterion of "contextual plausibility" is found in different forms in almost all catalogues of criteria, for example, as the "environmental criterion."

therefore discuss this criterion of Jesus' connection to his context within the framework of the problematic of historical relativism.

3. THE PROBLEM OF HISTORICAL RELATIVISM

Historical relativism says that all historical phenomena are interdependent. They stand in "relation" to each other or are "relative to each other." All must be derived from their prehistory, explained by their situation, and illuminated by analogies. Nothing is underivable, since everything is the result of past developments. Nothing is incomparable, since everything has analogies. Nothing is absolute. But Christian faith is based on Jesus as the mediator of an absolute certainty—the certainty of being confronted by the presence of God in him. Between this certainty of faith and the historical relativity of Jesus, Lessing's ugly ditch opens up anew. In Lessing's time, it was not yet clear how broad and deep it was. Not until the history-of-religions studies of the nineteenth century did we become aware of how deeply embedded Jesus was in his own time and religious history.

Despite all this, the study of the historical Jesus was confident that by means of the criterion of dissimilarity it had discovered in Jesus an unmistakably unique figure. But does not confidence in the unmistakable uniqueness and underivability of Jesus contradict the fundamental conviction of historical relativism, that everything is interdependent, that nothing is completely singular? As we have seen, doubts about the criterion of dissimilarity were further strengthened as it was seen to be misleading and incapable of being carried through consistently. It could not be carried through consistently because a universal negative judgment is inherent in it, a judgment that is impossible to verify.[13] It is misleading, since it suppresses everything Jesus had in common with either Judaism or Christianity. We cannot then get around historical relativism simply by appealing to the criterion of dissimilarity as practiced in Jesus research. This criterion itself is too problematic. Yet in its background there hovers a legitimate "idea:" the conviction of the individuality of everything historical.

Precisely with the help of historical relativism, we can establish and defend this conviction of the individuality of historical phenomena in a twofold man-

---

13. In order to show that a Jesus tradition is not derived from its environment, we would have to have a complete picture of this environment. This was seen early on. Cf. Hooker, "Christology and Methodology," 482: "Use of this criterion seems to assume that we are dealing with two known factors (Judaism and Early Christianity) and one unknown—Jesus; it would perhaps be a fairer statement of the situation to say that we are dealing with three unknowns, and that our knowledge of the other two is quite as tenuous and indirect as our knowledge of Jesus himself."

ner. The principle that everything is related to everything else means, in the first place, that a historical phenomenon can never be interpreted in isolation but only in the context of all the other elements contemporary with it—it is immaterial whether these are texts, people, or social movements. We meet here afresh an internal dialectic: even if individual elements are "derivable," it does not necessarily mean that the combination of elements would be "derivable." The combination could be unique. The more elements that are combined, the less is the probability of finding a comparable factual phenomenon anyplace else in world history. In the case of human beings, this seems to be a priori impossible, since every human being is such a complex phenomenon that the possibility of a "repetition" can be excluded. We thus approach historical reality with an a priori axiomatic conviction about its individuality.

Historical relativism, however, contains yet another idea that functions in the same way as an axiomatic conviction: the idea of development. The principle that everything is related to everything else applies not only to synchronic relationships between elements of a particular historical phenomenon, but also for the diachronic sequence of elements (traditions, ideas, motifs). Historical relativism says that everything can be derived from what has preceded. We can therefore place all historical material in a series of earlier and later elements and thus arrange them in stages of development. Now, if all elements were entirely alike, it would be impossible to place them in a temporal series. We would be incapable of distinguishing different stages within this sequence. The idea of development inherently implies the idea of the singularity of every individual moment of this development, for we can only think in this way if we are able to distinguish earlier and later, preceding and following, elements. Thus also from this point of view historical relativism necessarily implies an axiomatic faith in historical individuality. In fact, both ideas, that of development and that of individuality, were developed during the same period of historical scholarship: during the time of nineteenth-century historicism. They belong together in terms of their content.[14]

Our train of thought is therefore as follows: Behind historical relativism stands a very elementary axiom: we must interpret everything in context, in relation to everything else. This results, on the one hand, in a relativizing of all historical phenomena due to their being embedded in diachronic and synchronic contexts, and, on the other hand, in an individualizing of every historical phenomenon due to its singular location in diachronic lines of development and its complexity as a synchronic structure. If everything is interdependent, then everything is relative and everything is individual.

---

14. Cf. F. Meinecke, *Die Entstehung des Historismus*.

When we now turn from this general historical conviction to the concrete figure of Jesus, we arrive at this result: Jesus' singularity consists in a singular combination of Jewish traditions as well as in the fact that his words and deeds represent a unique stage in the development that leads from Judaism to Christianity.

The traditional criterion of dissimilarity does not do justice to this state of affairs, since methodologically it does not take account of both differences and agreements between the Jesus traditions and their Jewish context. "Contextual plausibility" includes both aspects. Only by taking both aspects into consideration can we avoid the paradoxical situation of having to make negative universal statements that we have no means of verifying. We can never demonstrate that any element in the Jesus tradition was not present in Judaism, could not be derived from Judaism, or is not comprehensible in Judaism. But we are presumably in the situation of making positive judgments about connections between our limited Jewish sources and the Jesus tradition. We can thus establish distinctive characteristics in the Jesus tradition in comparison to our limited data in the sources or locate its unmistakable place on the concrete line of development from Judaism to Christianity. In other words, we can investigate its embedded location in concrete synchronic or diachronic connections, and within these contexts show its individuality.

This idea of an inner dialectic of historical relativism can also be applied to the antidogmatic conviction on which it is based, namely, that Jesus was by no means "singular" and "without analogy." When one consistently thinks through this axiom, it tends to qualify and limit itself. This is shown by the development of history-of-religions research into early Christianity.

For a long time, it was considered a mark of "unenlightened" theological commitments to (1) defend the uniqueness of Jesus against all history-of-religions studies that argued for Jesus' dependence on his religious environment and (2) to resist the arguments that Jesus and early Christianity could be understood in terms of parallels from the religious world of their own day and could be integrated into that religious world without remainder. In contrast, today it is supposed that precisely in the overrating of parallels and lines of development from the history of religion, there is often an (unconscious) theological commitment to the uniqueness of Jesus and his central place in world history and the history of religions. The older history-of-religions studies had first (unconsciously) subjected many of its analyses to an *interpretatio christiana*, before they could be successfully evaluated on the basis of such a reinterpretation as explanations for early Christian phenomena. Thus scholars were persuaded that dying and rising gods were worshipped in the mystery cults. Today we see that what was expressed in the mystery cults was likely the longing for a new life (before or after death) but that there can be no talk of a "resurrection" of the gods they worshipped. It was rather a matter of compromises between death and life. Persephone (or Kore) had to remain in the underworld for one-third of the year and could return to life among the gods for only the remaining two-thirds. The corpse of Attis remained dead but did not know it; only his little finger moved. Osiris ruled in the underworld, thus belonged himself to the world of the dead, but, from his corpse, grain grew. Mithras is not at all a dying god and provides no parallel. His form is rather that of a "counter concept" for symbolizing the experience of death and the hope of life found in the other mystery cults. According to our present knowledge, only early Christianity knows a dying and rising deity. The proclamation about him found a resonance among people whose myths of dying gods had also expressed the longing for a new life. But only in early Christianity did this longing come to expression in the form of a resurrection from the dead. The older history-of-religions research thus unconsciously interpreted the mystery gods according to the model provided by the Christ figure. For them, Christ was de facto the key to the history of religion. And it is still always unconscious Christian (or anti-Christian) dogmatic theology that makes it difficult to perceive, analyze, and evaluate every historical phenomenon in its own terms.

The same applies to the incorporation of historical phenomena into developmental series in the history of religions. It is no accident that precisely a somewhat conservative "Biblical Theology" has made the tracing of such lines of development from the Old Testament to the New Testament into its own program. There too the question is raised of whether it is not a priori suggested that all the lines of development in the Old Testament and early Judaism converge on the single, unique figure of Jesus. Thus the few "Son of Man" texts in Dan 7, 1 Enoch 36–71, and 4 Ezra 13 are read all too quickly as "preliminary stages" of early Christian claims about Jesus as the Son of Man. Or Lev 16 and Isa 53 were read as pointers to the atoning death of Jesus, although perhaps the scapegoat ritual of Lev 16 requires an (impressive) *interpretatio christiana* before it can reveal that an animal that has been killed or driven away is a substitute for sinful humanity. Or everywhere in the Old Testament and the associated Jewish literature, messianic statements were found and so interpreted as though the messianic expectation stood at the center of the Jewish religion. In reality it was only one variation of eschatological hopes. It is only from a later Christian perspective that one can read the so-called "messianic" testimonies as though they were constantly growing and increasingly sublime messianic expectation. Biblical messianism is doubtless one line of development alongside others, but certainly not the only one. It was only for the early Christians that it became the central perspective.

The awareness of relativity from the perspective of the study of the history of religions thus today leads to "relativizing" the parallels that were drawn all too quickly and the lines of development that were constructed all too boldly. The great task still remains ahead of us of analyzing and evaluating each phenomenon in its own terms while, at the same time, integrating it into its comprehensive context without a priori centering these contexts around one figure. The line of argument has thus greatly changed in comparison with the beginning days of history-of-religions research: as the expression of an enlightened critical historical consciousness, the task today is considered to be elaborating precisely the distinctiveness of Jesus. The claim of an unparalleled singularity is seen to be just as theologically dogmatic as the attempt to let one of the most sharply profiled figures of ancient and Jewish history become unclear, obscured behind genuine analogies and lines of development.

3.1 The Criterion of Contextual Plausibility

The more a Jesus tradition fits into the context of contemporary events, local circumstances, Jewish traditions, and Jewish mentality, the more confidence develops within us that Jesus cannot be the creation of early Christian imagination. How else can a fictitious figure be distinguished from a historical personage except by localizing him in a particular time and place and relating him to other historical figures?[15]

The elements in the Jesus tradition that we named previously as examples of resisting the tendencies of the tradition can now serve as illustrations of the criterion of contextual plausibility: the baptism of Jesus at the beginning of his ministry, his opponents' criticism of his activities (including the reaction of Herod Antipas), and the end of his ministry by his death on the cross. The baptism, criticism, and execution of Jesus are associated with three names: John the Baptist, Herod Antipas, and Pontius Pilate. All three figures are also found in non-Christian sources,[16] so that the statements in Christian sources can be checked against those in other documents. The result is that, in the Christian documents, we undoubtedly have historically reliable information

---

15. Cf. R. G. Collingwood, *The Idea of History* (Oxford: Oxford University Press, 1961) 246–47.

16. The sources: (1) for John the Baptist: Josephus, *Ant.* 18.116–119; Matt 3.1ff. pars.; (2) for Herod Antipas: Josephus, *Ant.* 18.36–38, 101–105ff.; Matt 14:1ff. pars; Luke 13:31–32; 23:6ff. Antipas is also referred to in *Dio Cass.* 55.27.6 and 59.8.2 without mentioning his name. Two of his inscriptions have been preserved, cf. OGIS, nos. 416, 417. His coins can be seen in Y. Meshorer, *Jewish Coins and the Second Temple Period* (Chicago: Argonaut, 1967) 72–75. (3) Pilate is documented in Josephus, *Ant.* 18.35, 55–59, 62, 64, 87–89; *J.W.* 2.169–177. An inscription was found in Caesarea, cf. J. Lémonon, *Pilate et le gouvernement de la Judée: Textes et documents* (Paris: Librairie Lecoffre, 1981) 23–32. For his coins cf. Y. Meshorer, *Jewish Coins*, 102–6.

about these three figures, even if from a particular perspective. By analogy we can conclude that if the traditions regarding these three contemporary figures have a historical background, this will also apply to the same extent in the case of Jesus.

A further aspect of Jesus' conformity to his context is the embedding of Jesus traditions in a particular local context.[17] Local coloring is present, for example, in the report that John baptized in the desert (cf. Mark 1:4 NIV). The statement appears at first glance to be paradoxical. But sections of the Jordan are in fact bounded on both sides by the desert, separated from it only by the narrow river bank.

Above all, however, we are able to connect Jesus traditions with Jewish traditions and Jewish mentality. The *Assumption of Moses* was newly published (probably in an expanded edition) shortly before the public appearance of Jesus. In this writing, we encounter the expectation of the coming of the kingdom of God in a nonviolent form. The pious wait in the hope that God will act against Satan. The preaching of Jesus is related: for him, too, the kingdom of God means the end of Satan (in his exorcisms; cf. Matt 12:28), and here, too, without human violence. In the *Assumption of Moses* we thus get a fleeting glance into the milieu in which Jesus' own preaching was at home.

At the same time we find differences from the *Assumption of Moses*. In it, the kingdom of God is directed against the Gentiles. This opposition disappears in the Jesus tradition. On the contrary, in one of his sayings Jesus promises that people from all corners of the earth will stream into God's kingdom—Gentiles included—even if this promise also could well be directed to the Jewish Diaspora (Matt 8:10–11). The other half of our criterion of contextual plausibility calls attention to such individual traits within a demonstrable context.

3.2 The Criterion of Contextual Distinctiveness

Every comparison of Jesus with his context includes the noting of both similarities and differences. As is true in life generally, here too we recognize a person by his individual characteristic features—or, more precisely, a combination of individual characteristic features that we often grasp only intuitively. The fact is, in every day life we recognize particular people on the basis of small samples of their total identity, a few movements, their tone of voice, and such, without being able to describe discursively how we do it. So, too, in historical

---

17. On the basis of his preceding research, S. Freyne provides a survey of Jesus' Galilean environment in "The Geography, Politics, and Economics of Galilee and the Quest for the Historical Jesus," in B. D. Chilton and C. A. Evans, eds., *Studying the Historical Jesus* (NovTSup 19; Leiden: E. J. Brill, 1994) 75–121.

tradition we come across such "indications of individuality:" recurring traits that we find nowhere else. Here, too, it is often a matter of complex combinations of evidence. We here provide two examples. The first is based on synchronic connections among a plethora of elements; the second, on the special position of one element within a diachronic development. The idea of historical relativism hovers in the background of both kinds of "distinctive marks," a relativism that can understand one "element" in history only in relation to other related "elements."

Even when we are often unsure whether each individual saying really comes from Jesus, we are still amazingly sure that we recognize the linguistic forms of his proclamation—that is, the distinctive combination of literary (oral) forms, topoi, and basic structures associated with Jesus. If, in the case of each individual form, we can prove only a single instance to be authentic, we have thereby proven that Jesus used the genre as a whole. As a rule, several examples of a genre might well be authentic. Thus even when we are uncertain whether our judgment of authenticity is correct in a particular case, we could still have made the correct judgment in another case. It is extremely unlikely that none of the manifold examples of a particular genre is authentic. In other words, although we are uncertain whether in particular cases we have identified a "saying" (*parole*) of Jesus, we still know his "language" (*langue*) very well. We know that Jesus used parables and metaphors, woes and blessings, aphorisms and admonitions. There are parallels to all these forms in Judaism. Their combination, however, is unique. We know no other Jewish teacher in this time who united precisely this combination of structures and literary forms—and who, in addition, connected them with charismatic activity as a miracle worker and leader of a band of disciples.

In the second place, we provide an example of an unmistakably distinct location in a diachronic line of development in which the second guiding idea of historical relativism (the idea of development) functions as the means of recognition. Once again we choose Jesus' eschatology as an example. The kingdom of God often prevails by means of war against the Gentiles or other enemies. One thinks of the *War Scroll* from Qumran. The *Assumption of Moses* conforms to the thinking of a more peaceful time at the beginning of the first century C.E. Here the pious of Israel are absolutely nonviolent. They withdraw into a cave, where they wait for a great religious persecution, for death, and for the breaking in of the kingdom of God. Jesus continues this line of development: in his view the kingdom of God can coexist in a preliminary form with the Roman Empire. The kingdom has already begun and that means in a time when the Romans rule unchallenged.

For Jesus too, the people of the kingdom are nonviolent and are committed to nonviolence. It is, on the contrary, the kingdom of God itself that suffers violence—whether from opponents or its advocates (Matt 11:12–13). According to Jesus, the kingdom already begins with John the Baptist. The Christians after Easter went a step further. They identified the beginning of the eschatological events with the resurrection of Jesus from the dead. In this line of development from a futuristic understanding of the kingdom of God, brought in partially by human activity, to a present and "aorist" eschatology, the "Stürmerspruch" ("Violence Saying") has a unique stance by its speaking of violence *against* the kingdom. It takes up tendencies already present in Judaism, develops them further, and is then even further developed by early Christian faith.

The deeper one goes into the Jesus tradition in this way, the more irrefutable becomes the confidence that its fitting in with comprehensive lines of development and its specific combination of traditions and forms is found nowhere else. This confidence is justified, even if there is at work in it a quasi "a priori element," namely, the ideas of historical development and individuality. The criterion of dissimilarity is not criticized by us because it ascribes individuality to Jesus but because of three other reasons. First, the criterion of dissimilarity suppresses the dialectic of historical relativizing and individualizing. Both belong together, the embedding of historical phenomena in diachronic and synchronic contexts and the conviction of the individuality of all that is historical. Individuality is always contextual individuality. It is methodologically perceptible only by seeing it in a particular context. In the second place, the criterion of dissimilarity often presupposes an exaggerated idea of individuality. Jesus had his individuality as does every human being—especially every human being who has had an effect on history. The evidence for the individual and singular is misused, however, when it suggests that someone is more than human.[18] In the third place, the hermeneutical reflections on the criterion of dissimilarity do not make it apparent that the idea of individuality contains an a priori element. Here an idea comes into play that has been developed by historical consciousness, an idea that we find repeatedly confirmed in the sources but that we could never extract from the sources inductively. When it is recognized that historical research reconstructs historical reality on the basis of such a priori "ideas," tolerance will be created at the same time for the fact that the religious consciousness regards the historical figure of Jesus with "ideas" that proceed further and that interpret him in still more comprehensive contexts.

The theological "ideas" that proceed further can find support within the Jesus tradition itself from a well-documented conviction that bursts through

---

18. Sanders and Davies (*Studying the Synoptic Gospels*, 301–44) name their second "test" for the location of authentic Jesus material "uniqueness," but in their understanding it is a matter of a limited "distinctiveness." Cf. Sanders, "The Question of Uniqueness."

the framework of the merely historical: the Easter faith.[19] According to both early Christian statements (Rom 1:3–4) and present-day theological insight, here lies the actual basis for all those statements about Jesus that not only transcend historical consciousness but also go beyond what the historical Jesus said about himself. Within this book we cannot discuss the problematic of the Easter faith. Many want to consider it, too, a part of the historical realm—either with the critical result that this faith, because there are no historical analogies to it, does not point to any objective event, or with the "apologetic" result that it is placed on the same plane as other historical events in order to assure that it happened in the objectively real world. There can be no doubt that the Easter *faith* of human beings is a historical event. But the reality to which it wants to point is no more "historical" than the creation ex nihilo, which can never be the subject of historical research on the basis of sources. Events in the realm beyond death are fundamentally removed from the historian's work. This realm shatters our experienced world. The historical principles of immanence and analogy apply only to the experienced world. But this is not all. Whoever is convinced that they, in special "experiences," (in experiences with experience itself, i.e., with its boundaries and conditions) become porous to the transcendent world and have access to the greater encompassing Reality, such people can think of the Easter event as the breaking in of a transcendent reality—and at the same time investigate the Easter faith historically without "dissolving" that to which it refers into history itself. We can investigate the creation faith historically—and at the same time experience the wonder of creation as something entirely unique. The question of whether Easter and the Easter faith are withdrawn from consideration by the "ideas" of historical relativism is thus to be answered in a nuanced way: with the *Easter event* a Reality invades our world that is necessarily unavailable to historical relativism, if it is what it claims to be. With the Easter *faith*, on the other hand, we have the convictions of human beings that are subject to historical investigation, to which all the premises and methods of historical-critical research apply.

To return to our criterion of plausibility, however, we have seen that the traditional criterion of dissimilarity contains a legitimate nucleus when it works with the idea of individuality. Here it is dealing with a tried and true historical "idea." It may not, however, be "unofficially" burdened with a religious (or theological) idea that goes much further, according to which in the historical Jesus a transcendent reality breaks into our world. It is by no means the case that here "empirical experience" and "faith" square off against each other.

---

19. For a discussion of the historical and hermeneutical problems related to the Easter faith, we refer to G. Theissen and A. Merz, *The Historical Jesus*, 474ff.

Rather, in both cases it is a matter of "ideas" that function a priori; in both cases there is an appeal to confirming experiences. Both ways of approaching Jesus are legitimate. Historical "ideas" (which in every historical methodology serve as guidelines to what can be known) function as barricades to the approaches to historical reality. Religious ideas want to open up access to a transcendental reality. What we obtain as the result of historical investigation is overburdened if one stealthily injects into the historical idea of individuality the concept of "revelation" (i.e., the breaking in of the transcendent). But this idea is already built into the criterion of dissimilarity to the extent that "dissimilarity" means the nonderivability from Judaism and Christianity—that is, nonderivability from history as such. We therefore replace the criterion of dissimilarity by the criterion of plausibility, according to which Jesus traditions are authentic if they are recognizable as something individual within the Jewish context of the first century C.E. and can be plausibly understood as the source of the history of effects documented in the early Christian sources.

In regard to our project, the decisive thing remains: only by affirming historical relativism do we attain knowledge of the individuality of Jesus. This individuality is relativized by its location within the framework of Judaism. But theologically regarded, that is no disadvantage. The relation of Christianity to Judaism belongs to the essence of Christianity. So far as historical relativism is concerned, it does, at first, appear to be a deep ditch; but the leap into this ditch is also a gain. We must immerse ourselves in the cold waters of historical relativism: it binds Christianity to Judaism—and beyond that to all religions.

4. THE PROBLEM OF HISTORICAL STRANGENESS

The problem is not yet resolved by the above considerations, however. Let us assume that we possessed a historically reliable picture of the historical Jesus that did justice to his individuality within the framework of his Jewish context. The problem of his historical strangeness would still remain. The Jesus tradition leads us into another world. In this, it is not a special case. On the contrary, every historical tradition gets more and more distant and strange to us twenty-four hours per day. The strangeness of past history is no special problem confined to Jesus research. On the contrary, modern historical consciousness proceeds from the basic conviction of the strangeness of every historical tradition—and becomes skeptical precisely in the case of supposedly familiar traditions as to whether they really are as close to us as appears, or whether incidental agreements with our own life world have not all too quickly misled us to rediscovering something of ourselves in them. Every historical tradition, including those supposedly the most familiar, is approached with the postulate of historical strangeness. It is an axiomatic conviction of historical knowledge, one that has time and again proven itself in dealing with historical materials.

There is thus no greater sacrilege in historical science than "modernizing" strange life worlds and phenomena, instead of understanding them in their own terms and their own contexts.[20] That is all the more true, in that the greater an interest anchored in the present is present in the texts being studied, the greater interest there is in deriving orientation for the present from the texts from the past—and thus the danger of interpreting the past in the context of the present.

This is precisely the case in studies of the historical Jesus. Christian faith makes the figure of Jesus central to its own life's orientation—it does exactly what, from the perspective of a rigorous academic ethos, is guaranteed to corrupt objective scholarly work. The bringing of the past into the present appears here as an assault on history. Again Lessing's wide ditch opens up before us—this time in a particularly intimidating form. The overcoming of this historical distance appears already to be a vain effort, since it gets more difficult with every passing day. Jesus seems to recede more and more to the margin of our culture and to return to his own time, from which he has come into our time as a stranger.

Note well: the conviction of the strangeness of the historical is an axiomatic idea. We always bring this idea with us in our approach to the sources. But this idea works in the same way as other axiomatic ideas of historical consciousness. When thought through consistently, a dialect emerges that reveals its opposite counterpart as an inherent component in the idea itself. Only those who insist on the strangeness of historical traditions discovers in them a nearness that lets them be understood as an expression of the same cultural activity in which people of the present are also engaged. How is that possible?

Let us make the following mental experiment. Let us assume that we find in historical texts only our familiar life world or that their life world would always be identical with our own. The consequence would be that we would no longer experience our life world as the "historical" world (i.e., as a world in process of change and as a world changeable by us) but as the natural world, the world of nature that remains constant in its basic structures and is necessarily that which it is. It is only the strangeness of the historical that makes us aware that historical "life worlds" are meaningful worlds constructed by human beings. Paradoxically, it is through the historically strange that we first become aware of that which makes us contemporary with all the people of the past and future, namely, the meaning-producing activity of human beings, who

---

20. Cf. H. J. Cadbury, *The Peril of Modernizing Jesus* (New York: Macmillan, 1937).

never live merely in a natural environment but in a constructed life world that they themselves have built by interpretations and convictions, institutions and technologies—and that therefore manifest a great diversity.

In turn it is also true that we may not seek access to the past in some way that opposes the modern axiom of the strangeness of the historical—perhaps by falling back on "timeless truths" that are available only in historically changed form. We must instead commit ourselves unreservedly to this strangeness, even if at first it seems to drive Jesus to the margins of our own culture. The more strange a historical figure seems to be at first, the greater is the chance that, in struggle with his or her strangeness, we will discover new dimensions of our own cultural meaning-creating activities and that this discovery will not only confirm our understanding of human culture but broaden and deepen it.

Can this be demonstrated concretely in the case of the figure of Jesus—this dialectic of distance and nearness, strangeness and familiarity? Our thesis so far states that the strangeness of Jesus, as manifest in his exorcisms, radicalism, and apocalyptic expectations, drives him to the margin of our culture. But precisely these bizarre traits can be interpreted as an expression of a protest that represents the heart of our culture: its hidden center and its secret program.

4.1 The Strangeness of the Historical Jesus

The *strangeness* of the historical Jesus is seen in his expectation of a sweeping cosmic revolution: he believed that the kingdom of God was already present in a hidden way, but that in the near future everything would be dramatically changed. After that, nothing would be as it once was. This radical cosmic turning point could be spoken of in parables and metaphors as well as in straightforward discursive language. It appears as a *mysterium fascinosum* with vague contours. What is clear is that the kingdom is preceded by a final judgment. Not all will be able to enter. The judgment is a threat to all. Deliverance is possible by repentance. For the narrow circle of Jesus' followers, repentance includes a bizarre ethical radicality: the readiness to renounce self-defense and to love one's enemies, abandoning all anxiety with regard to the basic necessities of life, giving up one's possessions and accepting poverty, a break with family and familial piety—even leaving one's father unburied if the kingdom of God calls for it. Measured against God's kingdom, everything else is unimportant—normal life with work and vocation, house and family. This kingdom of God brings salvation to those who are presently outsiders: those possessed by demons are healed; the devil is defeated; demons flee. Sick people are healed in remarkable ways; the morally stigmatized are accepted; the poor and children are to be empowered in the kingdom of God. But this central content of his preaching, the promise of the kingdom of God, was not "fulfilled" by history—it didn't happen. Instead, Jesus moved to Jerusalem—perhaps in expectation of the end; perhaps well aware of the risk of a violent death. He was executed by the Roman authorities, to whom the Jewish aristocracy handed him over. After his death his disciples experienced appearances that generated in them the conviction that he had been raised from the dead. Who was this Jesus? In part, a sensitive poet, in part an apocalyptic prophet, in part a miracle worker and exorcist, and besides that, a charismatic leader and ethical extremist! We would experience his strangeness even more, if the Jesus tradition were not already so familiar to us.

4.2 The Nearness of the Historical Jesus

Despite Jesus' strangeness, it is precisely this Jesus, who remains a foreigner in our modern world, who can come near to us. We only have to relate the sense of the meaning of the world and life preserved in the Jesus tradition to the task that all human culture has, namely, to reduce the natural pressure toward "survival of the fittest." Culture begins where the opportunity is given for human life that would not otherwise be possible—facilitated through technological manipulation of the environment, social institutions that foster equality, and ethically motivated convictions. Culture begins where the weak, who would have no (or only a minimal) chance for survival, receive the opportunity for a new (or better) life by intentional human conduct. In this moment, human beings leave the realm of nature and enter the realm of culture—they cross over a threshold, with the ever-present threat that they will fall back into a "natural" existence.[21]

In the Bible this cultural obligation to reduce the pressure of natural selection becomes a sharp protest against the principle of selection, a protest that begins in the Old Testament and comes to its clearest expression in the figure of Jesus of Nazareth. The Christianity founded by him is—as F. Nietzsche astutely observed—the opposite principle to that of natural selection.[22] In Christianity the weak are not only protected but given priority: in the kingdom of God the poor, sick, hungry, and children will come into their own. The miracle stories may seem bizarre for us, but they deliver an unconditional protest against the natural dividing-up of the chances of survival—they give a

---

21. For an elaboration of these thoughts, cf. G. Theissen, *Biblischer Glaube in evolutionärer Sicht* (Munich: Kaiser, 1984).

22. Cf. F. Nietzsche, *The Antichrist* (1888). He defines Christianity as a religion of sympathy and writes, "Sympathy by and large opposes the law of development, which is the law of selection. It preserves that which is ripe for destruction."

failing and reduced life a new chance. Jesus' ethic may be too radical for us, but it only makes a break with previous biological evolution. It places a question against family solidarity founded on biology—love for those genetically related—and calls instead for love for enemies, love for those not genetically (or culturally) related—the very opposite of conduct governed by biology. The apocalyptic expectation of a cosmic revolution that has already begun—one that, though hidden in the present, is already underway—may strike us as bizarre and illusory, but it exactly fits the situation of human beings on the threshold between biological and cultural evolution, between the realm of nature and the realm of freedom. Wherever human beings rise up against the principle of selection,* they have already passed over this threshold—in many individual acts, hidden in the midst of a world that as a whole operates by other rules. The expectation of a final judgment portrays the separation of good and evil in an archaic and gruesome style. But it only represents the pressure of selection that stands over every human life—and that also continues to work in morality: evil has fewer chances for survival than good. But it is precisely this simple dividing up into good and evil that is challenged by the Jesus tradition. Only those who repent pass the judgment. Only those who confess their sins—and thus confess that they in fact have no chance on their own— are saved. The irritation of the early Christian Easter message fits into this picture—even gives it a new center: in it the Failed and Powerless One becomes the source of life. What has been excluded from life becomes the epitome of a new life. Selection means death and suffering, namely, reduced chances for life and survival. But the conquest of death is the conquest of selection.

If one sees in the figure of Jesus—precisely in the one who seems bizarre and foreign to us—an antiselection protest, then this figure turns out to belong not on the margin of our culture but at its center, at least for those who know that they must be committed to the program of reducing the pressure of selection of those of our fellow human beings who are weaker or who, as the "less well-adjusted," don't fit in. That people actually abide by this "program" is just as uncertain as is the idea that it is accepted as an obligation in the first place. National Socialism was a public betrayal of this program. And it was not only betrayed by those in power, but, often enough, even by Christian churches. Such betrayal always brings with it immeasurable suffering. Human culture is not simply the overcoming of the pressure of selection but the opportunity to overcome it—and at the same time the danger of artificially increasing it by collective cruelty.

---

*[Translator's note] Throughout this section, the German word *Selektion* can hardly be read without the overtones of not only the quote from Nietzsche above but also the unloading platform at Auschwitz.

We now summarize our train of thought: Personal certainty in relating to the historical Jesus is generated by the coming together of axiomatic convictions and accidental sources. The axiomatic convictions of modern historical consciousness at first deepen the chasm between us and the historical Jesus. The three premises—the fallibility of all historical sources, the relativity of all historical phenomena, and the strangeness of everything historical—lead to historical skepticism, relativizing, and distancing. The historical Jesus appears to sink into an unapproachable past. But these same premises include an internal dialectic that necessarily includes their own opposites. When consistently thought through, the fallibility of all human sources also places a limit on our historical skepticism; the incorporation of Jesus into historical contexts allows his individuality to be seen; and the struggle with his provocative strangeness leads to a surprising nearness. The ditch that separates us from the historical Jesus remains wide, long, and deep. We cannot leap over it. But falling into it is no catastrophe: we can swim in it and thus come nearer to Jesus. It does not mean that we are already on the other bank. All our knowledge is hypothetical, even the greatest certainty available to us. Everything stands under the qualification: it could have been otherwise. We have shown that, nevertheless—on the basis of axiomatic convictions—personal assurance is possible. These axiomatic convictions have, however, become historical. They are not timeless necessary truths, even if we cannot imagine that someday we might be able to approach historical subjects with other premises. For us, what we experience in their light is "certain"—as certain as any human certainty can be. But even this certainty is not unconditional certainty. A hypothetical element persists in it. Lessing's ditch has not been filled in. How can we come to terms with it? In other words, how can we come to terms with the hypothetical character of all knowledge and faith?

5. A PARADOXICAL RESOLUTION: COMING TO TERMS WITH THE HYPOTHETICAL IN LIFE AND THOUGHT

We ask first, In what ways has theology previously attempted to get past this ditch? What kind of arguments have been used? We will sketch four ways:

1. *Orientation to the biblical picture of Jesus.* All reconstructions of the historical Jesus are surrounded by an aura of hypotheses. In the confidence that the biblical picture is an effect of the historical Jesus, why should one not prefer this biblical picture to these reconstructions of scholarly imagination? Do we not have the "real Jesus" in the picture "effected by" him? Is the real Jesus the effective Jesus? Martin Kähler pleaded for this "biblicis-

tic" solution in his classic composition of 1892, *The So-Called Historical Jesus and the Historic, Biblical Christ.*

2. *The historical seal of approval of the biblical picture of Jesus.* The need has repeatedly arisen to guarantee the biblical picture of Jesus by the results of historical research. This concern was programatically represented by the "positive-critical" Jesus scholars: Joachim Jeremias, Leonhard Goppelt, and Werner Georg Kümmel. Historical research was expected to deliver assured results—precisely in the midst of an abundance of hypotheses and uncertainties: "Only the Son of Man himself and his word can give authority to preaching."[23]

3. *Kerygmatic reduction of the picture of Jesus.* Whoever has less confidence in the results of historical study to produce a consensus, and does not want the Christian faith to be dependent on the changing hypotheses of scholarship, can reduce the connection of Christian faith to the formal "thatness" of Jesus' existence (as does the kerygma theology of R. Bultmann). In the exercise of preaching and faith one can, of course, refer to the biblical picture of Jesus, but in theological argumentation and reflection, one can only refer to an invisible reference point.

4. *Symbolic understanding of the picture of Jesus.* This approach separates itself even more uncompromisingly from history. Poetic and metaphorical texts (such as Jesus' own parables) have their truth in themselves, independently from their historicality and authenticity. Why should one not interpret the New Testament witness to Jesus as an image and parable of timeless truths? For instance, the inner truth that one finds here the insight that human beings live out their existence and freedom from a grace that is not at their disposal needs no external confirmation. The image of Jesus is thereby not "demythologized" but "dekerygmatized." It is transformed from a message rooted in a particular historical situation into a timeless cipher. A plea for this solution is made—in dependence on the philosopher Karl Jaspers—by F. Buri.[24]

The courses that have been adopted so far all contain an element of truth but do not satisfy. The biblical and symbolic solutions contradict an irreversible critical attitude to historical sources native to modern mentality, one that insists on distinguishing between historical reality and the sources that witness to it. We can be satisfied neither with a wholesale expansion of the concept of reality that claims that basically all the biblical witnesses testify to something "real," nor with an expanded understanding of the symbol concept, according to which all the statements they contain—even those that clearly refer to a particular historical event—are to be interpreted basically as timeless symbols. In

---

23. J. Jeremias, *The Problem of the Historical Jesus* (Facet Books 13; Philadelphia: Fortress Press, 1964) 24.

24. F. Buri, "Entmythologisierung oder Entkerygmatisierung der Theologie," in H. W. Bartsch, ed., *Kerygma und Mythos*, vol. 2 (ThF 2; Hamburg: Reich & Heidrich, 1954).

both cases, the claim is justified that we can value the extant texts and that they—independently of how much historical reality they contain—preserve real experiences and experiences of the "real" in the broadest sense of the term.

Thus they mostly alternate between a positive-critical maximizing of the historical and its kerygmatic minimizing. The positive-critical solution, however, is not convincing in the long run, since it must repeatedly jump over the relativizing force of the hypothetical. It makes faith dependent on changing historical hypotheses. The kerygmatic reduction cannot be carried through consistently. Reducing the historicity of Jesus to the mere "thatness" [*Dass*] of his existence presupposes that a consensus already exists on the view that whoever it was that actually existed must have been of decisive significance. If this significance remains invisible within history, then it can only be expressed in a myth that transcends history. We illustrate that with the following picture: The kerygma theology sees the human situation as that of people who have been buried in an avalanche. For people buried alive, salvation means *that* [*Dass*] other people are already on the way to help. What they look like does not matter, just as their origin and concrete motivation do not matter. All that matters is that they reestablish the connection with the world of light and life. What is presupposed is the absolute certainty that the rescue team approaches with the intent to save. Similar unspoken presuppositions stand behind kerygmatic theology's reduction: it presupposes the conviction of a transcendent divine "world." It presupposes the certainty that salvation can come through contact with this "divine world." On the basis of both presuppositions, it can become the all-important issue *that* someone from this world enters into history. It is only internal to history that the mere "Dass" is a mere "Dass." Within the framework of an encompassing "myth" that transcends history, it is already filled with a particular content: it is the advent of a redeemer.

At the end of our book we can only attempt a personal answer. The inescapable hypothetical character of all our knowledge requires us to come to terms with this hypothetical character. We can introduce four arguments for this: one each on hermeneutical, philosophical, aesthetic, and religious grounds.

First, the hermeneutical reason. We are here using "hermeneutics" as a comprehensive term to include all the methods in the liberal arts and historical scholarship. Everything in Jesus research is more or less hypothetical. But the reverse side of all construction of hypotheses necessarily generates a certainty: that it is meaningful to develop hypotheses about the historical Jesus, that is, to weigh the merits of different possibilities and to prefer those that seem more probable. Precisely the relativizing built into all hypotheses, which says, "It could have been *otherwise*," makes us certain that "there was *something* that could have been otherwise"—or it would be meaningless to continue to develop historical hypotheses about this subject. So also the conviction of its historicity, that is, of its mere "Dass," is formulated by hypothetical balancing of the possibilities of *what* Jesus could have been. The pervasive character of the hypothetical thus becomes the foundation of certainty.

Our second reason is philosophical. It can also be said more precisely: it is a metaphysical reason, for it presupposes a picture of the whole of reality. We are quite aware that such pictures are somewhat brash anticipations of that which we ultimately cannot know. The decisive thing for us is that not only our knowledge but our whole life has a hypothetical character. The stream of life is a process of trial and error that attempts to fit in with the fundamental conditions of reality determined by God. The world and all of life are a hypothesis and promise that God is attempting to validate and fulfill. Our knowledge is also included in this, as is the New Testament and the Christian religion. Everything is hypothetical, penultimate, and in need of improvement. And precisely for this reason we can come to terms with the hypothetical character of our knowledge and our faith.

A third answer is based on aesthetic experience. All knowledge is provisional, including our knowledge of Jesus, but we can shape it aesthetically. It thereby attains a rounding-off that is valuable in itself, even when our knowledge is transitory. Our portrayals of Jesus should therefore have an aesthetic character. Poetry comes to terms with the transient, penultimate, and imperfect character of our knowledge.

A fourth and final answer rests on religious faith. All knowledge consists of hypotheses—and all life is a not-yet-validated hypothesis, a not-yet fulfilled promise from God. Everything hypothetical runs the risk of defeat. But Christian faith is convinced that God also accepts the defeated variations of life. From the divine side, God confers that validation of the hypothetical toward which all life strives. In the gospel, God offers the fulfilled validation and concord with himself, without qualification, unconditional and unlimited.

At the beginning of this chapter we spoke of Lessing's wide ditch. It is the chasm between hypothetical knowledge and unconditional faith. We cannot leap over this ditch. We can only jump into it—into the midst of a flood of hypotheses, attempts, and fragments. But we can swim through this flood and reach the far shore, if a helping hand is extended from the other side. Generations of Christians have repeatedly experienced this hand as God's grace, a grace that accepts our attempts even though laden with hypotheses. The Bible has again and again become for Christians the opportunity of taking up a dialogue with God—and it thus becomes the means of a certainty that transcends all historical plausibility.

Appendix

*A Collection of Formulations and Commentaries
on the General Theme of the Criterion of Dissimilarity,
Arranged in Chronological Order*

1521

Luther, Martin:

"Grund und Ursach aller Artikel D. Martin Luthers, so durch römische Bulle unrechtlich verdammt sind," 1521, in *WA* 7:308–457. Translation from *Luther's Works*, Vol. 32: *Career of the Reformer II*. Edited by George W. Forell. Philadelphia: Muhlenberg Press, 1958.

"They also say that I propose new ideas and it is not to be expected that everybody else should have been so long in error. That, too, the ancient prophets had to hear. If length of time were sufficient proof, the Jews would have had the strongest kind of case against Christ on that ground. His doctrine was different from any they had heard for a thousand years. The Gentiles too would have been justified in regarding the apostles with contempt, since their ancestors for more than three thousand years held to a different faith." (10)

Around 1550

Widman, Georg:

Chronica, cited according to Joachim Knape, *"Historie" in Mittelalter und früher Neuzeit. Begriffs- und gattungsgeschichtliche Untersuchungen im interdisziplinären Kontext*. SaeSp 10. Baden-Baden: Koerner, 1984.

"There are three things, so writes Georg Widman ca. 1550 in his 'Chronik,' that 'prevent the truth from being described' in histories:

"1. Instead of making a careful study of the sources, to listen to dubious rumors ('writing only on the basis of hearsay')
"2. Accepting the perspective of a party line ('to look on one side more favorably than the other')
"3. Placing concern for literary form so much in the foreground that the truth (i.e. the facts) suffer damage ('to want to be admired for literary grace more than for listening to the truth')." (Widman, 6, 18; in Knape, 381)

1555

Sleidan, Johannes:

Warhafftige und Eigentliche beschreibung der Geistlichen und Weltlichen sachen . . . Translated and edited by Marcus Stammler. Strassburg, 1557 (First printed 1555), cited according to Joachim Knape, "Historie" in *Mittelalter und früher Neuzeit. Begriffs- und gattungsgeschichtliche Untersuchungen im interdisziplinären Kontext.* SaeSp 10. Baden-Baden: Koerner, 1984.

"Where parties prevail / where war and murder are / there are found writings that accuse and writings that locate responsibility, and their counter arguments / as everyone already knows. Now whoever simply narrates / and favors no one / does no one any harm / but holds true to the course of *history* itself / for the insult or injury is in the feelings / as the laws themselves show / otherwise all the *histories* / from the beginning of the world must have been so / and those worthy of the name / would have been guilty / and would have been mistrusted. Thus not everything must be true / that one party says about the other / For wherever there is hostility / one can be sure / that neither side will spare the other / and should it all be true / what the Pope and others of his kind / teach against the Protestants and people / speaking and writing against them for thirty-five years / then they would have to be the most ungodly people on earth." (Sleidan's "Foreword," in Knape, 383)

1738

Chubb, Thomas:

The True Gospel of Jesus Christ Asserted. Wherein is shewn what is, and what is not that Gospel: what was the great and good end it was intended to serve; how it is exactly suited to answer that purpose; and how, or by what means that end has in a great measure been frustrated. London: Garland, 1738.

" . . . the *private opinions* of those who wrote Christ's history, and of those who were appointed and sent out to preach his gospel to the world, were in many instances very *abstruse* . . ." (49)

" . . . everything is not Christ's gospel which weak, or ignorant, or artful men have taken upon them to call by that name." (50)

1738–40

Morgan, Thomas:

The Moral Philosopher. Vols. 1–3. London, 1738–1740. Facsimile Reprint in One Volume. Edited by Günter Gawlick. Stuttgart: Fromman, 1969.

"[H]is (sc. Jesus') Disciples and Followers soon fell into very odd Notions about him, and reported several Things of him, that were neither consistent with his Character and general Design, nor with the Religion which he had preach'd and propagated. . . . they soon patch'd up a Religion very different from that of Nature, join'd Judaism and Christianity together, and in Favour of their old, national Prejudices, made Christ himself a false Prophet. . . . In a Word, they understood and reported every Thing that he said, according to their own Prejudices and false Opinions concerning the Messias; . . . for no two Religions in the world can be more inconsistent and irreconcileable than Judaism and Christianity; yet if a Man reads the New Testament as a plain, historical, and uncorrupted Account of Things, without any critical Remarks upon the State of Religion, and the Circumstances of that Time, he might be tempted to imagine, that Judaism and Christianity are both one and the same Religion." (1:439–441)

"[T]he biblical History has afforded more Matter of Dispute and Contention . . . than all the other Books in the World. But this could never have happened, had this sacred History been read critically, and interpreted by the same Rules of natural and Rational probability and Credibility, as we read all other History." (3:140)

1766

Reimarus, Hermann Samuel:

Die Vernunftlehre als eine Anweisung zum richtigen Gebrauche der Vernunft in dem Erkenntniss der Wahrheit, aus zwoen ganz natürlichen Regeln der Einstimmung und des Widerspruchs, 3rd rev. ed. Hamburg, 1766. Reprint edited by Friedrich Lötzsch. München, 1979.

"If the matter being reported brings distress, damage, or anything undesirable to the witness himself, or to those to whom he intends good, or if the matter being reported brings honor, advantage, or anything desirable to those he opposes—this is a sign that it is an honest report." (§247, 260).

"A document, or a passage in the same, is to be attributed to the purported author . . . if it has particular words and expressions, as well as opinions and materials that agree with the way people wrote at that time, and with their opinions; and a particular passage must also agree with its context." (§252, 266–267).

Ca. 1750, unpublished

Reimarus, Hermann Samuel:

Apologie oder Schutzschrift für die vernünftigen Verehrer Gottes. Vol. 2. Edited by Gerhard Alexander. Frankfurt: Insel, 1972 (= first complete publication). ET now available in *Fragments from Reimarus [microform] consisting of Brief Critical Remarks on the Object of Jesus and His Disciples as Seen in the New Testament.* Translated from the German of G. E. Lessing; edited by Charles Vonsen (Lexington, Ky.: American Theological Library Association, Committee on Reprinting, 1902).

"[T]he later system of the apostles [was oriented] not to the facts themselves, but the narration of the reported events had to be oriented to their changed system. Consequently, one must put aside everything in their account that bears the marks of the apostles' later system, and not judge Jesus on the basis of their accounts, if one wants to know his true views and intentions." (172) Translation by M. E. B.

1787

Gabler, Johann Philipp:

"Von der richtigen Unterscheidung der biblischen und der dogmatischen Theologie und der rechten Bestimmung ihrer beider Ziele (1787)." Pages 32–44 in *Das Problem der Theologie des Neuen Testaments.* WF 367. Edited by Georg Strecker; Darmstadt: Wissenschaftliche Buchgesellschaft, 1975.

On the investigation of the intention of the biblical authors; the principle of coherence in the process of their reconstruction:

"Finally, one must carefully distinguish whether the apostle speaks in his own words or in the words of another; whether he has in mind only to set forth a particular thesis, or to prove it; and in the latter case, whether he draws his proof from the inner nature and structure of the doctrine of salvation itself or from the statements of the books of the old doctrinal form (= the Old Testament), and of course whether these are adapted to the understanding of the first readers. . . . Only if we stick to these rules will we bring out the true and holy ideas that were entrusted to each author; of course not all (there would not be enough room in the books that have been preserved), but only those that the author had been impelled to write by the occasion or need—but nonetheless plenty enough. To be sure, other examples that have been passed by can easily be collected, when they present an unparalleled, clearly demonstrated principle that lies behind the various interpretations or that are connected with them by any sort of necessary consequence: the matter, however, requires much caution." (40)

1818

de Wette, Wilhelm Martin Leberecht:

Lehrbuch der christlichen Dogmatik in ihrer historischen Entwickelung dargestellt. Erster Theil. Biblische Dogmatik Alten und Neuen Testaments. Oder kritische Darstellung des Hebraismus, des Judenthums und Urchristenthums. 2d ed. Berlin: G. Reimer, 1818.

" . . . 1) that we distinguish the teaching of Jesus from the way it was understood by the apostles and evangelists." (§228, 209–210)

1835

Strauss, David Friedrich:

Das Leben Jesu, kritisch bearbeitet. Vol. 1. Tübingen, 1835. Appeared in English as *The Life of Jesus Critically Examined.* Translated by George Eliot. Lives of Jesus Series. London: SCM Press, 1973. Translation below by M.E.B.

"Since it is a matter of presenting the supernatural view of Jesus' person, as the only one of his kind, as independent of all external, human influences, as self-taught or better God-taught: so, among other things, every supposition that he might have borrowed or learned something from others must be decisively rejected." (301 in German text)

" . . . in situations where Jesus is being glorified—as is the case with our Evangelists—in disputed cases those statements are to be considered less credible . . . that most correspond to the goal of glorifying him. [This is] a criterion of greater probability." (473 of German text)

1864

Heinrich, J. B.:

Christus. Ein Nachweis seiner geschichtlichen Existenz und göttlichen Persönlichkeit, zugleich eine Kritik des Rationalismus, des Straussischen Mythicismus und des Lebens Jesu von Renan. Mainz: Kirchheim, 1864.

"Now Jesus Christ, as the Gospels picture him, has nothing in common with either the ideals of the Greeks nor the Jews; he towers above anything of which the legend ever dreamed, anything the poets ever created, or anything the philosophers ever thought. And, to be sure, the Gospels do not picture him with vague features and a cloudy profile, as though they simply suggested rather than letting one see precisely. Rather, the Gospels portray him in such particularity, clarity, and vividness that we can, so to speak, touch him with our own hands. Thus Christ stands before us in absolute divine originality, without having had anyone in the whole course of history as his ideal. And some people would have us believe that Galilean fishermen, unknown people from the dregs of humanity at the lowest point in the history of both Judaism and paganism, whether as intentional deception or unconscious fantasy, invented this Christ and this Gospel story!" (29)

1866

Keim, Karl Theodor:

Der geschichtliche Christus. Eine Reihe von Vorträgen mit Quellenbeweis und Chronologie des Lebens Jesu. 3d ed. Zürich: Orell, Füssli & Co., 1866.

Contrast to the Pharisees (21): "The fulfillment of Judaism for the triumph over Judaism" (26) " . . . a most respected eldest son of Israel, the consummating figure of the history of the Hebrew people, the proud treetop of the highest tree, the cedar of God already struck by the storm." (71)

"Then how is it that he became Jesus Christ . . . ? By contact with human beings, with the ideas of the time that aggrandized him, but having suppressed his characteristic individual identity under their uniformity, he escaped to become himself." (75)

1867

Keim, Karl Theodor:

Geschichte Jesu von Nazara in ihrer Verkettung mit dem Gesamtleben seines Volkes. Zürich: Orell, Füssli & Co., 1867.

"Theological historical research, which belongs at one and the same time to the general academic study of history and to a church that appeals to academic grounds for its foundation and justification, is entrusted with the assignment of writing the life of Jesus. . . .

"The basic rule of historical science, including its study of the life of Jesus, is called 'continuity,' while the key word for the church is 'discontinuity'; in the former case, a member of a series, in the latter case, uniqueness; in the former case, the human being, in the latter case, the divine personality.

"Still and all, these contrasts have been moderated and qualified in our time. For one thing, scientific historical study itself has backed off somewhat from its works that tend to level everything out, demoting the great figures of world history in favor of the masses and little people." (3–4)

"One may charge the Christian sources with having painted the life of Jesus in ideal colors, whether or not they intended to do so, while elsewhere [i.e. in Judaism and pagan sources] a sober, impartial view prevailed, and if not this, they at least presented a realistic critique from whose reflections, disclosures, accusations and objections a residue of historical truth can doubtless be extracted. In fact, when the differences neatly supplement each other, when the presumed exaggerations of Christianity are placed alongside the belittling and slandering statements of the opponents, from the one-sidedness of each set of statements it might be possible to draw out the objective reality from these two subjective views." (8)

1878

Wünsche, August:

Neue Beiträge zur Erläuterung der Evangelien aus Talmud und Midrasch. Göttingen: Vandenhoeck & Ruprecht, 1878.

"Every Talmudist has the experience of noting that many of Jesus' expressions and sayings can easily be translated into the Talmudic idiom, while for others it is difficult to find an appropriate Talmudic expression. Should this not present us with a criterion for the authenticity of each text? Should not expressions and sayings that can easily be translated into the Talmudic idiom have a primary claim to authenticity, or at least that they originate from someone at home in the idiom of the Talmud? And should not others, that can be translated into the language of the Talmud only by severe manipulations be considered of doubtful authenticity? At least one must acknowledge the possibility that terms and ideas that have come into our documents via the Greek language must have been modified in one way or another." (vi–vii)

1887

Beyschlag, Willibald:

Das Leben Jesu. 2d ed. Halle: E. Strien, 1887.

"Certainly, what we are looking for in the 'life of Jesus' is facts, not dogmas, and we attempt to discover these facts according to the rules of historical criticism, i.e., rules that are generally used to extract the underlying facts from the traditions in which they have been preserved. But in the process of doing this we encounter a peculiar characteristic of our subject for which our historical studies elsewhere have not equipped us. . . . We encounter in the sources the historical affirmation of the miraculous revelation of God in Christ, the miracle of the incarnation of God in human form. Do we have the right to declare in advance that this all belongs to the realm of fable, since on the other pages of history we find nothing so extraordinary and supernatural? Or should we be suspicious of New Testament declarations about Jesus because, say, in the traditions of the life of Buddha or Mohammed we find similar things, and that in these cases we do feel justified in denying credence to them in advance? After all, we are Christians, not Buddhists or adherents of Islam, and we know what privileges we have in this regard; . . . it is not the natural and human as such, but only the eternal and divine in the natural and human that can be the subject of prayer and religious faith. If we want to make the same a priori decision here to eliminate these elements as belonging to the realm of fable, this would be a denial in advance of the truth of Christianity. Who does not see that historical science, in making such an a priori rejection has simply gone beyond its own legitimate boundaries?" (7–8)

1898

Dalman, Gustaf:

Die Worte Jesu mit Berücksichtigung des nachkanonischen jüdischen Schrifttums und der aramäischen Sprache erörtert. Bd. 1. Leipzig, 1898. Appeared in English as *The Words of Jesus: Considered in the Light of Post-Biblical Jewish Writings and the Aramaic Language.* Translated by D. M. Kay. Edinburgh: T & T Clark, 1909.

"Whoever would know what was the Aramaic primary form of any of the Master's sayings will have to separate these latter Graecisms not less distinctly than the former Hellenistic Hebraisms. Thus may be reached a verbal form which is at least not unthinkable in the utterance of Jesus, and which is most closely identified with the original Aramaic tradition of the apostles." (19–20)

1900

Harnack, Adolf:

What is Christianity? Translated by Thomas Bailey Saunders. New York: Harper & Row, 1957. Sixteen Lectures Delivered to Students in All Faculties in the University of Berlin, in the Winter Semester 1899/1900. Original title *Das Wesen des Christentums = The Essence of Christianity.*

"Jesus Christ's teaching will at once bring us by steps which, if few, will be great, to a height where its connection with Judaism is seen to be only a loose one, and most of the threads leading [back] from it into [his] 'contemporary history' become of no importance at all." (16)

Weiss, Johannes:

Die Predigt vom Reiche Gottes. 2d ed. Göttingen, 1900. The first edition of 1892 appeared in English as *Jesus' Proclamation of the Kingdom of God.* Translated and edited by Richard Hyde Hiers and David Larrimore Holland. Lives of Jesus Series. Philadelphia: Fortress Press, 1971. The passage below is from the revised and expanded second edition, translated by M. E. B.

"Hopefully, from the theological side it will not be said that my discussions are directed to them or are intended to detract from Jesus' originality. However, it is time to get past the rationalistic tendency of attempting to see Jesus' importance in the novelty of his thoughts and teaching. A more free and vital historical view will consider it obvious that the new religion adopted the forms of thought and expression of its time. Its creative power does not lie in its theories, but in the faith with which it enlivens them. The greatness of Jesus is not that he invented the idea of the kingdom of God, but that he lived, suffered, and died for the conviction that the reign of God was about to appear and establish its eternal triumph." (34–35)

1901

Schmiedel, Paul Wilhelm:

"Gospels," *EncBib* 2 (1901): cols. 1761–1898.

"When a profane historian finds before him a historical document which testifies to the worship of a hero unknown to other sources, he attaches first and foremost importance to those features which cannot be deduced merely from the fact of this worship, and he does so on the simple and sufficient ground that they would not be found in this source unless the author had met with them as fixed data of tradition. The same fundamental principle may be safely applied in the case of the gospels, for they also are all of them written by worshippers of Jesus. . . . If we discover any such points—even if only a few—they guarantee not only their own contents, but also much more. For in that case one may also hold as credible all else which agrees in character with these, and is in other respects not open to suspicion." (cols. 1872–73)

1904

Wernle, Paul:

Die Quellen des Lebens Jesu. Halle: Gebauer-Schwetschke, 1904.

"[W]hat we have firmly in hand is the faith of the early church. It may be that it goes back to Jesus, in whole or in part; it may also be that it was retro-jected into the life and teaching of Jesus." (85)

1906

Jülicher, Adolf:

Neue Linien in der Kritik der evangelischen Überlieferung. Giessen: Töpelmann, 1906 (= Vorträge des Hessischen und Nassauischen theologischen Ferien-kurses H. 3).

"When we see characteristic traits that stand out from the general masses, when we encounter sayings with a distinctive cut and character, such as Mark 2:21–22 (old garments, old wineskins), then this is the surest evidence of authenticity. To be sure, the idea of 'that which could not have been invented' has been misused, but we cannot abandon it. That in the Gospels which has a characteristic freshness, pointedness, individuality has a prejudice in favor of its authenticity: should it really be so difficult in many cases to make a confi-dent decision as to whether an idea, or the way in which it is expressed, is the automatic reflex of a community of ordinary folk, or the penetrating creation of a single towering personality?" (73–74)

Kellermann, Benzion:

Kritische Beiträge zur Entstehungsgeschichte des Christentums. Berlin: Poppelauer, 1906.

Kellermann deems "it to be a methodological requirement of scholarship not to appeal to outstanding personalities in the context of their milieu as an explanation for historical events, as long as the milieu itself provides a sufficient ground for the phenomena, and there is no historical point of contact for the role that an outstanding personality would play." Kellermann sees the latter as the case for both Jesus and Paul. (34)

Neumann, Arno:

Jesus. London, 1906.

"For it is impossible (here every historian will agree) for one who worships a hero to think and speak in such a way as to contradict or essentially modify his own worship. Statements which do this can be nothing more or less than survivals of the truth, precious fragments which have been covered and well-nigh hidden for ever by the deposits of later times. For this reason a scholar of our own time, Dr. Schmiedel, has called these portions of the tradition, 'foundation-pillars of the life of Jesus.' The existence of such statements is the salvation of the Synoptic Gospels, giving them a definite value as sources. The Gospels cannot be pure sagas or legends when material so intractable is enshrined in them." (9–10)

Ninck, Johannes:

Jesus als Charakter. Leipzig: Hinrich, 1925 (1st ed. 1906).

"We can point to no single statement in the teaching of Jesus, and no characteristic of his life that he presented as something completely new, as though brought from heaven to the world below.

"And yet everything about this man is grand and new, and we may claim the highest originality for him. Everything traditional became new in his hands. . . . [A] good part of [Jesus' life and teaching] contrasts with Jewish life and teaching. . . . What he does not cite is more important that what he does cite." (277)

Schmiedel, Paul Wilhelm:

Das vierte Evangelium gegenüber den drei ersten. RV 1.8, 10. Tübingen: J. C. B. Mohr (Paul Siebeck), 1906.

"*Foundation for a truly scientific life of Jesus*. Every historian, in whatever area he may work, follows the basic rule that in a document dedicated to honoring its hero, that which goes against the stream of this tendency should be considered true, since it cannot be based on invention." (16–17)

1907

Holtzmann, Heinrich Julius:

Das messianische Bewusstsein Jesu. Ein Beitrag zur Leben-Jesu-Forschung. Tübingen: Mohr, 1907.

"For one should no longer doubt the historicity of a saying that finds a fully satisfactory explanation in the light of the fate he suffered." (70)

Klausner, Joseph:

Jesus of Nazareth: His Life, Times, and Teaching. Translated by Herbert Danby. New York: Macmillan Co., 1944.

"We have before us two facts: (a) Jesus was born, lived and died in Israel and was a Jew in every respect; (b) his disciples, and still more disciples' disciples, removed far away from Israel, or rather, the more numerous and more powerful Jews rejected the teaching of Jesus: they rose up against it during his lifetime, and, even when all the world drew nearer and nearer to Christianity, would not become Christians. Christianity was born within Israel, and Israel as a nation rejected it utterly. Why?" (9)

1909

Jülicher, Adolf:

"Die Religion Jesu und die Anfänge des Christentums bis zum Nicaenum," pages 42–131 in *Die Kultur der Gegenwart.* Vol. 1. Section 4. *Geschichte der christlichen Religion.* Edited by Paul Hinnenberg. 2nd ed. Berlin: Teubner, 1909.

"For the most part the original stands out so clearly from secondary material, the diamond from the polished glass, that confidence in deciding what is authentic, which shines forth its unique brilliance alongside all the glittering imitations, is actually no superficial judgment. . . . [I]n the Synoptic Gospels the writers struggle too vigorously with material they often do not understand themselves, and often with material that is even resistant to their own purposes. The real Jesus, whom they have received, stands so far above them, whose image they then have tidied up with additives from the Old Testament or Babylonian mythology, from Jewish literature and folk wisdom or early Christian theology and poetry, that the idea that here we simply have different layers of one and the same myth or acts that personify ideas, is more than merely bad taste. . . . The impression of the unique personality is still more powerful than the numerous difficulties that the history of the tradition has left behind for us. It is not an idea, not a dream, but a human being with mysterious grandeur who stands here, as everywhere, at the turning point of history." (46–47)

"Jesus' roots reach deep into Jewish soil, he was nourished with all that was offered by the religion of the Old Testament; but his treetop reached far above the highest that had ever grown in that forest, into trans-Jewish regions." (54)

"[Jesus] is honest enough to acknowledge openly a greatness peculiar to himself alone, something incomparable." (58)

"[I]n what does the new thing brought by Jesus consist? . . . Our first response is: the new was he himself, his personality." (60)

"[A]gain, his personality became the measure of his religious importance. And once again and finally, miraculously characteristic of him was his Jewish conquest of all that was Jewish." (68)

1910

Weiss, Johannes:

Jesus von Nazareth. Mythos oder Geschichte? Eine Auseinandersetzung mit Kalthoff, Drews, Jensen. Tübingen: Mohr, 1910.

"[T]o date the assignment has not been fulfilled of discovering a truly scientific principle of distinguishing between inorganic foreign bodies and new formations with authentic roots." (7)

Weinel, Heinrich:

"Ist unsere Verkündigung von Jesus unhaltbar geworden?" *ZTK* 20 (1910): 1–38, 89–129.

"Only such traits of the tradition are to be excluded as inauthentic that could not have originated from an interest of Jesus himself, but could only be the product of an interest of the church. This fundamental principle is . . . not to be expanded into another one, namely that everywhere that the church's interest is expressed—but where there is no reason to doubt that Jesus also had this interest—the whole tradition must be declared to be inauthentic. It is rather the case that, since what we are dealing with here is always a matter of ruling out material, the evidence must first be brought that the interest in question could only have emerged after Jesus' time." (29)

"The essential is distinguished . . . by an entirely different method than the authentic. That which is essential must still be separated out from the authentic material determined in the manner described above, and according to the principle: that which is essential is that which is original. It is not what Jesus shared with his people and his time—that, of course, is often authentic tradition—but what separated him from his people and his time, that is his own, that is the essential element in him and his preaching." (35)

1911

Holtzmann, Heinrich Julius:

Lehrbuch der neutestamentlichen Theologie. Bd. 1. 2nd ed. Edited by A. Jülicher and W. Bauer. Tübingen: Mohr, 1911.

"While earlier scholars sought analogies to Jesus' teaching in the classics and from that point of departure occasionally criticized Christianity for its lack of originality, today there has arisen an analogous way of posing the question from the ongoing comparison with the rabbinic literature. Both Christian and Jewish scholars vouch for the fact that the Midrashim and the Talmud offer numerous parallels to the sayings of Jesus in the Synoptic Gospels, while at the same time sharply opposing the attempts made from the Jewish side to divest the latter of all independent importance. But the tendency on the Christian side to minimize or completely deny the Jewish heritage, in order to find in the Gospels as much as possible that can be gaped at and admired as though fallen from heaven, is no less narrow-minded and unhistorical. It is rather the case that only an awareness of what has demonstrably grown and developed from the fruitful mother soil of contemporary Judaism can call forth the full impression of historical reality. A genius who is not rooted in his own time and homeland can not effect a transformation in his time. Whoever rejects this approach to things excludes himself from any truly historical understanding not only of early Christianity, but of Christianity as such. The general and abiding result of all biblical-theological studies for scholarship and life has indeed made us aware of the independence of what Jesus brought as pure fire on the altar. He brought a fire that has never been extinguished but has continued to burn despite the greatest variety of materials with which it has been fed, and thus could become the enduring and effective principle of a new religious life for the nations. But this same scholarship has made us aware that this independence can never be perceived apart from an awareness of the national, local, and temporal factors of Jewish theology, messianic legends, and eschatological perspectives." (408–9)

Weinel, Heinrich:

Biblische Theologie des Neuen Testaments. Die Religion Jesu und des Urchristentums. GThW 3.2. Tübingen: Mohr, 1911.

"The material is . . . constantly to be examined with the question of whether it contains elements that can be explained only in terms of later Christian tendencies or beliefs. Such elements in the tradition are to be excluded. This basic principle may not be twisted into a different one, namely, that everything is inauthentic that can be explained from a later Christian tendency. If there is no reason to doubt that Jesus also so thought, the tradition is to be kept. . . . When once what is authentic has been so established [in conjunction with the criterion of multiple attestation] to the extent that this is possible, then what is essential must be separated out from what is authentic. The essential is the new, the original. That which has historic significance is not what Jesus shared with his people and his time, but what he had that transcended them. This is the way every historical figure is perceived and characterized." (42)

1912

Heitmüller, Wilhelm:

"Jesus Christus I." *RGG* 3 (1912, 1st ed.): cols. 343–62.

"The basis for reconstruction must be that material that goes against the stream of the faith, theology, ethics, and cultus of earliest Christianity, or at least does not fully fit in with it. We may have absolute trust in such elements of the tradition. We may then extend this to everything that is organically integral to such material. Fairly often we deal with instances that are related both to the authentic elements in the preaching of Jesus and at the same time correspond to the later faith of the church: in such cases we will acknowledge the claim of the tradition and cautiously accept it as authentic. In contrast, the judgment of inauthenticity is to be made in every case where a story or saying all too clearly corresponds to the faith, the cultus, and the dogmatic and apologetic needs of the church, or even can only be explained on their basis." (361)

1921

Bultmann, Rudolf:

The History of the Synoptic Tradition. Translated by John Marsh. New York: Harper & Row, 1963.

"Accordingly, we cannot avoid raising the question of a possible Christian origin even for those passages where it seems intrinsically unlikely. Such an origin is the more questionable, the less we can discern any relation to the Person of Jesus or to the lot and interests of the Church, and the more, on the other hand we can trace a characteristically individual spirit." (135 [128])

"We can count on possessing a genuine similitude of Jesus where, on the one hand, expression is given to the contrast between Jewish morality and piety and the distinctive eschatological temper which characterized the preaching of Jesus; and where on the other hand we find no specifically Christian features." (222 [205])

1926

Bultmann, Rudolf:

"The New Approach to the Synoptic Problem," *JR* 6 (1926): 337–62.

"When once we have learned to make the distinction in the *Logia* between those utterances which express specific interests of the Christian community or which are shaped in terms of Jewish piety, and those utterances which transcend these interests and express great original ideas, it becomes possible to employ the *Logia* with critical intelligence, so as to derive from them a definite conception of the preaching of Jesus." (341–42)

1930

Goguel, Maurice:

"The Problem of Jesus," *HTR* 23 (1930): 93–120.

"Any statement is probably derived from very ancient tradition, and for practical purposes can be considered authentic, which is inconsistent with the forms in which the most ancient faith of the church is known to us—at least so far as concerns the essential points, such as the resurrection on the third day, the necessity of the redeeming death of Christ and his foreknowledge of his death, and his definite conception and open affirmation of his messiahship. . . . The texts and statements recognized by this process to be authentic become touchstones by which to test other elements of the tradition, centres of crystallization as it were, about which the solid materials contained in the tradition organize themselves." (112–13)

1934

Otto, Rudolf:

The Kingdom of God and the Son of Man. A Study in the History of Religion. Translated by Floyd V. Filson and Bertram Lee Woolf. London: Lutterworth Press, 1951.

The saying Luke 12:8 "is genuine, for no church would have invented at a later time a theology making a distinction so foreign to the feeling of the church, i.e. between the person of Jesus himself and that of the future judge. Furthermore, it is genuine because it corresponds to the criterion of unity." (163)

"[W]e find explicitly repeated in Jesus the ancient traits of the 'ish Elohim,' the man of God, the 'saint of God'; indeed in their mutual relationships they are traits characteristic of a holy man of his kind. This very circumstance is important, viz. that with Christ we have to do not with a mere congeries of traits but with a coherent group which belong together elsewhere in a typical manner in the charismatic man of God. It confirms the genuineness of the picture, and at the same time his category may serve as a criterion of what has been added or enhanced by legend." (336)

1937

Dibelius, Martin:

Jesus. A Study of the Gospels and an Essay on "The Motive for Social Action in the NT." London: SCM Press, 1963.

"Paul, and still more the church after him, already possessed other forms of expression and a new thought world; if little or no trace of such usage is to be found in the tradition of Jesus' words, this is the guarantee of the relative primitiveness in the tradition. It may well be that, occasionally, similar sayings from other sources, especially from the proverbial wisdom of Judaism, have been added to the authentic sayings of Jesus; but they have not affected their essential content. It is proper to speak of non-genuine sayings only where the later circumstances, conditions or problems of the already existing Church are clearly presupposed." (22)

1938

Baeck, Leo:

Das Evangelium als Urkunde der jüdischen Glaubensgeschichte, Berlin: Schocken, 1938.

"The following can all be regarded as belonging to a later layer than that of the historical Jesus: everything that is in conformity with the experiences, hopes, wishes, ideas, and imagery and concerns of the faith of later generations; everything in which the reported event could have been generated from a biblical text or developing Christian dogma; everything that is told in view of the Graeco-Roman world or the Roman authorities, revealing an adaptation to them or attempting to preserve the distinction between Christians and the Jewish people; everything that functions in the Hellenistic manner, such as Hellenistic prophets and miracle workers; and finally, everything that indicates an awareness of the catastrophic period, the time after the destruction of the temple—all this shows itself to belong to a later stratum. It belongs to the history of the church, but it does not belong to the old gospel. Conversely, the following types of material gives evidence of belonging to the oldest, original layer: everything that is different, in orientation or goal, from the generations that followed the first generation of disciples; everything that contradicts the forms in which these later generations constructed their faith; everything different from the intellectual, spiritual, and political world into which the earlier tradition entered, or even opposes it; thus everything that in its way of life and social form, in its attitude and way of thinking, in its language and style gives evidence of the time and place in which Jesus himself lived—all this is from the old, original period. It is in this tradition that we see the words and deeds of Jesus." (67–68)

Dodd, Charles Harold:

History and the Gospel, London: Nisbet & Co., 1938.

On the basis of the investigation of very different types of traditions, Dodd concludes: "But all of them in their different ways exhibit Jesus as an historical personality distinguished from other religious personalities of His time by His friendly attitude to the outcasts of society. This convergence of a great variety of strands of tradition is impressive. We may surely say, on strictly critical grounds, that we have here a well-attested historical fact." (94)

1954

Käsemann, Ernst:

"The Problem of the Historical Jesus," *Essays on New Testament Themes* (London: SCM Press, 1964) 15–47. Originally published as "Das Problem des historischen Jesus," *ZTK* 51 (1954): 125–153.

"With the work of the Form-Critics as a basis, our questioning has sharpened and widened until the obligation now laid upon us is to investigate and make credible not the possible unauthenticity of the individual unit of material, but, on the contrary, its genuineness." (34)

The only help it [Form Criticism] can give "is that it can eliminate as unauthentic anything which must be ruled out of court because of its Sitz-im-Leben." (35)

"In only one case do we have more or less safe ground under our feet; when there are no grounds either for deriving a tradition from Judaism or for ascribing it to primitive Christianity, and especially when Jewish Christianity has mitigated or modified the received tradition, as having found it too bold for its taste. . . . But in so doing we must realize beforehand that we shall not, from this angle of vision, gain any clear view of the connecting link between Jesus, his Palestinian environment and his later community. . . . However, it is even more important for us to gain some insight into what separated him from friends and foes alike." (37)

1955

Dahl, Nils Alstrup:

"Der historische Jesus als geschichtswissenschaftliches und theologisches Problem," *KuD* 1 (1955): 104–32. Appeared in English as "The Problem of the Historical Jesus." Pages 138–71 in *Kerygma and History: A Symposium on the Theology of Rudolf Bultmann*. Edited by Carl E. Braaten and Roy A. Harrisville, (Nashville: Abingdon, 1962).

"Everything which enlarges our knowledge of this environment of Jesus (sc. Palestinian Judaism) indirectly extends our knowledge of the historical Jesus himself." (154)

"The historical Jesus is to be found at the crossroads where Christianity and Judaism began separating from each other, although it only became gradually clear that the paths parted in such a way that Christianity appeared as a new religion alongside Judaism." (154)

"[T]he total tradition concerning Jesus must be taken into consideration. In its totality it is theology of the Church, but at the same time it is also in its totality a reflex of Jesus' activity—a maximum which contains everything of importance for our historical knowledge about Jesus." (156)

After citing Käsemann's formulation of the criterion of dissimilarity: "This radical criticism and its results may not be dogmatized, but must rather be regarded as one necessary heuristic principle among others. Whatever is discovered in this way is only a critically assured minimum." (156)

1957/58

Biehl, Peter:

"Zur Frage nach dem historischen Jesus," *TRu* 24 (1957/58): 54–76.

"According to the historical methods used so far, in the traditional sayings of Jesus we have material that is probably authentic if it cannot be explained either from early Christian preaching or from Judaism. It has accordingly . . . been made into a methodological presupposition that everything oriented to the post-Easter kerygma is out of the question as Jesus' own proclamation. . . . [H]ow then is the transition from the proclaimer to the proclaimed to be made [historically] comprehensible?" (56)

1959

Conzelmann, Hans:

"Jesus Christus," *RGG* 3 (1959): 619–653. Appeared in English as *Jesus*. Translated by J. Raymond Lord. Edited by John Reumann. Philadelphia: Fortress Press, 1973.

"For the reconstruction of Jesus' teaching . . . the following methodological principle is valid: whatever fits neither into Jewish thought nor the views of the later church can be regarded as authentic. This is the case, above all, for the sayings which express a consciousness of the uniqueness of his own situation. . . . Such observations guarantee above all the genuineness of the core of the parables. These are clearly distinguished from all Jewish parallels through style (narrative form, imagery) as well as thought, and reflect a sharply defined self-understanding in which teaching and action (miracle) are comprehended as an indissoluble unity." (16)

"Zur Methode der Leben-Jesu-Forschung," in Hans Conzelmann, *Theologie als Schriftauslegung. Aufsätze zum Neuen Testament.* BEvT 65. München: Kaiser, 1974. [= "Die Frage nach dem historischen Jesus," *ZTK* 56 (1959) Sup. 1:2–13.]

"In order to attain the required reliability the reconstruction must begin at a point where it does not get lost in the dispute about 'authenticity,' in other words, with the authentic nucleus of Jesus' parables. These offer, in turn, a criterion for the logia, especially those in which a very sharply profiled conception can be seen, a model of thought that is unrepeatable, a model so firmly connected with the personal existence of (the pre-Easter!) Jesus that it cannot be transferred without modification into the post-Easter situation. In other words: it cannot be a formation of the believing Christian community. With this, a sound basis has been established." (25)

1960

Cullmann, Oskar:

"Out of Season Remarks on the 'Historical Jesus' of the Bultmann School," in *USQR* 16, no. 2 (January 1961) 131–48.

" . . . how is this kernel to be established according to the procedure of the Bultmann school? We can reduce this procedure to two propostions: 1) Everything in the gospels which stands in tension with the tendencies of the tradition-making primitive church can be traced back to Jesus. . . . Here we are indeed on solid ground, and yet an important restriction must be observed. It is an authentic historical kernel which we seek in a given unit of tradition. This *kernel*, however, cannot subsequently be used as a reliable *criterion* on the basis of which we may determine in other less certain pieces of tradition what is churchly tradition and what is not. For the basis of those passages, fortuitously preserved for us, which stand in tension with the church's theology is *much too narrow* to allow this reliable kernel to serve as a criterion for its own further precision or extension, or for the gaining of a *total* picture of the historical Jesus. . . . On what basis do we know that a theological concern of the primitive church cannot have been *in the same form* a basic motif in the thought of Jesus? . . . Also, wherever a report or saying is found which both reflects a tendency of the church and is incompatible with the contemporary environment, one may conclude that he is dealing with a churchly tradition (in the sense that it lacks historicity) or with an alteration. Finally, wherever a generally valid law of legendary development is visible in a tendency of the church, historicity is to be questioned—with caution, of course." (141–43)

Hahn, Ferdinand:

"Die Frage nach dem historischen Jesus und die Eigenart der uns zur Verfügung stehenden Quellen" (1960 Lecture). Pages 7–40 in *Die Frage nach dem historischen Jesus*. Edited by Ferdinand Hahn, Wenzel Lohff, and Günther Bornkamm. EvFo 2. Göttingen, 1962.

" . . . a basic component is . . . thus first attained, when everything that can neither be explained from late Judaism nor early Christianity can be claimed for the historical Jesus. . . .

"The effects of Jesus of Nazareth and the content of his message are not to be explained from the tradition of the Judaism of that time, for they burst through the boundaries of Jewish thinking and faith in an entirely decisive manner. Neither do his message and acts simply agree without further ado with what the post-Easter community reported about him." (38)

Marxsen, Willi:

Anfangsprobleme der Christologie. 6th ed. Gütersloh, 1969 (1st ed. 1960). Appeared in English as *The Beginnings of Christology: A Study in its Problems*. Translated by Paul J. Achtemeier. Facet Books Biblical Series 22. Philadelphia: Fortress Press, 1969.

Regarding Conzelmann's methodological approach: "But this category would also include everything which (possibly) arose or was formulated in the earliest period of the primitive Christian community, perhaps on the basis of the Easter experience and in conjunction with the expectation of an immediate Parousia. This expectation stood, on the one hand, in contrast to Jewish precepts, but on the other hand could not have been said, or have been said in that way, in the later Christian community. Thus we do not have by any means a sure, positive criterion with this methodological principle. Its value as a negative criterion is also limited. Can one really say that a given word was not spoken by Jesus simply because it fits into Jewish thinking?" (14–15)

Zahrnt, Heinz:

Es begann mit Jesus von Nazareth, Stuttgart: Kreuz, 1960. Appeared in English as *The Historical Jesus*. Translated by J. S. Bowden. New York: Harper, 1960.

"We have no formal criteria with which to decide what material derives from the post-Easter faith of the community and what goes back to Jesus himself. Only radical criticism can help us here. . . .

"[W]e no longer have to prove the unauthenticity, but (and this is far harder) their authenticity. . . . On the whole we can feel ourselves to be on safe ground where a tradition can be derived neither from a Jewish environment nor from the thought-world of primitive Christianity.

"In this way we achieve a critically ensured minimum. This minimum, moreover, can serve as a measure with which to test the remainder of the tradition. . . . Generally speaking, it is impossible in every single case to draw an absolutely firm boundary between authentic and unauthentic, primary and secondary material." (107–8).

1961

Lohse, Eduard:

"Die Frage nach dem historischen Jesus in der gegenwärtigen neutestamentlichen Forschung" (1961 Lecture in Nürnberg) *TLZ* 87 (1962): 161–74.

Authentic words of Jesus are those "that can neither be derived from early Christian preaching nor from the presuppositions of the Judaism of that time. . . . This is not flatly to deny that the historical Jesus may have made use of a Jewish proverb or a common expression, or that he could have spoken a sentence that we would describe as specifically Christian. But in such statements, even if they could have been said by Jesus, we would not encounter the message that was distinctively his own, and that is what we are looking for." (168)

1962

Carlston, Charles Edwin:
"A Positive Criterion of Authenticity," *BR* 7 (1962): 33–44.

"As applied to the parables (and hence other sayings) the proposed criterion of 'authenticity' would be twofold:
"1. An 'authentic' parable will fit reasonably well into the eschatologically based demand for repentance that was characteristic of Jesus' message, and
"2. An authentic parable will reflect or fit into the conditions (social, political, ecclesiastical, linguistic, etc.) prevailing during the earthly ministry of Jesus, rather than (or, in some cases, as well as) conditions which obtained in the post-resurrection church." (p. 34)

"[T]he relative conclusions [i.e., no 'absolute historical certainties'] reached show the limitations of this method of historical study. Rather, the attempt has been made to state the criterion positively, because it seems to the writer that this will bring the relative nature of any results obtained clearly to the forefront at the very outset and thus avoid the temptation of using historical methods to prove, rather than to illustrate." (44)

1963

Bareau, André:
Recherches sur la Biographie du Buddha dans les Sutrapitaka et les Vinayapitaka anciens: De la Quête de l'Éveil à la Conversion de 'Sariputra et de Maudgalyana. Publications de l'École Française D'Extrême-Orient 53. Paris, 1963.

"[O]ne sees too many good reasons that the monks of later times would have had for inventing this story, and that is why one must be prudent on this point." (382)

Kümmel, Werner Georg:

"Der persönliche Anspruch Jesu und der Christusglaube der Urgemeinde" (1963). Pages 429–438 in *Heilsgeschehen und Geschichte. Ges. Aufs. 1933–1964.* Edited by W. G. Kümmel. Marburg: Elwart, 1965.

"[I]n my opinion it is entirely possible . . . with considerable confidence to distinguish between historically reliable old texts and ideas and those that developed later. The criterion for such decisions is bipartite: (1.) observing the tendencies characteristic of the development of early Christian faith that must have modified the Jesus tradition as it was passed along, and (2.) checking the accuracy of the results so obtained as to whether they may be combined into a united and coherent picture of the historical figure of Jesus and his message." (432)

Turner, H. E. W.:

Historicity and the Gospels. A Sketch of Historical Method and its Application to the Gospels. London: Mowbray, 1963.

"Where the teaching of Jesus diverges from contemporary Judaism or from that of the Primitive Church or preferably from both, we can be reasonably certain that we are on firm ground. We must not set the limits of contemporary Judaism too narrowly." (73)

"The difficulty of establishing a single (much more a double) negative considerably restricts the application of the criterion in this particular form.

"A modified form of this principle may, however, prove of greater importance. Where there is an overlap of interest between the Gospels and early Church, but a marked difference in the scale of treatment, we can be reasonably sure that we are on firm historical ground." (74)

"This suggested criterion is simply an application of the method of comparison which is a primary tool of all historical enquiry." (75)

1964

McArthur, Harvey K.:

"Basic Issues. A Survey of Recent Gospel Research," *Interpretation* 18 (1964): 39–55.

McArthur distinguishes the criterion "that the tendencies of the developing tradition should be discounted" (48) from "the criterion which suggests the elimination of all material which may be derived either from Judaism or from primitive Christianity." (50)

In regard to the latter, he says, "This is the most difficult of all the criteria to apply since it may easily be construed so as to leave no space between the Scylla of Judaism and the Charybdis of primitive Christianity. It is a radical criterion, since much of the teaching of Jesus must have been more or less standard Judaism, and the elimination of this from the portrait leaves only a fraction of his original teaching—though perhaps the most distinctive fraction. Finally, it is an ambiguous criterion since scholars differ as to whether a particular item is more 'natural' against the background of primitive Christianity or against the background of the ministry of Jesus. Nevertheless, this criterion has received widespread support, and some of its applications are relatively clear-cut." (50)

1965

Fuller, Reginald H.:

The Foundations of New Testament Christology. London: Lutterworth, 1965.

"As regards the sayings of Jesus, traditio-historical criticism eliminates from the authentic sayings of Jesus those which are paralleled in the Jewish tradition on the one hand (apocalyptic and Rabbinic) and those which reflect the faith, practice and situations of the post-Easter church as we know them from outside the Gospels." (18)

Teeple, Howard M.:

"The Origin of the Son of Man Christology," *JBL* 84 (1965): 213–50.

"If a saying reflects a situation or point of view which was characteristic of the early church and was not, as far as we know, characteristic of Jesus, the saying probably is not authentic." (219)

Coherence with the Palestinian environment: "If a saying reflects Gentile or Hellenistic attitudes, customs, and situations, rather than those which historical knowledge indicates would be characteristic of a Palestinian Jew in the first century A.D., it is probable that the logion is unauthentic." (219)

1966

Trilling, Wolfgang:

Fragen zur Geschichtlichkeit Jesu. Düsseldorf: Patmos, 1966.

He names the following as the three most important criteria of credibility:
"Jesus appears as a person of distinctively powerful character. His words
have a personal ring and an inimitable hue. . . . Many details of his sayings are
also found in other great speakers, in the classical prophets of Israel and in religious reformers. But when seen as a whole, his teaching has a characteristic
'style' that is found nowhere else. Above all, in many places a unique, imperi-
ous 'consciousness' shines forth, which lends to his 'style' a very demanding
tone, a tone that is without parallel. Consistent lines can be traced through his
life. . . . This comprehensive picture could not have been invented and must
as a whole be historically reliable." (45–46)

1967

Burchard, Christoph:

"Jesus," *KP* 2 (1967): cols. 1342–54.

"They [the Jesus traditions] become sources for the historical Jesus only by
separating the original elements from their secondary accretions. Since the
original layer has also been selected by faith and is permeated with it, it too
must be reduced (no longer by a process of subtraction) to what is authentic,
to what really happened." (1345)

"There are formal criteria for some sayings of Jesus . . .; even so, it is mostly
only the authenticity of the subject matter, not its forms, that can be demonstrated. The material criterion is that only that can be considered authentic or
really to have happened if it is not a postulate of faith. This can be determined
in comparison with Judaism and Christianity. In addition, the degree of overlap between Jesus and early Christianity must be determined . . . so that the
result is not a mere minimalist differential image. Jesus research and the investigation of early Christianity stand within the same circle." (1346)

Moule, Charles Francis Digby:

*The Phenomenon of the New Testament. An Inquiry into the Implications of Certain
Features of the New Testament.* SBT, Second Series 1. London: SCM, 1967.

"It would appear that there are certain features in the story of Jesus, the
retention of which can scarcely be explained except by their genuineness and
durable quality, since everything else was hostile to their survival.
"This is the principle seized on by P. W. Schmiedel. . . . Modern scholarship has accepted the principle, although without concentrating on
Schmiedel's particular instances." (62)

Perrin, Norman:

Rediscovering the Teaching of Jesus. New York: Harper & Row, 1967.

"[T]he nature of the synoptic tradition is such that the burden of proof will be upon the claim to authenticity. . . . Therefore, if we are to ascribe a saying to Jesus, and accept the burden of proof laid upon us, we must be able to show that the saying comes neither from the Church nor from ancient Judaism." (39)

Perrin then formulates the 'criterion of dissimilarity' as follows:
"[T]he earliest form of a saying we can reach may be regarded as authentic if it can be shown to be dissimilar to characteristic emphases both of ancient Judaism and of the early Church, and this will particularly be the case where Christian tradition oriented towards Judaism can be shown to have modified the saying away from its original emphasis." (39)

"[T]he criterion of dissimilarity . . . must be regarded as the basis for all contemporary attempts to reconstruct the teaching of Jesus." (43)

To this criterion of dissimilarity Perrin adds the "criterion of coherence" and the "criterion of multiple attestation." (43–46)

1968

Niederwimmer, Kurt:

Jesus. Göttingen: Vandenhoeck & Ruprecht, 1968.

Niederwimmer speaks of the specifically Jesus elements that are "without parallel" and refers to Käsemann's formulation of the criterion of dissimilarity. "For all that, no one denies that Jesus broadly shared the religious convictions of his environment. He was a Jew. . . . But all that is peripheral for understanding his work. One will instead attain the best access to the historical Jesus by looking for those elements of his message and conduct that brought him into conflict with the religious authorities of his time. That which the church shares with contemporary Judaism is not specifically Jesus-material. That which separates the church from Judaism is the 'essence' of Jesus' message and conduct. That also finally became historically effective, leading to the rejection of Jesus and the exodus of the Christian groups from Judaism, so that even the question of whether Jesus really said or did a particular saying or deed attributed to him in the tradition is relatively indifferent: if it only explains what the specific element in his work as a whole was, then we have obtained the most that this method is capable of delivering today." (25–26)

1969

Braun, Herbert:

Jesus. Der Mann aus Nazareth und seine Zeit. Expanded edition (by twelve chapters). Gütersloh, 1988. 1st ed. Stuttgart-Berlin: Kreuz Verlag, 1969.

"It is necessary to notice: does such a saying of Jesus share its content with surrounding Judaism? If so, this means it is untypical of Jesus. Or does its content stand out from the surrounding Judaism? If so, it is typical of Jesus."

Braun names the following possibilities: "The content of a saying is located on the Jewish level; then it is not exclusively typical of Jesus. Nonetheless, it could still very well be authentic. . . . the other possibility . . . a saying of Jesus has a content that, despite its Jewish formulation, is not derivable from Judaism or Qumran-Judaism, but contradicts Jewish thinking, as in the case of the command to love one's enemies (Matt 5:44). Here the assumption is very likely justified that in such a traditional saying we have something from Jesus' own mouth, an authentic saying of Jesus." (29–30)

Kümmel, Werner Georg:

Die Theologie des Neuen Testaments nach seinen Hauptzeugen Jesus—Paulus— Johannes. Göttingen, 1969 (= GNT 3). Appeared in English as *The Theology of the New Testament. According to Its Major Witnesses, Jesus—Paul—John.* Translated by John E. Steely. Nashville: Abingdon, 1973.

"Of course the decisive check on the correctness of such a setting apart of the earliest body of tradition can only be the proof that from the fitting together of the pieces of tradition thus gained a historically comprehensible and unitary picture of Jesus and his proclamation results, which also makes the further development of primitive Christianity understandable." (26)

1970

Kee, Howard Clark:

Jesus In History. An Approach to the Study of the Gospels. New York: Harcourt, 1970.

"Another formula of authenticity proposes a via negativa: Whatever in the tradition can be explained as originating in the early church or as taken over by the tradition from Judaism may not be regarded as authentic. [A reference to Käsemann] This criterion is weak, because it presupposes a more complete discontinuity between Jesus and Judaism on the one hand and between Jesus and the early church on the other hand than may actually have been the case. Since the tradition portrays Jesus as a critic speaking to Judaism from within, it would be surprising if his teaching did not take over from Judaism a great deal relatively unchanged. Similarly, although it must be acknowledged that the impact of the cross and the rise of the resurrection faith transformed Jesus' followers' understanding of him, it is not necessary to assume that the early church simultaneously transformed all facets of the message attributed to him or its recollection of events in his public activity. One would expect, on the contrary, considerable carry-over from the message and ministry of Jesus to that of the early church. The changes that occurred were generally modifications, not always innovations." (264–65)

Koch, Klaus:

Ratlos vor der Apokalyptik. Eine Streitschrift über ein vernachlässigtes Gebiet der Bibelwissenschaft und die schädlichen Auswirkungen auf Theologie und Philosophie. Gütersloh, 1970. Appeared in English as *The Rediscovery of Apocalyptic.* Studies in Biblical Theology. Second Series 22. London: SCM Press, 1972.

The New Quest of the 1950s "led to a general exclusion, from the very outset, of everything in the gospels which sounded apocalyptic as being alien to Jesus. This was possible by means of a method of reduction which was set up as a guiding line for synoptic research. According to this, the only sayings in the gospels which genuinely derive from Jesus are those which coincide neither with Jewish ideas, nor with the teaching of the primitive church. The only features which may be accepted as genuine are those which stand in visible contradiction to the directly preceding, or directly succeeding, periods." (68)

"This method of reduction suggests extreme historical conscientiousness. Is it not praiseworthy to work with a reliable minimum rather than with a multifarious maximum? The fascination of the principle for students and younger scholars is understandable. But the results are somewhat staggering. For what generally emerges is a picture in which Jesus is practically indistinguishable from a German kerygmatic theologian of the twentieth century. This suggests doubts as to whether it is really historical to lay down absolute discontinuity with past and future as the standard in tracing a historical personage and his influence."* (69)

* Footnote, p. 145:

"We only have to consider a hypothetical case: what would remain of Luther if one denied him every theme which can also be attested as medieval or early Protestant? If in Jesus' case more has been left up to now, that could be due to the fragmentary state of the comparable texts at our disposal. It is rather difficult to see why supporters of the reduction method hold fast so obstinately to the idea of the sovereignty of God as being Jesus' own; as if the relevant synoptic statements with their modification of this data were further removed from the apocalypses than their corresponding statements about the Son of man. Perhaps a reliable criterion for distinguishing the genuine sayings of Jesus can be found by linguistic and formal observations—i.e., through form criticism; the reduction method, as it is usually applied, has nothing in common with form criticism."

Perrin, Norman:

What Is Redaction Criticism?, London: SPCK, 1970.

"[M]aterial may be ascribed to Jesus only if it can be shown to be distinctive in Judaism or the church after him." (71)

1970/71

Hooker, Morna D.:

"Christology and Methodology," *NTS* 17 (1970/71): 480–87.

"[M]ost important, perhaps, is the demand that a saying must be given a reasonable 'pedigree', whether it is attributed to Jesus or the Church." (486)

1971

Jeremias, Joachim:

Neutestamentliche Theologie. Vol. 1. *Die Verkündigung Jesu*. Gütersloh, 1971. Appeared in English as *New Testament Theology: The Proclamation of Jesus*. Translated by John Bowden. New York: Charles Scribner's Sons, 1971.

"But it [sc. the criterion of dissimilarity] has one weakness: its comparison of the sayings of Jesus with the religious ideas of Palestinian Judaism and of the early church is one-sidedly based on the principle of originality; as a result, it only covers some of the sayings of Jesus that are to be taken as early. All the cases in which Jesus takes up already available material, whether apocalyptic ideas or Jewish proverbs or language current in his environment, slip through the net, as do the cases in which the early church handed down words of Jesus unaltered, as e.g., *Abba* as a mode of addressing God. Indeed, it has to be said that the way in which the 'criterion of dissimilarity' is often used today as a password is a serious source of error. It foreshortens and distorts the historical situation, because it overlooks the continuity between Jesus and Judaism." (2)

1972

Barbour, Robin S.:

Traditio-Historical Criticism of the Gospels. Some Comments on Current Methods. London: SPCK, 1972 (SCC 4).

"The use of the criterion of dissimilarity seems likely to give us a Jesus who presents a very distinctive figure, but not in the way in which the early Christian community regarded him as distinctive; who makes great claims, but not in terms of the titles which form the framework of early Christology. It is therefore likely to make the problem of continuity between the Jesus of history and the Christ of faith, about which the new questers of the historical Jesus are naturally so concerned, extremely difficult to solve except by means of a *tertium comparationis* like the concept of *Existenzverständnis*. . . ." (15).

"The use of the criterion of dissimilarity as a basic tool is not just a heuristic method, as seems to be supposed, but is in itself the adoption of an hypothesis about the historical Jesus and his relation to the early tradition. . . ." (19)

"The criterion of dissimilarity might become a tool, not indeed for exhuming some of those figures, but for burying the humanity, and especially the Jewishness, of Jesus." (20)

"The so-called 'criterion of dissimilarity' by which genuine material relating to Jesus is isolated can only be regarded as one among a number of heuristic criteria. . . . It may produce a critically assured minimum, but it cannot be said to produce an adequate historical core." (25f.)

"[T]he criterion of dissimilarity is being used in an attempt to establish those features of Jesus' words and deeds which are so distinctive that they could not have come from the reflection and proclamation of the earliest witnesses in their (of course legitimate) glorification of their Risen Lord. But in this theologico-philosophical context the traditio-historical techniques are in danger of becoming something much more than techniques; they are becoming metaphysical weapons." (33)

McEleney, Neil J.:

"Authenticating Criteria and Mark 7:1–23," *CBQ* 34 (1972): 431–60.

"[The] criterion of discontinuity [reveals] distinctiveness or discontinuity. . . . But this is no more than saying what any historian says of a period, that anachronisms must be ruled out or what the sources assign to a given person or movement belongs there. This is a positive use of dissimilarity without a simultaneous methodological pronouncement on the authenticity or nonauthenticity of other passages. Only with such limited usage can the criterion be successfully employed and its use reconciled with the use of the criterion of coherence. Understood in this manner, however, it does no more than state what is fairly obvious historically." (442)

Gager, John G.:

"The Gospels and Jesus: Some Doubts about Method," *JR* 54 (1974): 244–72.

"Two points in Perrin's formulation of the criterion [of dissimilarity] deserve mention. The statement that a saying will be authentic if it differs from characteristic emphases both of ancient Judaism and the early church seems unnecessarily complicated. To be sure, the early church was 'indebted at very many points to ancient Judaism.' [Perrin] But the only channel for this influence was Christianity itself, and it would be incongruous to assume that Christians borrowed concepts from Judaism which differed from their own views. In other words, a saying which is not consonant with the early church may be regarded as authentic, whether or not it is consonant with first-century Judaism. Thus the wording can be simplified to read 'dissimilar to characteristic emphases of the early Church.' A second problem is Perrin's further claim that 'if we are to seek that which is most characteristic of Jesus, it will be found not in things which he shares with his contemporaries, but in the things wherein he differs from them.' [Perrin] This is obviously a questionable assertion, based as it is on an implicit and unexamined model of human personality. The criterion of dissimilarity cannot guarantee that its results will reflect the kernel of Jesus' teaching. It can only promise to yield 'authentic' results." (257)

Latourelle, René, S.J.:

"Critères d'authenticité historique des Évangiles," *Greg* 55 (1974): 609–38.

"Even before looking at particular accounts, one may say that the Gospels, taken as a whole, present themselves as an instance of discontinuity, in the sense that they constitute something unique and original in relation to all other literature. The literary genre of the Gospel is in discontinuity with ancient Jewish literature just as it is with later Christian literature. . . . Their [the Gospels'] content is the person of Christ: a person who is classified neither according to the categories of universal secular history nor according to the categories of the history of religions. Jesus is found by the historian to be an absolutely unique being." (622)

"[I]t would be illegitimate, on the basis of this unique criterion, to eliminate everything that corresponds to the Jewish or Christian traditions." (625)

"There exists, in fact, in Jesus' language as in his actions, some characteristic *traits*, that constitute what one may call Jesus' *style*: a unique and inimitable style." (630)

Lentzen-Deis, Fritzleo:

"Kriterien für die historische Beurteilung der Jesusüberlieferung in den Evangelien." Pages 78–117 in *Rückfrage nach Jesus. Zur Methodik und Bedeutung der Frage nach dem historischen Jesus.* Edited by Karl Kertelge. QD 63. Freiburg-Basel-Wien 1974.

"With great probability such characteristic features of the Jesus tradition are original that distinguish Jesus from early Christianity and from his Jewish environment." (97)

"This criterion has the disadvantage that it can demonstrate only very minimal individual characteristics, if any at all. Recent research shows the close connections between Palestinian Judaism to Hellenistic Judaism and even more the connections between Jewish Christianity and its Hellenistic environment. Nonetheless, with this basic principle points of crystallization of the 'characteristically Jesus' can be discovered in Jesus' message and life." (99)

Mussner, Franz, et al.:

"Methodologie der Frage nach dem historischen Jesus." Pages 118–47 in *Rückfrage nach Jesus. Zur Methodik und Bedeutung der Frage nach dem historischen Jesus.* Edited by Karl Kertelge. QD 63. Freiburg-Basel-Wien 1974.

"Attention to the differences, which is what the principle of exclusion is concerned with, can indeed at first make Jesus' distinctive profile stand out clearly. But it must also be noted that the profile of a person is not formed merely by that which contrasts with the world around him, but also by what identifies him with it. Thus we have a continuum both backwards (tradition) and forwards (the history of effects). The principle of exclusion thus does not provide a holistic picture of Jesus.

" . . . The application of the criterion of exclusion can easily lead to an unconscious combination of historical criticism and theological judgments (or prejudices)." (132)

1975

Goppelt, Leonhard:

Theologie des Neuen Testaments. Edited by Jürgen Roloff. 3d ed. Göttingen, 1981 (the following quotation was already present in the first edition). Appeared in English as *Theology of the New Testament.* Translated by John E. Alsup. Edited by Jürgen Roloff. Two volumes. Grand Rapids: Eerdmans, 1981.

Goppelt calls for a critical analysis of the tradition that as its first step separates secondary material, for which he uses, among other methods, the CDC ("dependence on the situation of the community"). "On the other hand, we shall then attempt to draw together the various parts from a core of authentic material into a single, overall view through reasoned interpretation. The core of authentic material is distinguishable when one applies the generally accepted criterion of history-of-religions particularity in connection with both its milieu and the early Christian community."* Alongside this criterion Goppelt uses the criterion of multiple attestation, to which he then adds the criterion of coherence (additional traditions show themselves to be authentic "through a continuity of subject matter").

*Goppelt here adds the following footnote: "This particularity is no proof of a religious singularity. Distinguishing between traditional materials by this criterion is always relative, since judgments are dependent upon our knowledge of the milieu. Consequently, it is decisive that the particularity be identified not only statistically but also according to kind. Even when the distinction is not exclusive, it is possible that there are Jesus traditions that show contact with the milieu and are still authentic."

Lange, Dietz:

Historischer Jesus oder mythischer Christus. Untersuchungen zu dem Gegensatz zwischen Friedrich Schleiermacher und David Friedrich Strauss. Gütersloh: Mohn, 1975.

In reference to Käsemann: "The question must be stated as follows: In what way did Jesus transform Jewish tradition into something entirely new, yes even into its opposite, in a way that early Christianity neither dared to do, nor was capable of doing? Thus the usual hierarchy of criteria must be inverted: the material criteria are to be placed first, then the formal criteria; that Jesus expressed the new element in his preaching in the usual, folksy forms, is not only not to be excluded, but on the contrary is to be presupposed. After all, he was no literary figure, and his originality was not a matter of form, but content." (309–10)

Lührmann, Dieter:

"Die Frage nach Kriterien für ursprüngliche Jesusworte. Eine Problem-skizze." Pages in 59–72 in *Jésus aux origines de la christologie*. 2d ed. Edited by Jacques Dupont. BETL 40. Leuven, 1989 (1975 1st ed.).

"The value of the criterion of dissimilarity is that with its help the characteristic element in Jesus in contradiction to his time can be discovered, even if it is indeed only a distinctly minimal criterion, since it consciously foregoes much that is not expressed. . . . the criterion of dissimilarity [can] make clear the distinction between the community's confession of Jesus and Jesus himself, even if sometimes the impression of his followers slips in, who returned to their customary paths after the soaring flight of their master." (65)

Schillebeeckx, Edward:

Jesus. Die Geschichte von einem Lebenden. Freiburg-Basel-Wien, 1975. Appeared in English as *Jesus: An Experiment in Christology*. Translated by Hubert Hoskins. New York: Crossroad, 1979.

"The Criterion of Form Criticism: The Principle of Dual Irreducibility"

"This method, used almost exclusively by the exponents of Form Criticism to prise what is strictly peculiar to Jesus loose from what belongs to his Jewish contemporaries and the later local churches, . . . (92)

"There is absolutely no intention of denying, on the basis of this principle, that Jesus took over a great deal of what is in the Old Testament and in Judaism and that he stands in continuity with post-Easter Christian thinking; only that in such cases of continuity this criterion affords us no historical or critical certainty as to whether the source is Jesus himself or the Jewish Christian church. In other words, it must not be employed as a negative criterion. Used positively, it has a definite limited value. . . . (92–93)

"This criterion of the elements of Jesus' message and conduct that have no parallel in either the Judaism of his time or the early Church . . . (93)

"Even the earliest local churches could command from the store of their

Christianity irreducible elements of their own which stand apart from Judaism as well as from subsequent phases of the early Christian congregations." (94)

Schürmann, Heinz:

Jesu ureigener Tod. Exegetische Besinnungen und Ausblick. Freiburg: Herder, 1975.

"It is inherent in the method itself that the 'assured nucleus' obtained through the critical principle of exclusion [i.e., the criterion of dissimilarity as defined by Käsemann] can produce only a distorted picture of Jesus, a 'wholly other' Jesus who—in a way would be cause for alarm from the psychiatric point of view—lived in his Jewish world without making contact with it, and—from the historical point of view—had no effect on the history after him. It is very unlikely, however, that the post-Easter community was not decisively marked by the sayings and deeds of Jesus. Of course, we would like to ask about such a possible continuum, but a consistent application of this principle excludes the question in advance. . . . There is thus urgent need for a supplementary investigation of the 'residue' excised by this principle of exclusion, from which, with the help of positive criteria additional historically reliable material may still be gained." (23)

"Research that has been working with the principle of exclusion may no longer let itself be restricted in advance . . . to the traditional sayings of Jesus. . . . The actions of Jesus, along with his fate, is of decisive importance if one wants to arrive at any results in our quest." (25–26)

"It is important . . . to renounce the widespread methodological-monism, or, said more positively, to use the evidence of convergence, the evidence provided by the various observations and perceptions—whether of a hypothetical or morally certain kind—to construct a coherent comprehensive picture. Finally, it is possible to 'encounter' a historical personality—and this applies to Jesus in an even higher degree—only by means of a pluralism of methodological approaches. The understanding of a person in his unmistakable individuality is always more than the sum of all critically assured statements about his destiny, conduct, and speaking as well as the self-understanding of this person, because such a person is not a brutum factum that can simply be historically 'established.' Beyond all critical methods there thus remains a residue that can only be reached on personal terms, when we are talking about knowledge of a person." (25–26)

1976

Dahl, Nils Alstrup:

"The Early Church and Jesus." Pages 167–175 in Nils Alstrup Dahl, *Jesus in the Memory of the Early Church*, Minneapolis: Fortress Press, 1976.

"[T]he interest in the social function of the tradition has tended to result in a social isolation of Jesus himself. This tendency is further strengthened by the widely accepted principle that among sayings attributed to Jesus, those are most likely to be authentic which can not [sic] have originated either in contemporary Judaism or in the church after Easter ('the criterion of dissimilarity'). The irony of the matter is that the new application of rigid critical principles opens the doors to new versions of a modernized Jesus who is separated both from the church and from his Jewish environment but relevant for our time." (168)

"The 'criterion of dissimilarity' should only be used in conjunction with historical considerations of synchronic similarity and diachronic continuity." (171–172)

Demke, Christoph:

Im Blickpunkt: Die Einzigartigkeit Jesu. Theologische Informationen für Nichttheologen. Berlin: Evangelische Verlagsanstalt, 1976.

"We stand on relatively firm ground, where Jesus' words and his conduct go in the same direction, so that they mutually explain each other." (63)

France, R.T.:

"The Authenticity of Jesus' Sayings." Pages 101–143 in *History, Criticism, and Faith*. Edited by Colin Brown. Downer's Grove, Ill.: Inter-Varsity Press, 1976.

"If anyone else in the world of the New Testament could have said the saying in question, it cannot be taken as a saying of Jesus." (109)

1977

Catchpole, David R.:

"Tradition History." Pages 165–180 in *New Testament Interpretation. Essays on Principles and Methods*. Edited by I. Howard Marshall. Exeter: Paternoster, 1977.

On the criterion of dissimilarity as cited in Fuller, 1965: "Firstly, the deceptive simplicity of this test should not mask the fact that at most it can produce the distinctive Jesus but cannot guarantee the characteristic Jesus." (174)

"Dissimilarity is, as already noted, a doubtful tool when the relationship between Jesus and the post-Easter churches is under scrutiny. It also has some drawbacks in respect of a discussion of his relationship with Judaism, in view of the incompleteness of our knowledge of Judaism." (177)

"[T]here must also be a coherence of the context presupposed by a tradition with the context of Jesus' mission, as well as a coherence of content. But at least the use of coherence, after dissimilarity to Judaism has been explored, does offer certain advantages: (a) It allows for the incorporation of other material reflecting similarity between Jesus and Judaism. (b) It allows for the continuity between Jesus and some at least of the post-Easter Christian developments." (178)

Grant, Michael:

Jesus, New York: Charles Scribner's Sons, 1977.

"A further criterion requires the rejection from the lifetime of Jesus of all material which seems to be derived from the days of the Christian Church as it existed after his death. . . .

"[T]o distinguish between the authentic words and deeds of Jesus and the tendencies of the developing tradition which so easily overlaid them, was one of the principal tasks of the 'form critics'. . . .

"One way of attempting this task is to look out for surprises. For anything really surprising in the Gospels is quite likely to be authentic—anything, that is to say, which clashes with what we should *expect* to find in something written after the time of Jesus." (202)

"[T]he evangelists manifestly *do* include some unpalatable or even incomprehensible doings and sayings of Jesus, and incidents in his life . . . because they were so indissolubly incorporated in the tradition that their elimination was impracticable; in other words, because they were genuine." (203)

1978

Mealand, David L.:

"The Dissimilarity Test," *SJT* 31 (1978): 41–50.

"Sayings which are similar to the normal run of Jewish teaching or which are similar to the doctrine and practice of early Christianity are temporarily placed on one side. . . . The material which is 'distinctive', in the sense that it differs both from Judaism and from early Christianity, is singled out by the test of dissimilarity. This material is less likely to have been wrongly attributed to Jesus. . . ." (43)

Schottroff, Luise / Stegemann, Wolfgang:

Jesus and the Hope of the Poor. Translated by Matthew J. O'Connell. Maryknoll, N.Y.: Orbis Books, 1986.

"When one perceives Jesus in the context of the oldest Jesus movement, a large number of historical inferences can be made. Seen historically, Jesus may not be considered in isolation from his followers—and theologians are only too fond of doing just that. The alternative 'authentic = the historical Jesus—inauthentic = community formulation' . . . attempts to mark Jesus off and separate him from Judaism until he finally stands on the lonely pedestal of the heoric genius, whose genius becomes all the more clear the less he has to do with the people around him. But Jesus is fundamentally not separable from the particular groups of Jewish people, and especially not from his first disciples." (2)

1979

Dautzenberg, Gerhard:

"Der Wandel der Reich-Gottes-Verkündigung in der urchristlichen Mission." Pages 11–32 in *Zur Geschichte des Urchristentums.* Edited by Gerhard Dautzenberg, et al. QD 87. Freiburg: Herder, 1979.

"[T]he demarcation between the oldest, so-called "authentic" layer of the Jesus tradition—attained by historical methods and recognized criteria—and the early Christian kerygmatic layer of the post-Easter period to which it was directly attached [can] only be made in a rather vague manner, a matter no method can completely avoid. . . . In general, one must be content to judge the particular results as possible or probable, and to suppose that the general outline of the picture can be related to other data of the story of Jesus and early Christianity with some probability and without internal contradiction. One can then surmise that the results facilitate answers to questions discussed in this area." (14–15)

1980

Harvey, Anthony E.:

Jesus and the Constraints of History. The Bampton Lectures 1980. London: Duckworth, 1982.

"No individual, if he wishes to influence others, is totally free to choose his own style of action and persuasion: he is subject to constraints imposed by the

culture in which he finds himself. If communication is to take place, there must
be constraints which are recognized by both the speaker and his listeners. . . .
It is evident that he [sc. Jesus] succeeded in communicating with his hearers,
his followers, and indeed his enemies. To do so, he had to speak a language
they could understand, perform actions they would find intelligible, and conduct his life and undergo his death in a manner of which they could make some
sense. This is not to say, of course, that he must have been totally subject to
these constraints. Like any truly creative person, he could doubtless bend them
to his purpose. But had he not worked from within them, he would have
seemed a mere freak, a person too unrelated to the normal rhythm of society
to have anything meaningful to say." (6f.)

"[T]he criterion of 'dissimilarity' . . . may be crudely described as the principle that 'odd is true'. If we come across something in the gospels which
appears strikingly original and for which there is no known parallel or prece-
dent in the ancient world; and if we can see no possible reason for anyone to
have invented such a thing and foisted it upon the story of Jesus; then it seems
that we have at least an echo of something which happened in historical fact.
Its very oddity is an argument for its truth. The criterion needs to be used with
caution, since it is always vulnerable to the acquisition of new knowledge: what
was once thought to be unparalleled and unprecedented may be shown by new
discoveries to have been well established in the culture. Moreover, the criterion
must never be used in isolation. It would be impossible to build up a credible
portrait of Jesus entirely out of material selected because of its peculiarity: no
one has or could ever have a character composed entirely out of idiosyncrasies.
The method can be used only to supplement those more normal characteristics for which we have reliable evidence. But there are elements of the gospel
tradition (such as the episode of Jesus' mounted entry into Jerusalem) which,
as we shall see, are inexplicable unless they derive from authentic reminiscence,
and which provide us with invaluable clues to the specific options which were
actually chosen by Jesus amid the constraints to which he was subjected." (8f.)

Higgins, August John Brockhurst:

The Son of Man in the Teaching of Jesus. Cambridge: Cambridge University
Press, 1980.

In reference to Teeple, 1965: "Some writers give a high place to the criterion, according to which a saying of Jesus is genuine if it is explicable neither
from late Judaism nor from the situation of the early church. This standard is
questionable, for Jesus was himself a product of late Judaism, and so even a
saying containing apocalyptic elements could conceivably be genuine." (37)

Stein, Robert H.:

"The 'Criteria' for Authenticity." Pages 225–263 in *Gospel Perspectives. Studies of History and Tradition in the Four Gospels*. Vol. 1. Edited by R. T. France and D. Wenham. Sheffield: JSOT, 1980.

"In concluding our discussion of this tool, it would appear that despite many of the criticisms raised of late, when used correctly in conjunction with its innate limitations, the criterion of dissimilarity is nevertheless a most valuable tool in the quest for the ipsissima verba or vox of Jesus. It may in fact be the single most valuable tool for authenticity, for if a saying or action of Jesus in the gospel tradition meets the demands of this criterion, the likelihood of it being authentic is extremely good. It is true that this tool cannot necessarily deliver to us that which is characteristic in Jesus' teachings or even to produce 'an adequate historical core,' but it does give us a 'critically assured minimum' to which other material can be added via other criteria. Care must be taken, however, to apply this tool more objectively than in the past. . . ." (244)

Riesner, Rainer:

Jesus als Lehrer. Eine Untersuchung zum Ursprung der Evangelien-Überlieferung. WUNT II, 7. Tübingen: Mohr, 1981.

"Today it is widely recognized that a negative application of the 'criterion of dissimilarity' would be pseudo-critical." (90)

"Observations about dissimilarity can be especially valuable as indications of authenticity. According to all that we know, the majority of the Aramaic speaking members of the earliest church dealt with the Torah in a rather conservative fashion. Whenever sayings are found in a semitizing linguistic form that are critical of the Torah, they point back to Jesus with particular clarity. For all post-Easter communities, the messiahship of Jesus was a firm article of faith. Wherever only concealed or indirect messianic claims are found in sayings of Jesus, there the tradition is worthy of confidence." (91)

Schürmann, Heinz:

"Das Zeugnis der Redenquelle für die Basileia-Verkündigung Jesu." Pages 121–200 in *Logia. Les Paroles de Jésus—The Sayings of Jesus*. BETL 59. Edited by Joël Delobel. Leuven: Leuven University Press, 1982 (Konferenz 1981).

"As soon as we attempt to approach the earthly Jesus with the 'basic critical principle' of methodological doubt, more precisely with the 'criterion of dissimilarity,' he seems strangely to withdraw himself from this investigative look and the effort to seize him. When we want to draw inferences from the preaching of the kingdom of God found in the older layers of Q sketched above, the criterion of dissimilarity compels us to ascribe nothing to Jesus that he had in common not only with his environment—but also with the early Christian community. Against the use of this criterion are raised—precisely in this case—not a few critical objections that can be of further help. An authentic historical method cannot be satisfied with a fundamental skepticism, but remains obligated to the truth; it will therefore always seek for the 'greater probability' and on the basis of such will—with all due caution—look for evidence of congruence." (179–180)

"Kritische Jesuserkenntnis. Zur kritischen Handhabung des 'Unähnlichkeitskriteriums'," *BiLi* 54 (1981): 17–26.

"The . . . 'basic critical principle' [of methodological doubt] is concretized in the critical 'criterion of dissimilarity'—widespread unanimity prevails in critical Jesus research on this point. The Jesus tradition must be sorted out from two different sides, if an 'assured nucleus' is to be obtained: the Jesus material must stand out from and be separated from related Jewish material on the one side, and from the later early Christian community on the other.

"This 'criterion of dissimilarity' must of course be applied critically: There are two mutually supplementary procedures to be carried out, if a convincing result is to be obtained. In a first step (I.) with the help of the 'criterion of dissimilarity' the 'possibly non-Jesus material' is to be excluded; then (II.) the 'possibly Jesus material' is to be salvaged from the 'possibly non-Jesus material' by means of converging criteria. Only when both of these procedures are brought into play together can we speak of probabilities and end up with a relatively trustworthy critical 'picture of Jesus.'" (18)

"A radical and unreflective application of the criterion of dissimilarity oriented to history-of-religions study does not deliver an 'original' or 'unique' Jesus, but on the contrary an 'original' without connections or a meaningless figure, no longer understandable as a 'historical personality'—though Jesus in his personal uniqueness must certainly be understood to have been a historical personality. When applied consistently this criterion—in regard to both sides of its application, the Jewish and the Christian—simply violates the principle of 'correlation,' which is certainly a fundamental principle of all historical understanding." (19)

1983

Gamber, Klaus:

Jesus-Worte. Eine vorkanonische Logiensammlung im Lukas-Evangelium. StPatr-Ltg Beiheft 9. Regensburg: Pustet, 1983.

"The sayings of Jesus cannot have been invented. . . . The authentic sayings of Jesus . . . are 'words of eternal life' (John 6:69). Jesus' own preaching is conspicuous by it originality, its unmediated nature. . . . This is why the teaching of Jesus was so different from that of the Jewish teachers of the law. . . . The sayings of Jesus reveal themselves by their simplicity, their plainness. . . . The words of Jesus are quiet, simple, and natural, and yet possess an enormous power. His words are the most powerful and shaking that have ever been spoken." (7–8)

Strecker, Georg:

Die Bergpredigt. Ein exegetischer Kommentar. Göttingen, 1984. Appeared in English as *The Sermon on the Mount: An Exegetical Commentary.* Translated by O. C. Dean, Jr. Nashville: Abingdon, 1988.

"To be sure, it can be objected that the application of the differentiating criterion [i.e., the CDJ and CDC] isolates the words of Jesus from their Jewish environment as well as from the early Christian community, and also that it amounts to a reduction process that does not allow statements of the historical Jesus containing Jewish concepts to be put forward as genuine. The named criterion, however, is to be questioned above all because it presupposes a prior understanding both of Judaism at the time of Jesus and of the post-Easter church, which as such must be open to debate." (13)

Wilder, Amos N.:

"The Historical Jesus in a New Focus: A Review Article of 'The Silence of Jesus' by James Breech (Philadelphia 1983)," *USQR* 39 (1984): 225–36.

"[I]f his [i.e., Jesus'] impact was to prevail must it not have interlocked with the empirical reality of his theatre of action? What was creative and novel in his work—understood perhaps as deep structure—must have had to come to terms with the actual historical forces which he confronted. This would involve not only action, but debate, with their language patterns and symbol systems. To engender a new ethos in a new gathering of followers could hardly bypass the public options and passionate loyalties of that highly dynamic situation." (234)

Riches, John / Millar, Alan:

"Conceptual Change in the Synoptic Tradition." Pages 37–60 in *Alternative Approaches to New Testament Study.* Edited by Anthony E. Harvey. London: SPCK, 1985.

"A speaker or writer can employ familiar linguistic forms in new ways to express new thoughts while retaining the 'core' of their customary content.

Whether he does or not can only be determined by examining them in the light of whatever else the speaker or writer has to say." (46)

A kind of "criterion of coherence": "[T]he fact that a saying harmonizes with a body of sayings, which there are independent grounds for taking to be indicative of Jesus' teaching, counts in favour of the hypothesis that the saying in question, in respect of its content, is ascribable to Jesus. The kind of harmony which matters, however, has to do not just with superficial linguistic or literary features, though these are by no means irrelevant, but more importantly with patterns of thought. Exactly parallel consideration holds for the so-called principle of dissimilarity. It is commonly held that in order to determine which sayings are authentic to Jesus, we must first isolate a group of sayings which are sufficiently dissimilar to contemporary beliefs that they can be regarded as original to Jesus and then extend this group of sayings by adding others which harmonize with it. Where similarity or dissimilarity is concerned, again, what matters are patterns of thought. A group of sayings may be linguistically keyed to first-century Palestine and yet be radically distinct in respect of their content." (57)

Sanders, Ed Parish:

Jesus and Judaism. London: SCM Press, 1985.

Sanders lists the following difficulties of the "test of double dissimilarity": "We know first-century Judaism very imperfectly, and knowledge about the interests of the church between 70 and 100 CE . . . is slender indeed. . . . The test rules out too much. . . . The material which remains after the test is applied is biased towards uniqueness." (16)

"Secondly, the remaining material does not interpret itself or necessarily answer historical questions. It must still be placed in a meaningful context, and that context is not automatically provided by summarizing sayings which are atypical, as far as we know, of both Judaism and the Christian church." (16–17)

"I propose that a hypothesis which does offer a reasonable and well-grounded connection between Jesus and the Christian movement is better than one which offers no connection but which appeals, finally, to accident and to the resurrection experiences to explain why Jesus' mission did not end with his death." (22)

"[T]he only way to proceed in the search for the historical Jesus is to offer hypotheses based on the evidence and to evaluate them in light of how satisfactorily they account for the material in the Gospels, while also making Jesus a believable figure in first-century Palestine and the founder of a movement which eventuated in the church." (166–167)

On the problem of the "uniqueness" of Jesus: "[I]n order to derive meaningful information about Jesus . . . , scholars must suppose not only that they can reconstruct precisely what Jesus said and precisely what he meant by it, but also that they can eliminate the possibility that anyone else held such views. This enormously increases the dubiousness of the method which already requires hypothesis upon hypothesis. How can one argue historically that a certain attitude or conception is unique? A sober estimate in accord with the normal canons of the writing of history can go no farther than 'otherwise unattested'." (138)

"I worry a bit about the word 'unique'. . . . What is unique is the result. But, again, we cannot know that the result springs from the uniqueness of the historical Jesus. Without the resurrection, would his disciples have endured longer than did John the Baptist's? We can only guess, but I would guess not." (240)

Simonis, Walter:

Jesus von Nazareth. Seine Botschaft vom Reich Gottes und der Glaube der Urgemeinde. Historisch-kritische Erhellung der Ursprünge des Christentums. Düsseldorf: Patmos, 1985.

"The criterion of dissimilarity is acknowledged today by all scholars who are concerned to recover authentic Jesus material as methodologically necessary and useful. . . . [W]e have the greatest probability of dealing with authentic Jesus material when a saying, idea, or act of Jesus was neither current in contemporary Judaism, and thus possibly can be proven to come from him, nor overlaps the ideas, expectations and interests of the early churches that handed on the tradition or those of the Evangelists, so that it could also be seen as their composition. . . . The criterion of dissimilarity thus serves to trace out elements that have no positive analogies. . . ." (26)

"[W]e [have] in the process of the historical-critical reconstruction of the proclamation and work of Jesus as a whole only these pieces of tradition at our disposal . . . , which positively can be recognized as authentic or historical, whereas all other pieces are not to be considered in reconstructing the historical Jesus. That may at first appear as an arbitrary and unjustifiable decree, in reality however such a procedure means only taking seriously the inner logic of the criterion of dissimilarity itself and thus the historical difference between pre- and post-Easter." (27)

1986

Caragounis, Chrys C.:

The Son of Man. Vision and Interpretation. WUNT 38. Tübingen: Mohr, 1986.

"The criterion [of dissimilarity] stipulates that authentic words of Jesus must not correspond to characteristic emphases in Judaism or the Early Church. . . . We simply do not have an adequate basis for applying the criterion of dissimilarity in such a way that genuine results will be forthcoming. Another difficulty, the gravest of all, lies at the core of the criterion of dissimilarity, with its underlying assumption that Jesus' teaching must always be distinguishable or dissimilar from the teachings of Judaism and of the Early Church. This would seem to presuppose that no continuity between Judaism and Jesus is permissible, nor is even any lasting influence of Jesus on the Early Church recognized. Both of these assumptions would fly in the face of modern scholarly consensus." (155f.)

"[The criterion's] inexorably consistent use without restraint or check by other criteria, could only lead finally to the 'de-Judaization' of Jesus as well as the 'de-Jesus-ing' of the Early Church! In either case the Jesus of the criterion of dissimilarity would no longer be the Jesus of history." (157)

Segal, Alan F.:

Rebecca's Children. Judaism and Christianity in the Roman World. Cambridge, Mass.: Harvard University Press, 1986.

"The part of his teaching that can be identified as uniquely his [i.e., Jesus'] own and that most affected his contemporaries was apocalyptic. Since the later church would not eliminate authentic Jesus traditions yet at the same time did not favor apocalypticism, the presence of apocalyptic in early Christianity must be attributed to Jesus himself.

Theissen, Gerd:

Der Schatten des Galiläers. Historische Jesusforschung in erzählender Form, München, 1986. Appeared in English as *The Shadow of the Galilean: The Quest of the Historical Jesus in Narrative Form.* Translated by John Bowden. Philadelphia: Fortress Press, 1987.

"I doubt whether the criterion of difference is a practicable one. The fact that we cannot recognize any dependence of a saying of Jesus on Jewish tradition does not mean that there could never have been such dependence. Jesus could have been influenced by oral traditions. Or by traditions contained in writings which have been lost.

"Moreover the criterion of difference neglects all that Jesus has in common with Judaism, as though—in contrast to other men—he could not be understood from his historical environment. The 'criterion of originality' (another name for the criterion of difference) is dogma in disguise: Jesus seems to drop directly from heaven. And this dogma has an anti-Jewish slant: what puts Jesus in opposition to Judaism cannot be derived. . . .

"[T]raditions about Jesus have a claim to authenticity when they are historically possible within the framework of the Judaism of his time but at the same time have a special accent which enables us to understand how primitive Christianity later developed out of Judaism. Not only Jesus but the whole of primitive Christianity can be derived from Judaism." (141)

1987

Burchard, Christoph:

"Jesus von Nazareth." Pages 12–58 in *Die Anfänge des Christentums. Alte Welt und neue Hoffnung*. Stuttgart: Kohlhammer, 1987.

"[O]ne must . . . do for Jesus the same thing that one does for other people whose effects and heritage have been preserved, and must do it for early Christianity as well: one must enlarge the available sources by study of the contemporary history." (12)

"There are . . . two approaches to the historical Jesus: the history of the early church, to the extent that the effects of Jesus himself may be perceived in it, and the history of Palestine, inasmuch as it was the place where Jesus had an effect. . . . Jesus and the beginnings of Christianity themselves belong to the history of Palestinian Judaism." (13)

Schweizer, Eduard:

"Jesus Christus I.", *TRE* 16 (1987): 671–726.

"We can be most confident that material belongs to Jesus that is found neither in Judaism nor in the later church. That applies also to particular forms of speech . . . or action. . . . But this still results in only a minimal stock of materials, since Jesus obviously lived and taught as a Jew, and the later church learned from him. One can add to this basic stock the materials that fit in with it without suspicious traces of later development." (710)

"[B]ecause God is present in Jesus' whole conduct, work, preaching, and experience, . . . Jesus is 'the man who fits no formula'. . . .

"[P]recisely his refusal to fulfill the expectations and roles already present constitutes his uniqueness. . . ." (722)

Charlesworth, James H.:

Jesus Within Judaism. New Light from Exciting Archaelogical Discoveries. New York: Doubleday, 1988.

"I am convinced that we find our way to the greatest historical certainty by excluding (at least in the beginning) those Jesus sayings that can be attributed to the needs and concerns of the earliest 'Christian' communities. But it seems unwise to tighten this criterion further by eliminating material that has its roots in Early Judaism. If a particular saying is discontinuous with the needs or motives of the earliest Christians, it does not necessarily render it inauthentic if it has points of contact with Early Judaism. . . .

"In the past, a preoccupation with the notion of 'uniqueness' has caused many scholars to see this issue inaccurately. The historian's task is to sift through the accounts of those who wrote about Jesus to determine how much of their work may be reliably attributed to Jesus himself. My study of the Jesus tradition has led me to the conclusion that a considerable amount of that tradition which is discontinuous with the needs and concerns of the earliest Christians places Jesus squarely in the midst of Early Judaism, and that is precisely where one would expect to find a first-century Palestinian Jew." (6)

"From any of these sources [i.e., the Gospels], . . . an identifiable Jewish male emerges as a distinct historical personality. . . . [B]ehind the later editorial layer of the Gospels lie earlier historical traditions that clarify the distinctiveness of Jesus." (21–22)

"By using the principle of discontinuity, Jesus' authentic words were sought by using a net that released all Jesus' sayings that were paralleled either in Judaism or in the Church. By employing this methodology systematically, we begin with a tendency to portray Jesus as a non-Jew and as a leader without followers." (167)

Crossan, John Dominic:

"Divine Immediacy and Human Immediacy. Towards a new first principle in historical Jesus research," *Semeia* 44 (1988): 121–40.

"My proposal is to make a virtue of diversity and to formulate my basic question like this: what did Jesus say and do that led, if not necessarily at least immediately, to such diverse understandings?

This formulation suggests an alternative first principle to the criterion of dissimilarity, namely, the criterion of adequacy: that is original which best explains the multiplicity engendered in the tradition." (125)

Lee, Bernard J.:

The Galilean Jewishness of Jesus. Retrieving the Jewish Origins of Christianity. Vol. 1: *Conversation on the Road not Taken.* New York: Paulist Press, 1988.

"I will be trying to understand the Judaism of Galilean Palestine in the time of Jesus. . . . [I]f we understand the religious and cultural matrix in which his human consciousness awakened, we know something real about his subjectivity." (49)

"As Christians, we must finally ask what it is that is particular to Jesus in which our own faith finds adequate mooring. But even when we interpret what is particular to Jesus, we do not have a full answer to the question: 'Where do we Christians come from in our distinctiveness?' Only part of the answer is found in the particularity of Jesus. The other part is found in the historical and cultural conditions that accompanied and facilitated the evolution of Christian communities as entities outside Judaism, events from about two generations after Jesus. Those later events are crucial to questions about Christian identity. . . ." (96)

1989

Ernst, Josef:

"War Jesus ein Schüler Johannes' des Täufers?" Pages 13–33 in *Vom Urchristentum zu Jesus* (FS Joachim Gnilka). Edited by Hubert Frankemölle and Karl Kertelge. Freiburg: Herder, 1989.

"The questionable nature of the 'argument from embarrassment' is seen . . . in well-known counter examples, such as the preservation of the tradition of the baptism of Jesus or Peter's denial. The possibility that uncomfortable facts were suppressed cannot of course be entirely excluded, but if used as 'evidence' at all, it must be done only in a subsidiary manner." (33)

Holtz, Traugott:

"Jesus," *EKL* 2 (1989): 2:824–831.

"Only that which was important to the tradents was handed on, shaped by their interests. . . . The history of Jesus can be reconstructed only by critical analysis of the form and content of these individual units of tradition. The criterion is misleading that claims for Jesus only that which is neither Jewish nor Christian. It is primarily the inauthenticity of a tradition that must be shown, not the authenticity; an important positive approach is to show the coherence of the traditions considered to be original. In details, such analysis often remains uncertain, but can still lead to positive results. However, the character of the comprehensive picture of Jesus cannot be revised on the basis of a selection of particular traditions." (825)

1990

Downing, F. Gerald:

"Criteria," in *A Dictionary of Biblical Interpretation*. Edited by Richard J. Coggins and James L. Houlden. London: SCM Press, 1990.

"Criteria are standards for testing and for coming to a judgement on an issue. . . . In biblical studies the term 'criterion' itself tends mostly to be used in discussing tests for deciding whether sayings or stories attributed, say, to Jesus or to Jeremiah, are to be taken as genuine, or whether they should instead be ascribed to other contemporaries or to subsequent oral or editorial tradition." He names four standard criteria: "Dissimilarity; Authentic Context; Multiple Attestation; and Coherence. (The first of these in particular gets a number of titles, e.g., Dual Irreducibility, Dual Exclusion, Discontinuity.)" (151)

On the problem that the two first-named criteria contradict each other: "Still, if we find Jesus saying something distinctive about issues we know were live at the time, in an appropriate setting, then both criteria can work without canceling each other out." And in any case, these two criteria need not be applied alone. (152)

Gnilka, Joachim:

Jesus von Nazareth. Botschaft und Geschichte. HThK.S 3. Freiburg-Basel-Wien, 1990. Appeared in English as *Jesus of Nazareth: Message and History*. Translated by Siegfried S. Schatzmann. Peabody, Mass.: Hendrickson, 1997.

"The 'criterion of dissimilarity' holds that we are dealing with a tradition originating in Jesus if the tradition can neither be derived from Judaism nor attributed to the early church. . . . It is apparent that what matters here is absolute originality. Only what was truly new and distinct from what was already known can be regarded as valid. The presuppositions implied in this criterion may be based, consciously or not, on a particular christological concept. . . . This criterion is a helpful but sharp sword. What is certain is that, if it is applied radically, a lot of Jesus material would be severed from him. Had Jesus always been original, he would have resembled a missionary to China who refuses to speak Chinese. This criterion does, however, deserve our attention as a point of departure. . . ." (20)

Horn, Friedrich Wilhelm:

"Diakonische Leitlinien Jesu." Pages 109–26 in *Diakonie-biblische Grundlagen und Orientierungen. Ein Arbeitsbuch zur theologischen Verständigung über den diakonischen Auftrag*. Edited by Gerhard K. Schäfer and Theodor Strohm. Heidelberg: HVA, 1990 (= Veröff. d. Diakoniewiss. Instituts an der Universität Heidelberg 2).

"We can infer that we are dealing with sayings or conduct of the historical Jesus in those places in the Gospels that still preserve charges against Jesus from his Jewish environment. These charges are neither derivable from the interests of church theology, nor are they directed to the churches themselves; on the contrary, these same accusations, mostly preserved in scenes expanded as apophthegms, were difficult for the early church to interpret." (111)

Winton, Alan P.:

The Proverbs of Jesus. Issues of History and Rhetoric. JSNT 35. Sheffield: JSOT, 1990.

"The criterion of dissimilarity asserts that a saying can be regarded as authentic if it can be shown to be dissimilar to characteristic emphases both of early Judaism and of the early Church. It is also used negatively to claim that sayings similar to Jewish or Christian traditions are inauthentic, for it is presumed that their *Sitz im Leben* is in the life of the church, and not in the life of Jesus.

"Form criticism seems to provide the logic of this criterion, based on the principle that traditions about Jesus were retained and used in only so far as they met the needs and interests of the early church. However, this insight should not lead too quickly to a judgment about the origin of the material. The concept of *Sitz im Leben* can be overworked. *Sitz im Leben* relates to the characteristic function of a tradition: a judgment about the function does not necessarily lead directly to a judgment about origin." (109–10)

"It would seem that sayings dissimilar from both Judaism and Christianity are the least likely to help explain the transition from the one to the other. Sayings in continuity with Jewish teaching, and those which modify traditional ideas, would seem most helpful in understanding how Jesus as a Jew came to be seen as the founder of a renewal movement in first-century Judaism." (110)

"Our present principles dictate that in the case of material which appears to be unnaturally juxtaposed . . . The sayings which do not pass the dissimilarity test are considered inauthentic, because they fail to cohere with 'characteristic' material. There is an alternative, however, and that is to see how material which is 'unnaturally' juxtaposed might cause us to change our understanding of the whole picture. . . . This calls for a suspension of our negative judgment, until we have seen what the whole picture would look like. . . ." (112)

"We are suggesting that it would be helpful, for reasons of historical interest, to re-examine the framework in the light of the particulars. . . .

"Our study so far suggests that the dissimilarity test should be abandoned, unless one is self-consciously setting out to assess the uniqueness of Jesus— even then, the results of such work would always depend on an argument from silence. However, we have found, on the positive side, that any account of Jesus' teaching (as part of his overall impact) must help to account for the transition from Judaism to Christianity. . . . Our emphasis should be on understanding Jesus in continuity with his Jewish environment, while being aware that we need to give some account of the strong opposition to Jesus, and the rise of the early Christian movement with its eventual break from Judaism." (113)

Three tests for any attempt at historical reconstruction:

"1. It must set Jesus convincingly within the context of first century Palestinian Judaism.
2. It must show why his life ended in execution at the hands of the Roman authorities.
3. It must account for, or at least illumine, the birth of the Christian community." (123)

Meier, John P.:

A Marginal Jew. Rethinking the Historical Jesus. New York: Doubleday, 1991.

"The criterion of 'embarrassment' (so Schillebeeckx) or 'contradiction' (so Meyer) focuses on actions or sayings of Jesus that would have embarrassed or created difficulty for the early Church." (168)

"Like all the criteria we will examine, however, the criterion of embarrass-ment has its limitations and must always be used in concert with the other criteria. . . . [A] full portrait of Jesus could never be drawn with so few strokes. . . . [W]hat we today might consider an embarrassment to the early Church was not necessarily an embarrassment in its own eyes." (170)

"Closely allied to the criterion of embarrassment, the criterion of disconti-nuity (also labeled dissimilarity, originality, or dual irreducibility) focuses on words or deeds of Jesus that cannot be derived either from Judaism at the time of Jesus or from the early Church after him." (171)

"By focusing narrowly upon what may have been Jesus' 'idiosyncrasies', it is always in danger of highlighting what was striking but possibly peripheral in his message. . . ."
"Instead of 'if it is discontinuous, it must be from Jesus', we now have 'if it is discontinuous, it cannot be from Jesus'. Obviously, dogmatism in either direction must give way to a careful testing of claims in each case." (173)

"The criterion of Jesus' rejection and execution . . . [:] A Jesus whose words and deeds would not alienate people, especially powerful people, is not the historical Jesus." (177)

Merkel, Helmut:
"Die Gottesherrschaft in der Verkündigung Jesu." Pages 119–61 in *Königs-herrschaft Gottes und himmlischer Kult im Judentum, Urchristentum und in der hel-lenistischen Welt*. Edited by Martin Hengel and Anna Maria Schwemer. WUNT 55. Tübingen 1991.

"The principle of underivability formulated by Käsemann, also cited as the criterion of dissimilarity, the principle of distinctiveness or the criterion of dif-ferentiation, has meanwhile been widely accepted; it is probably regarded as the most important result of the methodological discussion so far." (132)

"At first glance this objection [of Klaus Koch, 1970, see above] seems to have a strong effect, but it does not hit the most important aspect. It is not the elements of medieval thinking that were doubtless still present in Luther that give us information about the distinctive historical significance of the reformer, but the elements that distinguish him from his medieval environ-ment! And obviously the old Protestant Scholasticism preserved many ele-ments of Luther's theology, but they are embedded in very different systematic conceptions in which they have different functions and implications than in

Luther himself. . . . And finally, the insinuation that an anti-Jewish tendency lies hidden in this criterion would ultimately have to lead to discrediting every single historical manner of posing the question. It would then be worthy of consideration only if one could prove that the criterion, which itself has a compelling logic, was being applied in a manner free of all tendencies." (133)

"A truly historical comprehensive picture of the proclamation of Jesus can . . . only be attained when one, in the sense of Heitmüller, regards everything as coming from Jesus that stands 'in organic connection' with the critically-attained minimum." (134)

Sauer, Jürgen:

Rückkehr und Vollendung des Heils. Eine Untersuchung zu den ethischen Radikalismen Jesu. Theorie und Forschung 133; Philosophie und Theologie 9. Regensburg 1991.

"Summary: to be sure, the condition of dissimilarity is a sufficient, but not a necessary condition of authenticity of Jesus material; the criterion of dissimilarity may well be able to show the authenticity of particular sayings of Jesus or the historicity of particular aspects of his life, but it cannot definitely exclude authenticity and historicity. . . .

"The application of the criterion of dissimilarity is thus indeed a necessary, but not a sufficient condition for the reconstruction of the proclamation of the historical Jesus." (88)

1992

Baasland, Ernst:

Theologie und Methode. Eine historiographische Analyse der Frühschriften Rudolf Bultmanns. Wuppertal/Zürich 1992: Brockhaus Verlag.

"The decisive question in research is thus rather this, whether one must construct his comprehensive view based on the criterion of originality (and coherence) or based on the criterion of longitudinal section (and coherence). We will here attempt to establish the last named solution more securely, which Bultmann also had suggested before 1920. For a truly historical understanding, the principles of coherence and consequences must be given a higher priority than the criterion of theological discrepancy. A historical consideration of Jesus cannot separate him from the Jesus movement and cannot remove him from his socio-cultural context. Thus within the framework of a comprehensive solution, the whole complex of characteristics must be seen together that explain Jesus' death and his effects on his disciples, Jews, and Romans; that make understandable the origin of early Christianity and its mission; that explain the origin of the tradition and the Gospels themselves: why is it that Jesus is presented there as the only teacher?

"As a control in providing a comprehensive historical view, alongside these questions related to the history of Jesus' effects there is the requirement that presumably historical data can be fitted into the historical milieu (the 'environmental criterion'); Jesus sayings, both in themselves and in comparison with his actions, must exhibit a coherent set (the criterion of coherence or cross-section). So also, a plausible explanation must be found for the (according to our ideas) 'dark sayings' and 'strange actions.' With the use of these criteria the judgment with regard to historicity will turn out to be more positive than in Bultmann's usage." (261)

1994

Borg, Marcus J.:

"Reflections on a Discipline: A North American Perspective." Pages 9–31 in *Studying the Historical Jesus. Evaluations of the State of Current Research.* Edited by Bruce D. Chilton and Craig A. Evans. Leiden: E. J. Brill, 1994.

"The decline of dissimilarity as the primary criterion of authenticity is generally characteristic of North American scholars today, with some exceptions" (here Borg refers to a few members of the Jesus Seminar). (26)

"My hunch is that the majority of scholars . . . will continue to be eclectic in making judgments about what goes back to Jesus rather than developing a rigorously methodical method. What seems to count most is a reasonable case that the tradition is early, plus a sense of 'fittingness' into a setting that makes sense in the context of the pre-Easter Jesus." (27)

1996

Becker, Jürgen:

Jesus von Nazaret. Berlin-New York, 1996. Appeared in English as *Jesus of Nazareth.* Translated by James E. Crouch. New York: Walter de Gruyter, 1998.

"The first and fundamental criterion of this kind for the analysis of an individual tradition is the criterion of dissimilarity. It is justifiably the most generally accepted criterion; indeed some use it exclusively. It claims a tradition as authentic Jesus material when its content is unique in two contexts, Early

Judaism and Primitive Christianity, and can thus lay claim to originality in both areas. The criterion is weakened when one does not apply it consistently—that is to say, when one compares it rigorously when comparing Jesus to the later church but only timidly when comparing him to Early Judaism.

"The criterion also self-destructs when the demand for originality is so unrealistic that the only thing left of Jesus is a solipsistic phantom. It should go without saying that we can use this criterion only when we understand that every person is part of a historical nexus and that the individuality of Jesus that we seek to discover occurred only within the culture of Early Judaism and thus must be understood today in that context. It is also true, of course, that the early church also lives in continuity with Jesus.

"We are not saying, therefore, that Jesus is to be understood primarily as a nomad in world history, which in the final analysis would be to understand him unhistorically. To use the criterion of dissimilarity is, rather, to elevate to the center of discussion of authenticity that which is especially and unmistakably characteristic of him in order to begin with the best possible basis for a more comprehensive understanding of Jesus. The criticism that this criterion has attracted, when examined in the light of day, speaks only to its misuse as the only criterion rather than to its use to secure a beginning nucleus of material. The criterion is by far without peer when we understand that its goal is to find an unmistakable nucleus of Jesus material that is at one and the same time an expression of his Jewish context and an antecedent that stands in continuity with Primitive Christianity." (13–14)

In a footnote Becker objects to a christologically tinted use of "uniqueness" and "singularity."

Bibliography

Aland, K. "Bemerkungen zum Montanismus und zur frühchristlichen Eschatologie." Pages 105–48 in *Kirchengeschichtliche Entwürfe*. Gütersloh: Mohn, 1960.

Allen, Ch. "The Newest Testament." *Washington City Paper* (4 September 1992): 20–23.

Althaus, P. "Akkomodation." *RGG*[3] 1 (1957): 209f.

Baasland, E. *Theologie und Methode. Eine historiographische Analyse der Frühschriften Rudolf Bultmanns*. Wuppertal/Zürich: Brackhaus Verlag, 1992.

Back, S. O. *Jesus of Nazareth and the Sabbath Commandment*. Åbo: Åbo Akademi University Press, 1995.

Baeck, L. *Das Evangelium als Urkunde der jüdischen Glaubensgeschichte*. Berlin: Schocken, 1938.

Bammel, E. "The revolution theory from Reimarus to Brandon." Pages 11–68 in *Jesus and the Politics of His Day*. Edited by E. Bammel and C. F. D. Moule. Cambridge: Cambridge University Press, 1984.

Banks, R. J. "Setting 'The Quest for the Historical Jesus' in a Broader Framework." Pages 61–82 in *Gospel Perspectives. Studies of History and Tradition in the Four Gospels*. Vol. 2. Edited by R. T. France and D. Wenham, Sheffield: JSOT, 1981.

Barbour, R. S. *Traditio-Historical Criticism of the Gospels. Some Comments on Current Methods*. SCC 4. London: SPCK, 1972.

Bareau, A. *Recherches sur la biographie du Buddha dans les Sùtrapitaka et les Vinayapitaka anciens: De la Quête de l'Éveil à la Conversion de 'Sàriputra et de Maudgalyàna*. PEFEO 53. Paris: École Française D'Extrême-Orient, 1963.

Barth, Karl. *Church Dogmatics*. Vol. 1. *The Doctrine of the Word of God*. 2nd half-vol. Edited by G. W. Bromiley and T. F. Torrance. Edinburgh: T & T Clark, 1956.

Bartsch, Ch. *'Frühkatholizismus' als Kategorie historisch-kritischer Theologie. Eine methodologische und theologiegeschichtliche Untersuchung*. SKI 3. Berlin: Selbstverlag Institut Kirche und Judentum, 1980.

Batdorf, I. W. "Interpreting Jesus since Bultmann. Selected Paradigms and their Hermeneutic Matrix." *Society of Biblical Literature 1984 Seminar Papers* (Chico: Scholars Press, 1984):187–215.

Baumbach, G. "Die Stellung Jesu im Judentum seiner Zeit." *FZPhTh* 20 (1973): 285–305.

Baumgarten, O. "Carlyle, Thomas." *RGG*[1] 1 (1909): 1578–86.

Baur, F. Ch. *Die sogenannten Pastoralbriefe des Apostels Paulus aufs neue kritisch untersucht*. Stuttgart: Cotta, 1835.

———. "Das Christenthum und die christliche Kirche der drei ersten Jahrhunderte (1853)." In *Ausgewählte Werke in Einzelausgaben*. Vol. 3. Edited by K. Scholder. Stuttgart: Fromman, 1966.

Baur, Ferdinand Christian. *The Church History of the First Three Centuries*. Translated by Allan Menzies. 3d ed. Theological Translation Fund Library. London: Williams & Norgate, 1878.

Beck, D. M. "The Never-Ending Quest for the Historical Jesus (A Review Article)." *JBR* 29 (1961): 227–31.

Becker, Jürgen. *Jesus of Nazareth*. Translated by James E. Crouch. New York: Walter de Gruyter, 1998.

Ben-Chorin, Schalom. *Brother Jesus: the Nazarene through Jewish Eyes*. Translated and edited by Jared S. Klein and Max Reinhart. Athens: University of Georgia Press, 2001.

———. *Jesus im Judentum*. SCJB 4. Wuppertal: Brockhaus, 1970.

Berger, K. *Einführung in die Formgeschichte*. UTB 1444. Tübingen: Francke, 1987.

———. *Exegese und Philosophie*. SBS 123/124. Stuttgart: Kath. Bibelwerk, 1986.

———. "Jesus als Pharisäer und frühe Christen als Pharisäer." *NovT* 30 (1988): 231–62.

———. *Wer war Jesus wirklich?* 3d ed. Stuttgart: Quelle Verlag, 1996.

Beyschlag, W. *Das Leben Jesu*. Vol. 1. 2d ed. Halle: E. Strien, 1887.

Biehl, P. "Zur Frage nach dem historischen Jesus." *TRu* 24 (1957/58): 54–76.

Blank, J. "Karl Barth und die Frage nach dem irdischen Jesus." *ZDT* 2 (1986): 176–92.

Blanke, H. W. "Aufklärungshistorie, Historismus und historische Kritik. Eine Skizze" In *Von der Aufklärung zum Historismus. Zum Strukturwandel des historischen Denkens*. Historisch-politische Diskurse 1. Edited by H. W. Blanke and J. Rüsen. Paderborn: Schöningh, 1984.

Bloch, M. *Apologie der Geschichte oder Der Beruf des Historikers*. Anmerkungen und Argumente 9. Stuttgart: Klett, 1974.

Borg, M. J. *Conflict, Holiness and Politics in the Teaching of Jesus*. SBEC 5. New York: E. Mellen, 1984.

———. "A Renaissance in Jesus Studies." *TToday* 45 (1988): 280–92.

———. "What did Jesus really say?" *BiRe* 5 (1989): 18–25.

———. "Reflections on a Discipline: A North American Perspective." Pages 9–31 in *Studying the Historical Jesus. Evaluations of the State of Current Research*. Edited by B. D. Chilton and C. A. Evans. Leiden: E. J. Brill, 1994.

———. *Jesus in Contemporary Scholarship*. Valley Forge, Pa.: Trinity Press International, 1994.

Boring, M. E. "Criteria of Authenticity. The Beatitudes as a Test Case." *Foundations and Facets Forum* 1 (1985): 3–38.

———. "The Historical-Critical Method's 'Criteria of Authenticity': The Beatitudes in Q and Thomas as a test case." *Semeia* 44 (1988): 9–44.

———. *The Continuing Voice of Jesus. Christian Prophecy and the Gospel Tradition*. Louisville, Ky.: Westminster/John Knox, 1991.

———. "The 'Third Quest' and the Apostolic Faith," *Interpretation* 50, no. 4 (October 1996). Repr. pages 237–52 in *Gospel Interpretation: Narrative-Critical and Social-Scientific Approaches*. Edited by Jack Dean Kingsbury. Harrisburg, Pa.: Trinity Press International, 1998.

Bornkamm, G. "Evangelium und Mythos." *ZdZ* 5 (1951): 1–5.

———. *Jesus von Nazareth*. 13th ed. UB 19. Stuttgart: Kohlhammer, 1983.

Bornkamm, Günther. *Jesus of Nazareth*. Translated by Irene and Fraser McLuskey with James M. Robinson. New York: Harper & Row, 1960.

———. "Die Bedeutung des historischen Jesus für den Glauben." Pages 57–71 in *Die Frage nach dem historischen Jesus*. EvFo 2. Contributions by F. Hahn, W. Lohff, and G. Bornkamm. Göttingen: Vandenhoeck & Ruprecht, 1962.

Botha, P. "Probleme van die vraag na die historiese Jesus. 'n Pleidooi vir meer demokrasie in die Nuwe-Testamentiese wetenskap." *ThEv(SA)* 20 (1987): 2–8.

Bousset, W. *Jesu Predigt in ihrem Gegensatz zum Judentum. Ein religionsgeschichtlicher Vergleich*. Göttingen: Vandenhoeck & Ruprecht, 1892.

———. "Thomas Carlyle—ein Prophet des 19. Jahrhunderts." *ChW* 11 (1897): cols. 249–53.

———. *Die Religion des Judentums im neutestamentlichen Zeitalter (1903)*. 2d ed. Berlin: Reuther & Reichard, 1906.

———. *Das Wesen der Religion. Dargestellt an ihrer Geschichte*. 4th ed. Lebensfragen 28. Tübingen: Mohr, 1920.

———. *Was wissen wir von Jesus?* 2d ed. Tübingen: Mohr, 1906.

———. *Jesus*, 3d ed. Tübingen: Mohr, 1907.

———. "Die Bedeutung der Person Jesu für den Glauben. Historische und rationale Grundlagen des Glaubens." Pages 291–305 in *Fünfter Weltkongress für Freies Christentum und Religiösen Fortschritt 5–10 August 1910*. Transcript of Proceedings. Edited by M. Fischer and F. M. Schiele, Berlin: Protestant. Schriftenvertrieb, 1910.

———. *Kyrios Christos*. Translated by John E. Steely. Nashville: Abingdon, 1970.

Bowker, J. *The Sense of God. Sociological, Anthropological and Psychological Approaches to the Origin of the Sense of God*. Oxford: Clarendon, 1973.

———. *The Religious Imagination and the Sense of God*. Oxford: Clarendon, 1978.

Bowman, J. W. "The Quest of the Historical Jesus." *Interp.* 3 (1949): 184–90.

Brandt, A. von. *Werkzeug des Historikers. Eine Einführung in die Historischen Hilfswissenschaften (1958)*. 10th ed. UB 33. Stuttgart: Kohlhammer, 1983.

Braun, Herbert. *Jesus. Der Mann aus Nazareth und seine Zeit*. Expanded edition (by twelve chapters). Gütersloh, 1988. 1st ed. Stuttgart-Berlin: Kreuz Verlag, 1969.

Brodbeck, M. "Methodological Individualism. Definition and Reduction." Pages 297–329 in *Philosophical Analysis and History*. Edited by W. H. Dray. Westport, Conn.: Greenwood, 1978.

Brown, C. *Jesus in European Protestant Thought 1778–1860*. Studies in Historical Thought 1. Durham, N.C.: Labyrinth, 1985.

Bruce, A. B. "Jesus." *EncBib* 2 (1901): cols. 2435–54.

Brunner, E. *Der Mittler. Zur Besinnung über den Christusglauben (1927)*. 4th ed. Zürich: Zwingli, 1947.

———. *The Mediator. A Study of the Central Doctrine of the Christian Faith*. Translated by Olive Wyon from the second, 1932 edition. Philadelphia: Westminster Press, 1947.

Bruns, I. "Kult historischer Personen." Pages 1–31 in *Vorträge und Aufsätze*. Munich, 1905.

Bubner, R. *Geschichtsprozesse und Handlungsnormen. Untersuchungen zur praktischen Philosophie*. stw 463. Frankfurt: Suhrkamp, 1984.

Buck, A. *Die humanistische Tradition in der Romania*. Bad Homburg: Gehlen, 1968.

Bultmann, R. "Ethical and Mystical Religion in Primitive Christianity." In *The Beginnings of Dialectic Theology*. Translated by Louis De Grazia and Keith R. Crim. Edited by J. M. Robinson. Richmond: John Knox Press, 1968.

———. *Die Geschichte der synoptischen Tradition (1921)*. 8th ed. FRLANT 29. Göttingen: Vandenhoeck & Ruprecht, 1970.

———. *The History of the Synoptic Tradition*. Translated by John Marsh. New York: Harper & Row, 1963.

———. "Die liberale Theologie und die jüngste theologische Bewegung" *GuV* 1 (1924): 1–25.

————. *Jesus and the Word*. Translated by Louis Pettibone Smith and Erminie Huntress Lantero. New York: Charles Scribner's Sons, 1958.

————. "The New Approach to the Synoptic Problem." *JR* 6 (1926): 337–62. Repr. pages 23–24 in *Existence and Faith: Shorter Writings of Rudolf Bultmann*. Selected, translated, and introduced by Shubert M. Ogden. New York: Meridian Books, 1960.

————. "Geschichtliche und übergeschichtliche Religion im Christentum?" *GuV* 1 (1926): 65–84.

————. "Zur Frage der Christologie." *GuV* 1 (1927): 85–113.

————. Die Bedeutung des geschichtlichen Jesus für die Theologie des Paulus." *GuV* 1 (1929): 188–213.

————. "Die Christologie des Neuen Testaments." *GuV* 1 (1933): 245–67.

————. "New Testament and Mythology." Pages 1–44 in *Kerygma and Myth: A Theological Debate*. Edited by Hans Werner Bartsch. New York: Harper & Brothers, 1961.

————. *Primitive Christianity in its Contemporary Setting*. New York: Meridian Books, 1956.

————. "A Reply to the Theses of J. Schniewind." Pages 102–23 in *Kerygma and Myth: A Theological Debate*. Edited by Hans Werner Bartsch. New York: Harper & Brothers, 1961.

————. *Theologie des Neuen Testaments (1948–53)*. 9th ed. Revised and expanded by O. Merk. UTB 630. Tübingen: Mohr, 1984.

————. *Theology of the New Testament*, Vol. 1. Translated by Kendrick Grobel. New York: Charles Scribner's Sons, 1951. Vol. 2, 1955.

————. *Das Verhältnis der urchristlichen Christusbotschaft zum historischen Jesus (1960)*. 4th ed. Heidelberg: Winter, 1965 (= SHAW.PH, 1960/3). Translated as "The Primitive Christian Kerygma and the Historical Jesus," in *The Historical Jesus and the Kerygmatic Christ: Essays on the New Quest of the Historical Jesus*. Edited by Carl E. Braaten and Roy A. Harrisville. Nashville: Abingdon, 1964.

————. *Glauben und Verstehen* (= *GuV*). Collected Essays.

GuV 1, 6th ed. Tübingen: Mohr, 1966.

GuV 2, 5th exp. ed. Tübingen: Mohr, 1968.

GuV 3, 3d exp. ed. Tübingen: Mohr, 1965.

GuV 4, 2d ed. Tübingen: Mohr, 1967.

Burchard, Chr. "Jesus." *KP* 2 (1967): cols. 1342–54.

————. "Jesus von Nazareth." Pages 12–58 in *Die Anfänge des Christentums. Alte Welt und neue Hoffnung*. Stuttgart: Kohlhammer, 1987.

Burckhardt, J. "Das Individuum und das Allgemeine." Pages 151–81 in *Weltgeschichtliche Betrachtungen*. Über geschichtliches Studium, Gesammelte Werke. Vol. 4. Darmstadt: Wiss. Buchges., 1956.

Buren, P. M. van. *A Theology of the Jewish-Christian Reality*. Part 3: *Christ in Context*. San Francisco: Harper & Row, 1988.

Buri, F. "Entmythologisierung oder Entkerygmatisierung der Theologie." Pages 85–191 in *Kerygma und Mythos*. ThF 2. Vol. 2. Edited by H. W. Bartsch. Hamburg: Reich & Heidrich, 1954.

Busch, A. *Die Geschichte des Privatdozenten*. The Academic Profession. New York: Arno Press, 1977.

Buttler, G. "Das Problem des 'historischen Jesus' im theologischen Gespräch der Gegenwart."*MPTh* 46 (1957): 235–44.

Cadbury, H. J. *The Peril of Modernizing Jesus*. New York: Macmillan, 1937 (= London: SPCK, 1962).

Calvert, D. G. A. "An Examination of the Criteria for Distinguishing the Authentic Words of Jesus." *NTS* 18 (1971/72): 209–19.

Cameron, A. "Introduction: the writing of history/Postlude: what next with history?" Pages 1–10, 206–8 in *History as Text. The Writing of Ancient History*. London: Duckworth, 1989.

Caragounis, Ch. C. *The Son of Man. Vision and Interpretation*. WUNT 38. Tübingen: Mohr, 1986.

Carlston, Ch. E. "A Positive Criterion of Authenticity." *BR* 7 (1962): 33–44.

Catchpole, D. R. "Tradition History." Pages 165–80 in *New Testament Interpretation. Essays on Principles and Methods*. Edited by I. H. Marshall. Exeter: Paternoster, 1977.

Charlesworth, J. H. "From Barren Mazes to Gentle Rappings: The Emergence of Jesus Research." *PSB* 7, no. 3 (1986): 221–30.

———. *Jesus Within Judaism. New Light from Exciting Archaeological Discoveries*. New York: Doubleday, 1988.

Chilton, B. D. and C. A. Evans, eds. *Studying the Historical Jesus. Evaluations of the State of Current Research*. NTTS 19. Leiden: E. J. Brill, 1994.

Chladenius, J. M. *Allgemeine Geschichtswissenschaft*. Reprint of the Leipzig 1752 edition, with an introduction by Ch. Friederich and a foreword by R. Koselleck. Klassische Studien zur sozialwissenschaftlichen Theorie, Weltanschauungslehre und Wissenschaftsforschung 3. Wien: Boehlau, 1985.

Chubb, Th. *The True Gospel of Jesus Christ Asserted*. London: Garland, 1738.

Collingwood, R. G. *The Idea of History (1946)*. Oxford: Oxford University Press, 1961.

Conzelmann, Hans. *Jesus*. Translated by J. Raymond Lord. Edited by John Reumann. Philadelphia: Fortress Press, 1973.

———. "Zur Methode der Leben-Jesu-Forschung." Pages 18–29 in *Theologie als Schriftauslegung. Aufsätze zum Neuen Testament*. BEvT 65. Munich: Kaiser, 1974. [= "Die Frage nach dem historischen Jesus." *ZTK* 56 (1959): Beiheft 1, 2–13.] Translated as "The Method of the Life-of-Jesus Research," in *The Historical Jesus and the Kerygmatic Christ: Essays on the New Quest of the Historical Jesus*. Edited by Carl E. Braaten and Roy A. Harrisville. (Nashville: Abingdon, 1964).

Crossan, J. D. *Four Other Gospels. Shadows on the Contours of the Canon*. Minneapolis: Winston Press, 1985.

———. "Divine Immediacy and Human Immediacy: Toward a New First Principle in Historical Jesus Research." *Semeia* 44 (1988): 121–40.

———. "Materials and Methods in Historical Jesus Research." *Foundations and Facets Forum* 4 (1988): 3–24.

———. *The Historical Jesus. The Life of a Mediterranean Jewish Peasant*. Edinburgh: T & T Clark, 1991.

Cullmann, O. "Out of Season Remarks on the 'Historical Jesus' of the Bultmann School." *USQR* 16, no. 2 (1961): 131ff.

Dahl, N. A. "Der historische Jesus als geschichtswissenschaftliches und theologisches Problem." *KuD* 1 (1955): 104–32. Translated as "The Problem of the Historical Jesus." Pages 48–89 in *The Crucified Messiah and Other Essays*. Edited by Nils Ahlstrup Dahl. (Minneapolis: Augsburg, 1974) and pages 138–71 in *Kerygma and History: A Symposium on the Theology of Rudolf Bultmann*. Edited by Carl E. Braaten and Roy A. Harrisville. (Nashville: Abingdon, 1962). A revised translation was published in Nils Alstrup Dahl, *Jesus the Christ: The Historical Origins of Christological Doctrine*. Edited by Donald H. Juel (Minneapolis: Fortress Press, 1991), 81–111, which is cited in this book.

———. "The Early Church and Jesus." Pages 167–75 in *Jesus in the Memory of the Early Church*. Minneapolis, Minn.: Augsburg, 1976.

Dalman, G. *The Words of Jesus Considered in the Light of Post-Biblical Jewish Writings and the Aramaic Language*. Translated by D. M. Kay. Edinburgh: T & T Clark, 1902.

Dautzenberg, G. "Der Wandel der Reich-Gottes-Verkündigung in der urchristlichen Mission. Pages 11–32 in *Zur Geschichte des Urchristentums*. Edited by Dautzenberg et al. QD 87. Freiburg: Herder, 1979.

Davies, W. D. and D. C. Allison. *The Gospel According to Saint Matthew*. Vols. 1/2. Edinburgh: T & T Clark, 1988/1991.

De Labriolle, P. *Les sources de l'histoire du Montanisme*. Collectanea Friburgensia 24. Paris: Ernest Leroux, 1913.

———. *La crise montaniste*. Paris: Ernest Leroux, 1913.

Demke, Chr. *Im Blickpunkt: Die Einzigartigkeit Jesu. Theologische Informationen für Nichttheologen*. Berlin: Evangelische Verlagsanstalt, 1976.

Dibelius, Martin. *From Tradition to Gospel*. New York: Charles Scribner's Sons, 1935.

———. "Mensch und Gott." Pages 16–23 in *Der Jude. Sonderheft: Judentum und Christentum*. 1926/4.

———. "Martin Dibelius," In *Die Religionswissenschaft der Gegenwart in Selbstdarstellungen*. Vol. 5. Edited by E. Stange. Leipzig: Meiner, 1929.

———. *Gospel Criticism and Christology*. London: I. Nicholson & Watson, 1935.

———. *Jesus*. Translated by Charles B. Hedrick and Frederick C. Grant. Philadelphia: Westminster Press, 1949.

———. *Jesus. A Study of the Gospels and an Essay on "The Motive for Social Action in the NT."* London: SCM Press, 1963.

———. *Wozu Theologie? Von Arbeit und Aufgabe theologischer Wissenschaft*. Leipzig: Klotz, 1941.

Diem, H. "The Earthly Jesus and the Christ of Faith." In *Kerygma and History. A Symposium on the Theology of Rudolf Bultmann*. Edited by Carl E. Braaten and Roy A. Harrisville. Nashville: Abingdon, 1962.

Dodd, Ch. H. *History and the Gospel*. London: Nisbet & Co., 1938.

Downing, F. G. "Criteria." Pages 151–53 in *A Dictionary of Biblical Interpretation*. Edited by R. J. Coggins and J. L. Houlden, London-Philadelphia: SCM/Trinity, 1990.

Droysen, J. G. *Historik. Vorlesungen über Enzyklopädie und Methodologie der Geschichte*. Edited by R. Hübner. Unveränderter Nachdruck, 7th ed. 1937. Darmstadt: Wiss. Buchgesellschaft, 1974.

Duhm, B. *Israels Propheten*. Tübingen: Mohr, 1916.

Dunn, J. D. G. *The Evidence for Jesus*. Philadelphia: Westminster, 1985.

Ebeling, G. "Die Frage nach dem historischen Jesus und das Problem der Christologie." *ZTK* 56, Sup. 1 (1959): 14–30.

Eisler, R. *IHSOUS BASILEUS OU BASILEUSAS. Die Messianische Unabhängigkeitsbewegung vom Auftreten Johannes des Täufers bis zum Untergang Jakobs des Gerechten nach der neuerschlossenen Eroberung von Jerusalem des Flavius Josephus und den christlichen Quellen*. Religionswissenschaftliche Bibliothek 9. Heidelberg: Carl Winters Universitätsbuchhandlung, Vol. 1, 1929; Vol. 2, 1930.

Eichhorn, A. *Das Abendmahl im Neuen Testament*. Leipzig: Mohr, 1898.

Ernst, J. "War Jesus ein Schüler Johannes' des Täufers?" Pages 13–33 in *FS* J. Gnilka: *Vom Urchristentum zu Jesus*. Edited by H. Frankemölle and K. Kertelge, Freiburg: Herder, 1989.

Evang, M. *Rudolf Bultmann in seiner Frühzeit*. BHT 74. Tübingen: Mohr, 1988.

Evans, C. A. "Authenticity Criteria in Life of Jesus Research." *CSR* 19 (1989): 6–31.

Faber, K.-G. *Theorie der Geschichtswissenschaft*, 2d ed. Munich: Beck, 1972.

Falk, H. *Jesus the Pharisee. A New Look at the Jewishness of Jesus*. New York: Paulist Press, 1985.

Fander, M. *Die Stellung der Frau im Markusevangelium. Unter besonderer Berücksichtigung kultur- und religionsgeschichtlicher Hintergründe*. MThA 8. Altenberge: Telos, 1989.

Ferrarotti, F. "Biography and the Social Sciences." *Social Research* 50 (1983): 57–80.

Flashar, H., K. Gründer, and A. Horstmann, eds. *Philologie und Hermeneutik im 19. Jahrhundert. Zur Geschichte und Methodologie der Geisteswissenschaften*. Göttingen: Vandenhoeck & Ruprecht, 1979.

Floris, E. *Sous le Christ, Jésus. Méthode d'analyse référentielle appliquée aux Évangiles*. Paris: Flammarion, 1987.

Flusser, D. *Jesus, in Selbstzeugnissen und Bilddokumenten dargestellt*. RoMo 140. Hamburg: Rowohlt, 1968.

Flusser, David, and R. Steven Notley. *Jesus*. Based on author's 1968 ed. of *Jesus, Selbstzeugnissen und Bilddokumenten*. Expanded and largely rewritten. Jerusalem: Magnes Press, 1997.

Fowl, St. "Reconstructing and Deconstructing the Quest of the Historical Jesus." *SJT* 42 (1989): 319–33.

France, R. T. "The Authenticity of Jesus' Sayings." Pages 101–43 in *History, Criticism, and Faith*. Edited by C. Brown. Downer's Grove, Ill.: Inter-Varsity Press, 1976.

Frend, W. H. C. "Montanismus." *TRE* 23 (1994): 271–79.

Freyne, S. "The Geography, Politics, and Economics of Galilee and the Quest for the Historical Jesus." In *Studying the Historical Jesus*. Edited by B. D. Chilton and C. A. Evans. NTTS 19. Leiden: E. J. Brill, 1994.

Fuchs, Ernst. "The Quest of the Historical Jesus." In *Studies of the Historical Jesus. Studies in Biblical Theology*. London: SCM Press, 1964.

———. "Einleitung: Zur Frage nach dem historischen Jesus. Ein Nachwort." Pages 1–31 in *Glaube und Erfahrung. Zum christologischen Problem im Neuen Testament*. Collected Essays. Vol. 2. Tübingen: Mohr, 1965.

Fuller, R. H. *The Foundations of New Testament Christology*. London: Lutterworth, 1965.

———. *The Mission and Achievement of Jesus. An Examination of the Presuppositions of New Testament Theology*. SBT 12. London: SCM Press, 1956.

Funk, R. W. "The Issue of Jesus." *Foundations and Facets Forum* 1 (1985): 7–12.

Funk, R. W., R. W. Hoover, and the Jesus Seminar. *The Five Gospels. The Search for the Authentic Words of Jesus*. New York: Macmillan, 1993.

Gabler, J. Ph. "Von der richtigen Unterscheidung der biblischen und der dogmatischen Theologie und der echten Bestimmung ihrer beider Ziele (1787)." Pages 32–44 in *Das Problem der Theologie des Neuen Testaments*. Edited by G. Strecker, WF 367. Darmstadt: Wiss. Buchges., 1975.

Gager, J. G. "The Gospels and Jesus: Some Doubts about Method." *JR* 54 (1974): 244–72.

Gamber, K. *Jesus-Worte. Eine vorkanonische Logiensammlung im Lukas-Evangelium*. StPatrLtg.Beiheft 9. Regensburg: Pustet, 1983.

Gawlick, G. "Der Deismus als Grundzug der Religionsphilosophie der Aufklärung." Pages 13–43 in *Hermann Samuel Reimarus (1694–1768) ein 'bekannter Unbekannter' der Aufklärung in Hamburg. Vorträge gehalten auf der Tagung der Joachim Jungius-Gesellschaft der Wissenschaften Hamburg am 12. und 13. Oktober 1972*. Göttingen: Vandenhoeck & Ruprecht, 1973.

Georgi, D. "Leben-Jesu-Theologie/Leben-Jesu-Forschung." *TRE* 20 (1990): 566–75.

Gerdes, H. "Die durch Martin Kählers Kampf gegen den 'historischen Jesus' ausgelöste Krise in der evangelischen Theologie und ihre Überwindung." *NZST* 3 (1961): 175–202.

Gnilka, Joachim. *Jesus of Nazareth: Message and History*. Peabody, Mass.: Hendrickson, 1997.

———. "Zur Frage nach dem historischen Jesus." *MThZ* 44 (1993): 1–12.

Goergen, D. *A Theology of Jesus*, Vol 1: *The Mission and Ministry of Jesus*, Wilmington, Del.: Michael Glazier, 1986.

Goguel, M. "The Problem of Jesus." *HTR* 23 (1930): 93–120.

Goppelt, L. *Theology of the New Testament*. Translated by John E. Alsup. Edited by J. Roloff. Grand Rapids: Eerdmans, 1981.

Grant, M. *Jesus: An Historian's Review of the Gospels*. New York: Charles Scribner's Sons, 1977.

Grimm, J. and W. "Genie." *Deutsches Wörterbuch* 5 (1897): cols. 3396–450. Reprint. Munich: dtv, 1984.

Grisebach, E. Gegenwart. *Eine kritische Ethik*. Halle: Niemeyer, 1928.

Grässer, E. "Motive und Methoden der neueren Jesus-Literatur." *VuF* 18 (1973): 3–45.

Gunkel, H. "Individualismus I, I. und Sozialismus im AT." In *RGG*[1] 3 (1912 1st ed.): 493–501.

———. Review of Everling, O., "Die paulinische Angelologie und Dämonologie." *TLZ* 14 (1889): cols. 369–71.

———. *Schöpfung und Chaos in Urzeit und Endzeit. Eine religionsgeschichtliche Untersuchung über Gen 1 und ApJoh 12*. Göttingen: Vandenhoeck & Ruprecht, 1895.

Haenchen, E. *Der Weg Jesu. Eine Erklärung des Markus-Evangeliums und der kanonischen Parallelen*. 2d ed. Berlin: de Gruyter, 1968.

Hagner, D. A. *The Jewish Reclamation of Jesus: An Analysis and Critique of the Modern Jewish Study of Jesus*. Grand Rapids: Zondervan, 1984.

Hahn, F. "Die Frage nach dem historischen Jesus und die Eigenart der uns zur Verfügung stehenden Quellen (Vortrag 1960)." Pages 7–40 in *Die Frage nach dem historischen Jesus*. Edited by F. Hahn, W. Lohff, and G. Bornkamm. EvFo 2. Göttingen: Vandenhoeck & Ruprecht, 1962.

———. "Die Frage nach dem historischen Jesus." *TThZ* 82 (1973): 193–205.

———. "Methodologische Überlegungen zur Rückfrage nach Jesus." Pages 11–77 in *Rückfrage nach Jesus. Zur Methodik und Bedeutung der Frage nach dem historischen Jesus*. Edited by K. Kertelge. QD 63. Freiburg: Herder, 1974.

———. "Umstrittenes Jesusbild? Problematische neuere Veröffentlichungen zur Geschichte und Gestalt Jesu von Nazaret (Lecture on Bavarian Radio and elsewhere)." *MThZ* 44 (1993): 95–107.

Harnack, Adolf. *What is Christianity?* Translated by Thomas Bailey Saunders. New York: Harper & Row, 1957.

Harvey, A. E. *Jesus and the Constraints of History*. The Bampton Lectures, 1980. London: Duckworth, 1982.

Harvey, V. A. and S. M. Ogden. "How New is the 'New Quest of the Historical Jesus'?" In *Kerygma and History. A Symposium on the Theology of Rudolf Bultmann*. Edited by Carl E. Braaten and Roy A. Harrisville. Nashville: Abingdon, 1962.

Hase, K. *Das Leben Jesu. Lehrbuch zunächst für akademische Vorlesungen*. (1829). 2d ed. Leipzig: Breitkopf & Härtel, 1835.

Hauck, F. and G. Schwinge. *Theologisches Fach- und Fremdwörterbuch*. 6th ed. Göttingen: Vandenhoeck & Ruprecht, 1987.

Hedrick, C. W. "The Tyranny of the Synoptic Jesus." *Semeia* 44 (1988):1–8.

Heine, R. E. "The Role of the Gospel of John in the Montanist Controversy." *SecCen* 6 (1987):1–19.

———. "The Gospel of John and the Montanist Debate at Rome." Pages 95–100 in

Studia Patristica XXI. Edited by E. A. Livingstone. Leuven: Akademie Verlag, 1989.

———. *The Montanist Oracles and Testimonia.* PatMS 14. Macon, Ga.: Mercer University Press, 1989.

———. "Montanus, Montanism." *ABD* 4 (1992): 898–902.

Heinrich, J. B. *Christus. Ein Nachweis seiner geschichtlichen Existenz und göttlichen Persönlichkeit, zugleich eine Kritik des Rationalismus, des Straussischen Mythizismus und des Lebens Jesu von Renan.* 2d ed. Mainz: Kirchheim, 1864.

Heitmüller, W. "Jesus Christus I." In *RGG*[1] 3 (1912, 1st ed.): 343–62.

Heitsch, E. "Die Aporie des historischen Jesus als Problem theologischer Hermeneutik." *ZTK* 53 (1956): 192–210.

Hengel, M. *The Charismatic Leader and His Followers.* Translated by James C. G. Greig. Edited by John Riches. Edinburgh: T & T Clark, 1996.

———. "Kerygma oder Geschichte? Zur Problematik einer falschen Alternative in der Synoptikerforschung aufgezeigt an Hand einiger neuer Monographien." *ThQ* 151 (1971): 323–36.

———. "Historische Methoden und theologische Auslegung des Neuen Testaments." *KuD* 19 (1973): 85–90.

———. *Zur urchristlichen Geschichtsschreibung.* Stuttgart: Calwer, 1979.

Herrmann, W. *Ethik.* 5th ed. GThW 5, vol. 2. Tübingen: Mohr, 1913.

Higgins, A. J. B. *The Son of Man in the Teaching of Jesus.* Cambridge: Cambridge University Press, 1980.

Hoffmann, D. M. *Renan und das Judentum. Die Bedeutung des Volkes Israel im Werk des 'Historien philosophe'.* Würzburg Diss. University of Würzburg, 1988.

Hoheisel, K. *Das antike Judentum in christlicher Sicht. Ein Beitrag zur neueren Forschungsgeschichte.* Studies in Oriental Religions 2. Wiesbaden: Harrassowitz, 1978.

Holeczek, H. *Humanistische Bibelphilologie als Reformproblem bei Erasmus von Rotterdam, Thomas More and William Tyndale.* SHCT 9. Leiden: Brill, 1975.

Holtz, T. "Jesus." In *EKL* 2 (1989, 3d ed.): cols. 824–31.

———. "Kenntnis von Jesus und Kenntnis Jesu. Eine Skizze zum Verhältnis zwischen historisch-philologischer Erkenntnis und historisch-theologischem Verständnis." *TLZ* 104 (1979): 1–12.

Holtzmann, H. J. *Die synoptischen Evangelien. Ihr Ursprung und ihr geschichtlicher Charakter.* Leipzig: Engelmann, 1863.

———. *Das messianische Bewusstsein Jesu. Ein Beitrag zur Leben-Jesu-Forschung.* Tübingen: Mohr, 1907.

———. *Lehrbuch der neutestamentlichen Theologie.* Edited by A. Jülicher and W. Bauer. Vol. 1. 2d ed. Tübingen: Mohr, 1911.

Hooker, M. D. "Christology and Methodology." *NTS* 17 (1970/71): 480–7.

———. "On Using the Wrong Tool." *Theol.* 75 (1972): 570–81.

Horn, F. W. "Diakonische Leitlinien Jesu." Pages 109–26 in *Diakonie-biblische Grundlagen und Orientierungen. Ein Arbeitsbuch zur theologischen Verständigung über den diakonischen Auftrag.* Edited by G. K. Schäfer and Th. Strohm. Heidelberg: HVA, 1990.

Hornig, G. *Die Anfänge der historisch-kritischen Theologie. Johann Salomo Semlers Schriftverständnis und seine Stellung zu Luther.* FSThR 8. Göttingen: Vandenhoeck & Ruprecht, 1961.

———. "Akkommodation." In *HWP* 1 (1971): cols. 125f.

Humphreys, R. St. "The Historian, his Documents, and the Elementary Modes of Historical Thought." *HTh* 19 (1980): 1–20.

Hübner, K. *Kritik der wissenschaftlichen Vernunft*. 3d ed. Freiburg: Alber, 1986.

Jaspert, B., ed. *Briefwechsel Karl Barth—Rudolf Bultmann. 1922–1966*. Zürich: tvz, 1971 (= Karl Barth–GA V (Briefe), vol. 1).

———. Rudolf Bultmanns "Wende von der liberalen zur dialektischen Theologie." Pages 25–43 in *Werk und Wirkung*. Darmstadt: Wiss. Buchges., 1984.

Jensen, A. *God's Self-confident Daughters : Early Christianity and the Liberation of Women*. Translated by O. C. Dean Jr. Louisville, Ky.: Westminster John Knox Press, 1996.

Jeremias, J. "Der gegenwärtige Stand der Debatte um das Problem des historischen Jesus." Pages 12–25 in *Der historische Jesus und der kerygmatische Christus*. Edited by H. Ristow and K. Matthiae. 2d ed. Berlin: Evangelische Verlagsanstalt, 1961. A slightly different version was translated as *The Problem of the Historical Jesus*. Facet Books 13. Philadelphia: Fortress Press, 1964.

———. "Appendix: Characteristics of the ipsissima vox Jesu," In *The Prayers of Jesus*. Studies in Biblical Theology. Second Series 6. Naperville, Ill.: Alec R. Allenson, 1967.

———. *New Testament Theology. The Proclamation of Jesus*. New York: Charles Scribner's Sons, 1971.

Jülicher, A. *Neue Linien in der Kritik der evangelischen Überlieferung*. Vorträge des Hessischen und Naussauischen theologischen Ferienkurses, H. 3. Giessen: Töpelmann, 1906.

———. "Die Religion Jesu und die Anfänge des Christentums bis zum Nicaenum." In *Die Kultur der Gegenwart*. Vol. 1, Part 4. *Geschichte der christlichen Religion*. Edited by Paul Hinneberg, with Introduction. 2d ed. Berlin: Teubner, 1909.

Kähler, Martin. *The So-Called Historical Jesus and the Historic, Biblical Christ*. Translated and edited by Carl E. Braaten. Seminar Editions. Philadelphia: Fortress Press, 1964.

Käsemann, E. "The Problem of the Historical Jesus." Pages 15–47 in *Essays on New Testament Themes*. London: SCM Press, 1964.

———. *Exegetische Versuche und Besinnungen*. Vols. 1 & 2. Göttingen: Vandenhoeck & Ruprecht, 1960.

———. *Essays on New Testament Themes*. London: SCM Press, 1964.

———. "Die neue Jesus-Frage." Pages 47–57 in *Jésus aux origines de la christologie*. Edited by J. Dupont. BETL 40. Leuven: Leuven University Press, 1975. 2d ed. 1989.

Kahlert, H. *Der Held und seine Gemeinde. Untersuchungen zum Verhältnis von Stifterpersönlichkeit und Verehrergemeinschaft in der Theologie des freien Protestantismus*. EHS.T 238. Frankfurt: Lang, 1984.

Kalthoff, A. *Das Christus-Problem. Grundlinien zu einer Sozialtheologie*. Leipzig: Diederichs, 1902.

Kealy, S. P. "Gospel Studies Since 1970." *IThQ* 56 (1990): 161–9.

Keck, L. E. "Bornkamm's Jesus of Nazareth Revisited." *JR* 49 (1969): 1–17.

———. *A Future for the Historical Jesus. The Place of Jesus in Preaching and Theology*. Nashville: Abingdon, 1971; London: SCM Press, 1972.

Kee, H. C. *Jesus in History. An Approach to the Study of the Gospels*. New York: Harcourt, 1970.

Keim, Th. *Geschichte Jesu von Nazara in ihrer Verkettung mit dem Gesamtleben seines Volkes*. Zürich: Orell, Füssli & Co., 1867.

———. *Der geschichtliche Christus. Eine Reihe von Vorträgen mit Quellenbeweis und Chronologie des Lebens Jesu*. 3d ed. Zürich: Orell, Füssli & Co., 1866.

Kellermann, B. *Kritische Beiträge zur Entstehungsgeschichte des Christentums*. Berlin: Poppelauer, 1906.

Kessler, E. *Petrarca und die Geschichte. Geschichtsschreibung, Rhetorik, Philosophie im Übergang vom Mittelalter zur Neuzeit.* Humanistische Bibliothek I/25. Munich: Fink, 1978.

Klausner, J. *Jesus von Nazareth. Seine Zeit, sein Leben und seine Lehre.* 3d ed. Jerusalem, 1952.

———. *Jesus of Nazareth: His Life, Times, and Teaching.* Translated by Herbert Danby. New York: Macmillan Co., 1944.

Knape, J. *'Historie' in Mittelalter und früher Neuzeit. Begriffs- und gattungsgeschichtliche Untersuchungen im interdisziplinären Kontext.* SaeSp 10. Baden-Baden: Koerner, 1984.

Koch, Klaus. *The Rediscovery of Apocalyptic.* Studies in Biblical Theology. Second Series 22. London: SCM Press, 1972.

Kölbing, P. *Die geistige Einwirkung der Person Jesu auf Paulus. Eine historische Untersuchung.* Göttingen: Vandenhoeck & Ruprecht, 1906.

Körner, J. *Eschatologie und Geschichte. Eine Untersuchung des Begriffes der Eschatologie in der Theologie Rudolf Bultmanns.* ThF 13. Hamburg: Reich, 1957.

Koester, H. "One Jesus and Four Primitive Gospels." *HTR* 61 (1968): 203–47.

Kraus, H.-J. "Das Alte Testament in der 'Bekennenden Kirche'." *KuI* 1 (1986): 26–46.

Kremer, J. "Die Methoden der historisch-kritischen Evangelienforschung und die Frage nach Jesus von Nazaret." *BiLi* 46 (1973): 83–91.

Kümmel, W. G. "Bibelwissenschaft II. Bibelwissenschaft des NT." In *RGG*[3] 1 (1957): 1236–51.

———. "Das Problem des historischen Jesus in der gegenwärtigen Diskussion." *DtPfrBl* 61 (1961): 573–8.

———. "Der persönliche Anspruch Jesu und der Christusglaube der Urgemeinde (1963)." Pages 429–38 in *Heilsgeschehen und Geschichte.* Ges. Aufs. 1933–1964. Edited by W. G. Kümmel. Marburg: Elwert, 1965.

———. *The Theology of the New Testament. According to Its Major Witnesses, Jesus–Paul–John.* Translated by John E. Steely. Nashville: Abingdon, 1973.

———. "Jesu Antwort an Johannes den Täufer. Ein Beispiel zum Methodenproblem in der Jesusforschung (1974)." Pages 177–200 in *Heilsgeschehen und Geschichte.* Vol. 2. Collected Essays. 1965–1976. Edited by W. G. Kümmel. Marburg: Elwert, 1978.

———. "Jesusforschung seit 1981. 1–3." *TRu* 53 (1988): 229–49; *TRu* 54 (1989): 1–53; *TRu* 55 (1990): 21–45.

———. *Dreissig Jahre Jesusforschung (1950–1980).* BBB 60. Königstein: Hanstein, 1985.

Ladd, G. E. *A Theology of the New Testament.* Grand Rapids: Eerdmans, 1974.

Lakatos, I. "Falsification and the Methodology of Scientific Research Programmes." Pages 91–195 in *Criticism and the Growth of Knowledge.* Edited by I. Lakatos and A. Musgrave. Cambridge: Cambridge University Press, 1970.

Lambeck, G. "Wie schildert der Historiker die Persönlichkeit im Rahmen der allgemeinen Geschichte?" *PrJ* 111 (1903): 277–95.

Landfester, R. *Historia magistra vitae. Untersuchungen zur humanistischen Geschichtstheorie des 14. bis 16. Jahrhunderts.* Travaux d'Humanisme et Renaissance 123. Geneva: Droz, 1972.

Lange, D. *Historischer Jesus oder mythischer Christus. Untersuchungen zu dem Gegensatz zwischen Friedrich Schleiermacher und David Friedrich Strauss.* Gütersloh: Mohn, 1975.

Lange, N. R. M. and C. Thoma, "Antisemitismus I. Begriff/Vorchristlicher Antisemitismus." *TRE* 3 (1978): 113–19.

Lapide, P. and U. Luz. *Jesus in Two Perspectives: a Jewish-Christian Dialogue.* Translated by Lawrence W. Denef. Minneapolis: Augsburg, 1985.

Latourelle, R. "Critères d'authenticité historique des Évangiles." *Greg* 55 (1974): 609–38.

Lee, B. J. *The Galilean Jewishness of Jesus: Retrieving the Jewish Origins of Christianity.* Vol. 1. *Conversation on the Road not Taken.* New York: Paulist Press, 1988.

Lehmann, M. *Synoptische Quellenanalyse und die Frage nach dem historischen Jesus. Kriterien der Jesusforschung untersucht in Auseinandersetzung mit Emanuel Hirschs Frühgeschichte des Evangeliums.* BZNW 38. Berlin: de Gruyter, 1970.

Lémonon, J. *Pilate et le gouvernement de la Judée: Textes et documents.* Paris: Librairie Lecoffre, 1981.

Lentzen-Deis, F. "Kriterien für die historische Beurteilung der Jesusüberlieferung in den Evangelien." Pages 78–117 in *Rückfrage nach Jesus. Zur Methodik und Bedeutung der Frage nach dem historischen Jesus.* Edited by K. Kertelge. QD 63. Freiburg: Herder, 1974.

Lessing, G. E. "Über den Beweis des Geistes und der Kraft." Pages 307–12 in *Lessings Werke III, Schriften II.* Edited by K. Wölfel. Frankfurt: Insel, 1967.

Liebeschütz, H. *Das Judentum im deutschen Geschichtsbild von Hegel bis Max Weber.* Tübingen: Mohr, 1967.

Lintzel, M. "Voraussetzungen des Individuums." *AKuG* 38 (1956): 167–73.

Lohse, E. "Die Frage nach dem historischen Jesus in der gegenwärtigen neutestamentlichen Forschung." *TLZ* 87 (1962): cols. 161–74.

Longenecker, R. N. "Literary Criteria in Life of Jesus Research: An Evaluation And Proposal." Pages 217–29 in *Current Issues In Biblical And Patristic Interpretation.* (FS M. C. Tenney). Edited by G. F. Hawthorne. Grand Rapids: Eerdmans, 1975.

Lührmann, D. "Die Frage nach Kriterien für ursprüngliche Jesusworte. Eine Problemskizze." Pages 59–72 in *Jésus aux origines de la christologie.* Edited by J. Dupont. 2d ed. Leuven: Leuven University Press, 1989 (= BETL 40).

Lukács, G. *Die Theorie des Romans. Ein geschichtsphilosophischer Versuch über die Formen der grossen Epik* (1920). 2d ed. Neuwied: Luchterhand, 1974.

Lundsteen, A. Chr. *H. S. Reimarus und die Anfänge der Leben-Jesu-Forschung.* Kopenhagen: O. C. Olsen, 1939.

Luther, M. "Grund und Ursach aller Artikel D. Martin Luthers, so durch römische Bulle unrechtlich verdammt sind. 1521." In *WA* 7 (308–457): English translation in *Luther's Works.* Vol. 32: *Career of the Reformer II.* Edited by George W. Forell. Philadelphia: Muhlenberg, 1958.

Ulrich Luz, *Matthew 8–20, A Commentary.* Translated by James E. Crouch. Minneapolis: Fortress Press, 2001.

Mackey, J. P. *Jesus, the Man and the Myth. A Contemporary Christology.* London: SCM Press, 1979.

Maier, J. "Gewundene Wege der Rezeption. Zur neueren jüdischen Jesusforschung." *HerKorr* 30 (1976): 314–19.

Marquardt, F. W. *Das christliche Bekenntnis zu Jesus, dem Juden. Eine Christologie.* Vol. 1. Munich: Kaiser, 1990.

Marrou, H.-I. *Über die historische Erkenntnis. Welches ist der richtige Gebrauch der Vernunft, wenn sie sich historisch betätigt?* (frz. 1954). Freiburg: Karl Alber, 1973.

Marxsen, Willi. *The Beginnings of Christology: A Study in its Problems.* Translated by Paul J. Achtemeier. Facet Books Biblical Series 22. Philadelphia: Fortress Press, 1969.

Massey, M. Ch. *Christ Unmasked. The Meaning of the Life of Jesus in German Politics.* Chapel Hill, N.C.: University of North Carolina Press, 1983.

McArthur, H. K. "Basic Issues. A Survey of Recent Gospel Research." *Interp.* 18 (1964): 39–55.

————. *The Quest Through the Centuries. The Search for the Historical Jesus.* Philadelphia: Fortress Press, 1966.

————. "The Burden of Proof in Historical Jesus Research." *ExpTim* 82 (1970): 116–19.

McEleney, N. J. "Authenticating Criteria and Mark 7:1–23." *CBQ* 34 (1972): 431–60.

Mealand, D. L. "The Dissimilarity Test." *SJT* 31 (1978): 41–50.

Meier, J. P. "Jesus Among the Historians." *New York Times Book Review* (December 21, 1986): 1, 16–19.

————. *A Marginal Jew. Rethinking the Historical Jesus.* Vol. 1: *The Roots of the Problem and the Person.* New York: Doubleday, 1991.

Meinecke, F. "Persönlichkeit und geschichtliche Welt." Pages 1–15 in *Menschen die Geschichte machten. Viertausend Jahre Weltgeschichte in Zeit- und Lebensbildern.* Edited by P. R. Rohden. 2d ed. Vol. 1. Wien: Seidel, 1933.

————. *Staat und Persönlichkeit.* Berlin: Mittler, 1933.

————. *Die Entstehung des Historismus.* Edited by C. Hinrichs. Munich: Oldenbourg, 1959 (= Werke 3).

Melville, G. "Kompilation, Fiktion und Diskurs. Aspekte zur heuristischen Methode der mittelalterlichen Geschichtsschreiber." Pages 133–53 in *Historische Methode.* Edited by Ch. Meier and J. Rüsen. Beiträge zur Historik 5. Munich: dtv, 1988.

Merk, O. "Anfänge neutestamentlicher Wissenschaft im 18. Jahrhundert." Pages 37–59 in *Historische Kritik in der Theologie. Beiträge zu ihrer Geschichte.* Edited by G. Schwaiger. SThGG 32. Göttingen: Vandenhoeck & Ruprecht, 1980.

————. "Bibelwissenschaft II." *TRE* 6 (1980): 375–409.

Merkel, H. "Die Gottesherrschaft in der Verkündigung Jesu." Pages 119–61 in *Königsherrschaft Gottes und himmlischer Kult im Judentum, Urchristentum und in der hellenistischen Welt.* Edited by M. Hengel and A. M. Schwemer. WUNT 55. Tübingen: Mohr, 1991.

Meshorer, Y. *Jewish Coins of the Second Temple Period.* Chicago: Argonaut, 1967.

Meyer, B. F. *The Aims of Jesus.* London: SCM Press, 1979.

————. "Review of A. E. Harvey, Jesus and the Constraints of History, 1980." *JBL* 103 (1984): 652–54.

Meyer, E. "The Development of Individuality in Ancient History." Pages 213–30 in *Kleine Schriften.* Vol. 1: *Zur Geschichtstheorie und zur wirtschaftlichen und politischen Geschichte des Altertums.* Halle: Max Niemeyer, 1910.

————. "Zur Theorie und Methodik der Geschichte." Pages 3–67 in *Kleine Schriften.* Vol. I: *Zur Geschichtstheorie und zur wirtschaftlichen und politischen Geschichte des Altertums.* Halle: Max Niemeyer, 1910.

Michaelis, J. D. *Einleitung in die göttlichen Schriften des Neuen Bundes.* 1, 2d ed. Göttingen: Vandenhoeck & Ruprecht, 1777.

Michaelis, W. "Notwendigkeit und Grenze der Erörterung von Echtheitsfragen innerhalb des Neuen Testament." *TLZ* 77 (1952): cols. 397–402.

Mödritzer, H. *Stigma und Charisma im Neuen Testament und seiner Umwelt.* NTOA 28. Freiburg/Göttingen: Universitätsverlag Freiburg Schweiz/Vandenhoeck & Ruprecht, 1994.

Moore, G. F. "Christian Writers on Judaism." *HTR* 14 (1921): 197–254.

Morgan, Th. *The Moral Philosopher.* Vols. 1–3. London, 1738–1740, One Volume Facsimile Reprint. Edited by G. Gawlick. Stuttgart: Fromman, 1969.

Mostert, W. "Luther III." In *TRE* 21 (1991): 567–94.

Moule, Ch. F. D. *The Phenomenon of the New Testament. An Inquiry into the Implications of Certain Features of the New Testament.* SBT, Second Series 1. London: SCM Press, 1967.

Muhlack, U. "Zum Verhältnis von Klassischer Philologie und Geschichtswissenschaft im 19. Jahrhundert." Pages 225–39 in *Philologie und Hermeneutik im 19. Jahrhundert. Zur Geschichte und Methodologie der Geisteswissenschaften.* Edited by H. Flashar et al. Göttingen: Vandenhoeck & Ruprecht, 1979.

———. "Historie und Philologie." Pages 49–81 in *Aufklärung und Geschichte. Studien zur deutschen Geschichtswissenschaft im 18. Jahrhundert.* Edited by H. E. Bödeker et al. Veröffentlichungen des Max-Planck-Instituts für Geschichte 81. Göttingen: Vandenhoeck & Ruprecht, 1986.

———. "Von der philologischen zur historischen Methode." Pages 154–80 in *Historische Methode.* Beiträge zur Historik, 5. Edited by Ch. Meier and J. Rüsen. Munich: dtv, 1988.

———. *Geschichtswissenschaft im Humanismus und in der Aufklärung. Die Vorgeschichte des Historismus.* Munich: Beck, 1991.

Murray, S. Ch. "History and Faith." Pages 165–79 in *History as Text. The Writing of Ancient History.* Edited by A. Cameron. London: Duckworth, 1989.

Mussner, F. "Die 'Sache Jesu'." *Cath*(M) 25 (1971): 81–89.

Mussner, F. et al. "Methodologie der Frage nach dem historischen Jesus." Pages 118–47 in *Rückfrage nach Jesus. Zur Methodik und Bedeutung der Frage nach dem historischen Jesus.* Edited by K. Kertelge. QD 63. Freiburg: Herder, 1974.

Neill, St. and T. Wright. *The Interpretation of the New Testament 1861–1986.* 2d ed. Oxford: Oxford University Press, 1988.

Neumann, A. *Jesus.* Translated by M. A. Canney, with a preface by P. W. Schmiedel. London: Black, 1906.

Niederwimmer, K. *Jesus.* Göttingen: Vandenhoeck & Ruprecht, 1968.

Ninck, J. *Jesus als Charakter* (1906). 3d ed. Leipzig: Hinrich, 1925.

Nipperdey, Th. "Kann Geschichte objektiv sein?" Pages 218–34 in *Nachdenken über die deutsche Geschichte. Essays.* Munich: Beck, 1986.

———. *Deutsche Geschichte. 1800–1866. Bürgerwelt und starker Staat.* 4th ed. Munich: Beck, 1987.

Oelkers, J. "Biographik-Überlegungen zu einer unschuldigen Gattung." *Neue Politische Literatur* 19 (1974): 296–309.

Orr, J. *English Deism. Its Roots and Its Fruits.* Grand Rapids: Eerdmans, 1934.

Otto, R. *Leben und Wirken Jesu nach historisch-kritischer Auffassung.* 4th ed. Göttingen: Vandenhoeck & Ruprecht, 1905.

———. *The Kingdom of God and the Son of Man. A Study in the History of Religion.* Translated by Floyd V. Filson & Bertram Lee Woolf. London: Lutterworth Press, 1951.

Pals, D. L. *The Victorian 'Lives' of Jesus.* San Antonio: Trinity University Press, 1982.

Patterson, S. J. *The Gospel of Thomas and Jesus.* Sonoma, Calif.: Polebridge Press, 1993.

Paulsen, H. "Traditionsgeschichtliche Methode und religionsgeschichtliche Schule." *ZTK* 75 (1978): 20–55.

Payne, Ph. B. "The Authenticity of the Parables of Jesus." Pages 329–44 in *Gospel Perspectives. Studies of History and Tradition in the Four Gospels.* Edited by R. T. France and D. Wenham, Vol. 2. Sheffield: JSOT, 1981.

Pelikan, J. *Jesus Through the Centuries. His Place in the History of Culture.* New Haven, Conn.: Yale University Press, 1985.

Perrin, N. *Rediscovering the Teaching of Jesus.* New York: Harper & Row, 1967 (= London: SCM Press, 1967).

———. *What Is Redaction Criticism?* London: SPCK, 1970.

Pfeiffer, R. *Die Klassische Philologie von Petrarca bis Mommsen.* Munich: Beck, 1982.

Pleitner, H. *Das Ende der liberalen Hermeneutik am Beispiel Albert Schweitzers*. Tübingen: Francke, 1992 (= TANZ 5).

Pólya, G. *Mathematik und plausibles Schliessen*. Vol. 2: *Typen und Strukturen plausibler Folgerung* (Engl. 1954). Basel: Birkhäuser, 1963.

Preuschen, E. "Idee oder Methode." *ZNW* 1 (1900): 1–15.

Rade, M. "Religionsgeschichte und Religionsgeschichtliche Schule." In *RGG*[1] 4 (1913): 2183–200.

Ranke, L. von. *Geschichten der romanischen und germanischen Völker von 1494 bis 1514*. 2d ed. Leipzig: Duncker & Humblot, 1874 (= L. v. Ranke's Sämmtliche Werke 33/34).

———. *Zur Kritik neuerer Geschichtsschreiber*. 2th ed. L. v. Ranke's Sämmtliche Werke 33/34. Leipzig: Duncker & Humblot, 1874.

Reble, A. *Geschichte der Pädagogik*. 15th ed. Stuttgart: Klett-Cotta, 1989.

Reimarus, H. S. *Apologie oder Schutzschrift für die vernünftigen Verehrer Gottes*. Vol. 2. Edited by Gerhard Alexander. Frankfurt: Insel, 1972 (= first complete publication). Fragments from Reimarus [microfilm] consisting of Brief Critical Remarks on the Object of Jesus and His Disciples as Seen in the New Testament. Translated from the German of G. E. Lessing; edited by Charles Vorisen (Lexington, Ky.: American Theological Library Association, Committee on Reprinting, 1962).

———. *Die Vernunftlehre als eine Anweisung zum richtigen Gebrauche der Vernunft in dem Erkenntniss der Wahrheit aus zwoen ganz natürlichen Regeln der Einstimmung und des Widerspruchs*. 3rd improved ed. Hamburg, 1766. Reprint edited by F. Lötzsch. Munich, 1979.

Reventlow, H. "Das Arsenal der Bibelkritik des Reimarus: Die Auslegung der Bibel, insbesondere des Alten Testaments, bei den englischen Deisten." Pages 44–65 in *Hermann Samuel Reimarus (1694–1768) ein 'bekannter Unbekannter' der Aufklärung in Hamburg. Vorträge gehalten auf der Tagung der Joachim Jungius-Gesellschaft der Wissenschaften Hamburg am 12. und 13. Oktober 1972*. Göttingen: Vandenhoeck & Ruprecht, 1973.

———. *The Authority of the Bible and the Rise of the Modern World*. Philadelphia: Fortress Press, 1985.

———. "Bibelexegese als Aufklärung. Die Bibel im Denken des Johannes Clericus (1657–1736)." Pages 1–19 in *Historische Kritik und biblischer Kanon in der deutschen Aufklärung*. Edited by H. Reventlow, W. Sparn, and J. Woodbridge. Wolfenbütteler Forschungen 41. Wiesbaden: Otto Harrassowitz, 1988.

———. "Wurzeln der modernen Bibelkritik." Pages 47–63 in *Historische Kritik und biblischer Kanon in der deutschen Aufklärung*. Edited by H. Reventlow, W. Sparn, and J. Woodbridge. Wolfenbütteler Forschungen 41. Wiesbaden: Otto Harrassowitz, 1988.

Riches, J. *Jesus and the Transformation of Judaism*. London: Darton, Longman & Todd, 1980.

———. *The World of Jesus. First-Century Judaism in Crisis*. Understanding Jesus Today. Cambridge: Cambridge University Press, 1990.

Riches, J. and A. Millar. "Conceptual Change in the Synoptic Tradition." Pages 37–60 in *Alternative Approaches to New Testament Study*. Edited by A. E. Harvey. London: SPCK, 1985.

Riesner, R. *Jesus als Lehrer. Eine Untersuchung zum Ursprung der Evangelien-Überlieferung*. WUNT II, 7. Tübingen: Mohr, 1981.

Ritschl, D. "Die Erfahrung der Wahrheit. Die Steuerung von Denken und Handeln durch implizite Axiome." Pages 147–66 in *Konzepte. Ökumene, Medizin, Ethik, Gesammelte Aufsätze*. Munich: Kaiser, 1986.

Roberts, R. *The Ancient Dialect. Thomas Carlyle and Comparative Religion.* Berkeley: University of California Press, 1988.

Robinson, J. M. *A New Quest of the Historical Jesus.* London: SCM Press, 1959.

———. *Kerygma und historischer Jesus.* 2d ed. Zürich: Zwingli, 1967.

Rürup, R. *Emanzipation und Antisemitismus. Studien zur 'Judenfrage' der bürgerlichen Gesellschaft.* KSGW 15. Göttingen: Vandenhoeck & Ruprecht, 1975.

Ruether, R. *Faith and Fratricide: the Theological Roots of Anti-Semitism.* New York: Seabury Press, 1974.

Rüsen, J. "Historische Methode." Pages 62–80 in *Historische Methode. Theorie der Geschichte. Beiträge zur Historik.* Edited by Ch. Meier and J. Rüsen. Vol. 5. Beiträge zur Historik, 5. Munich: dtv, 1988.

Sanders, E. P. *Jesus and Judaism,* London: SCM Press, 1985.

———. *The Question of the Uniqueness of the Teaching of Jesus. The Ethel M. Wood Lecture 1990.* London: University of London Press, 1990.

———. *The Historical Figure of Jesus.* Harmondsworth: Allen Lane, 1993.

Sanders, E. P. and M. Davies. *Studying the Synoptic Gospels.* London: SCM/Valley Forge, Pa.: Trinity Press International, 1989.

Sandmel, S. *A Jewish Understanding of the New Testament.* Cincinnati: Hebrew Union College, 1957.

———. *We Jews and Jesus.* London: Goolancz, 1965.

Sato, M. *Q und Prophetie. Studien zur Gattungs- und Traditionsgeschichte der Quelle Q.* WUNT 2. Tübingen: Mohr, 1988.

Sauer, J. *Rückkehr und Vollendung des Heils. Eine Untersuchung zu den ethischen Radikalismen Jesu.* Theorie und Forschung 133; Philosophie und Theologie 9. Regensburg: S. Roderer, 1991.

Scheuer, H. *Biographie. Studien zur Funktion und zum Wandel einer literarischen Gattung vom 18. Jahrhundert bis zur Gegenwart.* Stuttgart: Metzler, 1979.

Schildenberger, J. "Biblische Akkomodation." *LTK* 1 (1957): cols. 239f.

Schille, G. "Prolegomena zur Jesusfrage." *TLZ* 93 (1968): 481–488.

———. "Ein neuer Zugang zu Jesus? Das traditionsgeschichtliche Kriterium." *ZdZ* 40 (1986): 247–53.

Schillebeeckx, Edward. *Jesus: An Experiment in Christology.* Translated by Hubert Hoskins. New York: Crossroad, 1979.

Schilson, A. *Lessings Christentum.* KVR 1463. Göttingen: Vandenhoeck & Ruprecht, 1980.

Schleiermacher, Friedrich. *The Life of Jesus.* Edited by Jack C. Verheyden. Translated by S. Maclean Gilmour. Lives of Jesus Series. Philadelphia: Fortress Press, 1975.

———. "Dr. Schleiermacher über seine Glaubenslehre an Dr. Lücke. Zweites Sendschreiben." Pages 337–94 in *Theologisch-dogmatische Abhandlungen und Gelegenheitsschriften.* Edited by H.-F. Traulsen. Berlin: de Gruyter, 1990 (= Krit. GA, H. J. Birkner et al. (eds.), 1. Abt., Vol. 10).

———. "Über den Begriff des grossen Mannes. 24. Januar 1826." Pages 520–31 in *Werke. Auswahl in 4 Bänden,* Vol. 1. Leipzig: Eckardt, 1910.

———. Über die Religion. Reden an die Gebildeten unter ihren Verächtern. Pages 207–399 in *Id. Werke. Auswahl in vier Bänden.* Vol. 4. Edited by O. Braun and J. Bauer, Leipzig: Meiner, 1911.

———. *On Religion: Speeches to its Cultured Despisers.* Translated by John Oman. New York: Harper & Brothers, 1958.

Schmidt, K. L. "Jesus Christ." In *RGG*² 3 (1959): 110–51. Translated as several articles in *Twentieth Century Theology in the Making:* Vol. 1: *Themes of Biblical Theology.* Edited by Jaroslav Pelikan. New York: Harper & Row, 1969.

———. "Die Stellung der Evangelien in der allgemeinen Literaturgeschichte (1923)." Pages 126–228 in *Zur Formgeschichte des Evangeliums*. Edited by F. Hahn. WF 81. Darmstadt: Wiss. Buchges., 1985.

Schmidt, J. M. "Bousset, Wilhelm." In *TRE* 7 (1981): 97–101.

Schmidt-Biggemann, W. *Theodizee und Aufklärung. Das philosophische Profil der deutschen Aufklärung*. Frankfurt: Suhrkamp, 1988 (= stw 722).

Schmiedel, P. W. "Gospels." In *EncBib* 2 (1901): cols. 1761–1898.

———. "Die Person Jesu im Streite der Meinungen der Gegenwart." *PrM* 10 (1906): 257–82.

———. *Das vierte Evangelium gegenüber den drei ersten*. RV, 1. Reihe, 8. u. 10. Heft. Tübingen: J. C. B. Mohr (Paul Siebeck), 1906.

Schneider, J. "Der Beitrag der Urgemeinde zur Jesusüberlieferung im Lichte der neuesten Forschung." *TLZ* 87 (1962): cols. 401–12.

Scholder, K. "Ferdinand Christian Baur als Historiker." *EvT* 21 (1961): 435–58.

———. "Herder und die Anfänge der historischen Theologie." *EvT* 22 (1962): 425–40.

———. *Ursprünge und Probleme der Bibelkritik im 17. Jahrhundert. Ein Beitrag zur Entstehung der historisch-kritischen Theologie*. FGLP 10/23. Munich: Kaiser, 1966.

Schöllgen, G. "'Tempus in collecto est'. Tertullian, der frühe Montanismus und die Naherwartung ihrer Zeit." *JAC* 27/28 (1985): 74–96.

Schottroff, L. "Jesus von Nazareth aus sozialgeschichtlicher und feministischer Perspektive." *EvErz* 39 (1987): 27–36.

Schottroff, Luise, and Wolfgang Stegemann. *Jesus and the Hope of the Poor*. Translated by Matthew J. O'Connell. Maryknoll, N. Y.: Orbis Books, 1986.

Schulze, W. *Vom Kerygma zurück zu Jesus. Die Frage nach dem historischen Jesus in der Bultmannschule*. AVTRW 68. Berlin: EVA, 1977.

Schürer, E. *Geschichte des jüdischen Volkes im Zeitalter Jesu Christi*. Vol. 2. 2d ed. Leipzig: Hinrich, 1886.

———. *The History of the Jewish People in the Age of Jesus Christ (175 B. C.–A. D. 135)*. New English Version revised and edited by G. Vermes, F. Millar and M. Black. Vol. 2. Edinburgh: T & T Clark, 1979.

Schürmann, H. *Jesu ureigener Tod. Exegetische Besinnungen und Ausblick*. Freiburg: Herder, 1975.

———. "Kritische Jesuserkenntnis. Zur kritischen Handhabung des 'Unähnlichkeitskriteriums'." *BiLi* 54 (1981): 17–26.

———. "Das Zeugnis der Redenquelle für die Basileia-Verkündigung Jesu." Pages 121–200 in *Logia. Les Paroles de Jésus—The Sayings of Jesus*. Edited by J. Delobel. Leuven: Leuven University Press, 1982 (= BETL 59).

Schweitzer, A. *The Quest of the Historical Jesus*. First complete ed. Edited by John Bowden. Translation of the 6th Germ. ed., 1950. Minneapolis: Fortress Press, 2001.

Schweizer, E. "Die Frage nach dem historischen Jesus." *EvT* 24 (1964): 403–19.

Schweizer, E. *Jesus*. Translated by D. E. Green. Macon, Ga.: Mercer University Press, 1987.

———. "Jesusdarstellungen und Christologien seit Rudolf Bultmann." Pages 122–48 in *Rudolf Bultmanns Werk und Wirkung*. Edited by B. Jaspert. Darmstadt: Wiss. Buchges., 1984.

———. "Jesus Christus, I. Neues Testament." In *TRE* 16 (1987): 671–726.

Schwemer, U., ed. *Christen und Juden. Dokumente der Annäherung*. Gütersloh: Mohn, 1991.

Segal, A. F. *Rebecca's Children. Judaism and Christianity in the Roman World*. Cambridge, Mass.: Harvard University Press, 1986.

Seigel, J. P. *The Critical Heritage*. Edited by Thomas Carlyle. London: Routledge & Kegan Paul, 1971.

Semler, J. S. *Letztes Glaubensbekenntnis über natürliche und christliche Religion*. Edited with forward by Chr. G. Schütz. Königsberg: Nikolovius, 1792.

Setz, W. *Lorenzo Vallas Schrift gegen die Konstantinische Schenkung. De falso credita et ementita Constantini donatione. Zur Interpretation und Wirkungsgeschichte*. Tübingen: Niemeyer, 1975 (= Bibliothek des Deutschen Historischen Instituts in Rom 44).

Simonis, W. *Jesus von Nazareth. Seine Botschaft vom Reich Gottes und der Glaube der Urgemeinde. Historisch-kritische Erhellung der Ursprünge des Christentums*. Düsseldorf: Patmos, 1985.

Smend, R. *Wilhelm Martin Leberecht de Wettes Arbeit am Alten und am Neuen Testament*. Basel: Helbing & Lichtenhahn, 1958.

Soden, H. von. "Die synoptische Frage." Pages 159–213 in *Urchristentum und Geschichte. Ges. Aufs. und Vorträge*. Edited by H. v. Campenhausen. Vol. 1. Grundsätzliches und Neutestamentliches. Tübingen: Mohr, 1951.

Stanton, G. N. "Historical Jesus." Pages 285–90 in *A Dictionary of Biblical Interpretation*. Edited by R. J. Coggins and J. L. Houlden. London/Philadelphia: SCM/Trinity, 1990.

Stegemann, E. W. "Aspekte neuerer Jesusforschung." *EvErz* 39 (1987): 10–27.

———. *Der Denkweg Rudolf Bultmanns. Darstellung der Entwicklung und der Grundlagen seiner Theologie*. Stuttgart: Kohlhammer, 1978.

Stein, R. H. "The 'Criteria' for Authenticity." Pages 225–63 in *Gospel Perspectives. Studies of History and Tradition in the Four Gospels*. Vol. 1. Edited by R. T. France and D. Wenham. Sheffield: JSOT, 1980.

Stenger, W. "Sozialgeschichtliche Wende und historischer Jesus." *Kairos* 28 (1986): 11–22.

Strauss, D. F. *Das Leben Jesu, kritisch bearbeitet*. Vol. 1. Tübingen: Osiander, 1835.

———. *The Life of Jesus Critically Examined*. Edited with an introduction by Peter C. Hodgson. Translated from the 4th Germ. ed. by George Eloit. Ramsey, N.J.: Sigler Press, 1994.

———. *A New Life of Jesus*. London: Williams & Norgate, 1865.

Strecker, G. "Die historische und theologische Problematik der Jesusfrage." *EvT* 29 (1969): 453–76.

———. *The Sermon on the Mount: An Exegetical Commentary*. Translated by O. C. Dean Jr. Nashville: Abingdon, 1988.

Stöve, E. *Kirchengeschichte zwischen geschichtlicher Kontinuität und geschichtlicher Relativität. Der Institutionalisierungsprozess der Kirchengeschichte im Zusammenhang neuzeitlichen Geschichtsverständnisses*. Habil. Heidelberg, 1978.

Sullivan, R. E. *John Toland and the Deist Controversy. A Study in Adaptations*. HHS 101. Cambridge, Mass.: Harvard University Press, 1982.

Teeple, H. M. "The Origin of the Son of Man Christology." *JBL* 84 (1965): 213–50.

Theissen, G. *Biblischer Glaube in evolutionärer Sicht*. Munich: Kaiser, 1984.

———. *The Shadow of the Galilean: The Quest of the Historical Jesus in Narrative Form*. Translated by John Bowden. 1st ed. Philadelphia: Fortress Press, 1987.

———. "Gewaltverzicht und Feindesliebe (Mt 5,38–48/Lk 6,27–38) und deren sozialgeschichtlicher Hintergrund." Pages 160–97 in *Studien zur Soziologie des Urchristentums*. 3d ed. WUNT 19. Tübingen: Mohr, 1989.

———. "Die Tempelweissagung Jesu. Prophetie im Spannungsfeld von Stadt und Land." Pages 142–59 in *Studien zur Soziologie des Urchristentums*. 3d ed. Tübingen: Mohr, 1989.

————. *Lokalkolorit und Zeitgeschichte in den Evangelien. Ein Beitrag zur Geschichte der synoptischen Tradition*. NTOA 8. Freiburg (Schweiz)/Göttingen: Universitätsverlag Fribourg/Vandenhoeck & Ruprecht, 1989.

————. "L'herméneutique biblique et la recherche de la vérité religieuse." *RThP* 122 (1990): 485–503.

————. "Symbolpolitische Konflikte bei Jesus und in seiner Umwelt." *EvT* (1997/8).

Theissen, G. and A. Merz. *Der historische Jesus. Ein Lehrbuch*. Göttingen: Vandenhoeck & Ruprecht, 1996.

Thüsing, W. "Neutestamentliche Zugangswege zu einer transzendental-dialogischen Christologie." Pages 79–303 in *Christologie-systematisch und exegetisch. Arbeitsgrundlagen für eine interdisziplinäre Vorlesung*. Edited by K. Rahner and W. Thüsing. QD 55. Freiburg: Herder, 1972.

Thyen, H. "Rudolf Bultmann, Karl Barth und das Problem der 'Sachkritik'. Pages 44–52 in *Rudolf Bultmanns Werk und Wirkung*. Edited by B. Jaspert. Darmstadt: Wiss. Buchges., 1984.

Toland, J. *Christianity Not Mysterious, Faksimile-Neudruck der Ausgabe London 1730*. Edited by G. Gawlick. Stuttgart: Frommann, 1964.

Tracy, J. D. "Ad Fontes: The Humanist Understanding of Scripture as Nourishment for the Soul." Pages 252–67 in *Christian Spirituality II: High Middle Ages and Reformation*. Edited by J. Rait. World Spirituality: An Encyclopedic History of the Religious Quest 17. London: Routledge & Kegan Paul, 1987.

Trevett, Chr. *Montanism. Gender, Authority and the New Prophecy*. Cambridge: Cambridge University Press, 1996.

Trilling, W. *Fragen zur Geschichtlichkeit Jesu*. Düsseldorf: Patmos, 1966.

Troeltsch, E. "Ueber historische und dogmatische Methode in der Theologie." Pages 129–253 in *Gesammelte Schriften*. Vol 2. Zur religiösen Lage, Religionsphilosophie und Ethik. 2d ed. Tübingen: Mohr, 1922.

————. *Writings on Theology and Religion*. Translated and edited by R. Morgan and M. Pye. Louisville, Ky.: Westminster/John Knox Press, 1990.

Turner, H. E. W. *Historicity and the Gospels. A Sketch of Historical Method and its Application to the Gospels*. London: Mowbray, 1963.

Turner, R. St. "Historicism, *Kritik* and the Prussian Professoriate. 1790 to 1840." Pages 450–77 in *Philologie und Hermeneutik im 19. Jahrhundert II*. Edited by M. Bollack et al. Göttingen: Vandenhoeck & Ruprecht, 1983.

Vansina, J. *Oral Tradition as History*. Madison: University of Wisconsin Press, 1985. [Completely revised version of *Oral Tradition: A Study in Historical Methodology*. Chicago: Aldine Publishing Co., 1965.]

Verheule, A. F. *Wilhelm Bousset. Leben und Werk. Ein theologiegeschichtlicher Versuch*. Amsterdam: Ton Balland, 1973.

Vermes, Geza. *Jesus the Jew. A Historian's Reading of the Gospels*. Philadelphia: Fortress Press, 1973.

————. *Jesus and the World of Judaism*. London: SCM Press, 1983.

Vielhauer, Ph. *Geschichte der urchristlichen Literatur. Einleitung in das Neue Testament, die Apokryphen und die Apostolischen Väter*. Berlin: de Gruyter, 1975.

Vogler, W. *Jüdische Jesusinterpretation in christlicher Sicht*. Weimar: H.Böhlaus Nachf., 1988.

Vögtle, A. "Jesus von Nazareth." Pages 3–24 in *Ökumenische Kirchengeschichte*. Edited by A. Benoît et al. Vol. 1. Alte Kirche und Ostkirche. 4th ed. 1st edition, 1970. Mainz: Grünewald and Munich: Kaiser, 1983.

Vorster, W. S. "The historical paradigm—Its possibilities and limitations." *Neotest* 18 (1984): 104–23.

Walter, P. *Theologie aus dem Geist der Rhetorik. Zur Schriftauslegung des Erasmus von Rotterdam.* TSTP 1. Mainz: Grünewald, 1991.

Weidel, K. *Jesu Persönlichkeit. Eine psychologische Studie.* Halle: Marhold, 1908.

Weinel, H. "Ist unsere Verkündigung von Jesus unhaltbar geworden?" *ZTK* 20 (1910): 1–38, 89–129.

———. *Biblische Theologie des neuen Testaments. Die Religion Jesu und des Urchristentums.* GThW 3.2. Tübingen: Mohr, 1911.

Weiss, J. *Die Predigt vom Reiche Gottes.* 2d ed. Göttingen: Vandenhoeck & Ruprecht, 1900.

———. *Jesus' Proclamation of the Kingdom of God.* Translated and edited by Richard Hyde. Lives of Jesus Series. Philadelphia: Fortress Press, 1971.

———. *Jesus von Nazareth. Mythos oder Geschichte? Eine Auseinandersetzung mit Kalthoff.* Tübingen: Mohr, 1910.

———. "Das Problem der Entstehung des Christentums." *ARW* 16 (1913): 423–515.

Wellhausen, J. "Abriss der Geschichte Israels und Juda's." Pages 5–102 in *Skizzen und Vorarbeiten.* Vol. 1. Berlin: Reimer, 1884.

———. *Sketch of the History of Israel and Judah.* London: Adam & Charles Black, 1891.

———. *Israelitische und Jüdische Geschichte.* Reprint of 9th ed. Berlin: DeGruyter, 1958.

Wernle, P. *Die Quellen des Lebens Jesu.* Halle: Gebauer-Schwetschke, 1904.

Wessel, L. P. *Lessing's Theology. A Reinterpretation.* The Hague/Paris: Mouton, 1977.

Wette, W. M. L. de. *Lehrbuch der christlichen Dogmatik in ihrer historischen Entwickelung dargestellt. Erster Theil. Biblische Dogmatik Alten und Neuen Testaments. Oder kritische Darstellung des Hebraismus, des Judenthums und Urchristenthums.* 2d ed. Berlin: Realschulbuchhandlung, 1818.

White, H. "The Historical Text as Literary Artifact." Pages 41–62 in *The Writing of History. Literary Form and Historical Understanding.* Edited by R. H. Canary and H. Kozicki. Madison: University of Wisconsin Press, 1978.

Wilder, A. N. "The Historical Jesus in a New Focus: A Review Article of 'The Silence of Jesus' by James Breech (Philadelphia 1983)." *USQR* 39/3 (1984): 225–36.

Winton, A. P. *The Proverbs of Jesus. Issues of History and Rhetoric.* JSNTS 35. Sheffield: JSOT, 1990.

Wrede, W. "Die Predigt Jesu vom Reiche Gottes (1894)." Pages 84–126 in *Vorträge und Studien.* Tübingen: Mohr, 1907.

———. "Über Aufgabe und Methode der sogenannten Neutestamentlichen Theologie (1897)." Pages 81–154 in *Das Problem der Theologie des Neuen Testaments.* Edited by G. Strecker. WF 367. Darmstadt: Wiss. Buchges., 1975.

Wright, T. "'Constraints' and the Jesus of History." *SJT* 39 (1986): 189–210.

Wünsche, A. *Neue Beiträge zur Erläuterung der Evangelien aus Talmud und Midrasch.* Göttingen: Vandenhoeck & Ruprecht, 1878.

Zahrnt, H. *Es begann mit Jesus von Nazareth.* Stuttgart: Kreuz, 1960.

———. *Jesus aus Nazareth. Ein Leben.* Munich: Piper, 1987.

Index of Authors

Index of Scripture
and Other Ancient Documents